6th Battalion The Manchester Regiment in the Great War

6th Battalion The Manchester Regiment in the Great War

Not A Rotter In The Lot

John Hartley

Pen & Sword
MILITARY

First published in Great Britain in 2010 by
Pen & Sword Military
an imprint of
Pen & Sword Books Ltd
47 Church Street
Barnsley
South Yorkshire
S70 2AS

ISBN 978 1 84884 328 8

A CIP catalogue record for this book is available from the British Library.

Printed and bound in England
by CPI

Pen & Sword Books Ltd incorporates the imprints of
Pen & Sword Aviation, Pen & Sword Maritime, Pen & Sword Military,
Wharncliffe Local History, Pen & Sword Select, Pen & Sword Military Classics,
Leo Cooper, Remember When, Seaforth Publishing and Frontline Publishing.

For a complete list of Pen & Sword titles please contact
PEN & SWORD BOOKS LIMITED
47 Church Street, Barnsley, South Yorkshire, S70 2AS, England
E-mail: enquiries@pen-and-sword.co.uk
Website: www.pen-and-sword.co.uk

Contents

INTRODUCTION & ACKNOWLEDGEMENTS

THE GREAT WAR was a very short period in our history but one which still features in the public consciousness. Perhaps it is to do with the scale of death. Perhaps because it was the first technological war to be fought with weapons that we recognise today – aircraft, tanks, chemical weapons, heavy artillery – weapons of mass destruction if you will. Perhaps because, for the first time, it was an army of citizens who fought – men coming from all parts of the country and from all backgrounds.

Like many who develop an interest in the period, mine started by wanting to know "what did Grandad do in the war". Tom Brough joined the Manchester Regiment in January 1915, survived the war and lived to a ripe old age. He joined the 17th Battalion, the second of the so-called Pals Battalions, and saw action during the Battle of the Somme and, later, at Arras and Ypres. The Pals was an idea that caught the public imagination of the time and still does – allowing men who worked together, or played sport together or were neighbours, to join up and serve together.

But it was not a new concept, the Territorial Force and its predecessors had always been local community units. My own local unit in North Cheshire – the 6th Battalion, Cheshire Regiment, traditionally recruited working class men who lived close to Stockport town centre and who worked together in the mills and hatworks of the immediate area. Similarly, the 6th Manchesters recruited heavily from the area near to the battalion's barracks in the Hulme district, but these were mainly middle class men who worked in the city centre. Amongst its pre-war membership were many from the City's prominent families and others who held positions of authority within the area's major commercial concerns. Most of those who volunteered to enlist into the battalion in the weeks and months after the outbreak of war were men from the same social groups, often friends of serving Territorials. And so, when young middle class men from Stockport enlisted in August 1914, it was the Manchesters not the Cheshires that they chose to join.

I found it remarkably easy to research Grandad's war service. Much has been written about the Manchester Pals and, indeed, the Pals battalions of other regiments. But comparatively little has been written about Territorial units – the 'Saturday Afternoon Soldiers'. Two volumes of history of the 7th Manchesters were published after the war but, as with many books from that period, they are books written by officers, for officers. This book tells the story of the men of the 6th Manchesters whatever rank they held and uses their own words to do so. Many will have been

POST CARD.

This Space may be used for Correspondence.

The Address only to be written here

Dear Will am having a spanking time, have just arrived back at camp, time 6.45 pm from Anglesey where we have been ball firing, started 6 am. We arrived back in the pink and were cheered by the whole camp. The photograph is of some of my tent companions and of course yours truly Cyril.

Mr W. Dennis Jr
Plumber etc
Liverpool Rd
Irlam
Nr Manchester

The Manchester Territorials in camp, June 1914. Cyril Wilson, from Irlam, in shirtsleeves, would survive the coming conflict but his brother, James, would be killed on 5 June 1915. Neil Drum

known to the battalion's ex-commander, recently promoted Brigadier General Noel Lee. The book's title is taken from a letter home that Lee wrote just before the Manchesters attacked on 4 June 1915 towards the village of Krithia on the Gallipoli peninsula. "*We are having a very strenuous time, but I am more than ever proud of the Brigade and especially the 5th and 6th Battalions – the latter in particular. Not a single rotter in the lot and in such good spirits.*"

The battalion left Britain in September 1914 and did not return until April 1919. In that time, it saw service in Egypt, Gallipoli and on the Western Front in Belgium and France. The second line battalion, the 2/6th, had much shorter service arriving in France in the late spring of 1917. Until shortly before, it had acted as the reserve unit. This meant that the geographical connection with the Manchester area was retained in both battalions for most of the war. In the latter stages, after conscripted men were trained and ready to go overseas, replacement troops could and would come from all parts of the country.

A short rest while on exercise, June 1914. Cyril Wilson (right) and, probably, Corporal Edward Atherton (left). Atherton would rise to the rank of Lieutenant serving with the Machine Gun Corps before dying from pneumonia in 1919. Neil Drum

I've made extensive use of the diaries and other personal papers lodged with the principal relevant collections – the Liddle Collection at the University of Leeds, Imperial War Museum and, of course, the Manchester Regiment Archives held at Tameside Local Studies Centre and my thanks go to the staff at all for their assistance.

The official war diaries of the battalions and higher level units, held at the National Archives, have also been a major information source. Of previously published material, *The 42nd (East Lancashire) Division 1914 – 1918*, by Frederick P Gibbon, has provided the wider context in which the battalion served and I have drawn heavily on the book. Similarly, *Great Gable to Gallipoli* and *I Shall Not Find His Equal,* both published on behalf of the Trustees of the Regimental Collection, have contained useful insights into the battalion's activities in the earlier stages of the war.

Photographs in the book have originated from a variety of sources and copyright is noted where known. Amongst these, I am particularly grateful to the Trustees of the Manchester Regiment Archive Collection (MRA) for allowing me to reproduce a considerable number and I thank Captain Robert Bonner, Chairman of the Trustees, for encouraging me in this project throughout. Many of the other photographs of the men are taken from local newspapers. They are often reproduced from microfilm and are not of good quality. I make no apology for that – it is often all that is left to know what a man looked like.

The internet is now also a major source of background information and I have found much useful information on the Long, Long Trail (www.1914-1918.net) and, particularly useful for its On This Day section, www.firstworldwar.com. However, the greatest source of help and assistance has been the pre-eminent Great War Forum discussion board at http://1914-1918.invisionzone.com/forums/. Members have been consistently generous in offering advice on even the most obscure of topics and allowing me to use photographs, etc from their collections. I thank them all but must single out Des Blackadder, Mick Forsyth, Bernard Lewis and Tom Morgan. They read my first efforts and, by their positive responses, they gave me more encouragement to carry on than they can ever know. I also thank Dave O'Mara for advice and assistance on all matters map-related.

I hope my efforts in writing the book do justice to the memories of the men whose stories I attempt to tell.

John Hartley
Summer 2009

The Strongest Company. Evening News Dec 8/13

"C" Company (Captain N. G. Frank) of the 6th Manchesters, who held their annual dinner on Saturday evening at the New Shades Restaurant,, was the strongest company in the battalion this year, and finished four over establishment. The record of the company in battalion competitions was a capital one also, and a feature of the musketry was the keenness of young members who, having failed in their standard test at the first shoot, succeeded at the second attempt. The chief prize-winner of the year was Lance-Corporal Worthington, and the two premier sections were those commanded by Sergeant S. Wolstencroft and Sergeant W. R. Warburton. Saturday's gathering was attended by about 120 members and ex-members, and the gathering included eight past colour-sergeants of the company.

C Company's Annual Dinner, 1913 reported by the *Manchester Evening News*.

1951. 200,000. 7—10 H W V Forms [No. 14*.] E. 501 8/18 47 4

C Coy

From 2658 destroyed

Army Form E. 501.

TERRITORIAL FORCE.

4 years' Service in the United Kingdom.

ATTESTATION OF

No. 1643 Name Joseph Arnold Rowbottom Corps 6 Bn Manchester

Questions to be put to the Recruit before Enlistment.

1. What is your Name? — 1. Joseph Arnold Rowbottom
2. In or near what Parish or Town were you born? — 2. In the Parish of St Andrews in or near the Town of M/c in the County of Lancs
3. Are you a British Subject? — 3. yes
4. What is your Age? — 4. 17 Years 9 Months.
5. What is your Trade or Calling? — 5. Clerk
6. In whose employ are you? — 6. Gt Central Railway Co.
7. Where do you now reside? — 7. 58 Woodland Avenue Gorton
8. Are you now an Apprentice? if so, please state particulars — 8. no
9. Are you married? — 9. no
10. Do you now belong to the Army, the Marines, the Militia, the Militia Reserve, the Territorial Force, the Royal Navy, the Army Reserve (Regular or Special), or any Naval Reserve Force? If so, to what Corps? — 10. no
11. Have you ever served in the Army, the Marines, the Militia, the Militia Reserve, the Imperial Yeomanry, the Territorial Force, the Royal Navy, the Volunteers, the Army Reserve (Regular or Special), or any Naval Reserve Force? If so, please state Corps and cause of discharge — 11. no
12. Do you belong, or have you belonged, to any Cadet Unit? — 12. no
13. Have you ever been rejected as unfit for the Military or Naval Forces of the Crown? If so, on what grounds? — 13. no
14. Did you receive a Notice, and do you understand its meaning? — 14. yes
15. Are you willing to be attested for the term of 4 years (provided His Majesty should so long require your services) for service in the Territorial Force of the County of † Lancaster to serve in the ‡ 6th BATTN. MANCHESTER REGT. — 15. yes

Amendment for question 16.—Army Forms E. 501 and E. 501A (9/London County/323).

16. Do you understand—
(a) That during the first year of your original enlistment you will be required to attend the number of drills and fulfil the other conditions prescribed for a recruit of the arm or branch of the service which you have elected to join?
(b) That you will be required to complete such preliminary training by the 31st October next following your original enlistment, unless before that date you obtain permission from your Commanding Officer to complete it afterwards, but that in any case you must complete it within 12 months of your original enlistment?
(c) That in addition to such preliminary training you will be liable to attend the number of drills and fulfil the other conditions relating to training prescribed for the arm or branch of the service which you have elected to join, and be liable to be trained for not less than 8, or more than 15 days altogether, in every year, or, if belonging to a mounted branch for not less than 8, or more than 18 days altogether, in every year, as may be prescribed, ¶ and may for that purpose be called out, once or oftener, in every year?
(d) That if you, without leave or reasonable excuse, fail to attend the number of drills required to fulfil the conditions relating to preliminary or annual training prescribed for your arm or branch of the service, you render yourself liable to a fine not exceeding £5?
(e) That when a proclamation has been issued, in case of imminent national danger or great emergency, calling out the first class Army Reserve you will become liable to be embodied?
(f) That, if your term of 4 years' service expires when a proclamation ordering the Army Reserve to be called out on permanent service is in force, you may be required to prolong your service for a further period not exceeding 12 months?
(g) That you will be liable to serve in any place in the United Kingdom without further agreement, but not in any place outside the United Kingdom unless you voluntarily undertake to do so?
(h) That you will be required to deliver up in good order, fair wear and tear only excepted, at such time and place as may be ordered by the Commanding Officer, all arms, clothing and appointments issued to you, being public property (including the property of the County Association)? — 16. yes

¶ A further period of preliminary training may be prescribed during the first year of original enlistment by an Order in Council, the number of days being specified, and the period of annual training in any year may be extended by an Order in Council, due notice thereof having been given, and provided that neither House of Parliament has dissented, but the whole period of annual training shall not exceed 30 days in any year.

Under the provisions of Section 99 of the Army Act, if a person knowingly makes a false answer to any question contained in the attestation paper, he renders himself liable to punishment.

I, Joseph Arnold Rowbottom do solemnly declare that the above answers made by me to the above questions are true, and that I am willing to fulfil the engagements made.

J A Rowbottom SIGNATURE OF RECRUIT.

[signature] *Signature of Witness.*

OATH TO BE TAKEN BY RECRUIT ON ATTESTATION.

I, Joseph Arnold Rowbottom do make Oath, that I will be faithful and bear true Allegiance to His Majesty King George the Fifth, His Heirs, and Successors, and that I will, as in duty bound, honestly and faithfully defend His Majesty, His Heirs, and Successors, in Person, Crown, and Dignity against all enemies, according to the conditions of my service.

CERTIFICATE OF MAGISTRATE OR ATTESTING OFFICER.

I F M Blatherwick do hereby certify, that, in my presence, all the foregoing Questions were put to the Recruit, above named, that the Answers written opposite to them are those which he gave to me, and that he has made and signed the Declaration, and taken the oath at ______ on this 25th day of April 1913. F M Blatherwick *Signature of Justice of the Peace, Officer, or other person authorised to attest Recruits.*

If any alteration is required on this page of the Attestation, a Justice of the Peace should be requested to make it and initial the alteration under Section 80 (6), Army Act.

The Recruit should, if he require it, receive a copy of the Declaration on Army Form E. 501A.

Attestation papers of Joseph Arnold Rowbottom. Arnold served with the Battalion until he was commissioned as a 2nd Lieutenant in the 2/6th Battalion.

Chapter 1

MOBILISATION

ANNUAL CAMP was always the high spot of the year for the part-time Territorial soldiers of the Manchester Regiment. For many men, it would be their only holiday. For others, it was a time to renew old friendships. For all, it was a time of comradeship. When the trains took the men off to Caernarfon on Sunday, 31 May 1914, they cannot have known that, within a few weeks, their world would be in turmoil and that, for many, they would not meet again in such convivial surroundings.

There was a bond of friendship amongst the 6th Battalion's men. Many of them lived in the same fashionable areas of the city – the fairly new suburbs of Longsight, Gorton and Blackley – or in the small towns and villages of the surrounding area, commuting into work by train or tram. Others lived in the Hulme area, close to the battalion headquarters. They had 'good jobs' with many working as bank clerks, or

Market Street, Manchester.

Oxford Street and Palace Theatre.

were employed in one of the many accountancy, stockbroking or legal firms which had offices around the city's King Street, Spring Gardens and St Anne's Square areas. Others worked in the offices of cotton merchants and traders in the buildings around Princess Street. Cottonopolis, as the area was popularly known, was where much of the city's wealth continued to be generated. Keen sportsmen and, almost solidly middle class, their game of choice was not football or rugby league. Instead, they played lacrosse or hockey in the winter and, of course, cricket in summer. Moving easily in the same social circles, as well as regularly drilling together at Stretford Road, the 'Saturday Afternoon Soldiers' were true pals as well as comrades.

Sergeant Thomas Worthington.

Britain had a long tradition of part-time military service dating back to the Militias and, more recently, the Volunteer Battalions. Their role was one of home defence at times of national crisis. Some units had, however, fought in South Africa during the Boer War but individual men could not be obliged to serve overseas. In 1908, reforms to the army structure created the Territorial Force with a streamlined command structure and the continued primary role on British shores.

Sergeant Thomas Worthington had been a member of the battalion for some years. Aged 30, he was the son of the Collector of Rates for the Cheadle & Gatley Urban District Council. Worthington worked as an accountant for the practice of David Smith, Garnett & Co, 61 Brown Street, Manchester and was an Associate of the Society of Accountants and Auditors (a rival body to the Institute of Chartered Accountants). Unlike many of his friends in the battalion, his game was hockey rather than lacrosse and he is believed to have played for the Bramhall club. His father had taught him to shoot as a boy and he was skilled with the rifle. He had won 'C' Company's Challenge Cup in 1913. As the train travelled along the North Wales coast, he may have been thinking of winning it again. Worthington had been promoted shortly before and now led the company's 'crack' section previously commanded by Billy Warburton[1] (recently elevated to Colour Sergeant). He was, probably, wanting to make sure the section continued to be the regular winner of Company competitions. Travelling with him, was his friend and colleague, Sergeant James H Weston, of 15 Dean's Road, Swinton.

Tents had already been pitched at Coed Helen, the extensive estate owned by the Hughes family, and the men quickly settled into their routine. Monday was a restful day but, on the Tuesday, training began in earnest with a route march. It went well, although some men complained of ill-fitting boots. The men were fit and an officer was quoted in the Manchester Evening Chronicle as saying that he expected that, by the end of the camp, the men would be *'as hard as nails'*.

The weather was good over the coming days and the men undertook musketry practice, more route marches and other manoeuvres. There was also the opportunity for sporting competitions. The *Evening Chronicle* recounts one incident as the battalion was going on manoeuvres.

> *Maps were consulted and the officers had an impression that they had arrived at their destination. For a time, however, they could find nothing but fields with good crops and the little yellow flags indicating the land was out of bounds. They were about to give up the search when a field which had less grass upon it was come across. There was no yellow flag and the men promptly took possession of it. They had no sooner got on the land than a man, evidently the farmer, popped up from behind a hedge and, brandishing a stick, said 'Look you, I want five pounds for you coming on my land.' The farmer was very persistent in his demand and the situation was, to say the least, a very amusing one.*

The matter was resolved by some skilful negotiation and the eventual payment of one pound.

By the end of the first week, the weather had taken a turn for the worse and it became unseasonably cold and wet. It was a miserable time for the men to complete their manoeuvres. The last couple of days were spent undertaking a major exercise. The 5th, 6th and 7th Battalions would undertake landings from the sea and attack positions defended by the 8th Battalion. Although the men could not know it, it would be a foretaste of their early experiences the following spring when they would go into action at Gallipoli. Fort Belan is now self-catering holiday accommodation but a defensive structure had been here since the 1500s and the structure the men would attack had been built to guard the entrance to the Menai Straits against possible French invasion during the Napoleonic Wars.

It was a time for the men to work together and to work with their comrades in the other battalions of the Manchester Brigade. This was not always easy in the rigid social structures of Edwardian Britain. On the one hand, as already indicated, a substantial number of the 6th Battalion troops were relatively affluent middle class office workers. On the other hand, the 5th Battalion had significant numbers of poorly paid miners from Wigan and its surrounding villages. It could have been problematical but Colonel

Darlington, commanding the 5th Battalion, later wrote that both groups of men *'worked particularly well in spite of social distinctions. The 6th called us "the flashy fifth" and they were known as the "collars and cuffs"*. The exercise went well with a 'battle' being fought at nearby Llanfaglan. The next day, there was a further attack on a defensive position. In another foretaste of Gallipoli, the defenders successfully held on.

The exercises finished on 13 June and the officers and men settled down to a final evening's relaxation. It was a 'smoker' – an informal get-together under the chairmanship of Sergeant Major (later Lieutenant) William Wynne. They would have provided their own entertainments – songs, recitations, perhaps a humorous sketch or two, parodying the officers and senior sergeants. The next day, Sunday, it was time to return home and restart normal life.

The fortnight had gone well and the men of the 6th would have been pleased that they were in third place in the East Lancashire Division's 'Douglas Challenge Cup'. This was a competition named after the division's commanding general and scores were awarded for the best daily programmes put up by company officers and carried out efficiently. Because camps were being held in different weeks this year the final results would not be known until mid-August. However, the battalion had amassed 534 points, just one behind the 8th Battalion and the 5th Lancashire Fusiliers. These three were well ahead of all other units and, even though some others still had to hold their camps, it was confidently expected they would not be overtaken.

However, the fortnight had not been without its grumbles. Soldiers, even part-time ones, would not be soldiers without grumbles. There were a number of complaints that, this year, new orders meant the men were required to undertake the route marches carrying their greatcoats and entrenching tools. A number said they were considering resigning from the Territorial Force in protest.

Two weeks passed before news of the assassination in Sarajevo of Austrian Archduke Ferdinand and his wife was reported in the British press. Throughout July, the situation in Europe continued to deteriorate but there were no indications in the local press that this was other than 'foreign news'. On the 28th and 29th, armies in the Balkans started to mobilise, as did Austria. In Britain, Territorial camps were cancelled and the army issued orders recalling all regular officers from leave to rejoin their units. The deepening crisis started to have an effect in the local area with the Manchester Stock Exchange seeing a dramatic slump in the price of cotton. The 30th brought large increases in the price of flour, butter and bacon in Manchester's shops. Diplomatic efforts to avoid war continued but looked increasingly futile as Germany massed its army on the French border and refused to confirm to Britain that it intended to respect Belgian neutrality.

On 1 August, Germany declared war on Russia and, the following day, moved its troops across the French border. In response and in anticipation of further aggression, Britain ordered a general mobilisation of its forces and, by 11pm on 4 August, declared a state of war existed between the two countries. The world would never be the same again.

The army was thoroughly organised to undertake the mobilisation quickly. Few men would have realised that their 'calling up' notices had been made out just after they enlisted and that, month by month, home addresses were checked and envelopes rewritten where necessary. So, with postal deliveries then being twice daily, it would have been no surprise that many men had already arrived at Battalion Headquarters at Stretford Road, Hulme before the declaration of war was formally announced.

Battalion Headquarters at Hulme.

Across the region, there was a rush to enlist into the army and, for the first weeks of the war, men could pretty much pick and choose which regiment they joined. In Stockport, members of the lacrosse and cricket clubs met on the evening of the 7th and offered their services to the East Lancashire Territorial Association. They hoped to raise at least one company of players and their friends and they expressed the wish to join their sporting friends in the 6th Battalion. The group's organisers had contacted the press and asked them to publicise the recruitment drive and that interested men should contact R Lister[2], Oldfield, Mile End Road, Stockport. Their services were not immediately accepted but, undiscouraged, the men began to drill at the club grounds at Cale Green, under the direction of a Cheshire Regiment sergeant from the town's Armoury.

Elsewhere, a group of men employed by Westinghouse Ltd, a major turbine and generator manufacturer in Trafford Park, was also trying to enlist into the army and also wanted to join the 6th Battalion. They were not from the shop floor but represented the cream of the company's highly qualified staff. Amongst them, twenty seven year old Preston Horan[3], originally from Sunderland, was a fully qualified engineer and lived locally at Roseneath, Marlborough Road, Sale, Cheshire. They were, perhaps, encouraged by Alexander Doig whose service number, 1738, suggests he had joined the battalion a few months prior to the declaration of war. Aged 25, Doig lived at 128 Upper Brook Street, Manchester with his parents. He had a degree from Manchester University and had previously attended the Manchester Technical School (now UMIST – the University's Institute of Science and Technology). He worked for Westinghouse as an electrical engineer and was a keen member of the Eccles Borough Football Club.

Within days of war being declared, the Government realised that hundreds of thousands of new recruits would be needed for the army and approval was given for the creation of new battalions for each Regiment. Unlike the two Regular battalions and the six Territorial battalions, the new Manchester Regiment ones would be formed

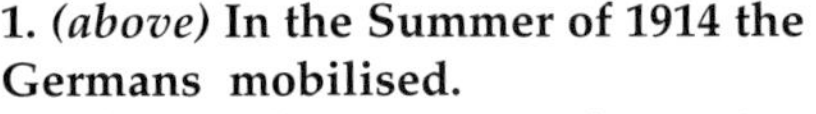

1. *(above)* **In the Summer of 1914 the Germans mobilised.**
2. *(above right)* **German infantry during training exercises.**

3. *(right and below)* **German artillery, cavalry and infantry in action against the Belgian, French and British defenders in the opening stages of the Great War.**

for the duration of the War only. They would be known as Service Battalions. The first of these, to be known as the 11th Battalion, was raised at Ashton under Lyne during August.

Meanwhile, those mobilised were spending their days around battalion headquarters, almost in idleness. The men who lived nearby were allowed home for a couple of hours each day for lunch (or 'dinner' as it was then almost universally called in the Manchester area). Ovens had been set up and there was usually roast beef and potatoes for dinner and bread, jam and cheese for tea in the early evening. Half of the men were sleeping at the drill hall on Stretford Road whilst the remainder were at a school on nearby Cavendish Street.

10 August was an important day for the Territorials. Lord Kitchener of Khartoum, the newly appointed Secretary of State for War, invited the men to volunteer for overseas service. There was no obligation on them to do so but, over the coming days, very many of them signed the forms indicating their readiness to fight for the duration of the war. They were anxious to be seen as 'proper soldiers'. It was also the day that the 6th Battalion deposited its 'colours' with Manchester's Lord Mayor for safe keeping at the Town Hall. The Mayor, Sir Daniel McCabe, responded

> *I feel it is a great honour to be entrusted with the colours of your Regiment. The very fact that you have joined the Territorials and made yourself efficient to defend and serve your country is evidence of your patriotism.'*

Within two days, 6,000 Territorials from the Manchester area had volunteered for active service abroad. Not all of them became Manchester Regiment soldiers. Across the River Irwell, Salford was the recruiting ground for the Lancashire Fusiliers and, south of the River Mersey, men from around Stockport and Stalybridge were long-serving Terriers with the 6th Battalion, Cheshire Regiment.

Although men were volunteering to go overseas in large numbers, the *Evening Chronicle* reported that there was concern amongst the men for their future once the war had ended. The Lord Mayor had met with a deputation from the regiment, headed by Noel Lee, a previous commander of the 6th Battalion and now commanding the Manchester Brigade. He was accompanied by Colonel G. G. P. Heywood, of the 6th Battalion and the commanders of the 7th and 8th Battalions.

> *They wanted reassurances from employers that all the men who return from service in the war will be re-instated in the positions they at present hold...the following organisations have already made such a promise – Messrs Tootal, Broadhurst Lee & Co, the Calico Printers Association and Messrs Rylands & Sons.'*

It is no surprise that Tootal Broadhurst led in this matter as Noel Lee was a director of the company. The Lord Mayor believed that many other employers had already agreed and that others would follow suit.

Within the week, over seventy percent of the full strength of the whole East Lancashire Division had volunteered for overseas service – some 14,000 from the total

Albert Square, Manchester. Major General Sir William Douglas takes the salute of a parade of the Manchester Brigade. Manchester Regiment Archives

Lord Kitchener.

establishment of 19,863. But, of course, in the fervour of patriotism, there were concerns about the men whose situation had prevented them from volunteering. It was an issue not restricted to the Manchester area and Lord Kitchener wrote to the country's Territorial Associations to reassure them. He confirmed that home defence was a matter of great importance and he did not wish that those *'who cannot, on account of their affairs, volunteer for foreign service should by any means be induced to do so, or on account of such inability, leave the Territorial Force.'*

For days, there had been rumours that the battalion would assemble with the rest of the brigade and other units of the division somewhere near Preston. However, it was decided to set up several smaller camps nearer to the City and, on the 19th, plans were made to march to Hollingworth Lake near Rochdale. They expected to be there for two months and then, like their Territorial neighbours, the 6th Cheshires, be sent to the Western Front.

The Lord Mayor hosted a lunch for the officers in command of the various Territorial units in Manchester and over fifty, headed by Brigadier Noel Lee, attended. Sir Daniel said that if he had allowed the Territorials to leave without public recognition he would not only have blamed himself but would have been blamed by the public as they were all very proud of their Territorials and, in particular, their early willingness to go on active service. Many people said that Manchester was only concerned with things that affected its pocket but they knew that commerce would be nowhere but for the open seas and access to other countries. Sir Daniel continued that it was very noble and very creditable that so many who had families and businesses should leave it all so that they could serve their country.

In reply to the toast 'Success to the Territorial Force', Lee said that Manchester had always been a leading centre of the voluntary spirit of military service, raising one of the first Volunteer Companies in 1859.

> *I receive many letters from parents stating that their sons have volunteered for active service and wanting to make conditions that it should be in such and such a place. Such a thing is not possible. We have volunteered our services to the King and we have to give those services wherever the King may require us, be it in England or at the front. It is not supposed that in the next month or two we shall be called upon to carry out that vow. We have much to do in brigades and in training in the next two months. But we must make ourselves efficient in these two months that our services may be of use whenever they may be required. If the King calls, those services will be readily given and we shall give an account of ourselves which will bring honour to our city.*

The *Rochdale Observer* reported their arrival at the new camp on the 20th under the headline 'Camping by the Lake. Manchester Territorials at Hollingworth. How Rochdale welcomed them'.

Battalion signallers, August 1914.

The Manchester Territorials made an early start. They were out and about soon after three o'clock and were in route formation by five. At that hour, the 6th Battalion moved away from their Headquarters in Stretford Road, half an hour later the 7th left Burlington Street and the men of the 8th from Ardwick, bringing up the rear. The departures were watched by crowds.

The 6th Battalion came through in orderly fashion. Officers riding, and one or two

The camp at Hollingworth Lake.

Camp life for new recruits. Published in the *Regimental Gazette*, November 1914.

mounted men were in the van, a cycling contingent followed and afterwards, four abreast, marched the 'Terriers'. A machine gun or two and quite a number of horse-drawn vehicles laden with stores brought up the rear. The 6th had scarcely passed along the Broadway into Smith Street before the 7th entered the Esplanade to the strains of a pulse-stirring march played by the Battalion Band. There was no ban on pipe or cigarette. Here and there water bottles were raised to dusty, ready lips. It must have been no joke this full kit march, with rifle, ammunition, other service requisites, and the greatcoat strapped behind the shoulders – a total weight exceeding 60lbs.

Coming round the bend of Hollingworth Lake, past the Fisherman's Inn, you get almost a bird's eye view of the camp of the Manchester Brigade. The white tents in rows along the greensward, stretching the length of a picturesque valley which culminates in the steep rise towards Blackstone Edge. The 6th Manchesters are at the foot of the short, sharp slope which falls from the east bank of the lake, and has the appearance of the edge of a basin or deep dish. Officers occupy separate territory on a sloping meadow to the right, and further along the straight the men of the 7th and 8th Battalions have fixed their tents. The eastern edge of the camp is occupied by the 5th Battalion and on this side also are the medicals and the Army Service Corps.

With the memories of Caernarfon still fairly fresh in their minds, the men quickly settled back into life under canvas. They undertook drills and other exercises designed to maintain their fitness. Food was good and plentiful and the Manchester Evening News reported that a man's daily ration included $1\frac{1}{4}$ lbs of fresh meat, $1\frac{1}{4}$ lbs of bread, 4 ounces of bacon, 3 of cheese and 2 of peas, beans or dried potato. There was also an allowance of jam, tea and sugar.

Hollingworth Lake had long been a tourist attraction. Created in 1800 as the feed for the Rochdale canal, by the middle of the nineteenth century it boasted hotels, pleasure grounds and small steamboats plied their trade, taking visitors on trips along the waters. The fact that it was now a massive army camp would encourage, rather than discourage, people from making a Sunday afternoon trip to gaze and gawp, as reported by the *Rochdale Observer* on 26 August.

Visitors are not encouraged is one of the statements issued by the Brigade staffs of the East Lancashire Territorials in camp at Turton, Bury and Littleborough, but at a spot like Hollingworth Lake it is a difficult matter to keep public interest at a distance. On Sunday afternoon the lake side presented a scene of the utmost animation; there was a continuous stream of people proceeding in the direction of the camp from all sides. Manchester and district visitors were very numerous and in the afternoon was heard expression of keen disappointment that the camp lines were closed to the public and the men kept within bounds. But the public must realise that there is a vast difference between the ordinary yearly training encampment and procedure in time of war.

The reason for keeping the men in close touch with headquarters was apparent early in the afternoon, when orders to strike camp were given. Instantly activity was general. Stores and equipment were collected and loaded, horses were saddled and loaded, and tents were tumbled down in wholesale fashion, though with a method that compelled admiration from civilian onlookers. Everybody, even the Territorials themselves, thought that once again they were to be on the move. Rumour was busy among the crowd. One excited individual would have it that the Germans were about to attack the South Coast, and that the Terriers as a defensive force, were called thereto. Others had it 'on good authority' that the training ground was to be changed. Few hit the right explanation that the whole thing was itself part of the training, designed to test how quickly, under conditions of actual necessity, departure from a camping ground could be accomplished. We believe the work was accomplished in record time and was to the complete satisfaction of the officers.

Over the weekend, some 51,000 people had travelled by train to Littleborough to visit. It led to a tightening up of discipline in the camp. There was even more physical exercise to concentrate the minds of the men and, as recorded by the *Evening News*, it became an offence for the soldiers to be found in a pub after 8pm.

Around the region, recruitment for the army continued at a brisk rate. In Stockport, the lacrosse players and their friends, drilling at Cale Green, now numbered around 150. Their intent was still to join the Manchesters but this was not finding universal favour in the town. The week's edition of the *Stockport Advertiser* noted that recruitment was generally going well but asked,

Why are the middle class hanging back at this time of national emergency. There must be any number of young men of good social standing in Stockport who are eligible for

service. Many of them are no doubt enlisting in Manchester but if they have any Territorial pride they should throw in their lot with the Cheshires.

Many of the men who worked in the mills and hatworks of the town were, indeed, joining the local 6th Cheshires but the newspaper's exhortations would have minimal effect on the town's young sportsmen. On 1 September, over fifty of them joined the 6th Manchesters. Many lived outside the Borough in the 'commuter villages' of Cheadle Hulme and Bramhall[4]. All had volunteered for overseas service.

The recruitment problem was not confined to Stockport. Numbers were drying up in Manchester and Liverpool and those who had come forward to enlist in the new Service Battalions were working class men from the factories and docks of the two cities. Lord Derby, then Mayor of Liverpool, hit upon the solution. He called for his city to raise a battalion of 'clerks and others engaged in commercial business, who wish to serve their country and would be willing to enlist…..if they felt assured that they would be able to serve with their friends…..' The idea latched on to the bond of friendship that existed in the Territorial battalions. It overcame the social barriers of the time and was an instant success. The 'Pals' Battalions had been born and it would take the Lord Mayor of Manchester only a day to adopt a similar strategy, not wishing to be outdone by the neighbouring city. Recruitment opened in the afternoon of 31 August and by the time the recruiting office had closed for the day on 1 September, the 1st City Battalion (later the 16th Battalion, Manchester Regiment) had been recruited from amongst the clerks and warehousemen employed by the city's major employers.

1 September was also the day that Ridley Sheldon joined the 6th Battalion. He later wrote[5] that, when war was declared, he had been on a cycling holiday in the Lake District with his father and a friend but, once back in Manchester, went to join up.

I wended my way to the Headquarters of the Battalion, situate in Stretford Road, only to discover that no more fellows were wanted for home service. I went again soon after, and this time found the place closed. This afforded every opportunity, as you may well imagine, for my ardour and zeal to cool down, but instead of this, the desire to offer myself only deepened all the more; so I went again, but was as unfortunate as ever, for it so happened that two or three other fellows were lounging about the entrance to the building, with mufflers round their throats – a sorry looking lot, and I suppose it was thought I was with them; at any rate, we were all told we were not wanted – our services were not required. This rather damped my feelings, but I was determined that I would not be beaten, so went once more, and I well remember the occasion; it was Tuesday, September 1st, 1914. This time I was successful, for the result of the Medical Examination was, that I passed the Doctor – being in the very pink of condition, was immediately accepted, and at once enrolled in the ranks of His Majesty's Army. Here, let me say, that finding out no more were required for home service, I signed on, along with all the others, or nearly all, for four years foreign active service. It was one of the very happiest days of my life.

During the war, the 'Manchester City Battalions Book of Honour' was published which included entries from employers listing their staff who had joined up. Woollen merchants, Sparrow Hardwick Ltd, list a man named R Sheldon who had joined the 6th Battalion and this was almost certainly Ridley.

The new recruits returned to Stretford Road the next day and received their uniforms and were allowed home for a final time. The next morning, they paraded at 8.15 and were given a stirring speech by Major (and Quartermaster) William Vass[6] before marching off to Victoria Station to catch the train to Littleborough. Private Sheldon had probably his first grumble of his army service. No kit bags had been issued and he later wrote of struggling with his belongings wrapped up in a large brown paper parcel.

For the new men, the next week was hard. There were drills, marches, parades and, even for the lacrosse players who had learned the rudimentary basics of drill, it was a difficult few days.

The newspapers were full of anti-German propaganda and, around Manchester, German and Austrian nationals had been rounded up and interned. It caused great problems for the city's top restaurants and hotels, many of whose waiters came from these countries. Nationally, J Lyons Tea Ltd had gone to the High Court and obtained an injunction against their competitor, Lipton's Ltd, preventing it from publishing anything to the effect that Lyon's was 'composed of Germans' and that by purchasing their commodities the public was assisting the enemies of Great Britain. Lyon's had

Clocks cost us £340,000.

Some of the toys and games for which we pay over a million every year to Germany.

We pay them £350,000 for glass bottles.

One way of dealing a heavy blow at Germany is to seize her trade while she is at war—and stick to it. Her foreign overseas trade is now stopped, thanks to the British Navy; and while Britain keeps command of the seas a large part of it should pass into British hands. In any case we should lose no time in making at home the many million pounds worth of goods that we have been importing from Germany every year. There should be no great difficulty about most of it.—(*Daily Sketch* Photographs.)

'How the British manufacturer can help to fight Germany.' *The Daily Sketch*, August 25, 1914, informed its readers of German imports.

Right: newspaper caption reads – These motor parts are made in Germany. Why shouldn't we make our own hooters?

taken out large advertisements in the newspapers headed 'Action for Libel' and proclaiming that their company was entirely British owned.

Rumours that the Manchesters would soon be on the move continued to circulate round the camp and as soon as one was dashed, another would start up. Would it be France? Would it be Belgium? The latest rumour was that it would be Egypt and this one seemed to have some basis in fact.

The *Rochdale Observer* continued to report the situation.

> *The Manchester Brigade are still in their lakeside camp at Hollingworth, though the 6th Battalion have moved from the ground immediately adjacent to the road bordering the lake. This spot was rather too shut in. Mornings have been occupied these last few days with hillside marches and manoeuvres, some good work having been accomplished. A dry camp is an appreciated boon. There is, however, plenty of ground mist in the early morning before the sun is up.*
>
> *Rumours of impending departure from the camping ground continue to circulate, but it appears that no definite orders have yet been received, in fact there has been addition to camp equipment within the last 24 hours.'*

It was not long before the rumours of Egypt were finally confirmed. On the 5th, the divisional commander, Major General Douglas, received a telegram from Lord Kitchener:

> *Inform the Division from me that I hope that they will push on hard with their training in Egypt as, before they are ready, there will be plenty of troops from India to garrison Egypt and I hope they will be one of the first Territorial Forces to join our Army on the Continent. All will depend on their fitness for service against the enemy in the Field.*

Douglas replied *'All ranks much gratified to receive your message. They are animated with keen desire to fit themselves to join our forces on the Continent.'* So, the plan was that the Territorials would go to Egypt which, legally still part of the Ottoman Empire, had been under British occupation for many years. Britain had invaded in 1882 and its troops were still stationed there to guard the strategically important Suez Canal. The Regulars currently on garrison duty could then be moved to France and Belgium. In due course, fully trained Territorials would also go to the Western Front, being replaced in turn by troops from India.

It was a busy few days, making ready to pack up and go. The new recruits meant that the 6th Battalion would go overseas at almost the full strength of a fighting unit – approximately 1,000 men, including about thirty officers. Some forty trains would be needed to take the various units of the East Lancashire Division from their camps to embark at Southampton. For the Manchesters, departures started from Littleborough during the afternoon of 9 September. For a while, there was chaos around the 6th Battalion's camp area. A steam lorry went out of control on the exit road, knocking down the wall and rolled over in the camp. It took another lorry and 200 men to get it lifted away.

Amongst the lacrosse players, many of whom were in the Battalion's 'F' Company, were three brothers – Sydney 'Cider' Heydon, Arthur Heydon and, the youngest, Frank 'Nip' Heydon. The brothers lived at the family home at 'Ebor', Kennerley Road, Stockport. 'Cider' had been educated at Stockport Commercial School but his employment is not known. Aged 25, he was a regular member of the lacrosse first team and had represented Cheshire, the North of England and, on one occasion, had played for England against Canada. Writing home, he told of the trip south

> *'After being on the train 14 hours, we arrived at Southampton and went aboard the SS* Corsican. *Arthur, Nip and myself and all our boys had a good sleep on the train. The boat we are on was one of the first boats to get to the* Titanic *when she went down. We sailed about nine o'clock when we were all in bed……'*

Lance Corporal Sidney 'Cider' Heydon, from Stockport.

SS *Corsican*.

Ridley Sheldon, the Heydon brothers and the other new recruits would undertake their basic army training while 'on the job'.

The men who had not volunteered for overseas service would form the nucleus of a new Battalion which would shortly be officially designated as the 2nd/6th. The original Battalion would become known as the 1st/6th but will continue to be referred to here just as the 6th. The history of the 2nd/6th is recorded in Chapter 7 and, until mid-1915, it undertook a dual role. Firstly, it took on the Territorial Force's responsibilities for home defence and, secondly, acting as the reserve battalion, trained new recruits to send overseas.

Sharing the cramped space aboard the SS *Corsican* were the Ardwick men of the 8th Battalion. The Wiganers of the 'Flashy Fifth' had boarded the *SS Caledonia* and the 7th and the brigade staff were aboard the *Grantully Castle*, owned by the Union-Castle Line and normally sailing between Britain and South Africa. The East Lancashire and Lancashire Fusiliers Brigades were aboard other ships, as were the units of the artillery, Army Service Corps and Royal Army Medical Corps. In total, the convoy had fifteen transport ships and their escorts. They were the first Territorial Division to go overseas.

The divisional history[7] recounts the convoy's departure:

HMS *Ocean*.

It was midnight when the troopships steamed out of the harbour, a dark night, all lights doused, no coastwise lights to guide, the blackness stabbed by scores of searchlights. The troops on board one of the ships began to sing and the whole convoy took up the strains. In the morning, the first arrivals lay-to off the Eddystone until, by late afternoon, a great fleet had assembled. At sundown the convoy sailed in three lines ahead, escorted by the battleship Ocean *and the cruiser* Minerva. *It is said that this was the first actual convoy that had left England since the Napoleonic wars.*

The weather was particularly bad for the first three days and it was a miserable time for the men. On 12 September, 'Cider' Heydon wrote

Woke up this morning and found it very rough…Nearly everyone on board is ill. Both Arthur and Nip have been ill all day and I have been sick, although I have not missed a meal and am feeling fit.

He was, perhaps, one of the fortunate ones – the divisional history notes that, although whole messes did not eat a meal in the three days, the daily indent of one bottle of beer per man was always drawn, to be saved for happier days.

The happier days for the brothers started on Monday, 14 September.

We should have had two hours drill every day, but we are only starting today. We get up at 6 o'clock, have breakfast at 7.15, dinner 12 o'clock and tea 5 o'clock and bed at 9. As for food, we do a lot better than at camp. For breakfast we have porridge or hashed beef and potato, bread and butter and jam and tea. Dinner, soup, roast beef and potatoes or stewed beef, rice and currant pudding. For tea, we have bread and butter, jam, tea or cold beef, pickles, so we do very well for food.

The *Corsican* had reached southern Spain by the 16th and 'Cider' included in his letter home that it was getting hotter and hotter. 'The only drink we can get on board is Bass, served out at 11 o'clock or lukewarm water. I would give anything to get a few bottles of iced lager or mineral water'. Heydon's drink preferences might surprise those who think of them as much later fashions. In fact, lager had started to be brewed in England in 1882, when the Wrexham Brewery was founded by German immigrants. It quickly gained a reputation as a thirst-quencher.

Early the next day, Gibraltar was sighted in the distance and the men hoped they would be amongst the few allowed ashore to collect the supplies of tropical uniforms and helmets. If Ridley Sheldon harboured thoughts of a spot of sight-seeing, his plans were quickly thwarted by the medical officer who was carrying on with his schedule of inoculations.

First of all, one of the RAMC men rubbed the places well with methylated spirits and iodine; the Doctor then filled a syringe with typhoid germs and injected the needle about half-an-inch under the skin, both in my chest and right side. The pricking was hardly felt at all; it was the injection that was so exceedingly painful, for it burned like fire. The next morning, I was awfully sore all over my chest, and could hardly move, but eventually I got over it.

The convoy had moored in the Bay of Gibraltar and whilst supplies were brought on board, large rowing boats came to the ships with locals selling grapes and tobacco. They spent six hours in the bay before steaming off at seven in the evening.

There was a party spirit onboard during the evening of the 18th, as recounted by Private Heydon,

*Mortimer got the officers to let him have a piano on deck and Fred Jeffreys played all night to the delight of all on board. Edgar, Jack, Vernon, Nip, Bleackley and Mortimer*8 *sang and recited and nearly all on board gathered round. The officers gave three cheers for the choir so you can tell we have already made a name for ourselves.*

The men's next hope for a walk on dry land was that the convoy would dock at Malta but the island was passed during the night of 21/22 August. The next day, a great convoy was seen steaming from the opposite direction. It was the transport for the Lahore Division bringing troops from India to Marseilles with, amongst the Sikh, Punjabi and Gurkha battalions, the 6th Battalion's regular army comrades from the 1st Manchesters. The convoys came to a halt and greetings were exchanged. The convoy escorts exchanged duties, with *Minerva* returning to Marseilles and the East Lancashires being escorted on by HMS *Weymouth*, a modern cruiser built in 1911.

The remaining three days of the voyage passed without incident and the men paraded for a full kit inspection and a final 'once over' from the medical officer. The ships arrived at their destination, Alexandria Harbour, during the morning of the 25th. The divisional history notes that as they entered the harbour, they passed an American battle-cruiser:

Though strict neutrality had to be maintained in respect of action, there was no attempt to observe it in sentiment. To the delight of the Lancashire men the Americans manned ship; their band played 'God save the King' and generally did us proud. The Division was keen to show its appreciation. The Band of the 8th Manchesters, uncertain whether 'Yankee Doodle', 'The Star-Spangled Banner' or 'My Country, 'tis of thee' is considered the national anthem of the United States, and doubting their ability to render either of the first two airs pleasingly – the third tune being that of our own national anthem, and therefore open to misconstruction – struck up 'Marching through Georgia'. All too late came the reflection that possibly the cruiser's complement had been drawn from States which might not appreciate this air.'

Disembarkation started soon afterwards with the first troops, Lancashire Fusiliers, being sent on to Cairo. For the men of the 6th, they would remain in Alexandria as part of its garrison but they would have one more night aboard the *Corsican* before their adventure continued.

---

1 298, William Rainsford Warburton. Later Company Quartermaster Sergeant and Captain and Adjutant.
2 Robert Lister, Stockport Lacrosse Club's first team goalkeeper. Wounded in action May 1915. Brother of John Bedford Lister, killed in action 5 June 1915.
3 2293, Private Horan served with the Battalion until 25 June 1915, when he received a commission with the Durham Light Infantry. Captain Horan was demobilised from the army on 1 March 1919 and returned to the family home at 1 Esplanade West, Sunderland.
4 They included Pte Frank Halliday, killed in action on 4 June 1915 and William Beecroft, killed in action on 22 July 1918, whilst serving as 2nd Lieutenant with the 6th Battalion, Gloucestershire Regiment.
5 William Musgrove Ridley Sheldon was born on 25 September 1896, at 11 Turkey Lane, Manchester. He was the son of William James Sheldon, a local minister of religion, and his wife, Elizabeth. After his early service, Pte Ridley Sheldon wrote an account of his service with the Battalion. A copy is held by the Regimental Archives which gives permission for the inclusion of extracts here.
6 William Vass did not see active service due to his age. He died, at 57, on 23 September 1917 and is buried in Southern Cemetery, Manchester.
7 'The 42nd (East Lancashire) Division, 1914-1918', Frederick P Gibbon, Country Life Ltd, London, 1920
8 Not all of these men can be identified but are possibly Harry Mortimer, living in the Stockport area, killed in action 30 June 1915; Fred Jeffreys will be Fred Jefferis, from Fallowfield. He had been educated at Hulme Grammar School and played lacrosse for Lancashire and the North of England. He was killed in action, 7 August 1915. Bleackley will be either Edward Bleackley, died of wounds, 25 July 1915, or his older brother known as Cliff.

Port of Alexandria in 1914.

Chapter 2

EGYPT

THE MANCHESTERS DISEMBARKED early on 26 September and paraded before General Maxwell, British Commander in Egypt, before moving off to barracks. Private Ridley Sheldon:

> *We had to face a walk of four miles in the broiling hot sun, with a weight of eighty-five pounds on our backs, in the shape of equipment, which included a hundred rounds of ammunition; and we were only allowed one rest during the whole distance and that was ten minutes. The distance may not seem very far, but then the fact must not be overlooked that the heat was something like eighty degrees in the shade, so that the walk was very trying. Our destination was Mustapha Barracks, which is a very large building, but rather awkward to locate on account of its situation, for you walk over nothing but sand, which is very trying to the feet; so we were very thankful to arrive at the end of our journey.*

Khaki pith helmets were quickly issued to the men on arrival at the barracks. But as all the tropical clothing had been loaded on to one ship at Gibraltar, it would take some time for all the men to receive their issue. As the divisional history has it,

> *The usual conditions of issue were experienced. When only the smaller sizes of headgear, boots and clothing are available, how is it that so large a proportion of big-footed, big-headed, big-framed men turns up?*

Whilst the men of the East Lancashire Division had had a pleasant voyage, the same could not be said for the division's horses. The ships had been poorly suited for the

Mustapha Barracks. A and B Companies occupied the buildings and C and D were in the tents. Manchester Regiment Archives

purpose and a not insignificant number had died on the way to Egypt. Most were disembarked in poor health.

Private David 'Dadie' Sinclair[1], B Company, spent his first night in Egypt looking after 150 horses. They were tethered on a quay some four miles from SS *Corsican* and Sinclair was one of fifty men detailed to provide a guard.

Very hot marching, perspiration running down in streams. We were in full marching order, which includes greatcoats, belt with pouches, mess tin, bayonet, entrenching tool, water bottle and rifle, with 100 rounds of ammunition. Guard consisted of watching about 150 horses to see that they did not lie down, also that they did not break away or fight. The reason for this is that they were nearly all sick after the voyage. Five died during the night.

Colour Sergeant Billy Warburton still waits for his pith helmet whilst his friend, Tom Worthington, has been issued his. Worthington family

The closing days of the month were spent moving the battalion's stores and the men's kitbags from the quayside to the barracks. Dadie Sinclair breakfasted on half a loaf of bread, tinned salmon and tea before starting the arduous day. Ridley Sheldon recorded that he and eleven others worked as a group to push a handcart loaded with kitbags the four miles to barracks. There was no rest break and nothing to eat 'and this, mark you, with an equipment of eighty five pounds on our backs…we were dead-beat and tired out'.

They only worked in the morning and were able to rest from the heat for the remainder of the day. Before they started work on the 29th, there was a bathing parade and the men enjoyed being able to swim in the warmth of the sea. Private David Sinclair:

It is well worth the hard work and the discomforts which we have passed through to get the change of air, scenery and the experience. Little did I think when I was bathing and golfing at home six weeks ago that I would be shortly sojourning on the shores of the Blue Mediterranean.

On the 30th, Sinclair got his tropical uniform. The tunic fitted quite well, but he found the trousers were three or four inches too long and they were a bit tight at the waist. Even so, he was on full battalion parade at 4pm and, along with everyone else, was put through rifle and marching drill until 5.30pm. They were then dismissed for their evening meal – bread, apricot jam and tea.

Training started in earnest the next morning. Reveille was at 5am and the men paraded twenty minutes later on the barracks square. They were drilled for three hours under the direction of the senior sergeants. This was all about improving the men's fitness, as much of the time was spent 'doubling' round the square as well as marching at normal pace. They were then released for breakfast – tea, bread, tinned paloney – 'the latter very enjoyable but most terribly scarce'.

During the day, a reorganisation of the battalion was announced. The previous set-up of eight companies would now be reduced to four, in common with the army's usual arrangements. Sinclair's B Company was merged with E; the new company still designated as B. Each company had four platoons and, within that, the men were split into sections under the charge of a sergeant and lance corporal.

> *"When we fell in on the afternoon parade, we had to form up in our new sections and the Lieutenant in our new platoon, Hellawell[2] by name, gave us a short lecture, the gist of which is that he wanted us to be the smartest in the Company.*

It was drill, drill and more drill for the next couple of days and army life seemed to be losing its appeal for Dadie Sinclair. He reported sick on the 3 October, suffering with a heavy cold, sore throat and what he described as a 'touch of colic'. The doctor gave him two unknown tablets which just 'burnt out my chest'. As other soldiers also record, he bemoans the fact that dinner almost every day since they arrived had been 'skilly' and potatoes. Skilly was porridge-like gruel or a thin stew and certainly would not have been in the usual diet of the middle class men of the battalion. On the 5th,

Bathing parade. Manchester Regiment Archives

Ras-el-Tin Barracks. Manchester Regiment Archives

reveille was at 5am. 'Good news. We were to have coffee and biscuit. Received the liquid; couldn't tell whether it was tea or coffee. Took their word it was the latter. Biscuit was good.'

One of Sinclair's company comrades, Tom Gresham, was having a better time of it. His diary[3] entry for 4 October records '*Went for a swim for 30 minutes, then lay in the sun and ate fresh figs.*' Born on 25 October 1895, he was educated at Manchester Grammar School and, in 1912, secured an engineering apprenticeship joining the Lancashire & Yorkshire Railway Company at its locomotive works at Horwich, near Bolton. Private Gresham had joined the battalion around the same time and was a member of the original E Company.

Sinclair's mood was no better on the 7th when breakfast had been little more than a cup of 'alleged tea' and dinner '*Skilly, again. If I ever get skilly served up to me after I get back, the server should look out for trouble.*' It was a busy day. There was company drill before breakfast and musketry practice and bayonet fighting drill for the rest of the morning. They paraded back at 3.30 and practised various marching formations, then had saluting drill.

The troops were now settled into their quarters and into the new routines and, over the next few days, there were no regular parades but training continued, particularly for the new recruits such as the lacrosse players. The 14th saw a very busy morning but the afternoon was a holiday and most of the battalion turned out to watch inter-company football matches. Private David Sinclair:

> *Parade at 5.35. Company drill then section drill and physical drill with rifles. Hard work but very enjoyable. I hope it is continued every day. Breakfast, after having a drink of hot milk which was good, was the best I have had since I came away. It consisted of tea,*

bread and tinned herring in tomato sauce. I also had bought two boiled eggs, so I had a very good feed. Musketry drill 9.55 to 10.45 then again 11.40 to 12.30. After dinner, went to see a football match between A and B Companies in which our Company lost 1-0. After this match, there was one between C and D, it was very good as there were some first class players.

Although closely allied with Germany, the Ottoman Empire had not entered the war in August but, on 1 October 1914, it had closed the narrow Dardanelles straits to Allied shipping, cutting off the Russian Black Sea fleet from the high seas. It became increasingly clear that Turkey was likely to declare itself for its ally. In Egypt, the fear was that with Turkey in the conflict, fellow Muslims in Egypt would be encouraged to rise against their British occupiers. It was decided to put on a deterrent show of strength to the local population with the whole of a heavily armed Manchester Brigade marching through the streets of Alexandria. They paraded at 7.45am on 16 October with rifles, fifty rounds of ammunition and their water bottles. As Dadie Sinclair wrote 'We were really out for intimidation purposes'.

We set off from the barracks at 8.05. The 5th, 6th and 8th Battalions, the 6th having the honour of leading the way. It was a very fine sight to see about three or four thousand men and some machine guns all marching along in fours. I was in the last file of fours of our Company so saw all the fun with people trying to cut through between our Company and C Company. One of our NCOs was marching behind our file and he had the job of stopping anyone going through. One Arab who had broken through was very funny. He had almost got on to the footpath when our chap got him by the back of the neck and he squealed like a stuck pig and threw up his hands.

Ras-el-Tin Barracks. Manchester Regiment Archives

Tom Gresham also enjoyed the day. 'We had been told to put as much 'swagger' into the march as possible and let the natives see who we were.'

As usual, Sunday the 18th began with church parades but unlike the previous weeks, where a service had been conducted for the whole brigade on the barracks' square, services for each battalion were held in the church. For most of the men, they had the rest of the day off, but for 120 of them, there was more work to be done. They were detailed, under the direction of Captain Kessler and two other officers to guard some German prisoners. Edgar Kessler[4] was a pre-war Terrier and had received his Captaincy only on 26 August, making him the junior Captain of the new A Company. Private Ridley Sheldon:

> *We donned our full marching order and made for Ras-el-Tin where, on arriving, we had something to eat and then went to our quarters. Soon, twenty tents came and these were immediately erected, eight of them being for the Germans to sleep in and the rest for the guard, which was at once mounted until the following morning. The fellows seemed quite happy and told us that they did not know England was at war with Germany until the* Duke of Edinburgh *captured their boat which was on a voyage from China to Germany.*

Sheldon was very pleased to have been selected for this duty. Not only did it mean he escaped the daily routines of parades and drill, but he also got the opportunity to see Malta as the prisoners were soon to be escorted there to go into prisoner of war camps on the island. It was a three day voyage and he was only able to spend a few hours on the island before the return trip.

Training exercises now started to take on a much more warlike aspect. On the 19th, and on several subsequent days, the battalion marched about five miles to manoeuvring grounds near to Victoria College (later the Army's 17th General Hospital). Here they practised outpost duty amongst the nearby sandhills. The exercise mainly consisted of skirmishing and taking cover.

After breakfast on 23 October, Captain Holberton, the battalion's 35 year old adjutant, gave the men a lecture on outpost duty before preparations were made for an exercise the coming night. Philip Vaughan Holberton[5] was the battalion's only regular army officer. He was born in the Brentford area of Middlesex in 1879 and had attended the Royal Military Academy at Sandhurst. Whilst there, he was awarded the Sword of Honour as most deserving cadet for the term ending 29 January 1901.

The night's exercise saw D Company attacking an outpost line defended by the other three companies. B Company held the centre of the defences and Dadie Sinclair and two others under the charge of a corporal were detailed as sentry pickets about 300 yards in advance of their platoon position. After a couple of hours, they heard noises in the desert and rushed back to the others to raise the alarm. Half an hour later, the defenders started to make out dark shapes moving towards them and orders were given to open fire although, of course, blank ammunition was being used. 'They were to all intents and purposes annihilated and had to surrender'.

Captain and Adjutant Philip Holberton takes an instruction class. Manchester Regiment Archives

Tom Gresham spent his 19th birthday at Alexandria docks guarding ammunition trains to ensure that supplies were not stolen. The next day, he undertook one of his required musketry tests but he did not think he had done very well. One test involved kneeling and firing five rounds at a target 300 yards away, taking cover and firing again over the cover. He scored sixteen out of twenty.

Perhaps insensitively to the local population, the exercise on 27 October was to assume that a nearby mosque was held by the enemy and they were to deploy as if for attack on it. It went very well and, as they were only a few hundred yards from the sea, the officers took the opportunity to reward the men with an impromptu bathing parade.

It had become increasingly clear that the Ottoman Empire's declared neutrality was little more than a sham. On the 29th, it entered the war as an ally of Germany. Two days later, Cairo saw an immense demonstration of British force, similar to that in Alexandria previously. On 1 November, martial law was declared throughout Egypt and, on the 5th, Britain formally declared war on Turkey. Cyprus was annexed two days later.

Early November also saw the men undertaking musketry practice. They were scored on shooting at various ranges and targets. It was slow progress for many of the new recruits. On the 6th, whilst the experienced men carried on refining their long distance shooting, the new recruits got their first taste of bayonet fighting. No injuries were reported. This pattern continued until the 10th when the men prepared for another exercise. Private David Sinclair:

> *Reveille 5.15. Cleaned up bayonet, rifle, etc. Breakfast – tea, bread, porridge. Parade at 7am, marched to desert, attacked a position, we were firing blank cartridges. Marched back 1.30. Dinner 2.30, roast, beans and potatoes. Parade 4pm under Sergeant Major, then bathing parade. Tea – tea, bread and jam. Played auction bridge all evening. Bed 10pm."*

It was not all exercises and, one evening, Sinclair was detailed to be on picket duty at Mustapha Station, where the men would catch a tram into town. His duty was to check the men were properly dressed but it was an easy job. The guard spent most of the evening sat in the hut, rolling cigarettes for want of something to do.

On 15 November, the battalion paraded at 7am, to move to Mex, about eleven miles away for a few days. Captain Claude Worthington[6], commanding A Company, recorded the day in his diary. He was clearly furious at the poor performance of his men.

Captain Claude Worthington was furious at the poor performance of A Company.

> *On arrival on company parade ground only three men. The rest drawing ammunition. Company not ready till 7.25am. Adjutant and Colonel[7] came to find reason. General waiting on parade ground. Company publicly disgraced on parade for being late by Commanding Officer. Enquired into lateness and found lack of organisation amongst Non-Commissioned Officers in loading wagons and distribution of ammunition.*
>
> *Made Sergeant Smyth acting Sergeant Major instead of Staff Sergeant Redden. Sergeant Walmsley No. 2 Platoon Sergeant. Lieutenant Kay, No. 1 Platoon Commanding Officer.*

Still angry the next day, he records 'Cursed all Non-Commissioned Officers for slackness the previous day and Staff Sergeant Redden.' Perhaps as punishment, the company were given drill for an hour and a half in the afternoon. No. 2 Platoon spent all night out on outpost duty under Captain Kessler.

As on previous exercises, the men were engaged in the hard task of digging through the sand to make trenches. Private Sinclair, the professional engineer, commented wryly in his diary that the army was trying to teach the men two new trades at once – navvy and grave-digger. There was more trench digging after breakfast on 20 November and most of the battalion then manned them in a defensive exercise. Sinclair avoided the digging this time and was part of the one and half companies under the command of Captain Bazley who attacked the defences. 'We would have been practically wiped out, as we were made to do some silly rushes of about 100 yards or more, over exposed ground.'

Walter Bazley was born in Salford in 1873 and worked as a cloth salesman in Manchester. He had long service with the Regiment, joining the mounted infantry

29 November 1914. German civilians at Ras-el-Tin barracks preparing to go into internment, probably on Malta. Manchester Regiment Archives.

company of the 2nd Volunteer Battalion in the mid 1890s and had seen action in South Africa with the 77th Imperial Yeomanry during the Boer War. Bazley had been promoted to Captain in September 1911. He lived with his wife, Rose, at 'Neardale', Middleton Road, Cheetham Hill.

There was a company inspection on 22 November which irritated some of the men. Sinclair recorded that the captains went along the lines of beds ensuring they were lined up to a piece of rope. '*It was a farce, plain and simple*'.

The next afternoon, Claude Worthington and Edgar Kessler rode along a proposed route of a march planned for the next day. The pre-war men went off on the march and undertook shooting practice. The newer recruits spent the morning again digging trenches and they were then attached to C and 'D' Companies to defend the position against a mock attack from A. There was now a sophisticated set of trenchworks, replicating realistic conditions with a front and second line, linked by communication trenches. The men found it much more enjoyable and interesting and seem to have had some good fun rushing about in the trench system.

A couple of days later, the officers had planned for the men to carry on with their shooting tests but it rained heavily and it meant A and B Companies had to move their camp to higher ground. Private David Sinclair:

> *The wind was very strong so it made the taking down and then putting up again of tents, a very tiresome business. Our eyes, mouths, ears and everything else were full of sand. It was my first experience of a sand storm and I hope it will be my last*

The battalion moved back to Mustapha Barracks on 4 December and B Company immediately prepared to provide the town guards for the coming two weeks. The men

Men of the original H Company take a break. Manchester Regiment Archives

would work twenty-four hours on duty and twenty-four hours off duty. The 24 year old Private Sinclair thoroughly enjoyed his time there and for nothing to do with military reasons.

I didn't think that there were so many nice looking girls in Alexandria until I came on this job. They are practically of all nationalities – French or Italian predominantly and all are very, very neat. Some of the better class Egyptian ladies are very nice looking though, of course, dark and are dressed practically the same in black flowing robes with a black mantle thing over their heads, also a white veil from the tips of their noses to their chests. As a rule, this veil is pretty transparent and you can see their faces quite well.

While B Company was away, life for the rest of the battalion carried on much as before with more route marches and training exercises in attack and defence. On the 17th, Egypt was declared a British Protectorate. The men of the 6th will have been less concerned about that than orders issued the same day that they would be confined to barracks on Christmas Day and Boxing Day. The next day some sad news came from their comrades in the 8th Battalion. The first of their number had died. Private Ridley Sheldon:

There was also the tragic side in regard to events which happened; this was the case whenever any of our fellows died. One was that of a lad belonging to the 8th Manchester Battalion. He had been inoculated and, lying in a draught, had contracted a chill, which developed into appendicitis; and at midnight he was so bad that a hurried operation had perforce to be performed. He rallied for a while, but passed away at two the next morning and his body laid to rest in the beautiful cemetery at a place called Chatby. Poor lad. He was only twenty one, without father and his mother's only son.[8]

As Christmas neared, a more relaxed atmosphere started to be felt amongst the men. Training continued but there were a number of half day holidays. Men took the opportunity to go sight-seeing. There were also sporting matches. A Company played C Company at hockey and, no doubt, Sergeant Tom Worthington will have been a leading light of the C team. The result is not recorded. As might be expected, lacrosse was played and there was a match on 23 December between the Cheshire and Lancashire men – the region's old rivals in the game. The River Mersey divides the town of Stockport into its two parts – mostly in Cheshire but across the northern bank, Lancashire. Bearing in mind the number of lacrosse players from the town, it's no surprise that they formed all of the Cheshire side and most of the Lancashire one. The Lancastrians won 11 – 6.

There was still work to be done and large scale exercises took place in the desert on the 21st and 22nd. It was the usual affair of attack and defence but, as part of his own training for the future, command of the battalion was undertaken by Captain Claude Worthington. Private Tom Gresham:

> *Captain Bazley was happy as a sandboy when we got in action. He was crawling about on his stomach trying to find a weak spot in the enemy's positions and shouting Come on you... run like hell, whenever we made a rush but he never lost his head. In fact, the more we see of him, the finer the soldier we find him.*[10]

Meanwhile, some of the men who had entertained their chums and comrades on the voyage from Southampton had been rehearsing for a big event. They would perform in a Pierrot entertainment at the barracks on the evening of the 23rd, in aid of the Military Hospital Fund. Amongst the troupe, were several of the battalion's characters.

As on the *Corsican*, Fred Jefferis would play the piano to accompany the singers. The only officer amongst them was A Company's 2nd Lieutenant Tom Mills. He would not only produce the show but also planned to sing a couple of songs. Aged 28, he had enjoyed a particularly privileged upbringing, even by the standards of the 6th Battalion. Educated at Harrow and Trinity College, Cambridge from which he graduated with a BA in 1907, he joined up on 4 August – the day war was declared – and was commissioned as an officer the same day.

Company Quartermaster Sergeant Frank Deacon.
Manchester Regiment Archives

Sergeant William Taylforth of B Company was used to performing in public as a member of Mr Cradock's Glee Club and Madrigal Choir in

The outer cover of the concert's programme is reproduced above. Tom Gresham sent a copy home together with explanations of some of the cartoons:

***Left hand page, top left* – 316 Arthur Fleming was the cooks' sergeant.**

***Left hand page, centre* – Staff Sergeant 'Evans is a Welshman and his favourite saying is 'I know you b…'**

***Left hand page, top right* – a good likeness of Private Gillbrand who, when off-duty, had a reputation for wearing 'the most awful' shirts**

***Left hand page, bottom left* – Dr Norris, Battalion Medical Officer.**

***Right hand page, top left* – a reference to tinned sardines always being amongst the rations when on exercises.**

***Right hand page, top right* – a good likeness of A Company's Dods[9]**

***Right hand page, bottom* – Sergeant Major Deacon, a strong drinker and loves his Johnnie Walker.**

Manchester. He was Assistant Headmaster at St Mark's School, Cheetham Hill and lived with his friend and fellow sergeant, George H Valentine. Taylforth originated from the area around Kendal and had joined the Regiment when he came to work in Manchester. He was a keen sportsman playing rugby at Sale and golf at Heaton Park. George was also to be one of the performers.

The concert itself was a roaring success and both entertainers and audience enjoyed themselves thoroughly. Tom Mills had sung 'All aboard for Dixie, which had only been written the previous year, and 'L'Entente Cordiale' (parody lyrics to the tune of the French National Anthem). William Taylforth also sang a couple, including the humorous 'Sergeant of the Line'. Sergeant Hartley sang 'The Matrimonial Handicap' in the show's first half and, after the interval, the recently written 'Toddling Home'. George Valentine recited two monologues and Corporal Joseph Dunworth performed a burlesque (a humourous skit, no doubt poking fun at the senior officers). Amidst the clamour of applause, there were calls for them to do another show. They'd be back in March for a second and final performance.

A few days prior to this, Ridley Sheldon had received a letter from home saying that a hamper of food was on its way to him and that nine mince pies would be included. This posed a dilemma for him as he shared a tent with eleven others and, of course, the luxury of food from England was always shared out. The parcel arrived just before Christmas Day and, on opening it, he found it full of other things as well as food

> *There were draughts and dominoes, and chess and ring board, in the way of games; then besides, there were cakes and sweets and chocolates, in the shape of eatables. Yes! There were nine mince pies. Nine mince pies to be divided amongst twelve men; just think of it! Whatever was I to do? For I did not want to cause any disappointment; still it was a very knotty problem to solve – how to make the nine pies go round for the twelve men, without either breaking or spoiling them. But, at last, after a great deal of thought and consideration, we got over the difficulty and this is the way in which we managed it. We decided to take pieces of paper and make a mark in the form of a cross on three of the*

Sergeants of the original F Company. **Manchester Regiment Archives**

Senior sergeants at Alexandria.
Manchester Regiment Archives

pieces. When this had been done, they were all placed into a hat and, well shaken up, we each drew in our turn on the distinct understanding that whoever got a paper with a cross on it would have to forego the pleasure of feasting on a mince pie…but those unfortunate enough to miss the pie had it made up to them by an extra supply of cake.

This was clearly a matter of great importance to Sheldon and he was pleased with the result, not least as he did not draw a paper with a cross.

The men's first Christmas away from home was celebrated in style. They breakfasted on porridge, bacon, eggs, bread, butter and tea and then attended church parade at 10am. Traditional dinner was served at 1pm, with the sergeants serving the food to the men and it was generally felt to be a fine feast, with mess huts decorated with palm branches, flowers, lanterns and chains of coloured paper. Private Ridley Sheldon

> *We had roast beef, carrots, cabbage, cauliflower and potatoes, followed by plum pudding and sauce, nuts and oranges. I had a mineral water to drink but for those who were not Total Abstainers, there was a pint of beer each and also tobacco for those who smoked. But tea was somewhat disappointing, for we only got bread, jam and cake with the tea…I thought they might have given us something else besides. After all, I missed the turkey and the other good things which I knew they were having at home and, certainly, the day*

6th Battalion on parade. Boxing Day, 1914. Manchester Regiment Archives

The officers of the Battalion on Boxing Day. Manchester Regiment Archives.

seemed very strange indeed. I well remember that I had not even the opportunity of going on church parade; for unfortunately, I was on Quartermaster's fatigue and my time was spent in peeling onions, potatoes and carrots and preparing cabbage to be cooked. Well, I suppose someone had to do it and it fell to my lot.

Sergeant Tom Worthington had enjoyed serving dinner to his men in C Company but he enjoyed Boxing Day even more as the men played hockey with a game in the morning and another in the afternoon. He then went to the cinema in the evening. Describing life in Alexandria in a letter home, he wrote

There are several rooms where we can read and write and enjoy ourselves and even make friends with the people here, so we are not cut off from the world as you might think. Indeed, we are just beginning to enjoy ourselves and will be very sorry to leave here. On Tuesday, a Bedouin funeral passed us. The women followed the coffin, shrieking and making a horrible noise and were waving their black robes and looking as weird as could be. Yesterday, we went to the Catacombs, which have only been unearthed a few years. There are some very fine Egyptian and Roman carvings in good preservation and the bones still lie in the places hewn out for them.

To close the festivities and to make another demonstration of strength, the 5th, 6th and 8th Battalions paraded through Alexandria in the morning of the 28th. Next day, it was back to work for the whole brigade with the men undertaking close order drill in the desert. Until now, the battalions had only practiced their own roles for an attack but training would now begin to concentrate on the battalions working together in much larger formations. New Year's Eve saw the first of the exercises with 6th Battalion defending against an attack by the Wiganers of the 5th.

In the opening days of 1915, there was a parade, possibly on 2 January when General Lee visited. It may be the event referred to in the Divisional History around this time.

> *On the occasion of some special parade the 5th Manchesters had to cross the very sandy parade ground before reaching the asphalt road that led out of barracks. Noticing the dusty state of their boots, the men of D Company of the 6th Manchesters darted into their quarters, which were close at hand and, producing brushes and rags, they quickly polished the boots of the Wigan men. It was a trifling incident, but still a perfect expression of good comradeship, and it had a wonderful and lasting effect. The two battalions were knit more closely together and later, in Gallipoli, there was a sense of absolute security in either Battalion in the knowledge that the other was in support.*

The final festive celebrations also took place on 2 January. Some expected parcels from home had not arrived in time for Christmas, including those that had been sent by the ex-colleagues of the Westinghouse men. They finally arrived complete with cards wishing 'Good health and fortune to the Westinghouse contingent'. It was going to be a feast and they would offer their thanks to the sergeants for serving Christmas dinner by inviting them to be their guests. The meal was turkey, sausages and mashed potato followed by Christmas pudding and brandy sauce. They finished off with mince pies, jellies and cheese. Alcohol was in plentiful supply as indicated by the number of toasts that were drunk:

The Duke of Lancaster	Proposed by Lance Corporal Bramwell
The Sergeants	Corporal Lewis
Absent friends	Private Horan
Our Allies	Private Tabb[10]
The Corporal	Private Doig (senior private)
The Lance Corporal	Private Boyetto[11] (second senior private)
The Ladies	Private Bock
The Boys at the Front	Private Beamish
The Colonials	Private McConnell[12]

The sergeants and other senior non-commissioned officers on Boxing Day.
Manchester Regiment Archives

Taking a break and enjoying a joke, apparently over the diminutive size of Sergeant Tom Worthington's fruit in his ration. Worthington family.

Hopefully, the Westinghouse men had clear heads the next day as the 5th, 6th and 8th Battalions paraded in the very early morning for the start of three days of exercises. The first exercise involved two companies of the Wiganers acting as defenders whilst they were attacked by their other two companies, C and D Companies of the 6th and some men of the 8th mainly providing the machine guns and support. A and B Companies formed the reserve under the command of Claude Worthington.

Ridley Sheldon reckoned the worst part of this exercise was when the men were ordered to lie down and he realised that he had crushed the bread in his rations.

> *The Corporal would yell out at the very top of his voice 'Lie down there and never mind your dinner', only he would use very strong and unparliamentary language…Soon came the order to fix bayonets and you would run like the wind with rifles at the slope, and overcoats scattered all around, up a very steep hill, for about five hundred yards and then the bugle sounded out the Stand Fast. This was followed by a well earned rest, during which we eat what was once a quarter of a loaf and cheese and water. Now we are fighting a Retreating Battle and the enemy is peppering us so much that the trench becomes too hot to hold; we wait our chance and then, under shelter of a hot covering fire, run like rabbits, only in good order, to the next position, which we had to hold until the enemy's fire again compels us to evacuate the position…. We have fallen back to our main position and are ordered to open a slow individual fire at fourteen hundred yards range but our fire is not heavy enough to keep the enemy back….Then comes the final*

order 'Fix bayonets'. And the enemy fixes bayonets and headlong they come, shouting and screaming, with the gleam of victory in their eyes. We fire faster and faster still. The enemy drop in scores but on they come. The enemy is upon us – we turn – we run - and then the Stand Fast sounds. We assemble and march back to camp and suddenly there flashes through your mind that you are going back – to SKILLY!

During the morning of 6 January 1915, the men practised bayonet fighting and had rifle practice. They paraded again at 3pm and marched off into the desert. The exercise was to test their ability to have undertaken a long route march and then dig-in for the night in darkness. It was not an overnight exercise and the men were back in camp by 11pm. A final attack and defend exercise took place on the 8th.

The battalion now started to prepare for a move to Cairo and spent time cleaning up the barracks. There was time for a route march to Aboukir and back. Sergeant Tom Worthington wrote it was a round trip of about twenty miles 'The country is very flat and seems well cultivated, but the people are dirty and the houses miserable. We saw one or two real mud huts.'

And, befitting a unit about to move to the seat of British power in the area, there was two days of 'smartening up' drill under the direction of the sergeant majors. Meanwhile, the officers were undergoing their own training in bayonet fighting. It was anticipated that they might soon need to put their training into practice. The move to Cairo was to bolster the city's defences in preparation for an expected attack by the Turks intent on capturing the strategically vital Suez Canal.

On the 19th, the Manchester Brigade moved to Cairo taking over from the 5th and 8th Battalions, Lancashire Fusiliers – Territorials from Bury and Salford, respectively. Arriving with the advance party at Abassia Barracks, Claude Worthington and Lieutenant and Quartermaster William Wynne found them to be 'disgustingly dirty'[13]. It would take days to settle down, clean and clear up the Barracks.

Private George Oliver Harrison, aged 23, had enlisted on 1 September 1914, leaving his job as a clerk with the Co-operative Wholesale Society and his home at 278 Great Cheetham Street, Broughton, Salford. His service papers are one of comparatively few of the battalion's still to exist at the National Archives. They show he was just over 5' 4" tall and weighed 138 pounds. He had brown eyes and blackish brown hair. Unusually for those days, Harrison had not indicated any religious denomination on the form. He was now one of C Company's stretcher bearers and kept a diary for the first half of 1915.[14] One of his first entries was made just after arriving on the 19th. *'Sorry to leave the sea, as Cairo much stuffier. Had bathed Christmas Eve and on January 1st at Alexandria.'* After church parade on the following Sunday, he took the opportunity for a bit of sight-seeing. *'Visited pyramids. Intensely interesting. Strenuous climb practically to the top and peep inside. Sphinx smaller than impression of photograph.'*

Prior to getting back to work, there was an equipment inspection on 26 January. The men's feet, socks and boots were also examined – they would all need to be in top condition as, the following, day, the whole of 42nd Division went on a route march of

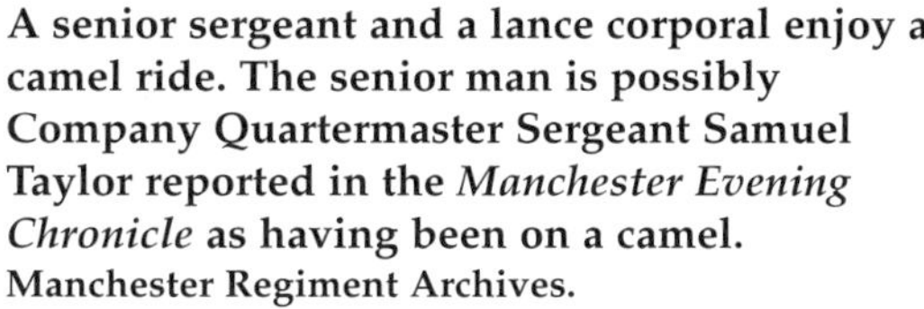

A senior sergeant and a lance corporal enjoy a camel ride. The senior man is possibly Company Quartermaster Sergeant Samuel Taylor reported in the *Manchester Evening Chronicle* as having been on a camel.
Manchester Regiment Archives.

Top right: climbing the Pyramids.
Manchester Regiment Archives.

Abassia Barracks, 1915.They found them to be filthy when they first arrived.
Manchester Regiment Archives

about twenty miles across the desert. Ridley Sheldon found his feet kept sinking into the soft sand and it made for a very tiring day. The 27th saw the largest exercise so far. The whole division practised disembarkation and then took up positions for an attack, with the Manchester Brigade holding the reserve position on the left. The remaining days of the month were quiet with only platoon drills to keep the men occupied.

British aircraft had been tracking the Turkish move across the Sinai and, late in January, there were some very minor skirmishes near to the Suez Canal at El Kantara. On 1 February, reports arrived that the expected Turkish troops, estimated at 12,000 strong, were close to the Suez Canal. Whilst British and Empire troops readied their defences, the Turks came under fire from British and French warships on the canal.

During the night of the 3rd, the Turks started to cross the canal on rafts but Indian machine gunners on the west bank inflicted very heavy casualties. The attack was restarted at dawn but was again easily beaten off and the Turks withdrew in the late afternoon. Some of 42nd Division's artillery had been sent to assist as well as some of its Royal Engineers. One man was killed. The Manchesters had remained at Cairo, scouting possible locations to dig defensive trenches in case the Turks had broken through.

With the threat of invasion removed, a period of relaxed calm returned to the troops

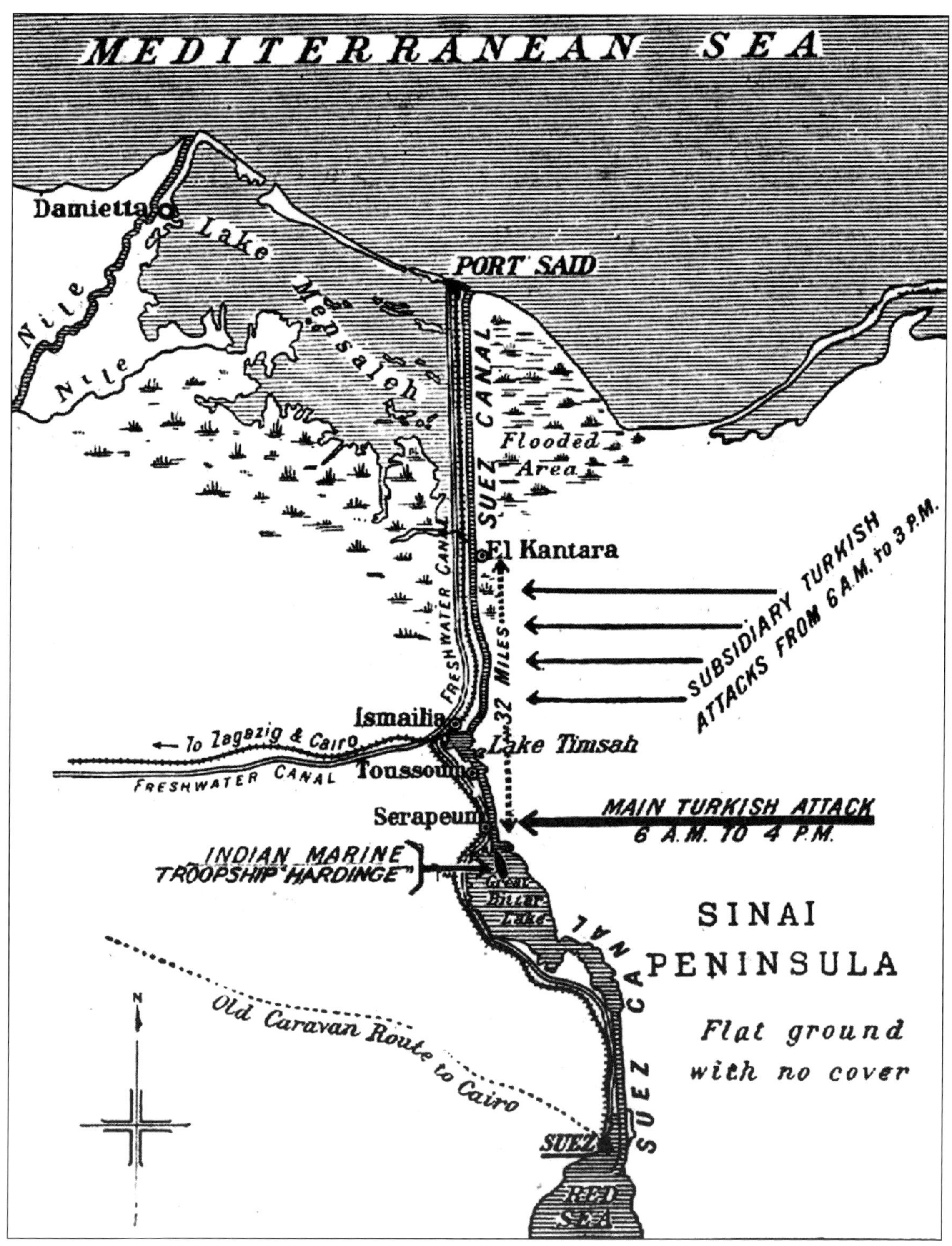

3 February 1915 – the Turkish attempt to cross the Suez Canal.

in Cairo, broken only by the occasional route march. The men took the opportunity for sight-seeing. George Harrison went to the zoo on 6 February. 'Very fine gardens and animals mostly better kept than English zoos.' Ridley Sheldon was initially impressed with the Pyramids and the Sphinx but soon unfavourably contrasted these man-made structures with the natural beauty of Ullswater and Helvellyn. The *Manchester Evening Chronicle* reported that Company Quartermaster Sergeant Taylor had been on a camel ride. In civilian life, he was the Assistant Inspector of Telegraphs at Manchester Post Office.

A few days of instruction classes followed, for both officers and men. The officers had classes on map reading and drawing and, also, on conducting courts martial. As there was no demanding physical work being undertaken, George Harrison and the other stretcher bearers had an easy time, with only sunstroke cases to deal with.

As early as December 1914, the British War Cabinet had been discussing the possibility of a major attack on Turkey. The strike would be delivered against the defences in the Dardenelle Straits, intended to knock out the shore batteries, thereby allowing free naval movement between the Mediterranean and the Black Sea. It would allow Russia to receive much needed munitions for the war in the east and for it to export her supplies of wheat. There would be the further possibility of Allied attacks on the Turkish capital Constantinople (now Istanbul), forcing Turkey out of the war. Winston Churchill, then First Lord of the Admiralty, successfully proposed that it would be an entirely naval attack. There were many dissenters and it would take another world war to restore Churchill's reputation after the subsequent costly failure of the forthcoming campaign.

This adventure would come as no surprise to Turkey. On 3 November 1914, even before a formal declaration of war, British ships had shelled the Turkish forts and gun emplacements. Unsurprisingly, the Turks, alerted to the possibility of a future larger scale attack, re-enforced the positions. On 19 February, a joint force of British and French ships opened fire on the outer defences around Cape Helles. It was not a success.

Men from C or D Company outside their tent. Manchester Regiment Archives

Company Quartermaster Sergeant Frank Deacon with several other sergeants. Manchester Regiment Archives.

Sergeant Hartley outside C Company store.
Manchester Regiment Archives

Under the headline 'Forcing the Dardanelles', the *Manchester Evening Chronicle*, in its edition of 22 February, reported the attack in somewhat scathing terms, concluding 'The whole operation is an extremely formidable one, not to be accomplished by sea power alone.' Articles continued the next day with a sense of foreboding.

> *Turkish preparations to defend the Straits have been well known to the British authorities for some time. The number of troops entrenched on both banks of the Straits is considerable as even in peacetime the garrison totals 13,000 men.*

24 February saw a return to large scale training exercises. All six battalions of the Manchester and East Lancashire Brigades paraded at 7.15am and marched off soon afterwards. They took up defensive positions in training trenches and were 'attacked' by the Lancashire Fusiliers Brigade. The exercise went well.

Smallpox had broken out in Cairo and, on the 25th, the battalion's first case was reported. Private Arthur Thompson was admitted to hospital and, immediately, the barrack rooms were disinfected. It didn't significantly alter the battalion's routine. Instruction classes were held in the afternoon for the men and officers undertook machine gun instruction. The day also saw the British and French Navies shell the Gallipoli forts with some success and a number of the shore batteries were silenced. Parties of Royal Marines landed to plant demolition charges at two of the partially destroyed forts and then withdrew.

It was an early start on the 26th with parade at 6.15am and another day of divisional

Sergeants at Abassia Barracks. **Manchester Regiment Archives**

training. The six thousand men of the Manchester and East Lancashire Brigades were the attackers this time and the defenders were yeomanry troops – territorial cavalry soldiers, who will have been acting as 'dismounted' troops, in the practice trenches.

March 1915 started with fresh instruction classes but, on the 2nd, it was time for another route march. These were usually along the road to Suez and the usual goal was 'Tower Three' about nine miles away. As the divisional history records:

> *Familiarity had bred not contempt but a whole-hearted loathing for that accursed highway and that distant mound. How the troops hated the sight of this detestable pile which, in the dust and glare, seemed to recede mockingly as they tramped towards it.*

Not only did they have to march back on this Tuesday, but they had to undertake the return as an exercise in fighting a rearguard action, against other battalions of the division. On the following Thursday, the men got a lie-in and did not have to parade until 9am. After a short time, they were dismissed and allowed the rest of the day off. A Company took the opportunity for a get-together for an evening 'smoker'. Their thoughts will have also been for Arthur Thompson, now desperately ill with smallpox. He died on the 8th and was buried next day at Cairo's British Protestant Cemetery (now Cairo War Memorial Cemetery, maintained by the Commonwealth War Graves Commission). About sixty of his comrades attended the funeral which was conducted with full military honours. A party of twelve men, under the command of Sergeant Smythe and Corporal Gray[15], fired volleys over his grave.

12 March saw the whole of the East Lancashire Division parade for a field exercise against New Zealanders. It was a long day for the men, starting at 7.15am and not

returning to barracks until 6pm. They would have had to rush to get ready for the second appearance of the battalion's Pierrot troupe which was to perform at the Continental Hotel that evening in aid of the Sick and Wounded Fund. In the event, there was an excellent attendance with about 600 men enjoying the evening.

The men had a rest from training the next day but were kept busy cleaning the barracks. Later, A Company's men had their boots and puttees inspected. Those who needed them would get replacements a few days later. Sunday, 14 March, saw a day of

Part of the programme for the second Pierrot show.

Captain Philip Holberton.
Manchester Regiment Archives

proper rest and, after church parade, the men were dismissed but it was back to training from the Monday. Instruction classes and musketry practice were the orders of the day and, on the 17th, physical exercises were supervised by Captain Holberton. He continued with these on the Thursday morning but there were informal football matches in the afternoon. No. 2 Platoon beat 3 Platoon two goals to nil. The match between 4 and 9 Platoons was drawn with each side scoring two goals.

On the wider front, the bombardment of the Turkish forts on the Gallipoli peninsula had resumed at the beginning of the month and had continued for several days with some apparent success. Naval commanders decided that the way was now clear for the warships to move through the Dardanelles and force their way through The Narrows. As the name suggests, the channel was only 1600 metres from shore to shore and the area to its south had been heavily mined. Five days were spent in clearing the mines and the joint British and French fleet sailed north on the same day as the battalion football matches. This would be the first of the failures of the forthcoming campaign. Unknown to the naval commanders, the Turks had laid another minefield some ten days before. HMS *Irresistible*, HMS *Ocean* and the French battleship *Bouvet* quickly sank. Several other ships in the fleet were badly damaged and orders were given for the remaining ships to withdraw. Even Winston Churchill accepted that the peninsula could not be neutralised by naval power alone and that an invasion would have to be undertaken. In London, planning started immediately and it was quickly decided that the initial landings would take place on 25 April.

For the Manchesters, routine continued much as

before with musketry practice assuming a greater prominence in the instruction classes. At this point, there was every intention that the Territorials stay in Egypt. The invasion would be carried out by Australian and New Zealand troops, the British 29th Division, together with a division of French infantry. Sir Ian Hamilton would command what was now to be called the Mediterranean Expeditionary Force. He had been aboard one of the ships on the 18th and had seen for himself that landing at

Battalion NCOs. Seated in the centre is a Sergeant wearing an instructor's badge above his stripes. The Quartermaster Sergeant (later Regimental Quartermaster) sits to his right. To his left, Company Sergeant Major Billy Warburton. To Warburton's left is another Sergeant, bearing a resemblance to Sergeant Hartley in the cartoon of the Pierrot troupe. The man, standing at the back, whose face is obscured by the damage is probably Tom Worthington. To his left, another man wears a medal ribbon for service during the Boer War. Worthington later sent this photograph home from Gallipoli and it is reproduced courtesy of his descendants. In a letter, he explained the damage. It had been in his tunic pocket when it was struck by a Turkish bullet. Luckily he was not wearing it at the time and had slung it over the parapet of his trench.

Taking a break at an oasis during an exercise in the desert. The unknown photographer has noted on the rear of the picture 'Snapped during an argument. The old gent with the camel was very annoyed about something and was worse still when he found out he had been photographed.' Manchester Regiment Archives

Gallipoli and securing the peninsula would be no easy feat. He recorded in his diary:

> *The Peninsula itself is being fortified and many Turks work every night on trenches, redoubts and entanglements. Not one single living soul has been seen, since the engagement of our Marines at the end of February, although each morning brings forth fresh evidences of nocturnal activity, in patches of freshly turned up soil. All landing places are now commanded by lines of trenches and are ranged by field guns and howitzers…(we) were startled to see the ramifications and extent of the spider's web of deep, narrow trenches along the coast and on either front of the lines of Bulair. My Staff agree that they must have taken ten thousand men a month's hard work from dark to dawn. In advance of the trenches, Williams in the crow's nest reported that with his strong glasses he could pick out the glitter of wire over a wide expanse of ground. To the depth of a mile the whole Aegean slope of the neck of the Peninsula was scarred with spade work and it is clear to a tiro that to take these trenches would take from us a bigger toll of ammunition and life than we can afford.*

Musketry and other classes of instruction continued for a few days but the men also had opportunities for rest and relaxation.

Sergeant William Taylforth took the opportunity to catch up with his correspondence. He had been a popular teacher and regularly received letters from his

ex-pupils. He continued to take an interest in their lives and wrote to Frank Ross[16] of 40 Daresbury Street, Cheetham hoping that young Frank had recovered from a recent accident and hoping there had been no disfigurement. He asked him to send a class photo and, ever the teacher, closed his letter: 'Just a word, professionally, all of you write your addresses too high on the envelope.'

Another major night exercise started on the 26th. Tom Gresham[17] recorded in his diary that the whole Division paraded and marched off at 2pm. The battalion made camp at 'Dead Man's Valley' and, as always when on exercises, the evening meal was tinned sardines. Sergeant Clegg[18] tended the section's fire and told the men of his time in South Africa during the Boer War. Later, they advanced through the night to undertake a practice attack. As they neared the defenders, they were ordered to crawl forward for a considerable distance. An umpire spotted Captain Bazley standing up and, much to Bazley's embarrassment, immediately told him

The Battalion Band. Seated to the right of the bass drum is Lieutenant Tom Mills, from Stockport. He had enlisted into the army on 4 August 1914 receiving his commission the same day. When in the front line, members of the band would usually undertake the dangerous role of stretcher bearers. Manchester Regiment Archives he was dead. They were back in barracks and ready for some sleep by the middle of the next morning.

Rumours of a major move started to fly around the various barracks but even senior commanders of the East Lancashire Division had no real knowledge of what was happening, although they were still hoping any move would be to France and the 'real war'. General Noel Lee wrote home expressing his frustration at being kept to one side.

> *Now the Dardanelles affair is beginning, and a Division of K's19 army has arrived (giving themselves tremendous airs as being 'Regulars', which does not take in anyone at all) and a French Division is arriving soon. If these K's are now given preference over us, I fear there will be trouble because we, the first TF Division in England to move out at our Country's call will be once more delegated to a back seat, after eight months training of the most strenuous kind. All are fed up with it if we are not going to be used.*

The whole division was inspected by Sir Ian Hamilton on the 28th and, no doubt, his good impression of the men confirmed to him that he would soon put them to use at Gallipoli, going in as part of the invasion's 'second wave' a few days after the initial landings. He recorded in his diary

> *Inspected East Lancashire Division and a Yeomanry Brigade (Westminster Dragoons and Herts). How I envied Maxwell these beautiful troops. They will only be eating their heads off here, with summer coming up and the desert getting as dry as a bone. The Lancashire men especially are eye-openers. How on earth have they managed to pick up the swank and devil-may-care airs of crack regulars? They are Regulars, only they are bigger, more effective specimens than Manchester mills or East Lancashire mines can spare us for the Regular Service in peace time. Anyway, no soldier need wish to see a finer lot. Maxwell will have a fit if I ask for them. He will fall down in a fit, I am sure.*

For now, Hamilton kept some of his thoughts to himself but his comments to the divisional commander, Major-General Douglas, were published in a special order of the day:

> *General Sir Ian Hamilton, having been accorded the privilege of reviewing the East Lancashire Division, wishes to congratulate the General Officer Commanding in Egypt, as well as Major-General Douglas, on the*

General Sir Ian Hamilton.

Unknown Battalion member.
Manchester Regiment Archives.

turnout and soldierly bearing of that force. He was able to observe today that the East Lancashire Division has made full use of the advantages which continuous fine weather and the absence of billeting have given them over their comrades now bearing arms, whether at home or on the continent of Europe.

Ever since the Siege of Ladysmith, General Sir Ian Hamilton has interested himself specially in the military output of Manchester and it is a real pleasure to him to be able to bear witness to the fact that this great city is being so finely represented in the east.

The month closed with intensive musketry practice and A Company's new recruits were supervised on the firing range by Lieutenant Tom Mills. There was now some urgency to this matter. If the men could not shoot to the army's required accuracy, then they should not go into action with the battalion.

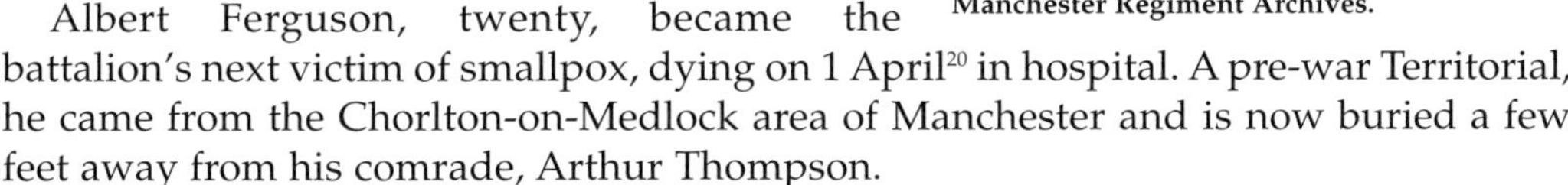

Albert Ferguson, twenty, became the battalion's next victim of smallpox, dying on 1 April[20] in hospital. A pre-war Territorial, he came from the Chorlton-on-Medlock area of Manchester and is now buried a few feet away from his comrade, Arthur Thompson.

The next day was Good Friday and it would be an eventful day. For a number of men, they would be packing their bags and heading home, deemed unfit for active service. Amongst them were Privates R Cordwell, P Denby, L Harrison, R H Jones, A Layton and T H Moorhouse, all of A Company.

The remainder of the battalion had hoped to spend the holiday weekend relaxing in Cairo but found themselves confined to barracks due to a riot by Australian and New Zealand troops in the city's brothel area in the Wagh-el-Bukh district. After several months training, the ANZACs had been told they would soon be in action, but only about a quarter of the men were granted leave for the day. The riot, popularly known as the Battle of the Wazza, appears to have been the men taking out their resentment on the local population for robberies, overpriced alcohol and a high incidence of venereal disease (often considered by the army to be self-inflicted injury subject to military punishment). The riot was, of course, fuelled by alcohol.

Ridley Sheldon, the vicar's son, was particularly disappointed on Easter Sunday. He had been on guard duty overnight and, returning to his barracks, immediately fell asleep. He missed all the opportunities to take Holy Communion.

There was little work to be done for the next few days, except for a night bivouac on the 9th. Captain Claude Worthington records an exercise on the 12th – 'Marched by night to Helonan. Some twenty-five miles. Men rather footsore'. Ridley Sheldon had a lot more to say:

> *We marched there in one day, with the idea of returning the next, but such a large number of our fellows had sore feet and blood-stained boots, with that awful walk, that the return journey had to be postponed until the following day...To begin with, the Battalion went out of its way five miles by getting astray, so when it had done twenty-three miles, it was about done up. Fortunately, I was not with them all the way; the explanation being that before starting from the barracks, we were standing in the sun for half-an-hour, when suddenly, I went very faint and nearly collapsed and, at that very moment, the order was given to the Battalion to march. I requested to be allowed to fall out but they asked me if I could not manage to stick it and did so until as far as a place called Wardi, twelve miles away. Here I was quite done for and was compelled to give in.*

Sheldon went the rest of the way on the ambulance wagon and was seen by the medical officer when they got to Helonan. They rested all the next day. The temperature was 101 in the shade and soared to 150 in the sun. Fully rested, Sheldon joined the return march on the 14th.

> *I felt in the pink of condition; the effect of the sunstroke having entirely gone. I have never known the officers to be so nice with the men, as they were on that march, for some of the men had terrible feet and they gave their horses for the use of the men, as did also the Doctor, who walked all the way, and Captain Pilkington*[21] *of C Company and Major Worthington of A Company did the same. We got to Kasr-el-Nil on the outskirts of Cairo just as it was coming light and we all felt very sleepy; then reaching barracks at seven am, we had a splendid breakfast of bacon and tomatoes and then having bedded down, we slept soundly nearly the whole of the day. I am very proud to be able to say that ours was the first Territorial Force to reach Heluan* (sic) *in one day after leaving Cairo; for the Lancashires, who had started off with that place as their objective to reach in a day's march, had been compelled to give up at Wardi and there they turned back.*

At dawn on the 25th, the first landings invading the Gallipoli peninsula were made. At the southern tip, around Cape Helles, the troops of 29th and Royal Naval Divisions had struggled to get ashore. Many had landed from small boats and had become easy targets for the Turkish machine gunners. As the professionals of the 1st Battalion, Lancashire Fusiliers reached the beach, they realised it was strewn with extensive entanglements of barbed wire. There was nothing else to do but wait until the men with wire-cutters had made ways through. Once paths were cleared, the Fusiliers stormed through, climbing the surrounding cliffs and winning a famous six Victoria Crosses before breakfast. Further north, the Australian and New Zealand troops had landed at Gabe Tepe (soon to be known to all simply as ANZAC after the Australian

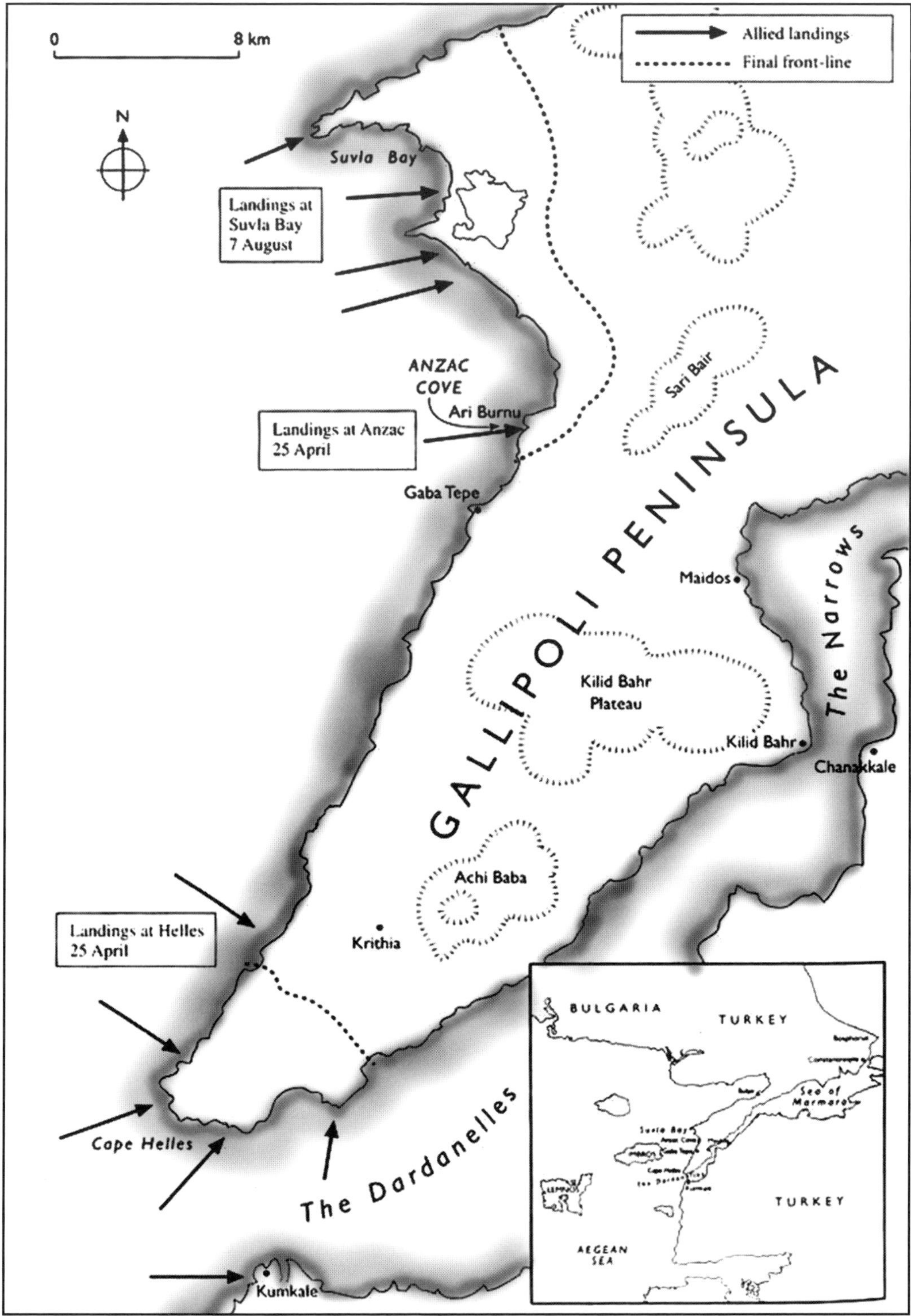
0
8 km
N
Allied landings
Final front-line
Suvla Bay
Landings at Suvla Bay 7 August
ANZAC COVE
Ari Burnu
Landings at Anzac 25 April
Gaba Tepe
Sari Bair
GALLIPOLI PENINSULA
Maidos
The Narrows
Kilid Bahr Plateau
Kilid Bahr
Chanakkale
Achi Baba
Krithia
Landings at Helles 25 April
Cape Helles
The Dardanelles
Kumkale
BULGARIA
TURKEY
TURKEY
AEGEAN SEA

Turkish machine gun team.

A beachhead established.

and New Zealand Army Corps).

Although a beachhead had been secured, the troops were unable to make much progress inland due to the strength of the Turkish defences and the ferocity with which they were defending their homeland. Over the next couple of days, they did advance about six miles but it was now clear to Sir Ian Hamilton that more troops were needed. Cables were sent to Lord Kitchener, the Secretary of State for War, back in London. He replied to the effect that General Maxwell would release troops from Egypt for Gallipoli and, on the 27th, Sir Ian cabled Maxwell asking him to hold the East Lancashire Division in readiness. The next day, another cable arrived from Kitchener *'I feel sure you had better have the Territorial Division and I have instructed Maxwell to embark them.'* Hamilton noted in his diary: 'The best buck up for the Army will be the news that the lads from Manchester are on their way to help us.'

THE EVENING CHRONICLE. TUESDAY, MARCH 9, 1915.
THE HAPPY TERRITORIALS IN EGYPT.

The orders to prepare to move reached the battalion on 29 April. As recorded by the divisional history

> *The news soon spread; it was no rumour this time, but the real thing, and on April 30 excitement was at fever heat. At last the Territorials were to be given the opportunity to which all ranks had looked forward so eagerly and toward which recent training had been directed. Little time was given for preparation, but no more was needed, as the Division was ready to take the field.*

The men got to work tidying up immediately. For their forty-eight year old commander, Colonel Gerald Heywood, there would be bitter disappointment. An architect by profession, he had been an officer in the old Volunteer Battalion from 1899 to 1908 and then served with the Territorials. A final medical examination revealed that his eyesight was too poor for active service. He was later diagnosed with Hypermetropia and Presbyopia. Whilst he had reasonably good vision with his glasses, he was unable to recognise faces even a few feet away without them. He was sent home and command passed to Major C R Pilkington. Like his nephew, Hugh Pilkington, commanding C Company, he had extensive business interests in several collieries in Lancashire.

By 2 May, everything was ready and all the barracks equipment had been returned to store. A and B Companies, under the command of Major Worthington boarded a train for Alexandria at 10am, arriving there at 5.40pm. The remainder of the Battalion left just before 3pm, arriving at the docks in the middle of the evening. From this point on, until the end of the War, the battalion maintained a war diary[22] and it forms the basis for the subsequent account in this book.

---

1 The papers of D C Sinclair, including an account of his service, are held by the Department of Documents, Imperial War Museum and have been consulted for this book. David Christi Sinclair was born in about 1890

and was the son of James, a baker, and Wilhelmina of Nairn, Scotland. He worked in Manchester as an engineer.

2 2nd Lieutenant (and later Captain) Henry Swindells Hellawell. Born in the Oldham area in 1885.

3 Thomas Bayley Gresham's diary is held by the Liddle Collection, University of Leeds and extracts are quoted with permission

4 Edgar Kessler was the oldest surviving son of P W Kessler, "Fernlea", Fallowfield and was a director of the family firm of merchants, Kessler & Co, Dale Street, Manchester.

5 Holberton was Mentioned in Despatches on five separate occasions during the war, twice for his service with the Battalion at Gallipoli. He was killed in action on 26 March 1918, whilst commanding the 2nd Battalion, Lancashire Fusiliers.

6 Claude Worthington's diaries, edited by Robert Bonner, are published by Fleurs de Lys Publishing on behalf of the Trustees of the Manchester Regiment Collection and are available as "Great Gable to Gallipoli". He died of wounds on 14 October 1918 whilst commanding the 5th Battalion, Dorsetshire Regiment.

7 Lieutenant Colonel Gerald Graham Percival Heywood

8 2270, Private Francis Shaw is commemorated on the Wilmslow War Memorial and the War Memorial inside St Bartholomew's Parish Church.

9 Almost certainly, 868 Private William Walton Dodd of Lingard Road, Northenden and an employee in the Manchester warehouse offices of Jones Brothers Ltd on York Street. Killed in action 7 August 1915, aged 24. No known grave. Commemorated on the Northenden War Memorial.

10 2472 Percy Tabb, killed in action 27 May 1915.

11 It has not been possible to identify a soldier of this name and it is probably a nickname for 1717, Cecil Boyes-Varley, known to have been a Westinghouse employee. Killed in action 13 July 1915.

12 2348, Private Arthur McConnell rose to the rank of Captain, serving with the Royal Engineers, and survived the war.

13 Great Gable to Gallipoli, page 12

14 George Harrison's diary is held by the Manchester Regiment Archives which gives permission to use extracts.

15 1669, Corporal James R Gray. Wounded in action and discharged from the army on 2 February 1916. He returned home to 37 Upper Medlock Street, Hulme, Manchester.

16 This letter is held by the Department of Documents, Imperial War Museum.

17 Gresham served with the Battalion's machine gun section, until 5 August 1915, when he was evacuated from Gallipoli with dysentery. On recovery, he transferred to the Machine Gun Corps and was commissioned as a 2nd Lieutenant on 28 January 1918. In 1920, he applied for his service medals and was then living at 5 Bishop's Road, Pendleton, Salford. Family history website, LancashireBMD, suggests he married Muriel Jones in 1922 at St George's Church, Tyldesley.

18 93, Sergeant John Clegg, killed in action 4 June 1915.

19 Kitchener's Army – the new Service battalions formed after the declaration of war and popularly named after the Secretary of State for War

20 Recorded erroneously as 1 March by the Commonwealth War Graves Commission. Ferguson's death certificate confirms 1 April.

21 Captain Hugh B Pilkington, 28. The son of Mr & Mrs Charles Pilkington, Headlands, Prestwich, Manchester. A director of the Clifton & Kearsley Colliery Companies. Joined the Battalion in 1909 and promoted Captain on 24 February 1914. Killed in action 4 June 1915.

22 National Archives refs: WO95/4313, WO95/4996, WO95/2660

Chapter 3

GALLIPOLI – INTO ACTION

FOR MANY OF THE MANCHESTERS, almost their last ever glimpse of a civilian would be when the wives and daughters of Alexandria's élite opened a buffet on the quayside and served tea and other refreshments from dawn on 3 May 1915 until all the troops had left in the late evening. The men were to board their ship, in the late afternoon. The *Derfflinger* was German and had been berthed in Port Said when war was declared and had been impounded and put to use as a troop transport. It was renamed *Huntsgreen* later in 1915.

The *Derfflinger*, shown here later in the war renamed *Huntsgreen*.

It had arrived at about 6.30am bringing over 500 Australian casualties and it must have been a sobering experience for the Territorials to see the badly wounded men being stretchered away to hospital. If further proof was needed that they were not about to embark on an easy expedition, the decks remained littered with bloody bandages and clothing. The nominal strength of the Battalion was 37 officers and 937 other ranks but not all would embark.

Some, like Colonel Heywood, were awaiting a return to Britain as being unfit for active service; others were temporarily sick and a few more would remain at Alexandria as a 'base detail'. The numbers actually boarding *Derfflinger*, at 4pm, were 31 officers and 846 other ranks. The Wiganers of the 5th Battalion were with them.

Captain Holberton aboard the *Derfflinger*.
Manchester Regiment Archives

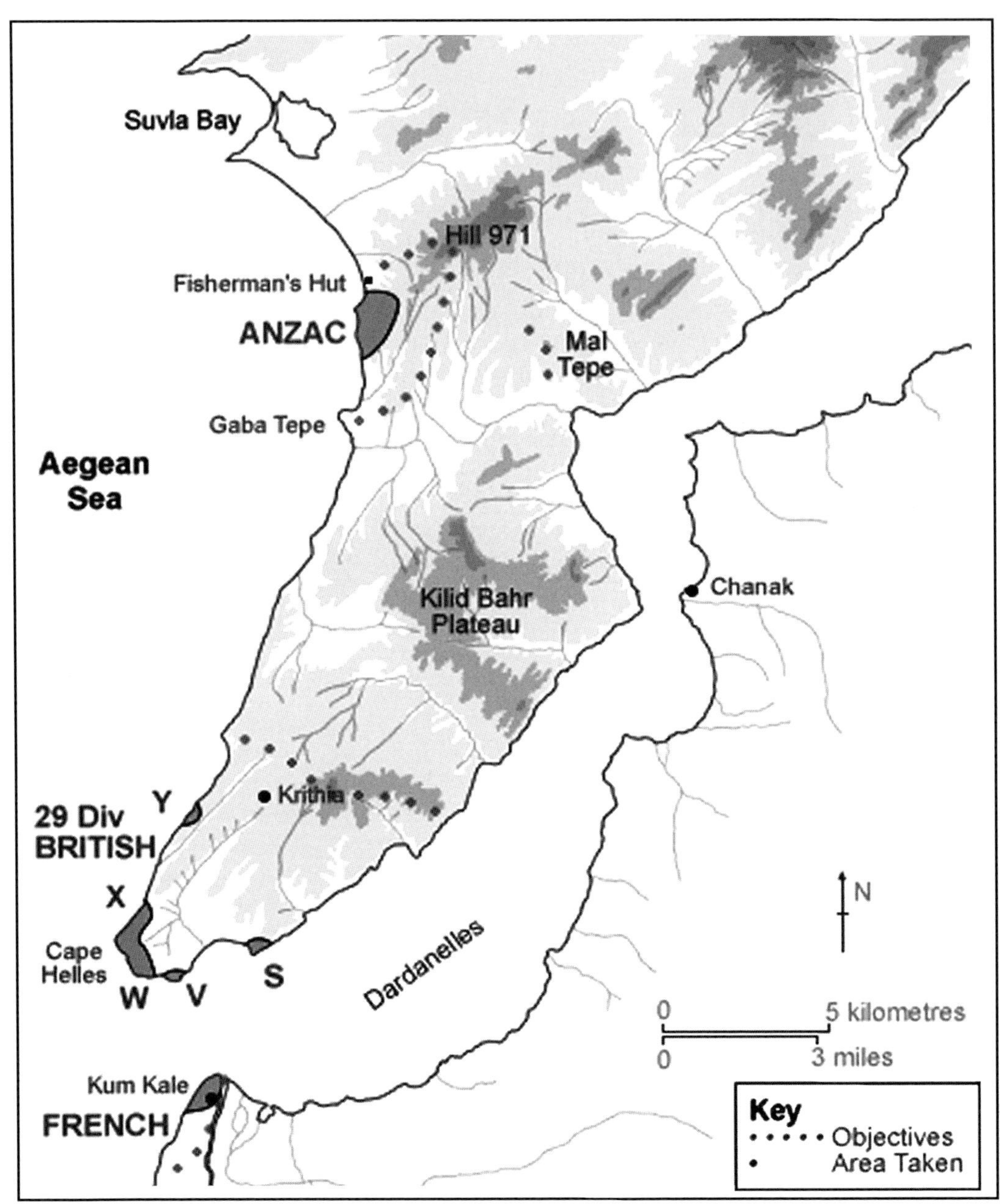
Suvla Bay
Hill 971
Fisherman's Hut
ANZAC
Mal
Tepe
Gaba Tepe
Aegean
Sea
Chanak
Kilid Bahr
Plateau
Krithia
Y
29 Div
BRITISH
X
Cape
Helles
W
V
S
Dardanelles
N
0
5 kilometres
0
3 miles
Kum Kale
FRENCH
Key
Objectives
Area Taken

Allied transports at Lemnos.

As the division was embarking, the commander of troops in Egypt sent a telegram to Major-General Douglas:

When you have the opportunity will you let the East Lancashire Division know that during the time they have been under my command I have been filled with admiration of their conduct, keenness, capacity for hard work, cheerfulness and soldier-like spirit. Now they are going on hard active service I am sure they will fight gallantly and uphold the great traditions of Lancashire and the Empire and prove, if proof be needed, that the trained Territorial soldier is second to none. Good luck and God speed to you all.

Derfflinger left her moorings at 9pm and sailed northwards. The next two days passed without incident and the men enjoyed the freshness of the sea air. Ammunition was issued – 200 rounds to each man – and, prior to landing, rations for two days. Just before departure, the battalion was issued with two new machine guns and the gunners took an opportunity to test them out on the voyage, firing off several hundred rounds. They arrived off the Gallipoli peninsula at about 5.00am on the 6th and, in an omen of the errors that would characterise the whole campaign, they had arrived at the wrong landing beach. They were some miles to the north, at Gaba Tepe, where the Australians and New Zealanders had landed a few days before. It took some while for the captain of *Derfflinger* to relocate to the correct spot – V and W beaches, off Cape Helles at the very southern tip of the peninsula.

Captain Claude Worthington noted in his diary:

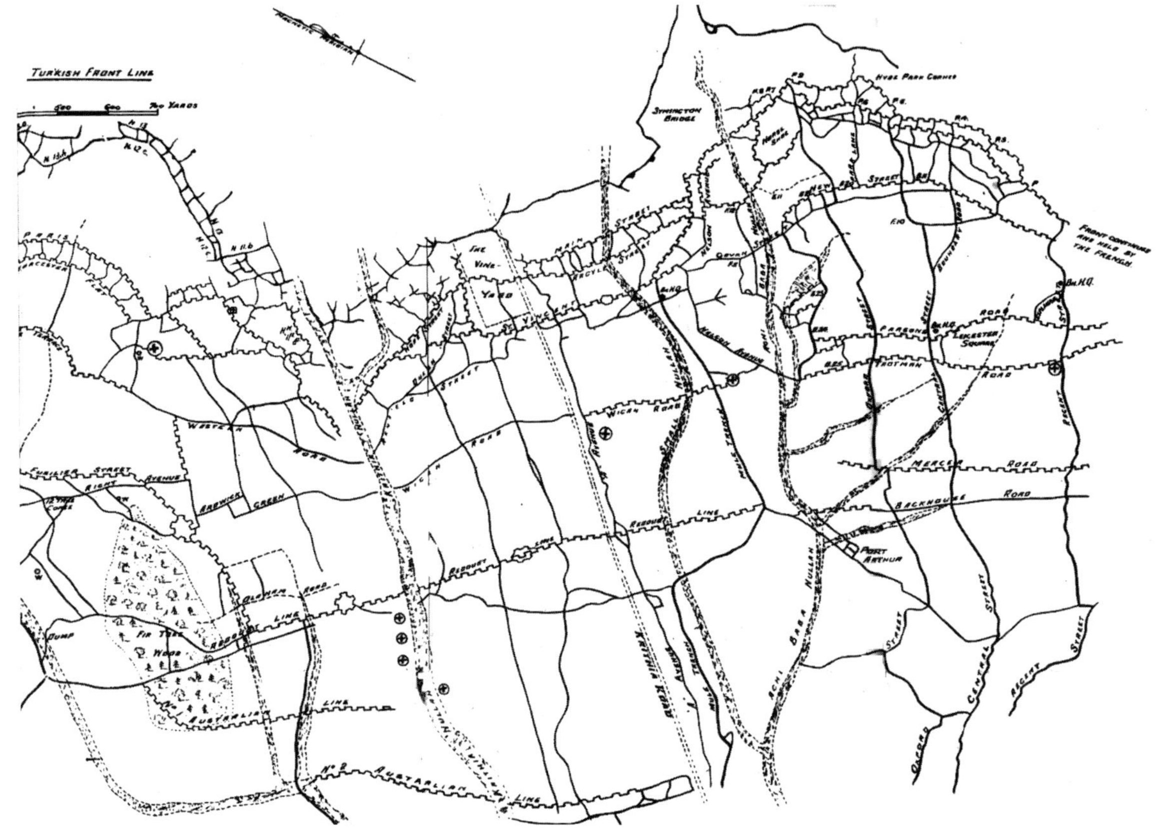

The central zone of the British positions, showing the Krithia Road running through the centre.

> *Saw shells bursting and rifle fire all along the line. Ships at Cape Helles a wonderful sight. Watched fight from ship till 4pm. Ships and batteries firing on Krithia and ridge to right.*

A and B Companies were the first to disembark, being taken to W Beach by small tugs at about 4pm. They were all ashore some four hours later and made their way to the cliff tops between V and W beaches. There was a problem landing C and D Companies at V but eventually they joined their comrades on the cliffs. In a letter home, an unknown soldier from Stockport wrote:

> *Our tug couldn't get to the landing stage and we lay from 6 o'clock to 9 o'clock in the bay, waiting for a chance to land…(once) landed they kept us on the cliff for another two hours and by that time we had begun to feel cold. The order to advance came just as I had unrolled my greatcoat and I marched about three miles along those cliffs with all my equipment in my hands. Then we made shallow dug-outs but sleep was impossible, we were so cold.*

It was now about midnight and the men passed a cold night. Their blankets, as well as the rest of the equipment, were still aboard *Derfflinger*. It was also a nervous time as there was every expectation that they would be in action next morning, providing support for an attack already underway. The attack would later be given the official designation of the Second Battle of Krithia.

In the event, the Manchesters remained where they were throughout 7 May. One platoon of men, under 2nd Lieutenant Hugh Heywood[1], started to bring the now unloaded stores up to the battalion positions, moving them by cart. About 4pm, enemy artillery shells started to fall close to their position. The Stockport man recorded:

> *We got our first experience of shellfire. One shell stopped a fatigue party and another burst harmlessly between the trenches. It made us nervous for a while.*

About 7pm, orders were received to take up a more advanced position in the third line of trenches about a mile away. However, when they reached the designated position, there were no trenches and the men had to try and quickly dig themselves in. The water table was very high and they could only get down about twelve inches before flooding started. They managed to gain a little protection by scraping a shallow hollow, only a few inches deep, and piling the earth up in front of them.

It was a relatively quiet night but, in the morning, enemy shelling started up again.

V Beach and the vast dump of materials. On April 25, 1915, the SS *River Clyde* was used to disembark 2,000 soldiers from the 29th Division. It was beached beneath Sedd el Bahr fort at V Beach, Cape Helles.

V Beach, present-day. **Chris Harley**

In a letter home, Lieutenant Henry Hammick[2] said *'I know I was in a beastly funk and I think most of us were really. We have not yet had a real shelling for which I am very thankful.'* In spite of this, he noted that, within 200 yards of the front line, he could see men 'strolling about', smoking pipes and carrying their rifles casually. Twenty-five year old Hammick was the son of Sir Murray Hammick and worked as a mechanical engineer for Westinghouse Ltd. Unlike many of his colleagues now with the battalion, he was a pre-war Territorial soldier, receiving his commission in 1913.

In the evening, the Manchesters were again ordered forward to take up positions as reserve troops behind the Royal Naval Division and some 400 yards behind the Australian troops then in the front line. A and B companies were the furthest forward with C and D a little way behind them. Private Ridley Sheldon:

> *But something happened a little later which fair made me quail; we had been told to lie down as low as we possibly could and just then bullets began to fly past as thick as hail, making a noise like a whistle as they whizzed through the air. This was my baptism of fire and I shall never forget it. Well, we lay low as we were told and I felt that I could not lie low enough: I have never trembled so much in all my life before and my legs beat such a tattoo, that I was afraid I should not be able to walk when once I got up. We stayed in that position for about an hour…but we did not escape altogether for one of our officers and two or three men were hit.*

The wounded officer was Hugh Heywood, who later wrote:

> *The bullets came pretty thick around us – probably ones fired at the front line trenches rained high and one of them picked me off in the lower left arm. It felt like a big stone being thrown at me hard – very hard, indeed – and I did not think it was a bullet till I felt the warm trickle of blood down my sleeve. Then I got the front man of my platoon who was lying near to me to get the field dressing from its place in my tunic and he was just going to put it on when Norris*[3] *turned up going forward and bound me up and put a sling on me and told me to walk back to the base, two or three miles away. The arm hurt a lot at first but it soon got to a dull throb.*

It took Heywood until midnight to get to the field hospital (Casualty Clearing Station) back at Helles. He recalled there being some very badly wounded men he felt rather a cad to have to occupy space. In due course, he was taken to the operating theatre – a small tent lit with an acetylene lamp and furnished with a wooden table.

> *(The doctor) ...washed the arm and then told me to 'get ready' and gave three rapid gashes with a knife whereupon blood flowed into a basin conveniently held by an orderly. The doctor then got a pair of sugar tongs or similar weapon and dived for the bullet in the gashes he had made in me. He caught hold of it at once and was pulling it out when the grips of the tongs slipped. He dived again. This time pulled it out all right. I've kept it as a memento.*

Hugh Heywood was evacuated away from Gallipoli and did not return to duty until 23 July. By then, many of his friends and comrades were dead. This painful but comparatively minor wound may well have saved his life.

It had been stretcher bearer George Harrison's first experience of treating men under fire and it had been a busy day, with about a dozen men wounded but only one of them seriously injured. Monday the 9th would be quieter and the men spent most of day improving the defences in the trench system. There was still work to be done by Harrison as shrapnel continued to fall on the Manchesters.

> *A few more men hit. Lost my way after attending Corporal McNaughton, but after hot time for half an hour with stray shells found dug-out and slept for three hours without greatcoat.*

William McNaughton, A Company, had been hit in the arm. It was another comparatively minor wound and he was soon back with his comrades. Born in Dalkeith in about 1885, his family had moved to the Gorton area of Manchester by the turn of the century. In 1912, he married Louisa Hickman and they set up home at 2 Mill Street, Reddish, Stockport. He's thought to have worked in the offices of Premier Waterproof and Rubber Co Ltd, Dantzig Street, Manchester. A long-standing member of the battalion, McNaughton had been awarded a First Class Musketry Certificate in October 1914. He was killed in action on 7 August 1915.

There was a Turkish sniper hidden somewhere in No Man's Land and he was very successful in keeping the heads of the Manchesters down, although no serious casualties were caused. Owen Evans[4] recorded in his diary

> *Troubled greatly by snipers. Marshall[5] had a very narrow escape – only a haversack prevented him being shot through the head. Saw some of our fellows of the 5th burying dead Turks.*

In the late evening, the battalion suffered its first fatality in action, when part of the trench collapsed burying five men while they slept. It was possible to quickly rescue Sergeant Ingham and three of the men, but when they managed to get to Private Murray Blaikie[6], he was dead. He was buried the next day but, over the course of the war, the location of his grave was lost and his name is now commemorated on the Helles Memorial to the Missing. The 10th had seen Owen Evans able to quickly bathe in a stream near to the French sector. Later he had a narrow escape when he 'fetched rations with Kay and Forbes[7]. Three shells burst near us on the way'. The most serious injury of the day was to Private Arthur Knight of A Company. He was evacuated from Gallipoli but died aboard a hospital ship the next day and was buried at sea.

After the landings, a number of troops had been detached to work at brigade or division headquarters and these, together with injuries and sickness, had reduced the effective strength of the battalion. By the morning of 11 May, the number of men in the trenches was 28 officers and 743 other ranks. Sergeant John Bennett was shot through the right arm during the day. It wasn't too serious a wound and, from hospital, he was to write home to his parents at 28 Chester Road, Swinton, telling of his experiences.

Sergeant John Bennett, C Company, would be killed in action on 7 August, aged twenty-three.

> *The country is quite pretty, very similar to Carnarvon…The most striking part of all is the peculiar nature of modern warfare. It is strange indeed to stand in the trenches and look ahead. Not a movement on the face of the country – the birds singing in the bushes, yet bullets are whistling and shells are bursting everywhere.*

In the early afternoon, orders were received that, during the evening, the battalion would go forward and take over a section of the front line for the first time. They would replace the New Zealand Canterbury Regiment and a battalion of the Worcestershire Regiment.

The move forward started at about 7pm with an experienced guide. It was to be a difficult and dangerous few hours. Even though they had the guide, they still lost their way and became entangled in barbed wire and it took some time to extricate themselves. Lewis Marshall had another lucky escape – he fell down a well and was fortunate not to be injured. There was then several hundred yards of rough ground and ravines to cross and it was not until after midnight that they approached the front line. The New Zealanders and Worcesters were not fully prepared to move and the Manchesters had to wait in the open for 30 minutes. Private Fred T Wilson[8]:

The enemy guessed a relief was taking place, for their machine guns found us and as the whine of bullets became more marked, we were ordered to lie down I lost my first friend at that moment and it is hard to realize he would never again share with me the things we both enjoyed. I flopped down, my equipment falling on top of me, I felt the handle of a spade on the ground. Instinctively I covered my head with the spade end and, burying my ear in the mud, felt very well protected. I saw the man in front of me lying still with head well down and waited with him for the next move. It came in the shape of a sergeant who, crawling up to both of us, wanted to know why the hell we didn't follow the others – we were keeping back all the men behind. I realized then my mistake waiting for the man in front and, crawling over him, I caught up with the others, who had waited after the break had been noticed.

Wilson's friend was, presumably, Lance Corporal Henry Plant, who is recorded as the only fatality during the day. In fact, Plant had not been killed outright although, badly wounded in the spine, he died a very short time later. Born near Kirkcaldy in Scotland, he had worked for cotton merchants, George Robinson & Co, 109 Princess Street, Manchester. He has no known grave. Whilst the men were lying in the open, the Turkish artillery opened fire and there were some twenty to thirty men injured by bullet or shrapnel. Private Fred T Wilson:

One by one, we dropped into the communication trench with a splash. Last night's rain still lingered, finding no outlet…The guns were silent again now and upon arriving at our appointed stations word came down the line to fire 'fifteen rounds rapid' at the enemy trench. With fingers cold, wet and fumbling, we loaded, fired as quickly as we could and got a volley in reply. This was our first shooting and proved so exciting that our discomfort was forgotten. The New Zealanders had now gone and we Territorials held the line, or rather our part of it, for the first time. A great honour and we meant, if possible, to do all we could to uphold that honour.

It rained heavily throughout the morning of 12 May and the men spent the time improving the defences of the trench system. There was occasional heavy fire from the Turkish machine gunners and the enemy snipers were again active. About 5.30pm, the British artillery opened up on the positions opposite as a prelude to an attack being made by the Ghurkhas. Shortly after, the infantry battalions in the front line also joined in to support the advance and the Manchesters fired off many rounds in the next hour. Of course, the Turkish artillery and riflemen were quick to respond and the front line became a very dangerous place until about 8pm. Two men were killed during these exchanges – Private Charles Cooper, B Company and Private Tom Penny, D Company.

Tom Penny, from Stockport. Killed in action on 12 May 1915.

Penny was the first of the Stockport lacrosse players to be killed. Playing in defence, he was a past Captain of the Club's A Team and had been hoping for a place in the First Team but, of course, the war had intervened before the season had started. Aged twenty-two, he is thought to have worked for the family printing company, the Edgeley Press Ltd, at its premises on Hardcastle Street.

His platoon commander, Lieutenant Arthur Brooke-Taylor[9], wrote to James and Catherine Penny:

I thought I would just like to say how much we shall all miss him here. As you no doubt know, we left Egypt a little over a week ago for active service and during the first few days which were necessarily trying to new troops, I could not help being impressed by the quiet courage displayed by your son, whilst his unfailing good temper and strict attention to duty in barracks had made him deservedly popular with us all. I was standing by him when he was killed. He had just put his head up to fire a shot when a bullet hit him in the temple and he died a few minutes later without regaining consciousness. He made no sound and I am sure that he did not suffer any pain at all. In your heavy sorrow, I should like to offer you and Mrs Penny my deepest sympathy.

Vickers machine gun with periscope attached.

It was a busy time for stretcher bearer, George Harrison. He treated Lance Corporals Cookson and Thomas[10], both of D Company, and got them away to safety down a gully. David 'Dadie' Sinclair was another of the wounded, injured in the leg.

Around 9pm, Captain Worthington made his way back from the front line to battalion headquarters to arrange for the machine gun teams to move up. Owen Evans was one of the gunners and recorded in his diary:

Trenches worse than awful. Everybody mucked up to their eyes. Mounted guns in pits on top of trenches. No. 1 opened fire first, then No. 2. Corporal Cross, No. 1, Corporal Shaw, No. 2 guns[11]. Used about 1,500 bullets. Had practically no sleep. Bullets came round us like hell.

Throughout the next day, snipers continued to be a problem for the companies in the front line. The battalion's war diary notes that they were managing to creep up to within fifty yards of the front line. The 8th Battalion, to the left of the 6th, tried to locate the enemy in No Man's Land but

Turkish snipers took a fearful toll of the invaders – invariably a shot to the head.

were unsuccessful, suffering another six men wounded of their own. Private Ridley Sheldon:

> *I had a terrible experience on Ascension Day, Thursday, May 13th, when along with a number of our fellows, I had to go on a ration party. There were ten of us detailed off for the work, with the Quartermaster Sergeant and you may have some idea of the dangers connected with what we had to do, when I tell you that though we had only about half-a-mile to go for the rations, it took us from half past seven in the morning until half past two in the afternoon to get back – seven hours altogether. The explanation is that the snipers were so awful and you had to watch your chance, dodging just a little at a time, otherwise you were bound to be picked off. For about three hundred yards, we were forced to wade up to our waists, in mud and water and one of my chums, happening to put his foot on someone's dead body, found the bottom of his puttee covered with blood. There was one part, about fifty yards in distance, where we had to run the gauntlet, which was fully exposed to the fire of the enemy's machine guns and here we had to dash across, one at a time.*
>
> *I managed to get across safely, but the Quartermaster and another man were both hit*[12]*. Then somehow the rest of us got separated and there were only six left to go for rations and wherever we could not help exposing ourselves, the snipers were potting at us immediately.*

Private Harry Coops, killed by a sniper.

During the morning of 14 May, it was the 8th Battalion which again attracted the main attention of the Turkish snipers. The British artillery started a very accurate shelling of

No Man's Land to try to dislodge them but the sniping continued at such a rate that George Harrison and his fellow stretcher bearers had to lend assistance to their comrades in the neighbouring unit. Their efforts were recognised in the battalion war diary entry for the day –

> *The work of Captain Norris and the stretcher bearers has been most praiseworthy. It is difficult to realize the danger and difficulties of getting wounded men out of the trenches at night; bringing them back over the rough ground, continually under fire.*

Twenty-seven year old Tom Marsden[13] was born in Holmfirth and spent most of his life there, working as a teacher at the Wesleyan Day School, where he had received his own education. More recently, he had moved to Glossop to work in his uncle's coal business. He had joined up in September 1914 and now took the opportunity to write home.

> *I am writing this from the trenches in the firing line, where we have been since Tuesday night. We had a very hot time getting here under cover of darkness, bullets flying in all directions, and anyone who got through that night without being hit I am sure is not intended to be hit. We have deepened the trench, so now we can stand up. We are getting decent food but are short of water and we scarcely get enough to drink. No bread, only hard biscuit. It has been very hard work up to now and our army has lost many men. We are now trying to take a hill in front, nearly like Holme Moss, and at the top of which is a huge fort. With this taken the rest will be comparatively easy. The Turks are fighting desperately and we have to be on the watch continually. This is a lovely country, a bit like the country at home for hills, but they are all covered with marguerites and poppies and, sad to say, little mounds of earth, with little crosses, where a number of our men are buried.*

All the available men spent the evening digging a new trench to provide better communication to the 8th Battalion's position on the left. The only casualty was Private Sidney Atkinson who received a comparatively minor wound and was back on duty before too long[14].

The following days remained relatively quiet, apart from the constant danger – shrapnel, and considerable effort was put in to improve the trench defences. An officer and thirty men from the Royal Engineers were attached to the battalion to give specialist advice and assistance. They identified that the trench parapets needed thickening as well as various improvements to the support and communication trenches. Work also started on improving the sanitary arrangements for the men. Metal biscuits boxes served as the front line latrines but there had been nowhere to dispose of the contents. A five foot deep cesspit was dug which was accessible from the front and support trenches.

There were two officer casualties on the 15th. Lieutenant Henry Hammick:

> *Old Aldous[15] got married to a French girl the day before we left Cairo and is now*

The Quartermaster's store near Krithia Nullah. Manchester Regiment Archives

> *wounded and will lose an eye, I am afraid. Dick Killick who was in Madras in Best & Co. was shot in the head and died soon after.*

Twenty-eight year old 2nd Lieutenant Richard Killick had been with his men in D Company, manning the most dangerous part of the line. Due to the very high water table, it had been impossible to make the trench very deep before it flooded. Efforts were being made to drain the trench but, in the meantime, the men were taking great care that they didn't expose themselves to the Turks. A Turkish infantryman took full advantage of what must have been Killick's momentary lapse of concentration and shot him through the head. He died within minutes. The Battalion War Diary records *'He was a thoroughly good officer, interested and thoughtful for his men and his loss will be greatly felt'*. The third son of Thomas and Euphemia Killick, of Bowden, Cheshire, he had worked in India for a number of years in the kerosene business of Best & Co. He had served as a Lieutenant in the Madras Guards – similar to a territorial battalion – transferring to the Manchesters when war was declared.

C Company's crack shots had an opportunity to show their deadly skill on the 17th. Corporal Newlove[16] spotted an enemy Maxim machine gun being dragged into position on a ridge some 350 yards away. He and his comrades opened accurate fire and, whilst they were not sure if they had hit anyone, the gun disappeared from view and was not seen again that day.

With Sergeant Northcote spotting targets through a telescope, D Company sniper Private Thomas Vivian Northcote was positive he had shot three men during the day at a range of 700 yards. They'd been seen to throw up their rifles and fall back in the Turkish trench. The two men were almost certainly brothers. Nothing is known of Horace V Northcote but Thomas had joined the battalion in 1911, when he was

The Battalion moving up Krithia Nullah towards the front line.
Manchester Regiment Archives

seventeen. Before the war, he had worked as a commercial traveller for the family firm of Northcote, Davies & Co, York Street, Manchester. The family lived in some comfort at 369 Moss Lane, Whitworth Park. Ironically, he became a sniper's victim only a few days later, on 29 May, when he was shot in the leg. Northcote was evacuated to hospital in Malta. He returned to Britain in July and, after further treatment at the military hospital on Manchester's Whitworth Street, he was discharged from the army on 26 March 1916. The surgery left him with one leg an inch and half shorter than the other.

The Northcotes were back in action again the next day, claiming another two victims. It was also a good day for the battalion machine gunners. Two more machine guns were issued to each battalion and, although the ones delivered to the 6th Battalion were the old-fashioned Maxims, they enabled much better covering fire to be given. Owen Evans had fired his rifle a few times during the day but, in the evening, was in place with the guns.

Came into action about 11pm with covering fire for the advance through the wood of the 5th Royal Scots and the Essex on the left. Did very well and drew the enemies (sic) *fire and shrapnel. Complimented by Major Pilkington, Brooke-Taylor and the Adjutant on last night's work.*

There were few casualties but George Harrison gave first aid to A Company's Frederick Kitson[17]. The twenty year old had been hit in the leg.

On the 19th, C Company finished digging the new trench to link up with the 8th Battalion. The day passed without incident except that, whilst digging, Harry Sutton was hit in the thigh, fracturing a bone[18].

Ridley Sheldon noted in his diary that the enemy were very quiet on the 20th but this changed in the early evening. Between 7pm and 7.30 a Turkish sniper accounted for four men. Two men in B Company were killed[19] and another two wounded.

After nine days in the trenches, the battalion was relieved by the 10th Battalion, on 21 May. Before they left the front line, there were two more casualties. Captain Bazley was shot in the head. Still alive, he was taken to 11th Casualty Clearing Station near Cape Helles, where he died on the 23rd. Shortly afterwards, Private Donald Lancaster,

The burial of Captain Walter Bazley at what is now Lancashire Landing Cemetery, near W Beach. The centre figure appears to be a nurse. Manchester Regiment Archives

A view looking north towards Achi Baba. Manchester Regiment Archives

serving with A Company, was also shot in the head. George Harrison went to attend to him but he was already dead[20].

Since the Manchesters had arrived at Gallipoli, they had lost ten men killed and nearly sixty wounded. Now in bivouacs, well away from the front line, they were again in relative safety, although there were still dangers from enemy shelling. Captain Claude Worthington:

> *Spent morning in improving dugouts. A good many shells fell on the bivouac. After a short sleep, went down to Y Beach and had a delightful bathe. A curious sight – most of the brigade bathing and the sound of shrapnel bursting not far off. At 9.00pm, 400 men from the Battalion went to make roads on the beach and also on the landing stage and returned at 1.00am. Saw a bible, which had been in man's pocket. Shot through the book and stuck in the leather binding on the inside…Whit Sunday: Spent a lazy morning reading illustrated papers and basking in the sun. At 2.00pm attended Captain Bazley's funeral, then went for a bathe. Rather nice having a Whitsuntide rest after 13 days in the trenches*

The men were also having a relaxing time. Private George Harrison comments, 'Had bath and washed clothes. Helped Lucas[21] finish off cake out of his parcel.' Owen Evans and his pal, William Bletcher, went to the base area where they bought milk, chocolate and oranges from a canteen run by Greek civilians. 'Prices most exhorbitant.'

Sergeant James Weston had received a letter from a colleague at the accountancy practice where he and Tom Worthington were employed. Worthington sent a postcard in reply

Weston showed me your note to him wishing us good luck and telling us how you were getting on at the office. For about a fortnight, we have been dodging about between the first and second line trenches, a most uncomfortable and dangerous job and too exciting to be pleasant. We are at present quite well and fit.

At this point, it is perhaps helpful to give a better impression of the daily hardships that the men experienced. The dangers from shell or bullet are apparent but the hazards from illness and disease increased with each day. It has been mentioned that the high water table made the digging of deep trenches impossible. Yet clean water was extremely scarce. There were a couple of farms which had wells but demand was so great that they quickly ran out.

A small supply for the brewing of tea was obtained by digging a hole in the trench, below the parados, and placing therein an old biscuit tin with perforated bottom. In this way a little water could be collected – and every pint was treasure. As there were many of our own and the enemy dead lying out in the open and also latrines in the immediate neighbourhood, it is a great tribute to the value of chlorination and typhoid inoculation that the men drank the water with impunity. (Divisional history).

A small stream ran through the division's area that provided some water for washing but, as it had previously flowed through the Turkish lines it couldn't be regarded as safe to drink and was very dirty.

During the initial weeks, there had been little attempt at proper sanitation arrangements; there were hardly enough men for combat and no-one really gave it much concern until it was too late. By then the flies had arrived. And, as the number of bodies lying in the open in No Man's Land continued to grow, a third army took to the field – rats.

Supplies of rations arrived by ship and were off-loaded to a divisional supply dump near W Beach. From here, the men of the Army Service Corps would transport them to battalion supply dumps about a mile inland, usually using pack animals. From there, men from the battalions would move the goods to their headquarters, also using pack animals. Carrying parties from each company would then take the stores to company headquarters where they divided first for platoons and then for sections. The loads consisted of boxes of bully-beef tins or Maconochie (tinned vegetable stew), sacks of loaves, tins of biscuits or jam, cheeses, bags of tea and sugar, sides of bacon and, periodically, mail bags of letters and parcels. Much of the work had to be undertaken at night to reduce the risk to the men but, even so, it was hard and dangerous as they crossed from trench to trench, often in the open, with the heavy boxes carried on their heads or shoulders. They would get caught on the barbed wire, fall down holes, all the while dodging rifle and artillery fire.

The food, once it arrived in the trenches, was a daily monotony and not well suited to the hot climate. As the divisional history comments 'Fruit – even good tinned fruit – and fresh vegetables would have done much to preserve the health of the men during the intense heat of summer.'

Firewood was also a scarcity as there were few trees or shrubs but it had to be found from somewhere so small fires could be made in the trenches to brew tea and cook food. It was not uncommon to see casefuls of tinned food stacked by the trackways, having been broken open so the valuable wooden packing case could be taken for fuel. Whenever and wherever it was safe to do so, official and unofficial salvaging took place. There would be official timber dumps often guarded by a sentry but the divisional history suggests that a few cigarettes might be offered in return for the sentry looking the other way for a few minutes.

One final shortage was of a direct military nature. There were no grenades (or bombs as they were then known) at Gallipoli. Battalions in Belgium and France had very limited supplies but for the men on the peninsula, there was not even one. The Royal Engineers started to make them out of old jam tins. They would be packed with old nails, bits of barbed wire and any other scraps of metal that could be found, together with an explosive charge. A time fuse was fitted to the top of the tin and this would have to be lit with a match and then quickly thrown. While the Battalion was at rest, each company supplied an officer, NCO and four men for grenade training. They would not actually get supplies of the bombs until an hour before the attack which would take place on 4 June. And, even then, the Division received only 225 bombs – less than one for each trained man.

Grenade making. Photo first published in the *Illustrated War News*.

On 25 May, the designation of the East Lancashire Division changed, becoming the Army's 42nd Division. At the same time the Manchester Brigade also lost its regional title, changing to 127 Brigade.

Private David Sinclair, wounded on 12 May, was now recovering at the Egyptian Government Hospital in Alexandria. He wrote home to his mother in Nairn:

> *It is now a fortnight since I got laid out and, I must say, I expected to be back in the thick of it by now but I am still as far off as ever. I can't move my leg yet or put it on the ground and they say that they don't know how long it will be before I go back. The trouble is, as far as I can tell, is that until I can hobble, they can't see what damage is done inside the knee as it is a case of wait and see.*

Sinclair recovered from his injuries and returned to duty to take part in an attack on 7 August 1915 during which he was killed. He has no known grave.

The day also saw the men's rest come to an all too brief end. In the early evening, they gathered up their rifles and belongings and started to make their way back to the front line to relieve their comrades from Oldham in the 10th Battalion.

Trench periscope in use at Gallipoli.

> *Just before leaving bivouac, a cloud burst on the Achi Babi Mountain and the dry dongas became roaring rivers. The trenches were waist deep in some parts and knee deep in others. The communication trenches were full of water and unusable. Consequently it was necessary to jump the parapet to get on. Cpl. Rutter was unfortunately killed in so doing.* (Battalion war diary)

Corporal Claude Rutter was one of several men across the battlefield who became victims of the alert Turkish snipers, who quickly picked off men avoiding the flood waters. Lieutenant Brooke-Taylor immediately went to his aid and found that he was still alive. However, Rutter died within a couple of minutes. He was buried near to the roadside but the location of his grave was lost during the course of the War. Born in the Eccles area, he was twenty-four and had lived in Ashton-upon-Mersey for a number of years. He was educated at Sale High School and later went to work at the local branch of Parr's Bank (now part of the Royal Bank of Scotland). Rutter had joined the battalion in 1912[22].

Corporal Claude Rutter.

When they reached the front line, they found that the 10th Battalion had advanced it by some fifty yards since they had been away. So, once again, the trench system was incomplete. One new communication trench, west of Krithia Nullah[23], had been dug in whatever position had been easiest and it had a significant bend in it which enabled the enemy to enfilade the occupants. 'This was a dangerous spot and a part of it particularly exposed was vacated until it could be traversed.' (Battalion war diary)

Machine gunner Owen Evans had also recorded the move forward in his diary. Terrific rainstorm had fallen and everything soaked through. Trenches deep in mud and water. Lost ammunition box in hole and fell up to waist in water. Bletcher, Cross, Nelson and I went into firing line to man two guns there.' It was not all bad news for

Evans 'Parcel arrived – cake, toffee, papers, parkin, stationery, H/Fs, chocolate'.

In a letter home, Lieutenant Hammick also wrote about the new position telling his parents that there were a number of Turkish bodies lying in No Man's Land. 'The smell was too awful'.

As recorded by the history of 42nd Divison, the army's first month at Gallipoli was

> *disappointing…After five weeks of toil and struggle, valour and self-sacrifice, unsurpassed in history, no more had been achieved than the securing of a mere foothold on the peninsula.*

This was recognised at the highest level and, for a number of days, senior commanders had been planning a new major offensive. As with two previous attempts, it would be designed to break through the Turkish line and capture the strategically important high ground of Achi Baba.

The sun came up early on the morning of the 26th and the trenches quickly started to dry out. It made digging much easier and progress was made in improving the defences, although many parts remained knee-high in water. Owen Evans, William Bletcher, John Donaldson[24] and another man[25] set up their machine gun just behind the advanced trench so as to give covering fire to the diggers. Even so, it was a day with high casualties. Over a dozen men were wounded, including Charles Taylor, from Whalley Range, who died the following day. Harry Coops, from Cheadle Hulme, was killed outright. His friend, Charles Turton, wrote to his parents telling them that Harry had been preparing food when he was shot through the neck and shoulder by a sniper[26].

Amongst the wounded was Captain Oswyn St Leger Davies. He was a long-serving officer of the battalion and its predecessor, having commanded the Mounted Infantry Company of the Volunteers, between 1904 and 1908. In 1911, he had written a booklet *The Theory of Musketry – a Plea for its Employment*. He was killed in action, aged forty-four, on 5 April 1918, whilst commanding the 8th Battalion, Lancashire Fusiliers. Originating from Llanwrda, South Wales, Davies had lived at Castleton, near Rochdale, before the War.

Whilst the stretcher bearers were attending to the wounded, one of their number, Private Frank Williams, was hit in the jaw. He was carried away by his mates to the field hospital near Helles where he died on 30 May.

At senior command level, details were being finalised for the forthcoming attack. The whole of the Allied line would advance, with French troops on the extreme right; to their left would be the British Royal Naval Division; the Manchester Regiment Battalions of 127 Brigade would be in the centre, attacking northwards astride the main road to Krithia; on their left to the western shore would be the troops of the 29th Division and a brigade of Indian troops. To bring the troops within charging distance of the Turkish front line, it would first be necessary for the Allies to make an advance to shorten the width of No Man's Land. This was planned for the 27th.

Once it was dark, Captain Pilkington ordered a reconnaissance patrol into No Man's

The road to Krithia with the entrance to Redoubt Cemetery on the left. Alan and Sue Curragh.

Land to prepare for the next day's advance. Lance Corporal Leonard Boardman and Private Sidney Atkinson[27] crept out and made their way to a bluff about 100 yards in front of C Company's position. They reckoned this would be a good firing position and came back to report that this should be a definite objective for the company.

Work on improving the trenches continued throughout the morning and afternoon of 27 May. The day's work was expensive with five men being killed[28] and others injured. The push forward was made under the cover of darkness at 9pm with C Company advancing about 200 yards on the left. On the right, Lieutenant Hellawell's platoon only had to move forward about seventy yards to keep in touch with the 5th Battalion's advance next to them. They started to dig in as soon as they reached their objective. Each man had an entrenching shovel and a sandbag. Once in position, they lay flat behind the scant protection of the bag and started to scrape a hole, five paces from the next man. As the hole was deepened, it was also widened and, in due course, all were linked together to form the new trench.

Zaccheus Holme was a twenty year old bank clerk, the son of a well-to-do shoe manufacturer. The 1901 Census showed the family, then living in Stockport, employing four live-in servants. He was one of the lacrosse playing group who had joined up the previous September. He wrote home to his mother:

We left the trenches we were in and advanced in the open at 9.45pm and, for the rest of the night, we had to dig in as hard as we could to get cover. Most of it had to be done lying

View towards Krithia from Redoubt Cemetery. The modern minaret in the village of Krithia can just be made out in the centre background. The village would remain an uncaptured objective throughout the campaign. Alan andSue Curragh

Private Zaccheus Holme, from Stockport. Killed in action on 4 June, aged 20.

flat and, I can tell you, it was awful work, but luckily for us the enemy did not spot us and we only got a few shots, but nobody in the company was hit. If we had been seen, it would have been frightful. The advance was quite a success as we were able to get the new firing trench dug and also the communicating trench to it. I can honestly say I have never worked harder before in my life as we were digging for seven solid hours.

As the trenches developed and became 'home' to the men, battalions started to give them names, often relating to their recruitment areas. So, on the western side of the peninsula, where the Essex Regiment and the Royal Fusiliers had troops, trenches became 'Chelmsford Street' and 'Fusilier Street'. Captain Worthington described the work as a 'splendid trench – with traverses every eight yards and three communication trenches'. And, in accordance with the new custom, it was named 'Stretford Road', after the battalion headquarters in Hulme. Elsewhere in the brigade sector, the trenches dug by the 8th and 5th Battalions quickly became known as 'Ardwick Green' and 'Wigan Road'.

At 11pm, the men were relieved by the 8th Battalion and went back to the support trenches a little way behind the front line. The men of the 8th continued the digging and suffered heavy casualties. Wilfred Hayes is reported to have recorded in his diary that one of the 8th Battalion men crawled back to Hayes' position after being shot through both thighs. He had a message that a Sergeant Fairhurst and four men were the only survivors in a trench and that if re-inforcements could not get there he would have to retire, but some supporting troops were sent to him within a few minutes[29].

During the daylight hours, the 6th Battalion men rested and tried to get some sleep but the Turkish artillery shelling made this difficult. At night, they dug new communication trenches to the front line. Mail arrived for the men during the 30th. Owen Evans had just finished reading a letter from his mother, when he heard that his friend Billie Barker[30] had been hit in the head.

George Harrison also lost a friend during the day – Arthur 'Phil' Collinge, was twenty-five and came from Crumpsall. He had worked for local merchants Heynssen, Martienssen & Co. Harrison went to the aid of Private Derwent who had been hit in the shoulder and carried him on his back down the trenches to the medical officer.

Ridley Sheldon later wrote of the general dangers of trench life:

> *On one occasion, when we were in the trenches, my section sergeant was using a periscope, which he held up too long; with the result that a sniper instantly put a bullet through the mirror, and the broken glass flew all over me and down my back, for I was standing between the sergeant and the parapet of the trench, but this was a very minor detail compared with much that I had to face in the way of danger. If you dared so much as to raise your hand above the parapet for one single moment…a bullet would come flying through the very place where your hand had been and if any of our fellows through thoughtlessness, happened to show the top of the head…he was almost sure to be singled out and either killed or wounded, in this way we lost a large number of men.*
>
> *My chum was preparing something to eat when, all at once, I heard his moan and was just in time to catch him in my arms as he reeled over, there were two holes, out of which blood was pouring firth like a tap, one in his forehead and the other just above the temple. I called for help; his wounds were bound up but he never regained consciousness and died at sunset. It was a very sad event and it might have been myself.*
>
> *On another occasion, there was one of our fellows lying on the floor of the trench, apparently asleep; so thinking he might be trodden on when darkness came, I called to him to get up. He took not the slightest notice; upon this, I went over and pushed him with my foot, but there was no response. When stooping down, I saw to my horror and dismay, that the back of his head had been blown away and his brains lay scattered under him. It was a sickening sight and these are things most horrible to relate…these incidents serve to show what awful realities of warfare mean.*

The final day of the month saw the battalion move back into the front line, taking over from the 8th Battalion. Rather than carry the machine guns in and out of the line, battalions were now leaving them in place for the relieving troops and Owen Evans took up his position ready to fire. He managed to get an hour's sleep – his first in twenty-four hours. Six men would be killed during the day, including Sergeant William Taylforth[31], the popular member of the Pierrot troupe.

The men spent their first full day back in the firing line improving the trench defences. Several took the opportunity to make diary entries: *Still digging. A very jumpy night. Turks reported going to attack.* (Captain Claude Worthington)

> *Certain death to show head above parapet. Three men killed[32]; only one hundred and fifty yards from enemy.* (Private Ridley Sheldon)

> *Fired the gun in the morning at the Turkish loopholes. Len Huff killed by wound in head. Quartermaster Sergeant Wilson killed, wound in head.* (Private Owen Evans)[33]

Edward Bleackley was one of the Stockport lacrosse players and was serving with his older brother, Cliff. A fit young man, aged eighteen, he was one of the battalion's runners, taking messages from headquarters to the companies. While he was crossing open ground on the way to the front line, he was shot in the head. Cliff dressed his wound and helped him to the dressing station. He then underwent two hours of surgery at the field hospital at Helles before his condition was stabilised sufficiently for him to be boarded onto a hospital ship bound for 15th General Hospital in Egypt. His condition improved there and he continued to recover for several weeks but, on 25 July, he suffered a relapse and died.

The men were now very tired, through lack of sleep and the physical exertions of digging and, during 2 June, the men of C Company and half of another were allowed to move back to Krithia Nullah to get some rest before the troops prepared for the coming attack. One platoon had not realised that they had bedded down too high up the bank of the nullah for safety. As dawn broke, they became easy targets for alert Turkish snipers. Within five minutes, 2nd Lieutenant William Cadman[34], Private Fred Collinge and five others had become casualties. Fortunately, none were dead. Cadman was treated by George Harrison and helped away. Harrison recorded that Collinge had received a minor wound in the thigh but it may have proved more serious as he was discharged from the army on 15 August 1916.

Private Edward Bleackley, from Cheadle Hulme, Cheshire. 18 year old Edward died of wounds on 25 July and is buried in Alexandria, Egypt.

During the morning of 3 June, detailed orders were issued for the next day's attack. The plan was that, from 8am, there would be an intense bombardment of the enemy trenches. At 11.20am, all the guns would fall silent and the infantry would cheer and wave their rifles above the parapet, as though about to attack. It was hoped that this would lure the Turks out of their dugouts and back into their front line which would then be bombarded again. The real attack would then take place. Half of each battalion would be in the first wave, ordered to take the enemy front line trench. The other half would be in the second wave following fifteen minutes later. They would press on the attack to take the Turkish second and third lines and, if possible, exploit any opportunities to advance even further, but all troops had orders not to penetrate the enemy defences by more than 800 yards.

All was ready and the Manchesters were in position astride the Krithia Nullah and the road to Krithia village. Holding the left flank was the 6th Battalion and, to their right, the 8th. Just to the right of the road was the 5th and the 7th was on the far right of the Brigade's sector. Also deployed along the road were eight armoured cars of the Royal Naval Air Service, each equipped with a Maxim machine gun.

The first wave of the 6th Battalion was in 'Ardwick Green' trench and consisted of three platoons of A Company and one platoon from each of B and D Companies. The remainder of the Battalion, forming the second wave, were now in Stretford Road, about forty yards behind. Printed copies of the orders were issued and every man knew exactly what part he was expected to play.

Brigadier General Noel Lee wrote home:

Official map showing the objectives for the attack on 4 June.

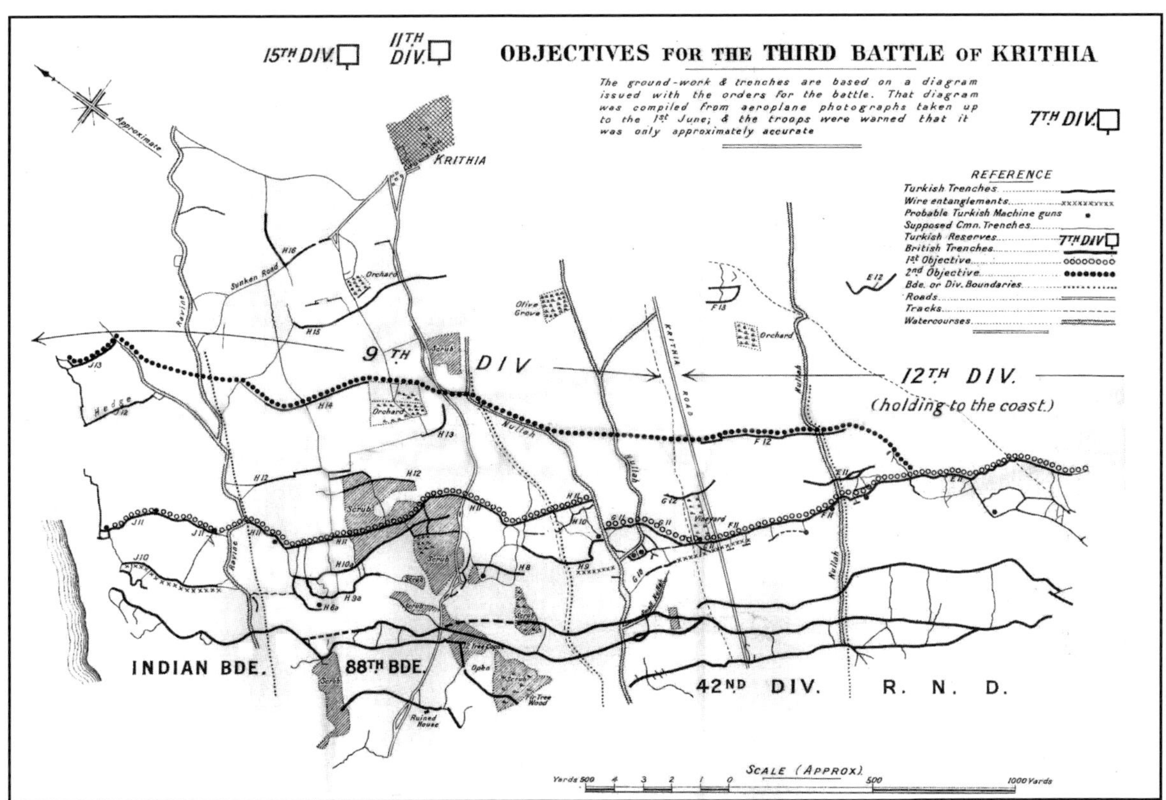

We are having a very strenuous time but I am very proud of the Brigade and especially of the 5th and 6th Battalions – the latter in particular. Not a single rotter in the lot and in such good spirits.

Tuesday, 4 June, was a fine summer's day although the heat was moderated by a stiff breeze from the north east. At 8am the British and French artillery opened up, starting a bombardment of Turkish strongpoints which lasted until 10.30. It was the heaviest barrage seen so far in the campaign with nearly eighty British field guns and howitzers firing. The French had also deployed six batteries firing their 75mm guns to support 42nd Division and the Royal Naval Division. From the sea, HMS *Exmouth*, *Scorpion*, *Swiftsure* and *Wolverine*, together with five French ships, pounded the Turkish defences. After a short break, the guns were now brought to bear on the Turkish front line, opening fire on them for fifteen minutes from 11.05am. Private Ridley Sheldon:

The Turkish trenches were almost destroyed; all the while this was going on, we kept our heads well down, but it was such an inferno of noise, that I was stone deaf for a fortnight afterwards; and there was a tornado of hellish fire, so fierce and terrible, that spread death and destruction all round. Any orders that were given had to be passed down the trenches from man to man, by his yelling into the ears of his mate as loudly as he

A French 75mm field gun cew in action at Gallipoli.

possibly could. The bombardment consisted of shrapnel and Lyddite[35] *and shells in thousands were dropped, blowing parts of the Turkish trenches to atoms and completely carrying away the barbed wire entanglements which the enemy had erected. Every shell that dropped seemed to tell, for we saw, hurled into the air, legs, arms, heads, bodies, parts of limbs and every imaginable thing. It was an awful and fearful sight.*

At exactly 11.20, the artillery stopped firing. For a few seconds, there was almost silence across the battlefield. In accordance with the plan, the British troops cheered and yelled and waved their rifles, already with bayonets fixed, above the parapet. The plan worked. The Turks believed the infantry attack was about to take place and rushed from their dugouts and opened heavy machine-gun and rifle fire, in the hope of cutting down their enemy as they left the trench. Ten minutes later, the British artillery opened fire again. It caught many Turks out in the open and casualties were heavy. The fire continued until midday, when the barrage lifted from the Turkish front line and started to play on their support areas, effectively preventing any reinforcements from making their way forward.

The Manchesters now climbed out of the relative safety of the trench and the men of A, B and D Companies charged across No Man's Land. In spite of the heavy bombardment, many Turks had survived and the machine guns instantly opened fire. Waiting with the second wave, Ridley Sheldon watched his pals go 'over the top'.

The fellows in the trenches leaped over the parapet and away they went. It was their work to cut the barbed wire entanglement, if necessity required it, bayonet any resisting forces and take the next line of trenches. The enemy's fire was terrific in the extreme and most deadly in its effect and our men went down before it like chaff before the wind.

Within a few minutes, they were in the Turkish front line and fierce hand-to-hand fighting was underway. Tom Marsden and his pal, Harold Jackson[36], had scrambled over the parapet with A Company and got across No Man's Land safely. In the charge, they lost sight of each other and Jackson's foot became tangled in the barbed wire in front of the Turkish front line. It was a little while before Jackson caught up with the man from Holmfirth.

The next I saw of him, he was leaning over the parapet of a side trench, shouting for the Turks inside to come out. I am afraid the menacing attitude he adopted scared them more than ever (if that were possible) and they would not come out. Then I came up and joined him and one fat Turk ventured out. Whilst Tom covered the remainder in the trench with his rifle, I disarmed and searched this one and sent him back to our lines.

When the others saw how he was treated they came out, one by one, readily enough, and a sorry spectacle they were. About five were wounded, though not severely, by our terrible artillery bombardment. Though half mad with fright, they seemed delighted to be taken prisoners. And their faces fairly lit up when we told them, by actions more than anything, to go to our lines. Several proffered to shake hands, the reinforcements were

The Battalion's charge across No Man's Land – midday, 4 June. Manchester Regiment Archives.

coming up then and the Turks turned several machine-guns on the spot we were occupying. The last Turk was out then and Tom and I took cover behind some gorse bushes whilst the heavy fire was on.

A fellow in our company, badly hit, I think in the lungs, called Tom to come and bind him up and Tom, like the brick he was, without any hesitation, got up and started to crawl across the bullet swept open ground. He had hardly left the shelter of the bush when the messenger of death struck him in the head. I could see death was instantaneous and it was useless to stay with him, so I hurried on to my company in the second Turk's line.[37]

It was now 12.15 and the second wave charged forward, passing the bodies of their dead comrades lying in No Man's Land. It was still exceptionally dangerous as recounted in the *Manchester Evening Chronicle* by an unknown soldier.

We were soon over the parapet and got going towards the enemy. The crack and bang of the rifles and crash of the bursting shells shut out all other noise. It is more like a nightmare than anything else. Chaps soon began dropping and this was the worst part, chaps you had mixed with, fed with, slept with for months, going down and dying…

Ridley Sheldon felt many of the same emotions as his unnamed comrade.

It is, indeed, terrible the first step you take right in the face of the most deadly fire and to realise that any moment you may be shot down, but if you are not hit, then you seem to gather courage and when you see, on either side of you, men like yourself, it inspires

you with a determination to press forward. Well, away we went over the parapet, with fixed bayonets – one long line of us, like the wind, but it was absolute murder, nothing less...This however did not deter us and on we went...we took six lines of trenches.

Sheldon never made it across No Man's Land. He was shot in the left thigh no more than twenty yards from the British front line and never fired a shot. Another soldier bound up his wounds and carried him back to the safety of the British line. There he was stretchered away to be treated by the medical officer and, afterwards, moved back to Cape Helles where, the next day, he was boarded on the transport ship *Ivernia* bound for hospital in Malta.

Sergeant Tom Worthington had led his men over and pressed on the attack towards the Turkish support line of trenches. He and the senior sergeant counted the men and found they had about forty. There were no officers left and it was up to the two sergeants to start to prepare the defences against an expected counter-attack. About 250 of the enemy had been taken prisoner and sent back to the British line.

The other battalions of 127 Brigade had also advanced according to plan. On the 8th Battalion front, A and B Companies had got across No Man's Land taking their first objective in the Turkish main trench. C and D Companies had leap-frogged them to continue the attack. Their second objective was high ground overlooking the original Turkish front line and they captured this with the help of some men from A and B who went forward with them. Early in the afternoon, General Lee, commanding the whole of the Manchester Brigade, was mortally wounded and Colonel Heys of the 8th took over. After an hour he had to return to the battalion as hardly any of its officers were left and, soon after, he was killed. The battalion held its positions throughout the day in spite of being heavily counter-attacked on several occasions. The divisional history records that, when the battalion was relieved on the 6th, one company comprising 200 men who had gone over the top had been reduced to just eighteen. The rest were dead, wounded or missing. eighty men from the battalion were dead. Of the seventeen officers who took part in the attack, nine were killed and another seven had been wounded.

To the right of the Krithia Road, the 5th Battalion also had success. C and D Companies had captured the Turkish front line and A and B had overlapped to take the second line of Turkish trenches about 500 yards further on. Thirty-eight men had been killed and over 130 wounded.

On the right flank, the 7th Battalion had also pushed forward. The battalion's war diary for this period is missing from its file at the National Archives and some of the details of the attack are now lost in consequence. A and C Companies took the first objective and, as with the other units, the remaining two companies now leapfrogged to attack the Turkish second line. They came under enfilade fire from the right as well as fire from their front. There were also pockets of Turkish troops to their rear who had not been mopped up and who fired on them as well. They also held their positions throughout the afternoon.

To the left of the Manchesters, the attack had gone less well. On the coast, the Indian Brigade had advanced with little artillery support. The battalions of Sikhs and Ghurkhas had got forward but the 1st Battalion, Lancashire Fusiliers, had been driven back by heavy enemy fire. To the immediate left of the Manchesters, the attacking troops suffered very heavy casualties from Turkish defenders firing from strong points which had been untouched by the artillery bombardment. The enemy front line was

Lucky to be alive. 6th Battalion men just relieved from duty in the front line. Note the dirt on the rifle butt. Manchester Regiment Archives.

Captured Turkish troops being interrogated after the Third Battle of Krithia.

taken but the troops were unable to press the attack further.

On the eastern coast of the peninsula, the French attack had been an almost complete failure. Although there had been sufficient artillery pieces, inaccurate shelling had left much of the Turkish defences intact. The attacking troops had suffered very heavy casualties as soon as they had begun to advance and, within a few minutes, they had been forced to fall back to their trench.

In between the French and the Manchesters, the Royal Naval Division had also left their trenches. The Anson, Hood and Howe Battalions led the first assault, capturing the Turkish front line but, in doing so, losing half their officers. The failure of the French attack now meant that the troops were coming under heavy enfilade fire and the second wave troops from the Collingwood Battalion were now ordered forward. The Official History of the War records,

> *At a quarter past twelve, in a long extended line, the Collingwoods moved forward as steadily as if on parade, but just before reaching the Turkish trenches, they were caught by murderous fire from their right flank. Practically the whole Battalion was annihilated. The few survivors, with parties of the Howe and Hood, pushed steadily forward and captured the brigade's second objective. But there too, enfilade fire made the position untenable and, by quarter to one, the remnants of the brigade were back in their old front line.*

Tom Worthington recounted his experiences in a letter home to his mother[38].

> *When I got to the second trench, we received word from the Captain that*

Lance Corporal James Wilson, from Irlam. Killed in action on 5 June, aged 22. He had been wounded in the leg and his brother, Cyril saw him making his way to the dressing station but he never reached it and nothing was ever heard of him again.
Neil Drum

reinforcements were wanted on the right and I and a party of twenty-five were detailed to give the necessary assistance. Well, off we went and shortly found ourselves with another force under our Company Sergeant Major also going with reinforcements. We therefore consolidated and together advanced to the Captain's aid. To do this, we had to go over the top of a ridge and here we found a machine gun posted and sweeping the top with bullets. However, I crawled along the top and got behind a bush, listening to the bullets. Next to me a youth named Casson[39] *was crawling on his stomach. When we looked round, we found all the others had retired and found a better way up a gully, leaving the two of us on the top. Then Casson managed to crawl out of range behind me until he was safe, I was too far up to back down so lay for a few minutes thinking things out and thinking pretty hard. Finally I decided to chance my luck and run for it, but with circumspection. The first move was to run for a bush about twenty yards off on my right and this I did – talk about evens – the machine gun rattled and the rifles blazed but my good fortune held out. The next rush was for another bush about twelve yards off but as this was only poor cover, I had to make for a further bush about another six yards off. As the enemy were waiting for me, I pretended I was hit and fell about a yard short of the first bush and rolled behind it. I immediately jumped up again and sprang for a second bush repeating the manoeuvre…I saw the edge of the donga and, still gripping my rifle and equipment, I rolled over and over as if hit and I finally fell into the donga about ten feet down. After collecting my wits, I walked up to where the reinforcements had gone.*

Private Thomas Holt Garner, from Bramhall, Cheshire. A very popular member of the village community, playing for the tennis, cricket and football clubs. Died of wounds on 5 June, aged 24.

It was now about 2pm. At the headquarters of 42nd Division, reports were being received of the success of 127 Brigade. The 6th Battalion held the most advanced position across the whole battlefield. However, it was a salient pushing well into the enemy lines and they were starting to come under pressure from Turkish forces on three sides of them. At senior level, it was agreed that the French would renew their attack at 4pm and be supported by the Royal Naval Division, which would be reinforced by its reserve battalions. The Manchesters would only have to hold on for another two hours.

General Sir Ian Hamilton, aboard HMS *Wolverine*, had watched the attack and wrote in his diary:

For the best part of an hour it seemed that we had won a decisive victory. On the left all the front line Turkish trenches were taken. On the right the French rushed the

'Haricot'– so long a thorn in their flesh; next to them the Anson lads stormed another big Turkish redoubt in a slap-dash style reminding me of the best work of the old Regular Army; but the boldest and most brilliant exploit of the lot was the charge made by the Manchester Brigade in the centre who wrested two lines of trenches from the Turks; and then, carrying right on; on to the lower slopes of Achi Baba, had nothing between them and its summit but the clear, unentrenched hillside. They lay there – the line of our brave lads, plainly visible to a pair of good glasses – there they actually lay!

The battalion machine gunners had been hit hard, with several men wounded in the early stages of the attack. Private John Hough was evacuated from Gallipoli but died of his wounds on 20 June at a field hospital on the nearby island of Lemnos. Brothers Charlie and William Cross were assigned to different gun teams and it would not be until the next day that William heard that Charlie had been killed. He was serving in the same team as Owen Evans and had been held in reserve in the British front line and they were not ordered forward until about 2pm. Evans told William that the team had moved up a little gully towards a position in the original Turkish second line where they were to set up the gun. The final twenty yards were exposed to enemy fire and the men had to make a dash for it. The first two men made it across safely. It was then Charlie's turn to make the run, carrying the gun. He nearly made it and was just passing over the gun into the trench, when a single shot rang out. There was a sniper hidden in the rough ground and he had shot Charlie in the stomach. George Shaw and Bill Kay[40] bandaged him up but, after asking for a drink, Charlie Cross passed into unconsciousness and died about twenty minutes later.

Private William Ashton, from Longsight, Manchester, aged 25. Chris Jordan

George Harrison and the other stretcher bearers were also having a bad time of it. It was just too dangerous to go into No Man's Land to try to treat or rescue the men. *'Wounded and dead were all over, but we could not get at many.'* They were doing what they could but suffering casualties of their own. Corporal Kent was badly wounded and lay in the open. They would not be able to get to him until the next day. Private Bickerton was one who was stretchered away. He was taken to the field hospital near Helles but died later in the day. Another comrade, Alec Charlton, needed medical attention but was fortunate that his wounds were not life-threatening[41].

Private Norman Bickerton, from Crumpsall, Manchester. Died of wounds on 4 June, aged 19.

When Tom Worthington caught up with his comrades, he found the captured position was,

...one of some danger, but we proceeded to dig ourselves in trenches and tried to hold on, but the machine gun ripped us and rifle fire crackled and then to complete the inferno, the shrapnel commenced to search every inch of the ground systematically until hardly a foot was left untouched. It was while trying to get a working party together here that I stopped a shrapnel bullet with my neck. It tore thro' my jacket, sweater and shirt and scarred my neck but not seriously – only a sticking plaster wound fortunately. As I was somewhat shaken by the blow and going back to the dressing station, I found the Sergt. Major who had been wounded in the head. After helping in several ways to get him back to the base, I finally carried him (6′ 4″ of him) on my back, down the rocky donga (for roads are minus here), pretty well shot to the world.

This was Company Sergeant Major Hurdley who had received a serious wound to the head and was partially paralysed. He had refused to be taken to the rear and continued to give orders and rally the scattered groups of men. For his bravery, he was awarded the Distinguished Conduct Medal, second only to the Victoria Cross. The citation, published in the *London Gazette* concludes 'It was largely due to his brave conduct that the advanced line was held'. He was also Mentioned in Despatches and was one of only six British soldiers to be awarded the Russian Cross of St George (2nd Class) during the whole War[42].

Hurdley recovered from his wounds and it is probable that he owed his life to Worthington's action. His injuries were such that he could never return to duty and he was discharged from the army on 27 April 1916. The damage to his skull was repaired

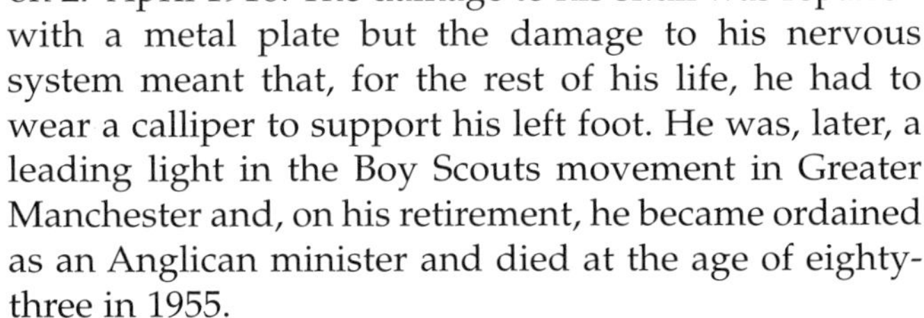

with a metal plate but the damage to his nervous system meant that, for the rest of his life, he had to wear a calliper to support his left foot. He was, later, a leading light in the Boy Scouts movement in Greater Manchester and, on his retirement, he became ordained as an Anglican minister and died at the age of eighty-three in 1955.

The expected second assault by the French had been scheduled for 4pm but this was delayed by an hour as they reported they were not ready. As 5pm neared, it became apparent that their losses had been so significant that another assault was going to be impossible. On the left, the Indian Brigade did try to push forward but again suffered heavy casualties. The 14th Sikhs lost almost all of their British and Indian officers and 380 out of the 514 other ranks. Across the battlefield, orders were received to dig in and consolidate the gains made so far. 127 Brigade still held a good position pushing their salient well into the enemy defences but, around 4pm, Turkish

Maor-General Douglas, 42nd Division commander, observing the attack with the aid of a telescope.

reinforcements started to arrive and were deployed against them. They were now coming under heavy attack from three sides.

Major-General Douglas, commanding 42nd Division, consulted with his superior and it was agreed that the position was becoming untenable. At 6.30pm, he ordered the withdrawal of the troops back to the position of the original Turkish front line. As recorded in the divisional history,

> *The retirement was made with the greatest reluctance; indeed, the few remaining officers had great difficulty in making the men realise that the order to withdraw must be obeyed. The idea of giving up the ground they had won was almost unbearable for the four Manchester battalions had resolved to hold on to their gains, whatever the cost might be.*

Captain Hugh Brocklehurst Pilkington, from Prestwich. Killed in action on 4 June, aged 27.

Sir Ian Hamilton later sent a private letter to Douglas which included the sentence *'As a matter of fact, I never saw any finer piece of work than that performed by the Manchesters that day'.*

C Company of the 6th Battalion, including many of the Stockport lacrosse players, occupied the position furthest forward. They were enfiladed by fire from the right and found it impossible to pull back.

> *Its commander, Captain H B Pilkington, was mortally wounded in the head but, propped up in the trench, he continued to direct and encourage the men. The company was practically wiped out.* (Divisional history)

Returning from the dressing station, Sergeant Tom Worthington tried to make his way back to C Company but,

> *As it was dark, and I could not see how far our men had retired, I attached myself to a party of the 8th as a guard on the donga to prevent any of the Turks coming down the donga and to intercept any of the British forces who might be returning that way. There were four of us on this guard and it was quite enough excitement to end the first day.*

Around 700 men of the Battalion had gone into action in the morning. By the evening, only 160 were left holding their sector of the new British front line. Many were wounded. Others were still unaccounted for and, like Worthington, may have temporarily attached themselves to other units. Others were dead but the figures are unclear. The Commonwealth War Graves Commission records fifty six members of the Battalion who died on 4 June 1915. It also records another eighty-three dying the next day, and a further ten on the 6th. Whilst casualties continued to mount on 5 June, it does seem likely that many of these were actually killed during the charge or in the fighting later in the day. In the chaos it would be hardly surprising that no-one was

Redoubt Cemetery. Situated on the west side of the Krithia Road and just behind the front line, it contains many burials of Manchester Regiment soldiers. Alan and Sue Curragh.

keeping an accurate record of the exact details of each man's death, even if it was possible to establish them.

Of the thirty-one officers who had arrived at Gallipoli a month before, ten had been killed during the day – Captains Robert Edgar, Joseph Holt, Stanley Jackson[43], Edgar Kessler and Hugh Pilkington; Lieutenants Arthur Brooke-Taylor, Tom Mills[44] and Arthur Taylor; 2nd Lieutenants Rowland Brooks[45] and Alan Donald.

Lieutenant Tom Mills, from Stockport.

Of the other ranks previously mentioned in this account, Zaccheus Holme was dead and Sergeant Arthur Fleming had been badly wounded. He died in hospital in Alexandria on 18 June. More fortunate was Sergeant James Weston, who had a lucky escape. He received a shrapnel wound to the head and spent several weeks in hospital in Malta before returning home. He wrote to his parents at 15 Deans Road, Swinton, to tell them he was being transferred to a hospital in Manchester.

The three Heydon brothers had all become casualties. Arthur and Frank were both wounded but Frank wrote home, from a hospital ship, to tell their parents about Sidney ('Cider').

Cider and I got to their first trenches together and it was fine to see the way the Turks bolted. We dropped on our knees and then began to get a bit of our own back. My right arm went useless and I found I had a bullet through it. Just in and out and nothing to trouble about. Cider went on and I met a chap on this boat who said Cider had bandaged him up in the Turks' third trench.

Heydon's death is officially recorded as 6 June but it probably occurred earlier[46].

Claude Worthington had recently been promoted to Major and was second in command of the battalion. Overnight, he went to brigade headquarters to try to obtain sandbags, barbed wire and, most importantly, reinforcements. He returned about 3.30am empty-handed to find the Commanding Officer, Major Pilkington, had received a minor head wound. Worthington now took command. There were only five other officers at duty – Lieutenants Henry Hammick and Edmund Young and 2nd Lieutenants Kershaw, Milne[47] and Sellars. A Turkish counter-attack was building nearby and, leaving the other officers to hold the line, Worthington led a small group of men forward up a nullah to fire on a party of about fifty Turks who were attacking the 5th Battalion's position. After a few shots, the Turks retreated.

It is possible that it was the same enemy group which was also able to pour enfilade fire onto the position being held by Tom Worthington and his small party. Sergeant Worthington's party had nine men killed and another four wounded. Sergeant Thomas Worthington:

As the officer in charge was killed and there was no one left of competent authority, I told our men of the 6th to follow me and clear out if we could. To get out of this shop was almost worse than the previous day but it had to be chanced if we wanted to get back to our own Battalion. The only way out was at an opening facing the Turkish position and again I had to jump for my life. This was at 7am after three hours of being shot at. Again, fortune favoured the fortunate and I only got a few shots at me. When I looked round for my men, I found they would not follow and they waited there until 10pm that night before moving and then only three out of six managed it. However, I collected another body of six stragglers and we made our way to our own Battalion to report and reinforce. There we found Mr Milne[48] and a party of 6th Manchesters nearly all that were left of the …[49]

V Beach showing the SS *River Clyde*. Manchester Regiment Archives

odd we started with, now reduced to under … Looking back at the hole I had got out of earlier in the day, I saw two bodies of men who had evidently tried to get out the same way I had done.

In the new British front line, the situation was comparatively quiet throughout the morning of the 5th. Of course, shelling and sniping continued with deadly effect. Lieutenant Young was shot in the head and died instantly. Work was undertaken to improve the defences and, in the afternoon, the men sniped at possible Turkish targets.

Second Lieutenant, George Moor VC.

Just before dawn on the 6th, the Turks launched a counter-attack. In front of Owen Evans, they had crept to within twenty yards under the cover of darkness and threw grenades. Luckily the range was just too far and they exploded a few feet in front of the parapet. To the left and right of the Manchesters' position, the Turkish attack was stronger and, in one nearby section, they recaptured the trench, forcing the British battalion into what was reported as being a rout. Order was only restored when a young Second Lieutenant, George Moor of the 2nd Battalion, Hampshire Regiment, ran across to the neighbouring battalion; stopped the retirement and led the men forward to recapture the trench. He is alleged to have stopped the retreat by drawing his revolver and shooting four British soldiers. Moor was awarded the Victoria Cross. Sergeant Tom Worthington:

After practically no rest for two days and only a biscuit for food, we manned the reserve trench and had another exciting experience. A young fellow named Smith and myself took upon ourselves to man the gully leading up to our trench from the donga. Before this, Mr Milne and a party of about eight men had worked part way down this under a heavy fire to a communication trench where were a number of Turks and these they were successful in clearing out while still under fire. Shortly they returned, leaving two or three wounded in the gully, up which the Turks were firing pretty accurately. As the position was rather warm Smith and I banked up the parapet with sandbags and waited. In due course the Turks came down the donga attacking our men on the opposite side of the hill and further down the stream. A party of them filled a dugout in the hillside and were blazing away at our fellows when we found the range and got three or four of them pretty quickly. The remainder looked round startled but did not clear away until we had got two or three more. Then as they cleared away down the donga we got a few more of them and also stopped a party of five or six going up a trench to the left. This rather disconcerted the Turks who began to run backwards and forwards much to their discomfort as we had by now got the range. After this we waited for a while to give them a chance to regain their confidence and come for more. In about ten to twenty minutes they, or a fresh party, arrived. The second party we treated the same way and then the

Turks seemed to smell a rat and placed a firing party on the opposite hillside. Then they proceeded to give it to us pretty hot for about twenty minutes, but we laid low in order not to give our position away. We finally had another go at them and I reckon that altogether we put about twenty to thirty out of action. Between whiles my companion brought in four wounded men from down the gully while I kept him covered from the top of the gully. Later in the day I spotted some snipers who were digging themselves in a pit in the middle of a field opposite our positions. With the help of a Borderer we managed to put 'paid' to their accounts. It is a great pity when you come to regard things afterwards that men should be coerced or compelled to kill one another for the gratification for a few others in power. The Turks against us seem a fairly intelligent lot of the peasant class and are not quite the blood-thirsty looking crew we generally suppose. Some of the wounded I saw (and there was a great number) looked really pitiful objects, and it is a regrettable fact that scores of both sides must have been left to die from sheer inattention as they lay between the two armies on the contended ground.

As the situation quietened down, it became a time for reflection. Owen Evans and William Cross went to find the body of William's brother and, together, they buried Charlie in the side of a Turkish trench. Later William wrote to his parents 'I am heart broken at having to break such news to you but the worst of things has happened…'[50]

It was also a time for General Sir Ian Hamilton, commanding the Expeditionary Force, to reflect. He cabled Lord Kitchener, the Secretary of State for War, stating that the attack had convinced him that substantial reinforcements would be necessary if he was to have success and expressed the view that the nature of the peninsula meant success would be very difficult, however strong the reinforcements were.

During the night of the 7th, half the battalion was relieved from the front line by the 8th Battalion, Lancashire Fusiliers (LFs) and moved back to their old positions at Stretford Road. In the early hours of the next morning, the remainder were relieved by the Royal Marine Light Infantry. Claude Worthington noted in his diary '8th LFs very jumpy. Had to put a guard on with fixed bayonets to turn back men who kept running away'.

Bathing at Cape Helles.

The men rested as much as they could during the day and, in the evening, withdrew to bivouacs in reserve. Even here, they were subjected to some long range shelling during the day but managed to bathe in the sea and catch up on more sleep.

On 10 June, Claude Worthington started to reorganise what was left of his command. He divided the 200 men into two companies. One would be commanded by Lieutenant Hammick, with Second Lieutenants Kershaw and Sinclair; the other commanded by Lieutenant Hellawell, assisted by Second Lieutenant Milne. Hellawell and Hammick would now have 'acting' rank as captains, whilst they commanded the companies. Worthington also wrote up the war diary and prepared the casualty list. He wrote a number of recommendations for commissions as officers for Company Sergeant Major Hay, Private Boyes-Varley and Private Boswell[51]. Gallantry recommendations were also made in respect of Captain Pilkington, Lieutenant Hammick, CSM Hay, Private A B Smith[52] and Private Stuart Forbes.

It would not take long for news of the casualties to reach the War Office in Britain and notifications would soon be on their way to the next of kin of the men. Telegrams would be sent to the families of officers but for the loved ones of the other ranks, it would take longer for letters to make their way. For the Yates family of Cheadle Hulme, there would be three letters – telling Arthur and Annie Yates that their three sons had been wounded. Wilfred had been shot in the foot and would be discharged from the army the following year. Billie had received a minor wound to the hand and was back at duty soon[53]. Chester had been injured in the thigh and, whilst his wound was the most serious, it was not thought to be life-threatening. He was evacuated to hospital on Malta, where his condition at first improved, but he died on 8 July.

For other families, the news from the War Office left room for hope. Men were posted only as 'missing' and it was possible that, perhaps wounded, they had been taken prisoner by the Turks. In some cases, these hopes would be dashed within a few weeks. As the front line moved forward in subsequent attacks, it would be possible to recover some of the bodies. The effects of the heat and rats would make visual identification difficult but many men had worn an identity disc, although this was often made of fabric and disintegrated over time. However, for many families, it would not be until a year later, in the summer of 1916, that the War Office would confirm that nothing further had been heard and the men must now be presumed to be dead.

A month later, Major-General Douglas wrote to Colonel Pilkington (by then recovered from his wound, promoted from major and back in command of the battalion)

> *I am still hoping that you may be able to collect evidence of some of the special acts of gallantry by officers and men of your battalion during the assault on 4 June. It is most unfortunate that, owing to the many casualties you sustained, many deeds worthy of the Victoria Cross, have not been reported. I hope that your men know this. The dash, steadiness, reckless bravery and endurance shown by the 6th Manchester and, indeed, by the whole Brigade, was equal to the best traditions of the British Army.*

In the event, it would appear that no VC recommendations were made for the battalion and, certainly, none were awarded. It is probable that the high level of casualties prevented finding three witnesses that were necessary for this award.

However, there had been a number of acts of exceptional bravery amongst the men. For those who were dead, there would be no official recognition as, at the time, the Victoria Cross was the only medal which could be awarded posthumously. But, for those surviving, there would be recognition by awards of the Distinguished Conduct Medal.

During the attack, Alexander Doig had taken six men with him to capture part of the enemy trench, which enabled them to fire on the Turks and help to repel a counter-attack. The medal citation concludes *'It was due to his action that the trench was not only taken but successfully held'*.

Fifty-six year old Sergeant Robert Gill was in charge of the machine gun section, commanding it in the advanced line throughout the period. He was instrumental in directing the fire which helped to repel the Turkish counter attacks. The local Manchester newspaper quoted him as saying *'Every minute we expected to be overwhelmed but eventually the Turks were beaten off and jolly glad we were'*. Gill's medal would be awarded not just for his bravery on 4 June but also on several subsequent occasions. He was wounded in action on 13 July 1915, losing his right eye, and was discharged from the army in April 1916. He originated from the Heaton Chapel area of Stockport but his close family had moved to Llanferfechan and he went there to convalesce.

Sergeant Robert Gill, DCM.

Company Sergeant Major Frederick Hay.

Privates Geoffrey Cutter and Randolph Hashlim had gone out under heavy fire and dug a shelter for a badly wounded officer and then rejoined the firing line. In September 1915, Hashlim left the Battalion to train as an officer, rising to the rank of captain with the Cheshire Regiment. In 1918, Cutter was promoted to Second Lieutenant, serving with the Battalion.

CSM Frederick Hay took over command of his Company when all the officers became casualties, holding the advanced line until the Battalion retired in the early evening of the 4th. 'He then brought his Company back in good order. He was twice wounded in the arm and later received a third slight wound but still continued to do duty.'

Three brothers called Senior took part in the attack. James Senior had been killed. Robert Senior had been wounded, but not seriously. He left the battalion in 1916 as his contracted time had expired but reenlisted into the Norfolk Regiment. He rose to the rank of second lieutenant and was killed in action on 27 March 1918. Lance Corporal William Arthur Senior was awarded the DCM for 'conspicuous gallantry on 4th June 1915, during operations on the Gallipoli Peninsula. He showed great bravery, coolness and resource in leading a party fighting from traverse to traverse which resulted in the capture of a Turkish officer and about sixty other

Corporal William Senior, DCM.

prisoners.' He was also 'Mentioned in Despatches'. Senior had joined the Territorial Force in 1908, originally serving with a local Army Medical Corps unit before transferring to the Battalion. He was then twenty-two and was working as a salesman for J & N Philips Ltd, Church Street, Manchester. Senior had been slightly wounded in the attack and spent some time in hospital in Alexandria before returning to duty. He was shot in the knee in the coming August and was evacuated home, being discharged from the army in February 1916.

During the evening of 10 June 1915, Major Worthington received orders that he was to prepare the battalion to move at short notice to the safety of the island of Imbros for rest and regrouping. Sergeant Tom Worthington:

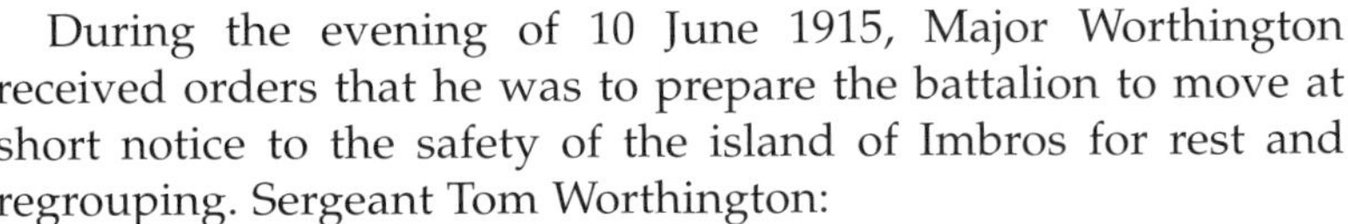

We received word that we were to be sent to the island of Imbros for a few days. I expect the reaction was too much for my nerves as I felt awfully seedy that day and the following day. Perhaps also it was because I heard of my friend A…[54] in the 7th Manchesters. I had the luxury of haircut and a right good one too. Even yet I can hardly decide whether it was a haircut or a shave. Anyway, if another bullet hits my hair, my head will have to catch it all.

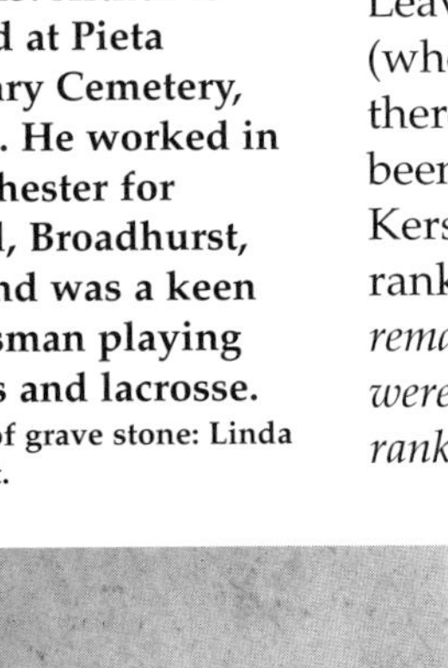

Private Arthur Chester Yates, from Stockport. Died of wounds on 8 July, aged 25. Arthur is buried at Pieta Military Cemetery, Malta. He worked in Manchester for Tootal, Broadhurst, Lee and was a keen sportsman playing tennis and lacrosse.
Photo of grave stone: Linda Corbett.

Rough seas prevented the men boarding for Imbros and they continued to rest in the reserve area. At about 3pm on the 11th, a shell exploded near battalion headquarters, wounding five men. They included Captains Hammick and Hellawell. Leaving aside Major Worthington and Captain Holberton (who had recovered from a minor wound) at headquarters, there were only three other officers at duty: Sellers who had been left in Cairo and only arrived at Gallipoli on the 2nd and Kershaw and Milne who had only been promoted from the ranks in Cairo. As Tom Worthington wryly observed *'It's remarkable that out of three officers left unwounded, two of them were privates six weeks ago, so apparently one learns things in the ranks that officers don't learn'*. Owen Evans spent the day sorting out the kit and personal effects of those who had been killed. Any kit that could be reused would be and the personal belongings would be parcelled up ready for their eventual return to families in Britain. The seas had calmed by the night of 12/13 June and, about 4.45am, the men embarked at V Beach where they had landed just over a month before. A number of men who had been treated at the field hospital at Helles were now fit enough to go with the Battalion and the strength was

"W" Beach, later known as Lancashire Landing Beach. Manchester Regiment Archives.

now eight officers and 286 other ranks. They arrived at Imbros four hours later but it was not until 2pm that they were landed. Tents were pitched and the new camp was ready before dark.

Sir Ian Hamilton's earlier cable to Lord Kitchener had been favourably received. Three divisions of troops still in training in Britain would be despatched to Gallipoli. They would not arrive until towards the end of July and, in the meantime, Hamilton was urged to continue to press the enemy but not to take unnecessary risks.

Major Worthington's first task on the 14th was to carry out another reorganisation of his diminished battalion, grouping the men from A and B Companies into the temporary No. 1 Company. The remainder were assigned to No. 2. He carried out an inspection later in the morning but everyone took the opportunity to rest. George Harrison liked Imbros *'Lovely place. Very hilly. Small harbour with few transports and gunboats. Picturesque natives with baggy trousers (including women)'.*

Back in Manchester, news of the attack had been reported in the press and it had been declared a success. From his hospital bed, Lieutenant Hammick wrote home 'The official account of June 4th is a gross misrepresentation of the truth. No casualties are published yet. They will not dare publish them in a lump'.

On the 17th, twelve new officers arrived from England to join the battalion. These were new recruits not experienced in the ways of the Territorial Force and, for a couple of them, their arrival would be the cause of some discontent. There were four captains (S A C Farrell, W Thompson, W H Waine and A J Walker[55]) and eight lieutenants. This enabled Worthington to form the battalion into four skeleton companies, but it was not until towards the end of July that any replacements for the rank and file casualties would arrive. He also took the opportunity to make a number of promotions amongst the Non-Commissioned Officers (NCOs).

General Sir Ian Hamilton was also concerned about the need for replacement troops. He noted in his diary

> *When a battalion which entered upon a campaign a thousand strong, – all keen and hopeful, – gets down to five hundred, comrades begin to look round at one another and wonder if any will be left. When it falls to three hundred, or less, the unit, in my experience, is better drawn out of the line. The bravest men lose heart when, on parade, they see with their own eyes that their Company – the finest Company in the Army – has become a platoon, – and the famous battalion a Company.*

He cabled the War Office:

> *A stage of wastage has now been reached in this Division, especially in the 127th Manchester Brigade, when filling up with drafts will make it as good or better than ever. If, however, they have to go on fighting in their present condition and suffer further losses, the remnants will not offer sufficiently wide foundation for reconstituting cadres."*

21 June saw the men of the 5th Battalion ordered back to Gallipoli and, the next day, the 6th Battalion left to join them, arriving back at Cape Helles at 11pm, where they disembarked and made their way to dug-outs. Lieutenant F A F Bone had been assigned to command Owen Evans' platoon and, unsurprisingly, he quickly became known to the men as 'Bones' (although, presumably, not to his face). One man who did not return to the dug-outs was stretcher bearer George Harrison. He had been assigned to Brigade Headquarters where he would work as a clerk until November when, like many of his comrades, he fell ill with dysentery and was evacuated to hospital in Alexandria[56].

Military hospital at Abassia Barracks, Alexandria.

On the 23rd, Major Worthington took the four new company commanders for their first look at the forward areas, showing them the support trenches which the battalion would occupy the next day. The 6th Battalion would be very much in the minds of people back in Manchester as a memorial service was held that day at the Cathedral for those who had died during the campaign. The men spent the next two days in the support lines before moving back to Pink Farm during the night of 26/27 June. Early on the 27th, they moved forward again, taking over a section of the front line, near Krithia Nullah, from a battalion of the King's Own Scottish Borderers. With only 200 men, it was impossible to adequately man the front line and two companies of the 5th Battalion were ordered forward to support them.

Private Frank Ollerenshaw had been wounded on 10 May and this was his first day back at duty.

> *In the line, the game was to watch all the time for movement on the other side and keep them guessing. At night we wore equipment with our packs and every third man was on look-out, while the other two slept in a sitting position, so that they could be easily awakened and, every hour, the look-out was changed so that with stand-to in the evening and at dawn, a man was lucky who got more than four hours sleep. Often during the night the Turks would commence a fusillade, which would mean an extra on the way of stand-to. In the daytime the flies and heat made it impossible to get any sleep and to get a meal in comfort one had to cook it immediately after stand-to in the morning or in the evening. To open a tin of jam during the heat of the day was to arouse a plague of flies.*[57]

To their left, 29th Division undertook an attack on 28 June which the 6th Battalion supported with rifle fire. The advance was successful but an immediate Turkish attack then captured part of the British front line. Attempts to dislodge the Turks failed and it now meant that both sides were within grenade-throwing distance of each other. Colonel Henry Darlington, commanding the 5th Battalion, wrote in a letter home about an incident on the 29th, when he was near to the 6th Battalion's positions. He recounted that a Turkish grenade had landed in the British trench.

> *One of the CSMs, who has already been wounded twice and got a DCM, picked up the bomb and tried to throw it back. He was too late and the beastly thing went off. It wounded the Sergeant Major in fourteen places and broke both his wrists. No-one else was touched luckily. The Sergeant Major was patched up and walked out of the trenches. He was a bank clerk at home58. Stout fellow.*

This was CSM Frederick Hay, one of the heroes of the 4 June attack. He should have left the battalion on 27 June to return to Britain to train as an officer but these orders must have been cancelled. He was, however, now on his way back but as a casualty. Once recovered, he did commence his officer training, later returning to serve with the regiment, rising to the rank of captain. Whilst in Britain, in the autumn of 1916, he married Amelia Battye in the Ormskirk area. In other grenade incidents during the day, CSM Hartley, recently promoted from Sergeant and an ex-member of the Pierrot troupe, and Private Harry Mortimer were both injured. Mortimer died early the next day and was the first fatal casualty following the Battalion's return to action.

Lieutenant Henry Hammick had almost recovered from his wounds and was at Imbros recuperating before a return to duty. He had heard of the some of the problems being caused by the newly arrived officers.

As their comrades snatch some sleep, two men try to tempt a sniper to give away his position

I have not seen them but hear they are a frightful lot. Neither gentleman nor brave…None of our men will be their servants[59] *at all. And, from what I hear, the men laugh at them for being funks.*

With the imminent return to command of Major Pilkington, Major Worthington took decisive action to deal with the problem. By agreement with Colonel Darlington, he transferred Captains Farrell and Thompson to the 5th Battalion, officially for instruction in company work by Darlington's experienced officers. In their place, he promoted Lieutenants Alexander Milne and G Kershaw. Walter Thompson would return to the battalion and serve under Milne in C Company until he was killed on 7 August. Farrell would never be promoted and was transferred away from front line service spending most of the war with a company of the Labour Corps.

An unfortunate accident happened during the early evening of 2 July. The battalion was in the front line, near to the positions held by the 4th Battalion, Worcestershire Regiment. The Worcesters were firing at a Turkish redoubt across the frontage of the Manchesters. In the twilight, their aim drifted off target and four Manchesters were hit. Fred Clark and George Smith[60] were killed and another two men wounded.

Over the coming days, the Battalion alternated between periods in the front line and undertaking fatigues in the support line, mainly digging to improve the trench system. It was a dangerous time, even in the support line, as the battalion was subjected to shelling and a considerable number of what the war diary records as 'overthrow bullets'. B Company's Sergeant Cecil Boyes-Varley[61] was shot in the head on the 13th. He died shortly afterwards whilst being carried to the dressing station and is buried at Lancashire Landing Cemetery.

Carrying a wounded man to the dressing station.

During the evening of the 15th, the battalion moved to dugouts about half a mile behind the support line. The war diary records it as a 'delightful place; breezy with a fair number of shady trees'. Several days were spent here and, each day, 100 men were sent to the front line as digging parties, improving the trenchworks. The remaining half of the battalion's strength was allowed to rest and go to the sea to bathe. Sergeant John Ingram[62] gave instruction classes in grenade throwing, training six men in each company.

One of the new weapons of war developed between 1914 and 1918 was what is generally called poison gas, although there were different types. The Germans were the first to use it, releasing chlorine gas on 22 April 1915 against French troops near the Belgian town of Ypres (now Ieper). Its main effect was as an irritant to the lungs which would incapacitate a man but which, unless there was prolonged exposure, would not be fatal. Now, some three months later and with British plans well under way to develop their own gas attacks, a colonel of the Royal Army Medical Corps came to Gallipoli to instruct the battalions in its use and effects. Representatives from each company made their way to Divisional Headquarters to hear the lecture.

A much needed draft of sixty-six replacement troops arrived from Britain on 23 July. They included four officers – Captains Arthur D Hunter and J H Helm, and Lieutenants Willoughby Reiss and Sidney McDougall[63]. Three of these four would never leave Gallipoli.

Lance Corporal Frank Thompson was amongst the sixty-two other ranks. Now aged twnty-one, he had lived with his parents, Herbert and Elizabeth, at 139 Claremont Road, Pendleton, Salford and is thought to have worked with his father at their chemist's shop in nearby Weaste. His service number, 1643, indicates he was a pre-war member of the Battalion, probably enlisting in about 1911. For some reason, he had not left England with his comrades in the previous September, remaining with the newly formed reserve battalion, the 2/6th. He would now meet some old friends, although many others were already dead[64].

River Clyde, the boat which was run ashore on the landing of the Australians is still ashore. We came ashore on barges made into bridges and marched the way the Australians landed. Senegalese, Algerian and British sentries we passed close to shore, guarding huge stacks of cases of food, thousands of cases. We landed in trenches at 5.30, heard for the first time the sound of guns. At first did not sound very much. Will probably liven up later in day…Met many fellows I know, among them Harry Dean, Stanley Road, who has not had a scratch. Very good trenches. My first taste of being under shellfire fairly pleasant – not as bad as expected.

Memorial erected by the family at the grave of Private William H Booth, from Moss Side, Manchester. Died on 13 June, aged twenty, from wounds received during the Third Battle of Krithia. He is buried at Pieta Military Cemetery, Malta.
Linda Corbett.

Second Lieutenant Hugh Heywood had fully recovered from his injuries and had travelled from Imbros with the draft. Like his comrade, Henry Hammick, he had something to say about some of his new brother officers:

I met, to my joy, the old crowd – Colonel Pilkington, 'Worthy', Holberton, Norris, Milne and Kershaw (and F Blatherwick[65] *and Wynne later on) but it rather distressed me to meet a whole new crowd consisting of Kitchener's Army officers who are not, most of them, very nice.*

He was attached to C Company under Alexander Milne and moved to Company Headquarters – a dugout on the forward side of the trench wall, fourteen feet long, four feet wide and six feet tall. On his first full day back in the trenches, he noted that the men were now battle hardened, accustomed to the sound of shells and knowing, generally, if they were going to fall near enough to need to duck.

Shells occasionally arrive here. One has just burst on the parapet near here and knocked four men down. When they picked themselves up, unhurt, the only remark made was by one man who asked 'Where's my damned fag?'

Heywood had dinner at battalion headquarters with Colonel Pilkington and some of the others. He records they had soup, steak and carrots, rice and jam and finished with fried sardines. As a contribution to the party, he took some chutney and cigars.

On the 25th, he took a party to bathe at Y Beach, noting that it was very crowded with other parties. While they were there, they came under some shelling which killed one man from another unit. Frank Thompson was one of the bathers and enjoyed the experience. He was still enjoying the food and recorded in his diary that he'd had steak, onions, biscuits and marmalade for breakfast; cheese and onions for dinner and marmalade and biscuits again for tea.

There was little of note in the closing days of the month. The battalion moved into trenches on the Redoubt Line (to the rear of the positions from which they had launched the June attack). Lieutenant Hammick was seconded as aide-de-camp to General Douglas, now commanding the whole of the Army's VIII Corps. Writing home on the 29th, Colonel Darlington, of the 5th Battalion, recorded

They gave us a good shelling this afternoon. A shell partially buried one of the 6th Manchester signallers, but his astonished face was sticking well out of the debris. His companion ran away. By the time I arrived at the spot, the companion was back with a spade and a camera. The camera was used first.

The same day, Captain Helm was walking down to the beach to bathe when a shell exploded nearby. He was badly injured in both arms and it was necessary to amputate his left hand. His war had lasted just seven days.

The next day, General Sir Ian Hamilton received news of a major British victory in Mesopotamia (modern day Iraq). Fighting had been underway for over a month, around a key Turkish supply point on the River Euphrates, at the town Nasiriyeh.

The main infantry attack was delivered on 24 July and the troops were supported by Royal Navy vessels firing from the river. The town was captured and the Turks retreated. By way of celebration, Hamilton ordered all troops to fire a volley (a *'feu de joie'*, as he recorded in his diary) at 5pm. Owen Evans, still with the battalion's machine gun crew recorded that, whilst his comrades in the infantry platoons fired a single shot, the machine guns fired twenty-five. Newly arrived Frank Thompson witnessed his first death of a comrade during the day. The Manchesters' trench had briefly come under enfilade fire in the morning and Lance Corporal Cyril Miller, B Company, had been killed. He was buried later in the day but, over the course of the war, the grave's location was lost and he is now commemorated on the Memorial to the Missing at Cape Helles.

General Sir Ian Hamilton spent the last day of the month 'clearing his desk' before setting out to visit troops of the divisions which had recently arrived from Britain and were now in camps on the various nearby Greek islands. He was putting the finishing touches to his plans for the forthcoming major offensive which would see the new troops committed in an attempt to finally break the deadlock on the Peninsula. Two divisions (nearly 40,000 troops) would land at Suvla Bay, a little to the north of ANZAC Cove. They would support a break-out to the north, by the Australian and New Zealand troops, who would be secretly re-inforced, almost doubling their strength. The two forces would support each other, breaking the Turkish stranglehold in the north. In the south, the troops around Helles would also attack northwards in a limited attack towards Krithia with the intent of tying down Turkish forces and preventing them being transferred north. The landings would take place on 6 August.

1 The son of a doctor, Hugh Christopher Lempriere Heywood was born in Oldham on 5 November 1896. He survived the war, rising to the rank of major serving with a battalion of Punjabi troops. He was later ordained as an Anglican minister. His papers are held by the Liddle Collection, University of Leeds and extracts are quoted with permission.

2 Henry A Hammick's letters are held by the Liddle Collection, University of Leeds and extracts are quoted with permission.

3 Captain Arthur Herbert Norris, Royal Army Medical Corps. Battalion medical officer.

4 1440 Private Owen Evans. Later commissioned as a Lieutenant in the Machine Gun Corps, he returned to civilian life on 31 July 1920. His papers are held by the Department of Documents, Imperial War Museum. Extracts are quoted with the permission of his son.

5 2074 Private Lewis Marshall. Served with the Battalion throughout the War and returned to civilian life on 29 January 1919. He is believed to have died in the Leeds area in 1923, aged 37. It is not known if he was married but his recorded next of kin was Mrs A Marshall of 17 Beeston Royds, Leeds.

6 Born in South Manchester in 1883, 2248 Private Blaikie had lived at Whalley Road, Manchester. His mother, Grace, was later known to be living at 16 Blair Road, Alexandra Park, Manchester.

7 2247 Private Stuart H Forbes from Stretford. Forbes would be Mentioned in Despatches and awarded the Meritorious Service Medal. He was killed in action on 5 June 1915, aged 19. Three men called Kay were serving with the Battalion and it is not known which Evans was referring to.

8 Published in the magazine "I Was There" in 1938/39. 1891 Private Fred Wilson later served with the Labour Corps until he returned to civilian life after the war.

9 Arthur Cuthbert Brooke-Taylor. Killed in action 4 June 1915, aged 27. Second son of Colonel and Mrs

Brooke-Taylor, The Close, Bakewell, Derbyshire. Had transferred to the Battalion from the 6th Sherwood Foresters in the spring of 1914. Educated at Manchester University and a qualified civil engineer. The Battalion's musketry instructor.

10 Both men survived the war. Jonathon Cookson trained for a commission in 1916 and served for the remainder of the conflict as a 2nd Lieutenant with the 7th Battalion. John W Thomas returned to duty with the Battalion, serving as a private until he was demobilised on 24 June 1919. He probably returned to his pre-war employment in the offices of Richard Haworth & Co, Dale Street, Manchester.

11 Each gun was operated by a six man team, under the command of a non-commissioned officer such as a Corporal. 914, William Cross would survive the War but his brother, Charlie, would be killed on 4 June whilst also serving with the machine gun section. 1306, George Shaw had joined the Battalion in 1910 aged 17. He lived at Parrin Lane, Winton, Eccles and worked as a warehouseman for S & J Watts at the Company's premises on Portland Street, Manchester (now the Britannia Hotel). Shaw was invalided away from Gallipoli at the end of July 1915, suffering from enteritis and was discharged from the army on 21 October as his contracted time as a Territorial had expired.

12 1998 Private John D Denham died of wounds, 17 May 1915. 502, Company Quartermaster Sergeant Henry St John Stokoe had joined the Territorials on 7 May 1908. He worked for Broome & Foster Ltd, Chorlton Street, Manchester. Stokoe never sufficiently recovered from his wounds to return to duty and was discharged from the army on 13 July 1916.

13 2277, Private Thomas Frederick Marsden

14 Killed in action, 7 August 1915

15 Captain F C Aldous. Although shot in the head and hand, his injuries may not have been as severe as Hammick believed as he later served as a Lieutenant Colonel with the Machine Gun Corps.

16 George Newlove. Killed in action 5 June 1915. A single man, aged 28, who lived at 6 Institution Place, Rusholme, Manchester. He was a member of Diggle Rifle Club and had shot competitively at Bisley.

17 Killed in action, 7 August 1915. The son of Frederick and Elizabeth, 4 Penelope Road, Irlam-o'-th'-Heights. Worked for William O'Hanlon & Co, Dale Street, Manchester. The Company made furnishing fabrics.

18 Almost certainly one of the Stockport lacrosse group, 20 year old Harry Sutton never returned to duty and was discharged from the army on 1 April 1917. He worked for Sutton & Torkington Ltd – the family owned firm of Stockport hat manufacturers.

19 2446, Walter Dawes and 2253, Thomas Henry Bebbington (an employee of S D Bles & Co, a firm of merchants and shippers with offices at 54 Princess Street, Manchester)

20 Walter Bazley left an estate of £1823 – worth over £500,000 at current values, based on the increase in average earnings. He is buried at Lancashire Landing Cemetery, Cape Helles. Donald Lancaster has no known grave but is commemorated on the War Memorial at Hale, Cheshire, where he lived with his parents, William and Ellen.

21 2265, Private Arnold Lucas. Commissioned in January 1917 and served as a Lieutenant with the Sussex Yeomanry. Survived the war and, in 1920, was living at Holly Mount, Ashton-upon-Mersey.

22 Claude Rutter's brother, Geoffrey, served with the Durham Light Infantry and was killed in action on 27 May 1918. Both men are commemorated on the Sale War Memorial.

23 Nullah – steep ravine or dry stream bed (Hindi)

24 Donaldson left the Battalion on 8 January 1916 to train as an officer and later served as a Captain with the Regiment. This may have been an "acting" rank and he was the Lieutenant of the same name, who had served with 8th Battalion and was killed in action on 25 March 1918, whilst attached to the Royal Warwickshire Regiment.

25 Evans' diary refers to this man as Maynall but it has not been possible to trace anyone of the name serving with the Battalion.

26 The son of Joseph and Hannah, 20 year old Coops was born in Manchester, moving to the Stockport area in the early 1900s. Educated at Cheadle Hulme School, he was employed by George Hewitt & Co (cotton manufacturers), Portland Street, Manchester. His social life centred on the local Wesleyan Church. Charles Turton, 26, was another member of the Church. The son of John and Margaret, he had also been born in Manchester but had lived in Cheadle Hulme for most of his life. He was killed in action a few days later in

the attack on 4 June.
27 2090, Leonard Lowe Boardman – left the Battalion in January 1916 to train as an officer and later served with the Regiment as a Lieutenant. Worked in the York Street warehouse of Jones Brothers Ltd, Manchester. 1556, Sidney Atkinson – killed in action 7 August 1915.
28 1903, Private Frank Allen, lived at Claremont Road, Pendleton. 2nd Lieutenant Roger Compton-Smith, worked for Tootal, Broadhurst & Lee Ltd. 1729, Private Stanley Kershaw, lived at Cromwell Road, Pendleton. 2164, Private Norman Lloyd, lived at Monton Green and 2471, Private Percy Tabb.
29 1676, Private Wilfred Hayes. Killed in action 4 June 1915, aged 19. The local Manchester newspapers reported that his diary had been picked up on the battlefield by a German officer attached to the Turkish army. Extracts are understood to have been published in the American newspaper "New York World" in December 1915.
30 1731, William Robert Barker – from Blackley, Manchester. His medal records held at the National Archives indicate that he died of his wounds next day (although the Commonwealth War Graves Commission records his date of death as being 12 June 1915)
31 Taylforth has no known grave and is commemorated on the Memorial to the Missing at Helles. He is also commemorated on the Kirkby Lonsdale war memorial.
32 Records show that five men were killed in action during the day.
33 1441, Private Leonard Huff. 57, Company Quartermaster Sergeant John William Wilson, aged 40 – the husband of Hannah Wilson, 71 Meadow Road, Lower Broughton and father of their four children. He worked at the showrooms of Orme & Sons, a manufacturer of billiard and snooker tables, at Blackfriars Street, Manchester. Wilson was a keen sportsman and member of the Broughton Harriers Club.
34 William Henry Cadman, the son of Mrs Cadman, Bryncliffe Lodge, Little Orme, Llandudno. Later promoted to Captain.
35 High explosive
36 2425, Private Harold Haygarth Jackson. Left the Battalion on 20 December 1915 to train as an officer. Returned to the Regiment, serving as Captain and then Major.
37 Tom Marsden is believed to be buried at Twelve Tree Copse Cemetery and is commemorated on a special memorial there.
38 Extracts included with permission of the family
39 19 year old Thomas Casson was one of the Stockport lacrosse players and worked as an audit clerk for the Co-operative Wholesale Society. He was wounded in the shoulder on 9 June and invalided home. Still on sick leave in the autumn, he applied to become an officer, joining the 1/6th Battalion, Cheshire Regiment in May 1916. In the July, he took part in a raid on enemy trenches for which he was awarded the Military Cross. In September 1916, he was invalided home with "trench fever". After recovering, he was appointed to the Brigade Bombing School in Oswestry where, on 17 May 1917, a faulty grenade exploded killing him. He is buried in Willow Grove Cemetery at Stockport.
40 1306, Sergeant George Shaw – joined battalion in 1910, aged 17. Evacuated from Gallipoli on 1 August suffering with enteritis. Discharged from the army on 24 November 1915. 1405, Private William Kay – joined battalion in 1911, aged 22. Worked in the warehouse of Jones Bros. Ltd, York Street, Manchester. Discharged from the army on 18 April 1916, his contracted time as a Territorial having expired.
41 361, Corporal W Kent, recovered from his injuries and returned to duty. Later promoted to Company Sergeant Major, he left the army on 27 January 1919. 2198, Private Norman Bickerton, 19, is buried at Lancashire Landing Cemetery. He had previous worked for Tootal, Broadhurst Ltd. 2237, Private Alexander Chapman was discharged from the army on 19 June 1916.
42 The Mayor of Salford presented Hurdley with the Russian medal in April 1917. At the time, he was living at 2 Brindleheath Road, Pendleton. The author has previously written about Worthington's rescue of a Sergeant Major. After the article was published on the internet, a descendent identified him as John Hurdley. In 2008, Hurdley's medals were offered for sale at auction. Their current location is unknown.
43 Stanley Jackson, 27, was married with a young daughter. They lived at "Elmscote", Timperley, Cheshire and he was a stockbroker, dealing on the Manchester Exchange. His body was not found and recovered until a considerable time later.
44 On Sunday, 19 March 1916, the congregation of St Mary's Church, Stockport, held a memorial service for

Tom Rethanan Mills. A plaque was unveiled which is inscribed "Tell them I have done my best". He has no known grave.

45 Brooks' brother, Archibald, was killed 7 October 1917, whilst commanding a company of the battalion.

46 Arthur and Frank Heydon recovered from their wounds. Arthur was later commissioned and served as a Lieutenant with the Battalion. "Nip" achieved the same rank serving with the Lancashire Fusiliers. Both are believed to have survived the War.

47 Alexander Nicol Milne from Cheadle, Cheshire. He had worked as the managing clerk for local solicitors, Taylor, Kirkman and Co, before enlisting at the beginning of September. He had been commissioned on 25 April and was promoted to Lieutenant in the field on 5 June.

48 Worthington's formal reference, in this private letter, to Milne who was a near neighbour in the small community of Cheadle and of similar age and social standing is, perhaps, surprising. It may be that Worthington was just showing the respect due to his rank.

49 Worthington left blanks in the letter, probably realising the army censor would delete information about casualty numbers.

50 This letter is held by the Department of Documents, Imperial War Museum. Attempts have been made to trace the copyright holder, without success. Charles Allen Cross has no known grave and he is commemorated on the Helles Memorial.

51 Percy Boswell did not become an officer but was promoted to Sergeant. He was killed in action on 7 August 1915.

52 Andrew B Smith. Killed in action, 7 August 1915.

53 William Yates returned to duty with D Company and was killed in action on 7 August 1915.

54 Worthington has not included the full name of his friend.

55 Arthur John Walker, from Henley on Thames, was 19 and had been educated at Wellingborough School where he had been a keen sportsman, playing cricket and football. He was killed in action on 7 August 1915.

56 George Oliver Harrison never fully recovered from his illness and was discharged from the army on 27 June 1916. He is believed to have returned to Broughton and may have been the George O Harrison who, in 1920, married Gladys M Shaw at Salem Church, Broughton.

57 Written in a letter to a friend and published in the Stockport Advertiser, 1 October 1915.

58 Possibly the F Hay employed at the Head Office, in Manchester, of the Lancashire & Yorkshire Bank (as recorded in the Bank's entry in the Manchester City Battalions Book of Honour).

59 The term "batman" did not come into widespread army usage until after the War.

60 Clark was aged 27 and lived at "Southgate", Meadow Road, Urmston. He was a keen sportsman being a member of Flixton Cricket Club and Davyhulme Golf Club. Smith lived at Crofts Bank Road, Urmston. Ref: Eccles Journal, 23 July 1915.

61 Boyes-Varley was born in South Africa and educated at St Edmund's College in Hertfordshire. Commemorated on the Metropolitan Vickers (Westinghouse) war memorial.

62 1408, John Alfred Ingram, an employee of Reiss Brothers, a Manchester firm of yarn merchants. Left the Battalion on 23 September 1916 to train as an officer. Killed in action on 23 April 1917, serving as a 2nd Lieutenant with the 16th Battalion, Manchester Regiment.

63 Hunter was a longstanding officer of the Regiment, having received his Captaincy in 1904 with the 2nd Volunteer Battalion. He had been attached to the reserve Battalion when war was declared. He was married, with a young daughter. Reiss was born on 8 May 1890 and educated at Charterhouse School, where he had been a member of the Officer Training Corps. He was now a partner in the family firm in Manchester. He had first attended for drill with the Battalion on 14 February 1910, at which time his address was "The Hermitage", Holmes Chapel, Cheshire and he had given his occupation as "gentleman".

64 Frank Thompson maintained a diary for 1915 and a transcript is in the possession of the author. The location of the original is unknown. Extracts from the diary prior to his arrival at Gallipoli are in Chapter 7.

65 2nd Lieutenant Frank Moir Blatherwick. Worked for J H Agnew & Brother, cloth merchants, 5 Mount Street, Manchester.

Chapter 4

GALLIPOLI – THE FINAL MONTHS

LIEUTENANT ARTHUR BROOKE-TAYLOR had been killed on 4 June. As his friend and comrade, Hugh Heywood, came to the front line on 1 August he could see Brooke-Taylor's body lying in No Man's Land. '*So far, sad to relate, no-one has been able to get at him to bury him.*' Heywood knew that, within a few days, he would have to risk his life crossing this ground in the forthcoming attack. The Turkish front line trench was on slightly higher ground, silhouetting it against the sky. It made targets easy to spot for the battalion snipers and they claimed a couple of victims. However, it was not all 'one-way traffic'.

During 2 August, a number of accounts record that the men could hear singing or chanting from the Turkish trenches which they presumed were prayers. Whenever it was heard, many of the Manchesters struck up 'Ragtime' tunes to annoy their opponents. Perhaps in over-enthusiasm, one of the new replacements, Richard Cooper, let his head show above the parapet and was promptly shot and killed by a sniper (taking the advantage that the high ground afforded him). Cooper, twenty-two, came from the Manchester suburb of Blackley and worked in the city for Dehn & Co.

Private Richard Cooper, from the Manchester district of Blackley. Killed in action on 2 August, aged 22. Buried in Redoubt Cemetery.

During the evening, seven men, under Captain Holberton, started out on a most dangerous mission. Since the attack in June, the British front line was what had previously been the Turkish front line. It meant that, in front of the British, there was no longer an open No Man's Land but one crossed by the old Turkish system of support lines and communication trenches. On both sides, barricades had been built in the trenches and these were manned by sentries. The aim of the raid was to get to the other side of one of the barricades and then dig away a traverse in the Turkish part. This would enable the British to have a clear field of fire down fifty yards of trench.

Holberton and Corporal Hartshorn acted as the covering party, keeping down the heads of any Turks in the area by throwing grenades from time to time and firing their guns. Once the digging was completed, the men withdrew behind the British barricade and waited. In the early hours of the next morning, a party of Turks moved towards where the traverse had previously provided cover for their grenade throwing. Now in full view, the Manchester men opened fire on them. A

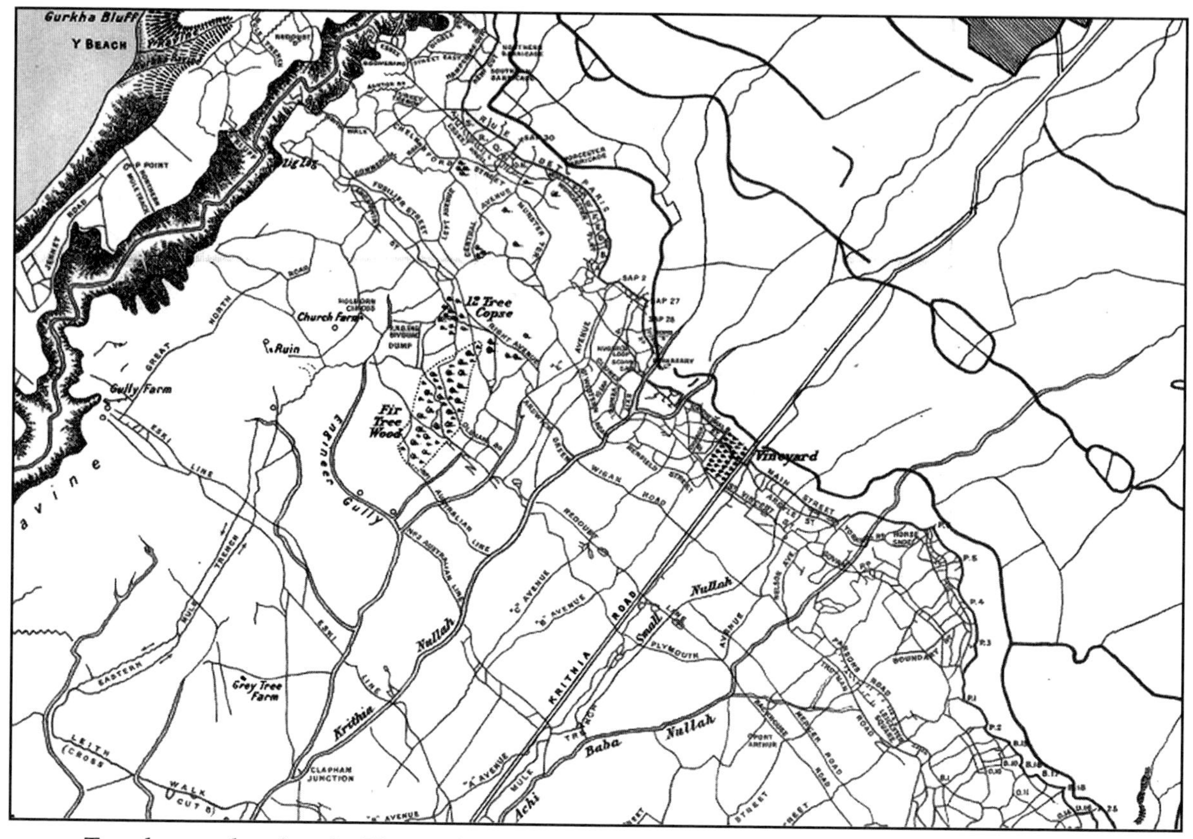

Trench map showing the Vineyard almost in the centre.

similar fate befell several more who came down the trench in the morning. Hartshorn[1] was awarded the Distinguished Conduct Medal for this action and for his conduct during the forthcoming battle.

The landing of the new troops at Suvla Bay during the evening of 6 August was largely unopposed. They included the Regiment's 11th Battalion, raised mainly in August 1914. In the south, the plan remained that, during the afternoon, the troops would undertake an attack intended to pin the Turks down, preventing them from moving reinforcements north. The attack would, however, be conducted over two days. After a short artillery bombardment, 88 Brigade, supported by the 5th Manchesters, attacked to the left of the Vineyard at 3.40pm.

The attack was unsuccessful. The war diary of the 5th Battalion notes that the artillery bombardment 'entirely failed and the infantry attack made against entirely unsubdued rifle and machine-gun fire'. Several British artillery shells had landed in the Manchesters' trench before they attacked. The battalion made its charge at 3.50pm and reached its objective on the other side of No Man's Land. However, once here, they found it to be a trap. It was an unmanned dummy trench and, without cover, they were immediately exposed to heavy enfilade fire. They suffered 229 casualties – dead, wounded or missing.

To their right, the men of the other Manchester battalions could only wait and contemplate that it would be their turn the next day. As in the previous attack in June, the Manchesters would attack northwards astride the road to Krithia. Their first objective would be the Turkish front line lying just in front of a vineyard (the engagement would later be given the official name of the Battle of the Vineyard). The second objective would the Turkish support lines on the far side of the vineyard. A handful of men expected this to be their last attack for some time. At least five, including Acting Company Sergeant Major Tom Worthington, had been selected to leave the battalion in a few days to train as officers.

Frank Thompson had watched the artillery bombardment:

> *The scene over the parapet was indescribable. It seemed as if some huge fire had taken place and, the flames having died down, the smouldering still remained. The whole of the Turkish front was hidden in clouds of smoke. The noise was deafening and everyone was advised to keep their heads down and get as good cover as possible, preferably against the side of the trench facing the enemy. At 6.0 we had to pack our valises and take them into the gully to be stored away. We had to wait until a shell burst and then dash to the place where our packs were to go and then scurry back to shelter. It was rather palpitating but of no consequence.*

By 7am on 7 August, Thompson and his comrades were ready for the attack. The British artillery bombardment opened up at 8.10am but the Turks, clearly anticipating another attack after the failure of the previous day, had already started to shell the Manchesters' front line trench. There would be many casualties here even before the troops charged the seventy yards across No Man's Land. Private Frank Ollerenshaw:[2]

> *We were up at four, preparing breakfast and getting ready generally. We had already greased every separate cartridge and clip to allow of easy loading… C Company was the first assaulting party and we were to go over at 9.40. Besides my rifle I had to carry a pick, so somebody evidently thought we had a 'sweet thing' on. We were all ready on the*

View of the Vineyard from the approximate British front line position. Chris Harley

View of the Vineyard from the Krithia Road. Twelve Tree Copse Cemetery can be seen in the background. Many of the burials here are from the later months of the campaign.
Alan and Sue Curragh.

> *ladders and steps that had been put there and, when the word came, we went up together and ran as fast as we could down into our own firing line, then up again and on. As right-hand man of our Battalion I was given a mark – some posts in the trench half-right and for these I had to make. On the left, the Turks were being reinforced but, in front of us, they had retired and there were very few in the trench when we jumped in.*

The battalion machine gunners provided covering fire for the attack and Owen Evans noted in his diary that he had fired about 2000 rounds. However, many of the Manchesters had got no more than a few yards from their trench before being hit by enemy machine-gun bullets. C Company's commander, Alexander Milne, led the remainder of his men on to the Turkish trench where fierce hand-to-hand fighting took place. His second in command, Walter Thompson, probably never made it across and was later posted as being 'missing'. Milne attacked a Turkish redoubt from which grenades were being thrown, firing four shots from his revolver before he was killed with a shot to the head. Second Lieutenant John Rainbow[3] and Company Sergeant Major Tom Worthington were both very badly wounded in the trench and were later also posted as 'missing'. Nothing was ever heard of either man again. Frank Ollerenshaw continued:

Captain Alexander Milne, from Cheadle. Killed in action on 7 August, aged 31.

> *We had only one officer left by this time[4] and, as we were being bombed from the sap on the left and the trench was being searched by shrapnel,*

it became imperative to move. The officer jumped up on to the top of the trench but was immediately hit and fell back. Then a few of us tried to get over but another burst of shrapnel came and about three were left standing. The man next to me was killed outright, shot in the head and a sergeant-major of the 8th had the inside of his thigh blown away. My helmet saved me for it was blown to atoms and, whilst my head was pretty badly cut and a bled a lot at the time, it turned out no damage was done. I was too sick for a while to take any interest in what was going on but when I came round I found plenty of dressing to do.

B and D Companies, about 100 strong, now left their trenches to go across No Man's Land as re-inforcements. A Company had been held in reserve but also sent a few men forward to help with the consolidation of the gains, not knowing, of course, that there were really no gains to consolidate. Lance Sergeant Archibald McDonald was probably one of the re-inforcements. During the day, he twice crossed No Man's Land, which was being swept by enemy fire, to bring fresh supplies of grenades to the advanced troops. On the third occasion, he found a wounded officer who he carried back to safety. He was awarded the Distinguished Conduct Medal for this 'conspicuous gallantry'.

Lance Sergeant Archibald McDonald, DCM.

The battalion war diary records that the re-inforcements started 'splendidly, but were mown down by very heavy fire' and few managed to get across to the Turkish trenches. Many of the dead were lying no more that twenty to forty yards from the British trench. Battalion headquarters was having a difficult time trying to establish what was happening as the view across No Man's Land was badly obscured by smoke and dust caused by the shells which continued to explode from the firings of the artillery on both sides. Second Lieutenant Hugh Heywood, battalion machine gun officer:

After a time, one or two wounded began to crawl in from in front. One poor fellow crept back very slowly under a heavy fire and rolled fainting into our arms over the parapet. When we came to dress him, we found he had three huge holes in his stomach and half his insides were outside. We did him up as fast as we could – it took five field dressings to do it – and sent him back on a stretcher.

It was now about 11.00 and the Turks had started to launch a counter-attack.

Our left could not make any headway because of machine guns which made the gully, up which they should have advanced, a certain death trap and, as we were enfiladed from that position, we were ordered to retire and those of us who could did so. How I got back without being hit is as much a marvel as the advance itself. Out of 160 of us who went over, thirty-two were unwounded or only slightly so. (Private Frank Ollerenshaw)

By 11.30am, the 6th Battalion's attack was over and, around this time, the 5th and 7th Battalions were ordered to take up the assault with the men of the 6th offering what

Private Robert Davies, from Manchester. Killed in action on 7 August, aged 21.

support they could. However, this renewed attack barely got off the ground as it was quickly realised it was certain to fail.

Back in the trench, Frank Ollerenshaw found one of his pals who had been shot in both legs and an arm. He bandaged him up and carried him to the aid post. Whilst at the post, the medical officer checked Ollerenshaw's head wound and confirmed it was minor. He remained with the Battalion, as a private, until 28 May 1918, when he left to train to become an officer and was commissioned as a second lieutenant in the Cheshire Regiment. He survived the War. Second Lieutenant Hugh Heywood:

You can pick out at least thirty bodies lying in a space of twenty yards square – one of them is Milne. He is on the parapet of the Turkish trench. Later in the day, a shell burst over them and four of them got on fire and only their charred bodies are left. I'm afraid there isn't much chance of getting Milne's body in.

Nearly 150 men, over half the effective strength of the battalion, had become casualties. Although many were listed as "missing", later records show that 75 were dead. Amongst them were Alexander Doig who had won the Distinguished Conduct Medal for bravery on 4 June, B Company's David 'Dadie' Sinclair; and John Bennett who had recovered from his wound received on 11 May. Of the men who had only arrived on 23 July, B Company's Captain Willoughby Reiss was mortally wounded. He died the following day having been hit in the chest, left arm and both feet. Frank Thompson had been killed. The only later entry in his diary was for Friday, 19 November 'Edie's birthday. Hope to be home'.

During the evening, the survivors still at duty were withdrawn to the support line, where the next two days passed relatively quietly. The Turks counter-attacked during the evening of the 8th but the men were not required to go forward to support the front line. The general exceptions were the machine gunners who opened fire to help fight off the attack. Owen Evans fired 1300 rounds from his gun and caused some casualties.

The village of Disley lies alongside the A6, then as now the main road between Manchester and Buxton. At the time of the War it had a population of around 3500 and the news in recent weeks had had a devastating effect on the community.

The *Manchester Evening Chronicle* reported,

All the Disley lacrosse players have figured in the casualty lists. There were nine of them and all joined the 6th Manchesters. Seven have been wounded and two are missing.

Private Frank Goude, from Flixton. Killed in action on 7 August, aged 21.
Neil Drum

Corporal Frank Holyoake of the Ram's Head Hotel and Corporal W Arnold are reported missing on August 7 with 54 others of C Company[5]

At least six men had been due to leave the Battalion on the 11th to return to Britain for training to become officers. Tom Worthington had been killed but five other men did go. Frank Crossley and Archibald Bowers-Taylor had been colleagues at Tootal Broadhurst Ltd. Bowers-Taylor was later killed in action on 7 June 1917 commanding a company of the London Regiment. Crossley returned to serve with the Battalion until he left the army in 1919. Frank Stockdale served with the 2/6th Battalion and is mentioned again in Chapter 7. The other two men, William Braithwaite and Thomas Crossley would also survive the war.

It's often suggested that senior officers during the war were out of touch with the reality of the fighting. The suggestion is usually wrong and, particularly at Gallipoli, brigade staff were only a little way behind the front line. They would have been keenly aware of the situation and, on 11 August, of the casualties that the brigade had just incurred. It is, therefore, surprising that the Major H L Knight, the Brigade Major, should issue the following insensitive orders to battalion commanding officers:

Great slackness has been noticed among the troops in saluting officers – some do not even remove their pipes from their mouth. Lack of respect to supervisors and to the King's Commission is highly unsoldierlike and the practice must cease. This slackness can only have a [illegible] *owing to want of supervision on the part of officers. Any officer who, when a soldier of whatever unit does not salute, fails to check him, is guilty of a grave neglect of his duty, namely the maintenance of discipline. Commanding officers will take immediate steps to impress this upon all company officers to inform the men that any neglect in this respect will be severely dealt with.*

The next day, the Turks launched a counter attack on part of the Vineyard, capturing some of it from the neighbouring 1/4th Battalion, East Lancashire Regiment. Major Claude Worthington noted in his diary, about the other Manchester Regiment battalions 'The 8th and 9th got very panicky, rushed up the

Friends and comrades – Leonard Norbury and Harry Forrest.

Both men played for the Chorlton Lacrosse Club. Norbury was wounded, on 7 August, in the cheek, arm and shoulder. Forrest suffered a compound fracture of the ankle and had to hop and crawl for 450 yards to escape back to British lines. Both men were evacuated to Malta for treatment. Norbury returned to duty and served with the Battalion until March 1919. Forrest's wounds were more severe and he was discharged from the Army in 1916 – no doubt, a bitter blow as he was a noted sprinter in the Manchester area.

6th Battalion men in the reserve area. Manchester Regiment Archives

vineyard and our supports also rushed up'. The war diary notes that Lieutenant Sidney Collier[6] did some 'good work' with four men of the East Lancashires in helping to drive off the attack with the use of grenades. For this, and other acts of gallantry with the battalion bombers, he was awarded the Military Cross at the beginning of 1916.

Henry Hammick had also had an eventful night and one which earned him the Military Cross:

A private and myself were sent for and congratulated for bravery for a scrap we had the other night. We were reinforcements and went through a battalion who were in a panic and two privates and myself held a barricade in a trench while another was built behind us for bombing from. Meanwhile Turks were bombing us, though we could not reach them with our bombs. The other officer[7] had his face blown in beside me. I never thought I should come out alive and pray to God I am never again in a place like that. I have lost what little bravery I had and simply stuck it out on pure will-power.

The private, John Murphy, was awarded the Distinguished Conduct Medal. He had arrived at Gallipoli on 23 July, as part of the reinforcing draft and, before the war, had worked for textile manufacturer, A K Dyson Ltd, 88 George Street, Manchester. Subsequently promoted to Corporal, Murphy remained with the Battalion until he returned to civilian life 4 March 1919.

Hugh Heywood recorded an unfortunate incident in his diary on this day:

I came across two men cleaning their rifles and one of them was just putting back his bolt and thoughtlessly shoved it back home without examining the breech, then pulled the trigger. Of course, the magazine was charged and the gun went off and the bullet passed right through the other man's neck. He fell spouting blood at my feet. The man who shot him promptly got hysterical so we bandaged the poor fellow up and sent for the bearers, but he died before they turned up. The man who shot him went quite mad – for he was his best friend.

A little later on two men were digging a little higher up the trench and one of them hit the other on the head with a pick and killed him.

It has not been possible to identify these men with any certainty. There does not appear to be anyone who died on 12 August near the front line but they may have been Privates John Kelsey and John Tyldesley, both recorded as having died on the 11th. Of course, Heywood may be referring to men from a different battalion.

During the afternoon of the 13th, the battalion was relieved to bivouacs near X Beach, where they would spend the next several days. Its companies had been reduced to less than the strength of platoons and only twelve officers were still at duty. The attacks around Helles had been a costly failure. There had been no significant advance and, with the attacks petering out, the Turkish army could now transfer troops north to ANZAC and Suvla Bay. There had been no break out at ANZAC and the forces at Suvla soon found themselves contained by an ever strengthening opposition. An Allied attempt to link up these two groupings would be made towards the end of August but, as with all previous attacks in this campaign, it failed. General Sir Ian Hamilton would again request additional troops but, even amongst the most ardent supporters of the campaign, it had become clear nothing was going to succeed and his request was refused, indicating that any available reserves would be sent to the

Cleaning up in the reserve area. Manchester Regiment Archives

Lance Corporal Stanley Cooke. John Cooke

Western Front in preference to Gallipoli. Plans now started to be laid for an eventual withdrawal and there would be no further major attacks. From now on, the main killers would not be the Turkish Army but disease, dysentery and other illnesses.

Hugh Heywood found it a most relaxing time after the stresses of the past weeks and enjoyed bathing in the sea several times a day and, also, being able to sleep in pyjamas each night. A large draft of nearly 200 replacement troops arrived on 18 August. They had trained with the reserve Battalion (the 2/6th) and had embarked from Plymouth on the 2 August, aboard the *Franconia*. The ship was a classic cruise liner belonging to Cunard and had been commandeered as a troopship at the outbreak of war. Among the men, was Lance Corporal Stanley Cooke[8]. He kept a diary during the war and his first entry on arriving at the Peninsula reads,

> *6.0am. First thing we draw rations, then breakfast, then lay kit out and clean rifles for inspection at 9.00 by Colonel Pilkington.*

He also wrote home to his father saying that, if anything happened to him, he wanted anything in his bank account to go to Winnie. It's not known who she was but she is often fondly mentioned in the diary. I am not attempting to write her anything in the nature of a farewell letter as it is too painful a task and could not improve matters in any case.' Lance Corporal Frank Waring[9] had also just arrived and, in a letter home, recounted his first meeting with Company Sergeant Major A McDowell, DCM.

> *A real soldier who inspired my complete confidence…He introduced me to the men for whom I was to be responsible. As there was no cookhouse, each one of us cooked his own meal on little rubbish fires on the fire-step. This gave us something positive to do and helped relieve the boredom. On the first night, it became clear that there were no dugouts to sleep in. Each put his blanket over his shoulders, sat on the fire-step and went to sleep…The nights were chilly but the days were tropical. As we were wearing our heavy khaki serge, we decided to conform to local custom, firstly by cutting the trouser legs to above the knee and cutting off the sleeves of our grey flannel shirt."*

The battalion returned to the front line on 19 August, taking over trenches in a sector new to it near Fusilier Bluff. This was now the northern most position around Helles and was just inland from the sea (on the western side of the peninsula). They would undertake tours of duty in the trenches, alternating with periods at nearby Y Ravine. The Ravine gave access to Y Beach and enabled the men to easily get to the sea to bathe.

A significant change in tactics on both sides started to develop around this time.

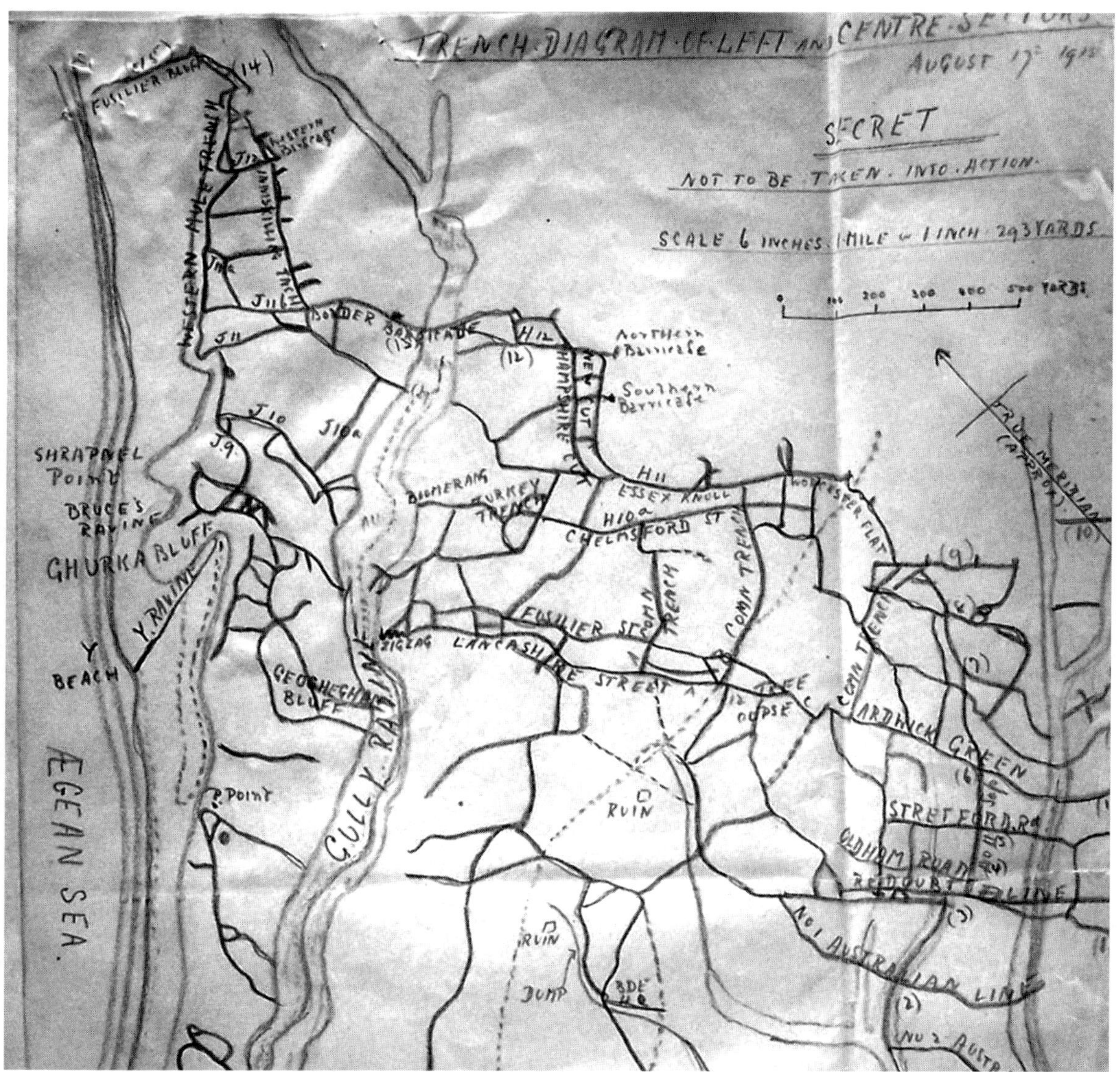

The Adjutant's copy of the trench map, attached to the war diary, showing Fusilier Bluff in the most north westerly position and Gully Ravine running south.

Instead of large scale attacks, the opposing sides began to dig tunnels towards the other line with the intent of planting explosives under or near the trench. At Fusilier Bluff the excavations were being undertaken by specialist troops from the Royal Engineers but the Manchesters were providing vital working parties, bringing supplies for shoring up the tunnel and, also, carrying away the spoil.

> *This part of the line is extremely close to enemy trenches for about 100 yards. The Turk is mining here and there are countermines in two places.*

Gully Ravine; a convenient natural feature giving access to the beach.
Manchester Regiment Archives.

> *It is most essential that the mining fatigue parties are properly organized, that good men are selected and that they are made to understand that they are doing most important work as otherwise the work of the miners is stopped through being made to clear his stuff. Another point worthy of consideration is that the hours of work for the mining fatigue are necessarily long and it is essential that care is taken the men have their food just before going on. Fatigues should be taken from the supports and the men given as little sentry go as possible.* (Battalion war diary)

Owen Evans had a very lucky escape from the clutches of military discipline on 23 August. He was on duty as a sentry but, during the night, dozed off and was caught fast asleep. To be asleep whilst your comrades were relying on your vigilance was regarded as a most serious military offence normally tried by courts martial. The maximum sentence was execution by firing party and, during the war, over 400 received death sentences for this offence but, with the exception of two, they were all commuted to periods of imprisonment. It would seem that Evans received no more than an admonishment from the officer who discovered him.

As the month drew to a close, the Manchesters again moved to Y Ravine. The men were put to work repairing some of the trackways. It was relatively safe but Stanley Cooke knew there was still a risk from stray shots. 'One chap in C Company got hit in the backside, but only a flesh wound.'

On the 29th an unknown benefactor sent presents to all the battalion's officers – a pipe, fifty cigarettes, a bottle of Horlicks, tin of coffee and two pounds of chocolate. There was also a welcome battalion issue of tinned pineapple to the men – two tins to be shared by twenty one men.

Lieutenant Henry Hammick:

We have had a large draft who are shaking down but they are a rotten lot compared with the old ones. They have not had half the training and have not any discipline worth speaking of…I got one man 21 days Field Punishment and loss of pay for general inefficiency and cheek. That woke the rest of them up a bit. The subaltern who came and is attached to C Company is not a bad fellow – but unable to look after himself – drinks my water, smokes my cigarettes and, then, wants my rations as he has lost his own.

The first death of a close comrade of Stanley Cooke occurred in the early hours of 1 September. Richard W Turner, aged twenty and from Longsight, was on guard duty when he was killed. In a letter home, Lance Corporal Frank Waring describes the fatal shooting of a man and, whilst Waring suggested this occurred on 19 August, an examination of the casualty information confirms no member of the Battalion was killed on that day and that it is most probable he is describing Turner's death:

The sentry was a very pleasant young bank clerk and he must have failed to notice a Turkish sniper who had crawled into No Man's Land in the dark and awaited the first light of dawn. Sniper waited for sentry to raise his head. He whirled round and fell with a heavy crash to the bottom of the trench. He had been hit in the neck and blood was pumping out. I took out my field dressing and, using it and a pad, tried without success to stem the flow. Two stretcher bearers arrived quickly, pronounced him a 'goner' and took his body away.

Captain Harold Cawley.

Most of the next two weeks was spent in reserve at Gully Ravine where working parties continued to be provided for the tunnellers. On 8 September, a popular pre-war member of the Battalion joined its ranks for the first time since the campaign began. Captain Harold Cawley had been born in the Crumpsall area of Manchester in 1878 and, after education at Rugby School and New College, Oxford, practiced as a barrister. In the 1910 general election, he was elected as Member of Parliament for the Heywood constituency but had volunteered for overseas service with the battalion in August 1914. He had recently been serving as aide-de-camp to the divisional commander, Major-General Douglas. Several of his old school friends had been killed in the recent attacks and he requested a posting back to his battalion where he felt his duty lay. He's reported to have written:

> *'I have always felt rather a brute skulking behind in comparative safety while my friends were being killed'.*

The same day, the small group of just over 100 men remaining from the 1/4th Battalion, East Lancashire Regiment, were temporarily attached to the Manchesters and were distributed to the four companies. On the 10th, the battalion moved back to the front. Lance Corporal Stanley Cooke:

> *A long dusty march up gully until we arrive at the head where D Company go into dugouts in a nullah as supports. A and B occupy the firing line. On arriving, am detailed as guard at the wells and move up to the guards' dugout for the usual two hours on, four hours off. My well is about thirty yards behind the firing line. Troubled greatly with diarrhoea.*

Many of the men were also suffering from diarrhoea and dysentery and battalion strength was falling by the day as they reported sick. For now, B Company's Corporal Frank Waring continued on duty. On the 8th, he and one of the men he had trained with, Jim Kirk[10], had made pancakes with some eggs and flour that they had found. 'I feel very bloated on them'. It would not be long before he was writing home again:

> *You don't have no fear about me keeping my head down. I have seen quite enough fatalities not to know better. My bowels are the chief source of trouble. I have had*

An ambulance wagon brings wounded men down Gully Ravine for treatment.

diarrhoea continuously since I have been here. It has the effect of making me very lazy.

Private Leslie Whitbread was one who had to report sick. He had only arrived on 18 August but had been troubled by dysentery from almost the first day. He was aged 23 and, before joining up, had been studying to become an architect. He was evacuated away from the peninsula aboard a hospital ship but died on 11 September and was buried at sea.

Corporal George Broome, from Pendleton. Died of dysentery on 10 September.

Around this time, the divisional history recounts that Captain Holberton, as adjutant, placed a newly arrived subaltern in charge of a working party. An hour later, to his surprise, he saw the party returning from the task. He expressed surprise to the junior officer that he could have finished so soon. The young Second Lieutenant had replied that the men had said they were tired and would work better after a rest and tea. 'Yes', said Holberton, 'they wanted to find out if they had to deal with an officer or a damned fool. Now they know.' The history praises Holberton for his constant thought for others and his cheery words of encouragement during this period 'stimulated weary comrades to carry on hopefully and made him an inspiration to officers and men alike'.

Sanitary conditions continued to deteriorate and the numbers of men reporting sick each day continued to rise.

> *The seasoned veterans fared better than the new reinforcements, who succumbed at an appalling rate. There had been no break in the hot dry weather. Many of the wells had gradually become defiled, others had run dry and this no doubt contributed greatly to the amount of sickness. The insanitary conditions inseparable from the type of warfare waged in so confined and exposed a space, the continuous strain exacted from all, the lack of sleep, the tropical heat, the monotonous and unsuitable food, the lice and, above all, the plague of flies, with which no sanitary measures could cope, all were in their degree responsible for the deplorable results. The country was one huge graveyard in which hundreds of corpses of friends and foes lay unburied and the air was heavy with the stench. Flies clustered in noisome masses on everything that attracted them, on the food and in the mess-tins as these were carried to one's mouth, on sores, on faces and hands – blue and green monsters too lazy to fly or crawl away and to kill fifty was but to invite five thousand to attend the funeral. Under such conditions men lived and moved and even kept a stout heart.* (Divisional history)

The identity of the officer chastised earlier by Holberton cannot be known but one newly arrived young man was twenty-three year old Lieutenant Robert Harold Bedford[11], who had lived with his parents at 1396 Ashton Old Road, Manchester. He had been serving with the reserve 2/6th Battalion and an indication of his popularity with the men can be drawn from the following report, of his leaving for Gallipoli,

Lieutenant Robert Bedford, a most popular officer. Killed in March 1918.

published in the Battalion magazine, the *Sphinx*:

A deep plot was hatched. He was lured to the door of the Sergeants Mess and, regardless of his protests, lifted bodily into the air and carried shoulder high by a score of his men to the C Company parade ground where the whole of C Company had assembled. When the tumultuous cheering had at last subsided, Mr Bedford was permitted to make himself heard and those who were present will never forget his manly words. Thence, once more into the air – but this time escorted by a hundred men – to the Officers Mess…The Mess reached, the Company was not to be satisfied till a hundred men had wrung the hands of their popular officer.

The Manchesters returned to the front line on 18 September, taking over from the 7th Battalion. Mining and counter-mining would be the significant activity over the coming days. As the men were just settling in, a Turkish mine went off under No Man's Land. Immediately, the Manchesters started to dig a sapping trench towards the crater to see if they could occupy the crater for use as a grenade throwing post. The next day, British tunnelers broke into a Turkish tunnel and set explosives to destroy it.

The major incident of this tour of duty occurred at 6pm on 20 September when the Turks exploded another mine, blowing in a British tunnel. The crater was just next to the one created on the 18th and work again started to dig towards it. At dusk, Captain Cawley took four men and they occupied the crater overnight, with the intent of preventing the Turks from garrisoning it. They were no more than ten yards from the Turkish front line and well within range of their grenade throwers. Of course, it meant

Cawley's Crater. In this photograph, taken from the approximate position of the Turkish line, the crater's position is in the middle distance, where the line of bushes extends from the right into the field. Andy Crooks, 2007.

Private Jefferson Seal. Photograph taken in September 1915. Jeff Seal was commissioned as a second lieutenant in the 10th Battalion in October 1916.
Manchester Regiment Archives.

that the Turks were also well within grenade range for Cawley and his men. It was a dangerous time, with both sides keeping up grenade fire, until about midnight when the British trench mortar battery opened a heavy and extremely accurate shelling of the enemy front line. Stanley Cooke was one of the men with Cawley. 'Bombs were flying thickly and I had some narrow shaves. Poor Ted Heeley[12] met his death just about 5.30am, shot through the head.'

The troops withdrew back to their own lines shortly after this but action continued throughout the day. The Battalion war diary makes special mention of fifteen men, including four of the attached East Lancashires, who behaved with particular gallantry. Amongst the Manchesters were three men who would become officers later in the war – Corporals Alfred Featherstone, Ambrose Gordon Willcocks and Private William Yarwood. Ted Heeley was also mentioned as was George Heeley who may have been his brother (and later served with the Royal Air Force).

It is probable that Willcocks is the man referred to as Gordon by Stanley Cooke in a letter home:

> *Gordon and I had one night sentry go on this job and we don't want another in a hurry. Gordon's shift was on the far side of the crater nearest the Turks and mine on the near side, part of my duty being to warn a party of engineers engaged in repairing the trench when enemy bombs came over. I had two bombs exploded seemingly right in my face, blinding and deafening me for a few moments and how I escaped being hit escapes me. Gordon's job was more risky as he had to climb over the lip of the crater to get into it and cross it and with snipers about it was a ticklish job.*

The original headstone on Harold Cawley's grave. Perhaps surprisingly, the date is incorrect.

At dusk, the troops again occupied the crater lip and, towards midnight, there was a suspicion that the Turks were digging a trench out towards it. Captain Cawley went to the crater to confirm the situation but was shot and killed with a bullet through the temple. *'His body was lying close to me and I have a clear memory of his face as he lay in the*

Private William Bourne, one of the Stockport lacrosse players. Almost certainly wounded during the Cawley Crater incident, he died of these wounds aboard the Hospital Ship Gascon. William, aged twenty, was buried at sea.

bright moonlight – his face chalky white and the whole of his nose glistening with blood.' (Corporal Frank Waring)

The crater would become known officially as 'Cawley's Crater'.

Early the next morning, the battalion was withdrawn to bivouacs at Gully Ravine. They took the body of Harold Cawley with them and it was buried at Lancashire Landing at 3pm. The funeral was attended by Major General Douglas, Brigadier General Elliott commanding 127 Brigade and members of the battalion.

Ted Heeley is believed to be buried near the front line at Twelve Tree Copse Cemetery and is commemorated on a special memorial there.

Some time during the previous days, twenty year old William Bourne had been injured by one of the mine explosions. He was another of the Stockport men, playing for the Lacrosse Club's B team and, also, for the Cricket Club in the summer. He wrote home just before starting what would be his final tour of duty in the trenches and commented that it was now a year since he had left Southampton.

> *Twelve long months but on looking back I cannot think but what they have passed away very quickly. Months full of new experiences, not to say perils, that at one time I should never have dreamt would befall to me. In these experiences there has been much to learn and I am almost certain I have benefited by them. The chief thing I have learnt is to appreciate home. I have never regretted joining when I did. To be known as one of the first is an honour. It would be galling to be one of the 'White Feather Brigade'. I have no particular news of myself: am in good form though, a bit worn out which is, of course, only natural, my rest long since worn off. But I am hopeful to arrive home some day, looking fitter than I left. I've dropped weight and got as hard as iron and as brown as a penny piece.*

Bourne was evacuated away from Gallipoli. He died on 30 September, aboard the Hospital Ship *Gascon* and was buried at sea.

Back home, news of the casualties continued to be reported in the local press and, on 18 September, a campaign had opened to recruit ten thousand new Territorials. The *Manchester Football News* reported this under the headline ARE OUR LIVES TO BE WASTED? It continued 'They mean to win but they must have help and from them comes the call to the young men still at home.'

The month concluded with the receipt of a congratulatory message from Major-General Douglas, noting the excellent work undertaken at and around Cawley's Crater in the immediate aftermath of the explosion. He had been particularly impressed by the Battalion's bombers, several of whom, like Private William Yarwood[13], had only

(3) Census of Battalion Serving
30 9 15

original members who have not left the Bn	77
original members who have been away and returned	58
First draft (50 strong)	9
Second draft (63 strong)	6
Third draft (188 strong)	70
excluding 21 on detached duty	220

CASUALTIES TO Sept 30 1915

Particulars.	K.	W	M	Total.
original members	91	375	79	545
1st Draft	6	12	8	26
2nd Draft	12	12	13	37
3rd Draft	3	3	–	6
Total	112.	402	100	614

Lance Corporal A S Ballingall. Died of wounds on 12 September in a military hospital at Alexandria, Egypt.

Lance Corporal Harry Williams, from West Gorton. Died of dysentery on 17 October, aged 19. Buried at Portianos Military Cemetery, Lemnos, Greece.

just returned from a one day instruction course.

At the end of the month, the Adjutant took a census of the Battalion which showed the high rate of casualties, in particular noting that only 135 of the original strength were still at duty and that, of these, only seventy-seven had not been away from duty due to sickness or injury.

October would be a quiet month as the following summary of operations, attached to the war diary, indicates:

> *The operations during the month had resolved themselves into mining and bombing activities. The enemy artillery was, on the whole, very quiet and our casualties were remarkably few, only four men being wounded.*
>
> *Jaundice was still prevalent causing us to lose many men, mainly of the last two drafts and dysentery, which had caused so many losses during the two previous months, was almost absent. The weather was fine and warm but not oppressive, except for one or two showers during the latter days of the month.*
>
> *During the period that the Battalion occupied the extreme left of the line, we were able on more than one occasion to report enemy movements to the Navy which succeeded in checking and destroying the enemy workings.*

As indicated in the summary, mining was the main offensive tactic on both sides. On 2 October, the Turks exploded a large mine at the top of Fusilier Bluff and occupied the crater. On the 7th, the British retaliated with a mine of their own at nearby Boyes Point. The mine exploded at 7am, but the men of B Company had orders not to occupy the crater unless there was a clear advantage in doing so. Perhaps unsurprisingly, the men stayed in the safety of their trenches. The next day, the Turks exploded a mine in the same area in another seemingly pointless exercise as they also did not occupy the new crater. Lance Corporal Stanley Cooke:

> *My first twenty four hours here on getting up the line was to go down a mine as a listening party. Our job was simply to sit down and listen if we could hear the Turks working as we knew they were mining towards our trenches and were only a few feet away and it's a race to see which blows up the first. I went on at three in the afternoon and got no relief until nine at night so thus had six hours on my own in pitch blackness…The work is very nerve trying and three men have been took off with a nervous breakdown. One particular chum of mine came up with nerves quite gone and started blubbing like a child.*

On the 12th, Lance Corporal Owen Evans and his machine gun team took over the gun in the firing line. They fired off 250 rounds at the crater just to deter the Turks. Over the next couple of days, two of the six man team reported sick. It's not known when B Company's Private Harry Williams, nineteen, fell ill with dysentery but he had been evacuated to hospital on the nearby island of Lemnos where he died on 17 October. Before the war, he had worked as a telegraph clerk at Manchester Post Office and lived at 70 Forbes Street, West Gorton.

Colonel Pilkington was another who had to report sick after feeling unwell for several days. Command passed to Captain Holberton as Major Worthington had been taken off the peninsula at the end of August suffering with dysentery. Holberton was himself taken aboard a hospital ship on the 20th suffering with jaundice.

Around this time, Frank Waring recorded that another man had a narrow escape but this time, it was again from the possibility of facing a courts martial:

> *One night, my Company Sergeant Major came with me on my rounds. We entered a trench with a sentry in the usual position, looking over the top and resting his head on his hands. He did not seem to be aware of our entry so the CSM took away his rifle from his side and asked him if everything was alright. At the second time of asking, without response, the CSM gave him a thump which knocked him off the firestep onto the floor. He had no idea where he was until the CSM asked him why he was sleeping at his post and whether he knew he could be shot for it. The sentry strongly denied sleeping. The CSM asked him to produce his rifle. The man looked round wildly then broke into sobs. The CSM produced the rifle and told him not to do it again and the matter was closed.*

Waring, promoted to Lance Sergeant on 2 October, wrote home saying he was now earning two shillings a day – double a private's pay. But '*out of twelve chaps of No. 8*

Gully Beach. Manchester Regiment Archives

Platoon at Crowborough who came out here with me, only three are left, including myself. The rest are in hospital.' It would not be long before he joined them, spending two weeks in bed suffering from dysentery, before going to convalescent quarters on the island of Lemnos at the beginning of November[14].

On the 23rd, Owen Evans reported sick with a 'bad leg' and was admitted to 17th Stationary Hospital in the reserve area at Helles. He would spend over three weeks there and, on the 29th, get to meet the divisional commander, General Douglas, who had a few words with him. The same day, Evans noted the death during the evening of a man from the 10th Battalion who had been badly wounded by a grenade. This will have been Private Ralph Burgess from Oldham.

The next day, Claude Worthington returned from sick leave and took command of the battalion. The ship that had brought him from the port of Mudros, on the nearby Greek island of Lemnos, had also brought a draft of forty-three badly needed reinforcements. One of Worthington's first acts was to write recommendations for commissions for two men who had served at Gallipoli since the landings. Private J Campbell Barrett became an officer on 1 January 1916 and rose to the rank of Lieutenant serving with the Regiment. Harold Haygarth Jackson, previously an employee with James Hutton & Co, 14 Lloyd Street, Manchester, had been wounded in the fighting earlier in the year. His commission dates from 20 December 1915 and he would rise to the rank of Major, serving on the Army Staff.

Private Leslie Whitbread, the son of George Whitbread, a Methodist minister. Another victim of dysentery. Manchester Regiment Archives

All of the Manchester battalions at Gallipoli were now severely weakened by illness and, to maintain effective control, the 5th and 6th Battalions had been effectively merged into one, under Worthington's command. They moved back into the firing line on 29 November. Stanley Cooke was not amongst them. He had reported sick with frostbite that morning and was on his way to hospital at Mudros. The next day, they came under Turkish shelling and Lieutenant Clarke had a narrow escape when a shell hit his dug-out but, fortunately, he was not injured.

The weather turned noticeably colder in early November and, this brought some brief respite in the numbers reporting sick. In his diary, Colonel Claude Worthington records that he ignored orders which had been given to him by Colonel Tufnell, of the divisional staff.

> *Colonel Tufnell came round line and told Sergeant Major Ingham and me that there should be a man ready to fire alongside each observer. There is an order to this effect and as it would mean two men on and six by day, I gave*

instructions for it not to be carried out but always to have two men in a traverse besides the sentry who could be roused up to fire.

A case of the front line commander have a better grasp of what was required than the man from the reserve area.

On 12 November, the battalion moved to bivouacs at Gully Beach and fifty of the men were permitted to travel to Mudros for a full rest. The remainder would start to dig again, preparing winter quarters in Gully Ravine. The 52nd (Lowland) Division successfully undertook a major attack on the 15th. This was in the centre of the line – around the area where the Manchesters had been during the summer. Several Turkish trenches were captured and held. There was a very heavy downpour during the night. Men's belongings were washed away and the dugouts were under two feet of water. Next day was spent trying to clean rifles and other equipment as well as sort out clean, dry blankets and kit. It happened again on the 17th, just after Owen Evans had returned to duty from hospital.

The 24th saw two long awaited football matches. The Ardwick men of the 8th Battalion beat the Wiganers of the 5th. And, in the other match, the 7th beat the 6th , 4-2. It would seem that there was no opportunity for a Final to be held between the 8th and 7th teams.

During the morning of 30 November, the Manchesters moved back into the firing line. It had been their easiest month since arriving – levels of sickness were down, nobody had been killed and only four men had been wounded. Claude Worthington recorded in his diary 'Froze hard all day, very cold. Some men started with incipient frostbite. Rifles would not shoot owing to being clogged in bolts with dust, rain, oil and frozen hard. Had them put right.'

Captain Hammick was also concerned about the condition of the men's feet as the weather alternated between being very cold and being very wet. He felt that the soldiers did not appreciate the damage that could be done by wearing damp boots for days. He was obviously feeling the cold himself:

You would laugh to see me as I have two pairs of socks on and trench boots to my knees with trouser puttees inside them, a sandbag tied round each knee, two vests, three waistcoats, a tunic which will hardly button, cuffs, mittens and a muffler, a Burberry and mackintosh cape over the lot.

The weather warmed up slightly as December progressed but the thaw and the heavy rain meant there was much work to be done in maintaining the trench system but this was a quiet time until the 7th when the Turks opened a heavy artillery barrage on the British front line. The shelling continued the next day but only one man was wounded in the trenches. Private Robert Corbishley was not so lucky. He was working in the battalion's reserve area at the transport lines and was killed by an exploding shell. Before the war, Corbishley, twenty-two, had worked for textile merchants, Sparrow, Hardwick & Co.

On the 10th, the battalion again took up duties on mining fatigues. The heavy work and depleted numbers meant that the stretcher bearers and officers' servants, normally excused from this type of work, had to be pressed into service.

> *We are just back in bivouac at a place called Geoghan Bluff. Not a bad spot but 100 men a day are on mining fatigues, carrying fatigues, etc, which is heavy work for men just out of the firing line. Never getting away from the firing line very far means that one has six weeks on end sleeping in uniform. Not very pleasant nor calculated to rest one thoroughly.* (Captain Henry Hammick)

The next evening, at about 7pm, Private Robert Beresford Hind was shot by a stray bullet whilst the men were at the bivouac area. He was hit in the head and died almost immediately. Hind was a popular member of D Company and one of the stretcher bearers. He was buried next day, Owen Evans recording this as being 'opposite HQ'[15]. The location of his grave was lost in the following years.

There would be some welcome relaxation and entertainment on the 16th, when there was a camp concert. 'Rum punch was served to men and much appreciated.' (battalion war diary). The day would also bring news that would end the anguish for a number of families who were waiting to hear news of their men posted as missing after the attack on 4 June. The front line now having moved forward, it was safer for patrols to start to search for bodies of men who had fallen in the original fighting areas. One such patrol, from the 5th King's Own Scottish Borderers, spent several days doing this and brought in a number of bodies, including at least six members of the Battalion. One was Thomas Garner, the son of a farmer from Bramhall, Cheshire and an

British troops awaiting their turn to leave.

employee of the Vacuum Oil Company in Manchester. Colonel Worthington wrote to his parents:

> *I am glad to inform you that your son's body which has been missing since June 4th was found on December 16th. Your son took part in a very gallant charge on June 4th and died a soldier serving his King and country. No-one could look for a nobler death. I am very glad his body was found and am sure it will be some consolation to know that it has been found buried. Please accept from the officers, NCOs and men of the 1/6th Manchester Regiment our very deep sympathy in your loss.*

Three days later, the battalion acted as support for an attack undertaken by the 6th Lancashire Fusiliers. A mine was exploded next to Crawley's Crater and the Fusiliers successfully went forward to occupy the crater, which was quickly named Boyd's Crater after their commander. The Turks later counter-attacked and forced the Fusiliers to withdraw but they regrouped and captured it once again. The Manchesters did not have to go into action but the war diary notes that, during the day, one of the men was killed but it has not been possible to identify any fatality in other official records.

To the north, the withdrawal of troops from ANZAC and Suvla Bay had been underway for several days and the final groups of men slipped away in the early hours of 20 December. The evacuation had probably been the most successful part of the whole campaign and, although large quantities of supplies and artillery had to be left behind there was hardly a casualty. This left only the troops at Helles and plans were already well underway for their withdrawal.

Most of the Battalion remained in the support trenches but a small contingent, commanded by Captain Hammick, was in a forward position. They were relieved during the afternoon of the 21st but, just before the relief, one man died when a shell exploded close by. Private John Young would be the last of the Battalion's men to be killed in action at Gallipoli. Hammick recorded his feelings about this period in one of his letters home:

> *I have had two days in the first support line behind a place where we were having a* [illegible]. *The result was we got shelled. Four hours under heavy howitzers was the worst. I never have been in four hours such agony. The men I had with me were good men. I had seen them under fire but there was not a man amongst us who could have held a pen to write with at the end, we were so shaken.*

On the 23rd, arrangements were made to celebrate Christmas early. Still in the trenches, the men ate a hot meal in two shifts – at 12.30 and 2.30pm – and had the opportunity to drink a bottle of beer with it. Christmas Day itself was spent in the front line. It was quiet all day and orders had been issued to pretend that they were evacuating the trenches at night. Not a shot was fired between dusk and moonrise at 9.30pm, when the British artillery opened a barrage and the Manchesters joined in with rifle fire.

The actual evacuation orders came on the morning of the 28th. Other battalions would remain on the peninsula until 9 January but the Manchesters left the trenches during the early evening. Major Davies and Captain Maskell were the last to leave, signing over all the stores to the 9th Worcestershires. The men moved to V Beach where Owen Evans recorded that he won a turkey in a draw. 'Section had it for dinner.' In the late evening of 29 December, they boarded their transport ship and left for the island of Lemnos at 5am the next day.

Everyone pleased to have left the Peninsula, though some left it with regrets. (Battalion war diary)

---

1 2016, Eric Ponsonby Hartshorn. Born in the Hayfield area in 1894. Educated at Manchester Grammar School and employed by Blakeley & Beving Ltd, cotton printers. Left the Battalion on 24 August 1915 to train as an officer, later serving as a Lieutenant with the 5th Battalion and a battalion of the Gurkha Rifles.

2 Writing in a letter home, published in the Stockport Advertiser.

3 John Rainbow, 19, had lived with his parents, Alfred and Sarah at Croft Bank, Castleton, Nr Manchester. He had been educated at Manchester Grammar School.

4 Presumably Alexander Milne.

5 The Commonwealth War Graves Commission records Ernest Walter Arnold as serving with "D" Company.

6 Sidney Collier worked for Tootal Broadhurst, Lee & Co and was the son of the Rev. S Collier and Mrs H Collier.

7 Lieutenant Edmund Woods, 1/4th Battalion, East Lancashire Regiment.

8 Stanley Cooke worked for Alfred Young & Co, 74 Whitworth Street, Manchester. His diary and letters home are held by the Department of Documents, Imperial War Museum and extracts are included with the permission of his son.

9 Frank Waring's letters home are held by the Liddle Collection, University of Leeds and extracts are quoted with permission

.10 Almost certainly 3117, Private James Kirk, then aged 18 and a resident of Denton. He had worked as a warehouse clerk for Ogden & Madeley Ltd, Manchester. Kirk would be evacuated away from Gallipoli in the November suffering from frostbite. He would serve with the Camel Corps and later train to become an officer, returning to serve with the Regiment's 2nd Battalion in October 1918. On 4 November, Kirk undertook an act of great bravery for which he was awarded the Victoria Cross, Unfortunately, it was a posthumous award.

11 Captain Robert Bedford was killed in action on 25 March 1918. He has no known grave.

12 2637, Arthur Edward Heeley, from Chorlton-cum-Hardy, Manchester. Heeley's death is officially recorded as the 23rd, although by this date the Battalion had been relieved from the front line. Such errors in the records are not infrequent.

13 Yarwood left the Battalion on 22 November 1916 to train for a commission and subsequently served with the Royal Flying Corps and, later, Royal Air Force.

14 Shortly after this, Frank Waring was transferred to the Royal Flying Corps. He is believed to have survived the war.

15 Beresford Hind had been born in Derby but spent his school years living in Stretford. After education at Manchester Grammar School, he worked for the Scottish Widows Fund, in the city centre. He is believed to be now buried at Twelve Tree Copse Cemetery and is commemorated on a special memorial there.

Chapter 5

EGYPT AGAIN

SHORTLY AFTER ARRIVING at the port of Mudros on the Greek island of Lemnos, the adjutant, Captain Maskell, took a census of the battalion strength: on 31 December 1915, there were twelve officers and 153 other ranks – less than a normal company. Of the men, only eighty-two were part of the original contingent who had landed at Gallipoli in the previous May. Of these, just twenty had been with the battalion for the whole period, never leaving to recover from wounds or sickness. They were Acting Regimental Quartermaster Sergeant Billy Warburton, Company Sergeant Majors A McDonald and T Smith, Sergeants S Meldon, F Webb and A Yates, Corporals H Lingard, A Lucas and P Mullins, Lance Corporal R Johnson and Privates C Brooks, G Chadwick, F Davies, L Durham, E Garner, J Gibson, R Langton, A McKenzie, F Stretch and A Vernon. This group would generally continue to have good fortune and, with the exceptions of Mullins and Yates, survived the war.

The recent weeks had taken a toll on the men's health and they were not in good physical condition. Rest and regular light exercise were needed and they got both in

The port of Mudros on the Greek island of Lemnos.

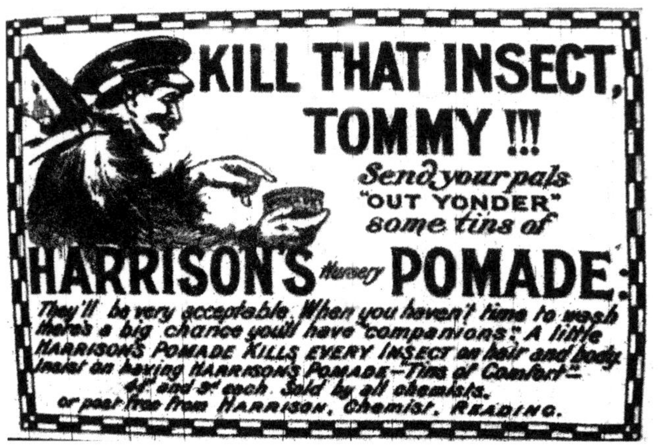

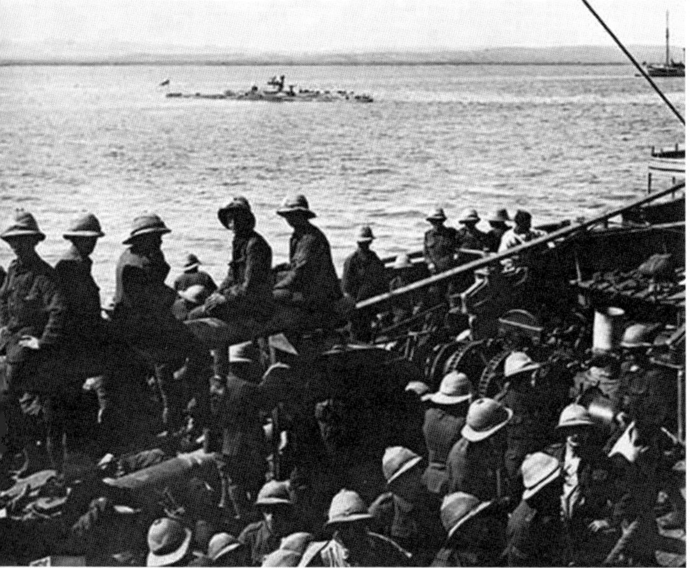
Troopship leaving the port of Mudros.

the first few days. Owen Evans and his friend, Private Thorp, managed to get some beer from the Quartermaster's Store and they went for a walk while they drank it. On 6 January, there was a football match between A Company and B Company and A Company won by two goals to one. Over the following two days, the men started to undertake some drill exercises but also had the luxury of being able to get hot baths and fumigated uniforms and blankets. A welcome relief from lice at least for a while.

By 13 January 1916, preparations were well under way for a move back to Egypt. The battalion should have embarked on the 15th but a very heavy rain storm prevented it. The men waited outside for hours and were soaked to the skin. There was a real danger of men falling ill from exposure and, later, they marched to a camp about two miles away where there were able to take shelter in some huts. With nothing to eat but their iron rations, they passed a miserable twenty four hours. The battalion was then able to board the ship but it remained in harbour until the morning of the 18th. The Manchesters arrived at Alexandria during the evening of 20 January and travelled overnight by train to Cairo. Once in the city, a transfer to trams took them to Mena Camp, close to the Pyramids. Colonel Claude Worthington noted in his diary that the officers occupied tents whilst the other ranks went into grass huts.

Although the men undertook some exercises, much of the next few days was devoted to relaxation in what the divisional history describes as the 'flesh-pots of Egypt'. Owen Evans and a friend went in to Cairo one evening where they had dinner and then went to the cinema. For Frank Stretch, the stay would be brief. He was a member of Evans' gun crew but left the battalion on 25 January to return to Britain as his contracted time as a Territorial had expired. A clerk with the Vacuum Oil Company, he had joined the battalion in 1911, aged eighteen. In the latter stages of the war, 'time expired' men were not exempt from conscription back into the army and he may have been the man of the same name who later served with the Regiment's 5th Battalion and, in the closing stages of the war, with the Lincolnshire Regiment[1].

The stay at Mena was fairly short and, on 1 February, the battalion moved to El Shallufa, just north of the town of Suez, as part of the defence force for the Suez Canal. The whole of 42nd Division went into a tented camp on the eastern side of the canal. The men spent 3 February bringing stores across on a small ferry and generally settling in to their new surroundings. Routines were established and Colonel Worthington noted in his diary that the men paraded at 7am and spent thirty minutes undertaking physical exercises. The rest of the day was spent as follows:

9.00am – 9.30am	Squad drill and guards
9.30am – 10.00am	Musketry
10.00am – 10.30am	Squad drill
11.45am – 12.20pm	Tactical exercise in holding a post
2.00pm – 3.00pm	Fire discipline
6.30pm – 7.30pm	Lecture on discipline

Stanley Cooke celebrated his twenty-fourth birthday on 6 February. It was spent attending church parade in the morning and, for the rest of the day, as one of the men sent to the advanced outpost line of defences. Major General Douglas, commanding the Division, came to inspect the lines during the afternoon. On the 8th a draft of new troops arrived. There were four new officers and 152 other ranks. Over sixty of the men were experienced troops – many previously serving with the two regular battalions and now returning to duty after recovery from wounds. A few more had previously served with the 6th Battalion and were also returning to duty. Most, however, were newly trained troops coming from the 3/6th Battalion (the second of the reserve battalions). Fifty of these men brought with them a new weapon of war – the Stokes trench mortar. The mortar had been invented the previous year and had seen its first significant use, in northern France, at the Battle of Loos in September 1915. It was a short range weapon which was particularly effective in suppressing enemy machine gun posts. Within a few weeks, however, the army decided to concentrate the control of these specialist weapons at brigade level and separate trench mortar batteries were formed under the higher command.

On 16 February, the whole battalion crossed back to the western side of the Suez Canal to the stores area where they drew supplies and a total of 160,000 rounds of ammunition. The next day, along with men from the 5th Battalion, 200 of them set out for a position they had named Manchester Post. This was some two miles into the desert, where they dug a defence line. Stores and equipment were carried on a camel train and Colonel Worthington described the whole thing as 'quite a procession'.

Machine gunner Owen Evans had been promoted to sergeant and had taken over duties as the Orderly Sergeant so did not go into the desert, remaining at Shallufa where he instructed a new officer in the use of the Vickers machine gun. He had made some notes to assist him, in particular describing what needed to be done when taking over a new position:

1. Post an observer by the gun immediately
2. Ascertain targets and ranges
3. Ascertain position and amount of bulk ammunition
4. Get receipt for tripod handed over
5. Fill barrel casing with water and glycerine
6. Inform each member of section as to targets, ranges and bulk ammunition
7. Allot sleeping places for section
8. Clean gun before mounting.

Evans' diary ends at this point. He continued to serve with the battalion until 24 December 1917, when he received a commission as an officer in the Machine Gun Corps in which he served as a lieutenant. He applied for his service medals in 1922 when he was living at The Alders, Chinley, Derbyshire and was in business as a partner in the firm of Diggles & Evans, 8a Charlotte Street, Manchester.

Manchester Post was one of a series of small garrisons which formed the first line of defence against any Turkish attack on the canal. Along with the Manchesters was a battery of artillery, a squadron of Yeomanry cavalry and some Royal Engineers. In due course, these defence positions took on an air of permanence, with water supply pipes running back to the fresh water canal, which took its supply from the Nile and ran alongside the main Suez shipping canal.

Late February and early March continued to see men return to Britain as their time as Territorials had expired. Newly trained replacements arrived in their place. On 2 March, Claude Worthington notes the draft included nine new officers. Amongst them were Second Lieutenants Richard Hankinson, aged twenty, and Richard Mawson, thirty. Both men had enlisted in September 1914 and served with the 2/6th Battalion. Hankinson had lived with his parents at 'Rosemere', The Cliff, Higher Broughton and had been educated at Lincoln Collge, Oxford. Almost immediately, he had applied to become an officer. Thirty-one year old Mawson originated from Leeds and had served with the local Volunteer Battalion, the Leeds Rifles, before moving to the Manchester area some years before the war. He was a single man who lived at Keppel Road, Chorlton and worked as a commercial traveller for S & J Watts Ltd. In spite of his long experience, he had not been selected to train as an officer until October 1915.

Colonel Worthington and a few of the other officers rode to Suez on 5 March and spent several days there socialising in the Mess of 9th Army Corps and with other guests at the Sinai Hotel where they were staying. They were fortunate to escape injury on their return to Shallufa as they did not hear a challenge from a sentry. Following his usual orders, the sentry opened fire but it was a warning shot over their heads.

Lance Corporal George Gibbons. Neil Drum.

The men at Manchester Post continued to develop the defences, digging a more extensive trench system, incorporating the nearby sand dunes into the overall structure. Back at Shallufa, the remainder of the battalion undertook training courses with many of the men trying out the new Lewis machine guns. Unlike the heavy Maxims and Vickers guns that Owen Evans had fired, the Lewis gun was lightweight and operated by only a two man team. One man fired the gun whilst the other carried and loaded the circular ammunition magazines.

Towards the end of the month, Lieutenant S Collier and Corporal J Swinchatt attended a four day specialist grenade course and qualified as first class instructors. They returned about the same time as the men at Manchester Post returned to Shallufa and, on the 24th, orders were received that the battalion would move to a new position to the northwest of Suez. It was an eleven mile march which they undertook on the night of 25/26 March. The rest of the 26th was spent in settling in to the camp, which was being erected by a Belgian contractor and, working under the direction of the Royal Engineers, the contractor's Egyptian employees rapidly put up huts and stables. The 27th was declared to be a holiday and Colonel Worthington went into Suez where he had lunch at the Bel Air Hotel and then spent the afternoon at the Club Port Tewfik.

It was back to work as usual the next morning with the men on parade at 5.30 for ninety minutes physical exercise, bayonet fighting drill and musketry practice. There was further drill after breakfast and, again, in the afternoon. The pattern continued for the closing days of the month – exercise, route march, drill, fatigues.

The men awoke on 1 April 1916 and may have thought someone was playing a bad April Fools Day joke on them. There was no water and no water meant no breakfast. They would have grumbled at every opportunity through the early morning parade which had started at 5.30am. Supplies had been restored by mid-morning and the men spent a relaxing afternoon. There was an inter-battalion competition for the men with the various transport sections, with awards for smartness, horse riding and wagon driving. In the afternoon, there were football matches. Football and rugby now became the main games played by the battalion's men. Lacrosse was hardly played as most of the pre-war players were now either dead or recovering from wounds. There was a concert in the evening which everyone thought was a good end to the day.

Four senior NCOs left the battalion on 2 April to briefly return to Britain. Regimental Quartermaster Sergeant White, Company Sergeant Majors Kent and Smith, together with Sergeant Houghland, had all decided to re-engage with the battalion even though their time as Territorials had expired. By now, they would know that the coming conscription would mean that they might be taken back into the army as privates and sent to other units. In return for volunteering, they were all entitled to a month's leave at home and to retain their rank.

During the morning of the 6th, parties of men were sent to Port Tewfik to be fumigated and have hot baths. There were no duties in the afternoon and there were battalion football matches. There was also a hockey match between the officers and sergeants. The results are not recorded.

The remainder of the month appears to have been very easy on the men with little more than a weekly route march, some musketry drill and plenty of time for sporting competitions. Two hockey matches were played against the East Kents, with the Manchesters winning both. However, the sporting stars of 42nd Division were now the rugby team of the 5th Manchesters. Even the battalion's officers were able to form a team which beat a team of officers drawn from the rest of the brigade. Stanley Cooke took part in events on 29 April and reached the final as a member of his company's tug-of-war team, but they were beaten by D Company. Colonel Worthington took the next day off and went fishing with another officer named Allard.

Claude Worthington received a letter from Captain Henry Hammick in the middle of May. Hammick had not left Gallipoli with the remainder of the battalion but had stayed on to assist with the supervision of the evacuation of the other troops from Gully Beach. He had been one of the last to leave the peninsula in early January. Hammick had then returned to Britain for leave and, whilst there, he was seconded to the Royal Engineers where, perhaps, he hoped that his professional skills as a mechanical engineer could be directly utilised. However, it was his organisational skills that would be valued and he wrote to Worthington saying he was going to France as a Railway Transport Officer, directing the movement of trains that served the

Outpost duties in the desert. Manchester Regiment Archives.

western front from the channel ports. Hammick remained with the Engineers for the remainder of the war, rising to the rank of major.

There were several specialist courses for the men in the middle of May. The brigade signalling officer ran one for battalion signallers and Lieutenant Collier put a number of prospective grenade throwers through their paces on the 15th of the month. Other went to the divisional school to learn about the new trench mortars and how they were intended to support the infantry.

Captain Tom Blatherwick[2], brother of Frank, and Lieutenant Stanley Bridgford arrived back from Britain on 21 May. There was also a draft of 69 other ranks. Bridgford was one of the replacement officers who had joined the battalion the previous August. At the end of the following month, he had been evacuated away suffering, as many others, from jaundice and had spent time in hospital in Malta before returning to Britain becoming a patient at Osborne Military Convalescent Hospital on the Isle of Wight.

Within a couple of days, Blatherwick had taken up the duties of adjutant. His administrative skills were in great demand as the battalion received orders for a move back to Shallufa on the 26th. He organised fatigue parties to check equipment and load the wagons ready for the march. This was finished by early afternoon on the 25th and a guard was posted on the wagons. The brigade moved off a couple of hours later and marched overnight, arriving at Shallufa at about 6am on the 26 May. The men had breakfast and then crossed to the camp on the eastern bank of the Suez Canal. The rest of the day was spent bringing supplies and equipment by ferry across the canal. It was going to be a brief stay and, almost immediately, orders were received that, the following day, the battalion would move to Salford Post, one of the outposts in the desert.

The men managed a few hours rest in the tents before they had to be dismantled and made ready for the journey. Once done, the battalion war diary records 'men dossed down in open until 20.00'. They moved off at dawn on 27 May and reached the railhead at Genneffe, about eight miles away, at 8am. They had breakfast there and then A and C Companies completed the final two miles train ride to Salford Post. B and D Companies remained at the railhead to deal with the baggage that would arrive on the wagons.

Except in an emergency, the battalion would not be involved in defence work at Salford Post but spend its time digging to improve the trenchworks. 28 May was a Sunday and in view of the heavy work undertaken by the men in recent days, they were allowed to rest until the late afternoon. At 4pm, they started digging. It was hard work as the sand constantly collapsed into the newly dug trench. They hammered wooden posts into the ground and fixed matting hurdles to them to retain the sand. Their efforts were watched with some amusement by the men defending

Salford Post – territorials from the Chelmsford area serving with the 1/5th Battalion, Essex Regiment. As late spring turned to early summer, the weather became appreciably warmer. The men continued to dig trenches each day, working between 5am and 8am and, again, between 4pm and 6pm. In between, they rested and sought as much shelter from the sun as they could find.

The first entry in the battalion's war diary for June shows, perhaps, an exasperation and disappointment with the orders of the higher command:

> *The G.O.C[3]. 54th Division inspected the post. As a result of this visit, scheme of defence was altered and it was decided to throw out the idea of continuous fire support trenches round the Post and build separate strong posts which would be self-contained and connected by communication trenches to one central position. This entailed the demolishment of a large portion of the work already done by the unit.*

The feelings of the men who will have seen their recent efforts totally wasted are not recorded. Over the following two weeks, the men filled in the trenches they had dug and started to dig the now required communication trenches. It was hot work and temperatures continued to rise. On the 12th, the temperature in the shade reached 118F (48C) but digging had to continue. By 20 June, two posts had been completed, including the necessary dug-outs and water storage tanks. It was time for this tour of duty to end and for the men to return to Shallufa.

They had had one afternoon of rest on 3 June. This was as a commemoration for the men who had died on 4 June 1915 at Gallipoli. There had been a special dinner in the evening and, afterwards, an impromptu concert. The next day was a Sunday and, during the church parade, the chaplain, Padre Davey, gave an address in remembrance of their fallen comrades.

Back in Manchester, similar remembrance commemorations also took place on 4 June. The Pleasure Gardens at Belle Vue had opened in the early 19th century on the then eastern outskirts of the city. By the time of the war, the gardens had been extended. There was now a zoo, funfair and a very large ballroom, making it the whole area's most popular place of entertainment. It was an ideal place for the start of the commemorative procession, as reported by the *Manchester Evening Chronicle*:

> *It was therefore fitting that the East Lancashire Territorials now in convalescent camp at Heaton Park, recovering from their wounds, and other soldiers from the Division, should take part in an organised procession…Many of the men were limping, others bore the marks of recent illness; all showed some signs of the martyrdom of Gallipoli through which they had passed with such courage and fortitude. A number of the men were in mufti and walked with the aide of crutches.*

The men marched down Hyde Road to the Town Hall in Albert Square. The entire route was lined with thousands of people, clapping and waving flags. The Lord Mayor presented a number of medals, including the Distinguished Conduct Medal to Company Sergeant Major Frederick Hay and Lance Sergeant Archibald McDonald.

For many Mancunians, the long wait for any news of their loved ones who had been posted missing at Gallipoli was about to be over. Months had passed since the evacuation. The British Government had made enquiries through neutral countries and the Red Cross about men possibly taken prisoner. Of those about whom there was no information, the Government now felt able to conclude that they must have been killed on the day they were posted as missing. Letters were sent to the families informing them of this decision and death certificates were issued so that probate for a man's will could now be granted. It also meant that a widow's status was clear and, in times when many women depended on a husband's earnings, she could now consider remarriage. Many did so very quickly. The families of Robert Davies and Walter Musgrave received letters on the same day. The young men were both aged twenty and were pre-war members of the battalion. They had been killed on 7 August 1915 during the Battle of the Vineyard. Davies lived with his parents at 47 Bridge Street, Chorlton on Medlock and worked at the local chemist's shop belonging to Boots Ltd. Musgrave had only arrived at Gallipoli on 23 July 1915 as one of the reinforcements. He also lived with his parents at Whitney Street, Crumpsall and worked in the offices and warehouse of cotton manufacturers, Bannerman Ltd, York Street, Manchester.

The men dismantled their tents on the morning of 22 June so they could be loaded onto the wagons for transport back to Shallufa. At 17.15, they paraded and started their march back overnight. They were back in time for an early breakfast. It was a busy day, unloading the equipment and erecting the tents in their new camp. The battalion's war diary notes that the next three days 'were spent resting at Shallufa West

The Suez Canal at Port Said; a vital artery of the British Empire and vulnerable to attack by the Turks.

and great advantage was taken by all ranks of the good washing facilities. This rest, after all the heavy digging work, was greatly appreciated by all.'

In the late afternoon of 28 June, camp was struck and all the equipment was taken to the railway station ready for another move. At 8.30pm, the men of the 6th and 8th Battalions boarded open trucks for a journey to El Ferdan, towards the southern end of the Suez Canal. They arrived at 1am on the 29th and were directed to a camp where tents had already been erected for their use. As always, after a move, the next two days were spent unloading stores and equipment.

After so many days working as labourers, it was decided that the men needed 'smartening up' and were put through some light drill during the morning of 1 July 1916. It would be a day or so before they heard news of fellow Mancunians fighting hundreds of miles to the north in France.

In what would become known as the First Day of the Battle of the Somme, sixteen British divisions, in conjunction with the French Army, had attacked, at 7.30am on 1 July, in what was the largest assault of the war. It resulted in the highest casualty figures sustained in the history of the British Army. Amongst the dead and missing were almost 700 Manchester Regiment soldiers. Most of them had died fighting with the newly formed Pals battalions in their first time in a major action. Many of the Manchesters worked for the same employers as the 6th Battalion men and would have been well known to them. Although the attack on the 1 July was generally seen as a failure with many divisions not reaching their objectives, the Manchester Regiment battalions, fighting in the south of the battlefield, were successful. They had trained extensively for the attack, practising on a life-size replica of the trench system including at least once without any officers, and each man knew exactly what was expected of him.

On 6 July, most of the battalion left to spend several days at a rest camp at Sidi Bishi, near Alexandria. Approximately 200 men, mostly from very recent replacement drafts remained at El Ferdan, under the command of Captain Molesworth. He put them to work, digging trenches and grenade-throwing pits. Colonel Worthington spent much of his holiday visiting a dentist in Alexandria but also had time to visit a number of the prominent British families in the city. The rest period was all too short and the men were all back at El Ferdan by the late afternoon of the 13th.

The next day, the battalion took over guard duties on the eastern side of the canal, patrolling along the bank. There was specialist training for the Lewis gunners and the grenade throwers. One of the patrol duties was to ride a camel alongside the railway track, brushing it clear of sand and any obstructions. One soldier was fortunate to escape injury on the 18th, when he was accidentally fired on. Colonel Worthington investigated the next day and established that another unit had fired 80 rounds across the canal not realising someone was there.

Towards the end of July, Colonel Pilkington, who had been on sick leave since the previous October, returned to duty as battalion commander and Claude Worthington reverted to being his second-in-command and to his substantive rank of major. Around the same time, the British Army received intelligence that a major Turkish offensive was imminent.

> *A large enemy force, led by German officers and armed with German and Austrian artillery and machine guns, was moving, with a rapidity that was surprising when the difficulties of the march of an army across the desert are realised, westwards from El Arish. Before long, aircraft located Turkish troops at Oghratina Hod – a hod being a plantation of date-palms – about ten miles east of Romani, held by 52nd Division…The Turks meant to force a fight in the worst possible season for British troops and their march across the desert was a notable achievement.* (42nd Division History)

In preparation for meeting this threat, the division was formed into a mobile column, ready for operations east of the fortified posts

Turkish troops marching into Egypt.

and, on 25 July, the battalion moved north to Kantara, near to Port Said. Equipment and stores were cut down to a minimum and what remained would be carried into the desert by camel train. The men stayed in this area before taking up a more advanced position on 27 July at Gilban. To the east, the British 52nd Division and brigades of Australian Light Horsemen and New Zealand mounted riflemen held defensive positions around the railhead town of Romani. The Turkish infantry forces were encamped at an oasis a further ten miles to the east and had been there for several days, waiting for their artillery to catch up with the infantry. The attack was clearly imminent and, in response, orders were issued to 42nd Division to prepare to reinforce their comrades at Romani. During the evening of 3 August, the 6th Battalion was sent by train to Pelusium, six miles north west of Romani. They started to prepare defensive positions in case of a Turkish breakthrough and made preparations for the arrival of the rest of the brigade.

Under the cover of darkness, the Turks managed to bring their leading troops close to the positions of the Australian Light Horsemen in front of Romani and launched their attack shortly after midnight. Fierce fighting continued throughout the night with the Australians beating off wave after wave until they were finally forced to slowly withdraw. Noise of the artillery fire could be heard miles away and orders soon reached the reserve troops that they were to move forward. The 5th, 7th and 8th Battalions arrived at Pelusium in the middle of the afternoon. Just as the last battalion was detraining, they were ordered to move forward immediately to support the Romani garrison which, though under severe pressure, was about to launch a major counter-attack. The order was received at 3.27pm and, just three minutes later, the troops set off across the desert.

> *They moved off without any transport – as none of the camels had arrived – and also without their dinners, the stew which had been prepared for them being left untouched. They passed through the 6th Manchesters, who were ordered to remain in their positions covering Pelusium, in order to escort and assist in organising the expected camel transport. Artillery, cavalry and engineer detachments arrived at Pelusium and moved forward, but nothing was seen or heard of the camels until 11pm, when two long files, each of 1000 camels turned up. It was pitch dark, the transport was new to the Division and the task of sorting out the animals, allocating them to the various units, loading them with rations, ammunition and blankets was a stupendous one. But the 6th Manchesters understood what every moment's delay in delivering the goods – especially the water – might mean to their comrades and they put their backs into it. By 4am, the camel convoys for 127 Brigade and the attached troops had been despatched on their trek into the desert.* (Divisional history)

Meanwhile, the other battalions of Manchesters had marched across three miles of soft sand under a scorching sun and gone into action just ninety-three minutes after receiving the order at Pelusium. By then the Turkish attack had already stalled in the face of determined fire from the ANZAC troops and the British reinforcements had

The hills of Romani as seen from Qatiya. Terry Kinloch.

Battle of Romani, 4 August 1916.

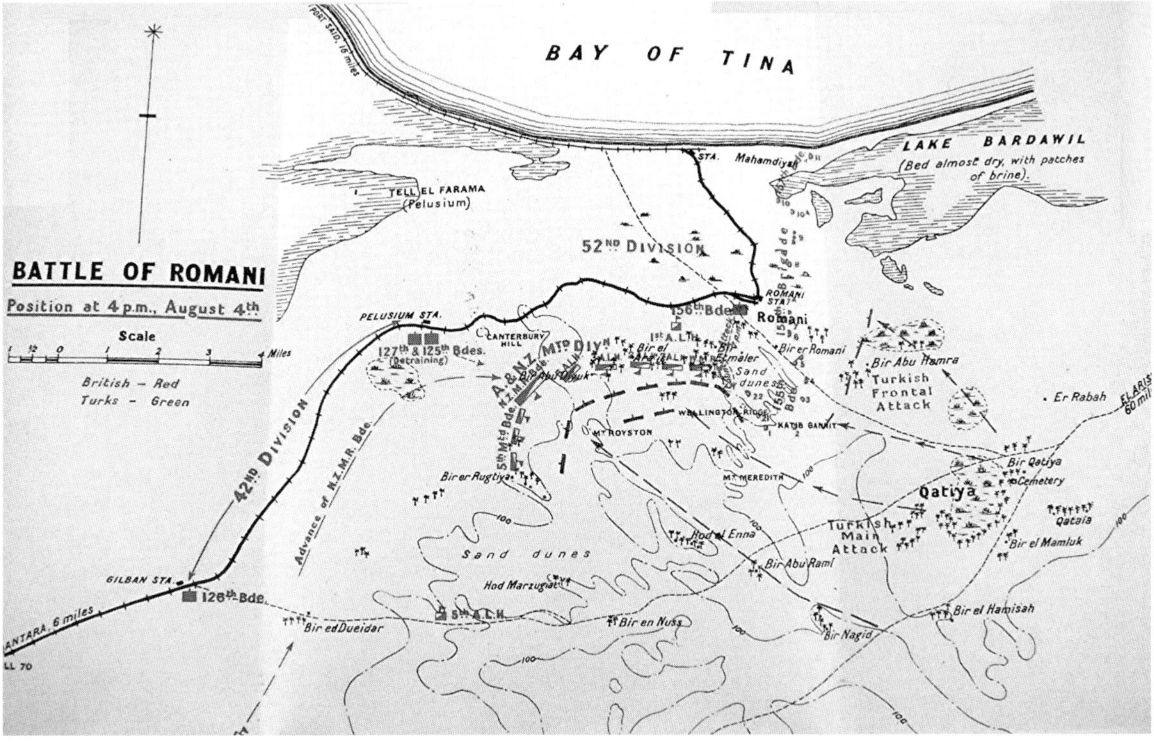

only a minor role to play. The three battalions advanced, with the 7th on the left, the 5th on the right and the 8th in support.

But the Turk did not wait. Worn out as he was by the marching and fighting of the past few days, the sight of new British troops moving steadily towards him, line after line in regular waves, shook his faith in the assurance of victory. (Divisional history).

The Battle of Romani was effectively over and many Turkish soldiers surrendered whilst the bulk of the force undertook a brave and well-organised fighting retreat.

The camel train had been escorted by A Company of the 6th Battalion and, at 7am on 5 August, the rest of the battalion marched off to join them. There were no camels left for transport, so the men only took what equipment they could carry – rifles, 120 rounds of ammunition and their own water bottles. They halted at Mount Royston, scene of the some of the earliest fighting during the night of 3/4 August. After an hour, they moved on again, but after another mile, the intense heat meant the men and horses simply could not go on any further and they rested for the afternoon in a small palm grove which was fortunate to have its own well.

There were many signs around this position of the complete rout of the Turks on the previous day; many dead camels carrying ammunition and camel guns, also dead horses were lying about on the ground. Large quantities of ammunition were also thrown about. (Battalion war diary).

British troops marching from the Suez Canal into the desert to meet the Turks.

Major Claude Worthington rode forward and was able to establish the location of the other battalions of the brigade now at Mount Meredith. He noted in his diary that they had taken some 300 prisoners. 'At night had 1/2 pint water, 3/4 pint tea and tin bully and 1/2 biscuits – all since breakfast'.

Worthington was not alone in having too little to eat and, more importantly, too little to drink during the day. Fourteen men had already fallen out; victims of the heat and thirst. There was no improvement in the situation when the battalion joined the rest of the brigade during the early evening. Food was scarce and water was rationed to one pint per man. It was going to have to last them through the night and, probably, all the next day. The men were warned to drink sparingly. There was little time for sleep and the men were roused at 2am on the 6th but were able to replenish their water bottles. They moved off again at 4am, as part of the force pursuing the retreating Turks. Claude Worthington recorded the day in his diary:

> *Terrible march in heat, had no rations and practically no water. Halted for three hours in blazing sun, while cavalry went round and on to Katia, then went forward in extended order to the outskirts of Katia, where halted in palm grove.*
>
> *Ground like a battlefield. At 12.00 brigade moved on about 1½ miles to Katia and I was left behind to clear ground of sick men and collect and march on in cool. Collected eighty-six men of the 8th, about fifty of the 5th and 110 of ours with about forty of their collecting party, also a lot of 7th. Got these in by 10.30pm and reported to brigade.*

The battalion war diary described this advance as the most trying it had been called on to perform during the war. 'The fearful heat and the complete absence of water and want of food was responsible for many hundreds of casualties in the brigade.' Although many men were now in a poor state, as far as can be established, all of the battalion's soldiers recovered from their ordeal. They had, of course, expected to get some rest once they reached Katia and its fresh water wells but they were ordered forward to take up an outpost line. Rest finally came on the morning of 7 August when the battalion moved back to bivouacs at Katia. Enemy planes flew over the British positions during the morning and dropped bombs, in an unsuccessful attempt to destroy the wells. Later in the day, A and B Companies again took up defensive positions on the outpost line.

Mount Meredith. **Terry Kinloch**

The battalion remained here for the next seven days. Conditions quickly improved with good supplies of rations arriving. Although it was clear the Turks had retreated from the area, it was still necessary to exercise caution and outposts were manned overnight by small groups of men. There was still work to be done during the day and the battalion was employed on burial parties – men from both sides who had died during the fighting and, also, many horses and camels. By 14 August, the area was deemed safe enough from Turkish attack for the 42nd Division to be withdrawn from the area and they marched back to Romani. The next day, the battalion paraded and there was a full inspection of rifles, ammunition and iron rations still held by the men.

Many official congratulations were sent to the troops who had been involved in the Battle of Romani. The King wrote to General Sir Archibald Murray, commanding British forces in Egypt:

> *Please convey to all ranks engaged in the battle of Romani, my appreciation of the efforts which have brought about the brilliant success they have won at the height of the hot season and in desert country.*

General Sir Archibald Murray.

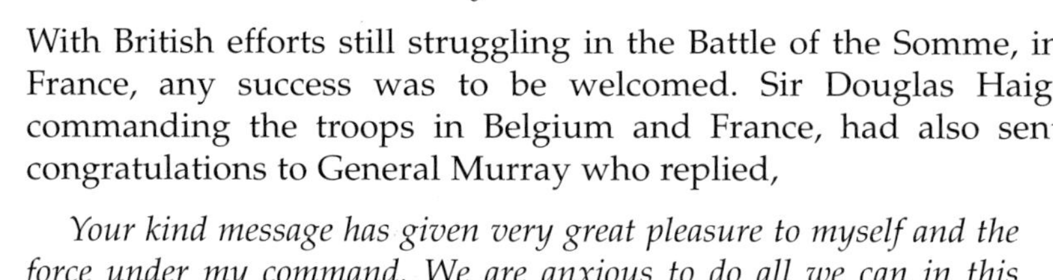

With British efforts still struggling in the Battle of the Somme, in France, any success was to be welcomed. Sir Douglas Haig, commanding the troops in Belgium and France, had also sent congratulations to General Murray who replied,

> *Your kind message has given very great pleasure to myself and the force under my command. We are anxious to do all we can in this theatre of operations to help directly or indirectly towards the decisive action in the Western Front and we watch with intense interest and admiration the sure and certain progress which nothing can stop of the force under your command.*

The pattern for the remainder of the month was set on the 16th and recorded in the battalion war diary. 'Short parades were held in the morning and evening, the rest of the day being spent quietly in camp.' The situation improved further from the 18th, when Lieutenant C Burdett and a party bringing the field cookers, water carts and other stores arrived from Pelusium. The next day, Second Lieutenant William Braithwaite and sixteen other ranks, who were still unwell from the exertions earlier in the month, and unable to march, were sent to Kantara to be attached to a divisional composite battalion. The only major activity in the latter half of the month was a night exercise which started the same evening and involved holding a practice outpost line and deploying for a rearguard action on their way back to camp early in the morning of 20 August.

With the battalion at nearly full strength, training schemes started again at the beginning of September 1916. Two officers and sixteen men were sent for a few days to the Grenade Training School at Kantara, whilst Major Worthington and three men went on a practical signalling exercise at Pelusium. Orders were issued on 8 September that the battalion was to prepare to move forward once more as part of a "mobile column". The men who formed part of the column would need to be very fit, as experience of the previous month had shown. About eighty men were deemed unfit to march and they would remain behind and be temporarily attached to 125 Brigade. Lieutenant Hugh Vipond and eighteen other ranks would also stay behind so they could join a grenade instruction course. 127 Brigade moved off in the late afternoon of 10 September, reaching El Rabah by about 8pm. After a few hours rest, the column started off again. Until now, they had been following the railway line, but now struck up a direct route across the desert to reach their new garrison positions at Negiliat, some twenty kilometres to the east of Romani.

In the two years since war had been declared, the technology of killing had developed at an ever increasing pace. Poison gas had been used by both sides the previous year; within a few days, tanks would make their first ever appearance in combat; and the use of airplanes as both a weapon and, more importantly, for reconnaissance was now commonplace. To conceal the troops as much as possible from enemy aircraft, the battalion did not make camp in a single place, but the men were scattered over a fairly wide area in groups no larger than section or platoon. Stores and animals were also kept in small groupings.

Even though the men were generally attempting to conceal themselves, they would fire at any enemy aircraft that flew within range of their rifles or Lewis machine guns. To ensure that no unfortunate errors were made, a telegram was received on the morning of 12 August advising that the Royal Flying Corps had a new plane in the area which was very similar to an enemy one. The 'Martinsyde' could be distinguished from the Turkish plane as it had a semi-circular tail, instead of triangular one.

The Martinsyde fighter plane.

> *Further orders were received to reduce the size of bivouacs which were now to be made to hold no more than two men. In a report from an airman it was found that if the bivouacs are made for two or three men, with no more than two, or at the most three, blankets and are surrounded and covered with scrub, brushwood or palm leaves, they are most difficult to discern from an aeroplane.* (Battalion war diary).

The day also brought news of a medal awarded by the King of Serbia to the battalion's ex-adjutant, Philip Holberton, now brigade major with 126th Brigade. Company Quartermaster Sergeant Alfred Featherstone was similarly honoured.

There was some excitement during the morning of 18 August when a telegram arrived giving a description of an alleged German spy supposedly on board the train due to arrive at Negiliat. The guard was turned out and the train thoroughly searched but there was no sign of anyone fitting the description nor, indeed, anyone seeming at all suspicious. On the 21st, the brigade took over the advanced defence line. B Company held the outposts while C and D took up positions behind them in the main defence line. A Company remained in reserve at battalion headquarters. They had relieved the 1/4th Battalion, East Lancashire Regiment and, as these troops were marching away, they were bombed by an enemy aircraft. 'Fortunately, no damage to white troops was done but four native camel drivers were killed' (1/6th Battalion, Manchester Regiment war diary).

Towards the end of the month, the divisional artillery brigades received new guns and howitzers. Standard practice was to register the guns on likely targets – firing several test shots to check the accuracy of range and barrel elevation. Possibly as a safety matter, the infantry holding the defensive line were ordered to withdraw from their positions and move back behind the artillery. This did not find favour with the infantry officers who felt that, in a combat situation, registration would take place over the heads of the troops. As Captain Tom Blatherwick recorded in the battalion war diary, 'This seemed an unnecessary move and one liable to cause the troops to think that the defensive positions which they were holding was really not an important one'. Clearly somewhat disenchanted with the decisions of higher command, Blatherwick also writes on the same day

Thirteen men evacuated to Field Ambulances as permanently medically unfit. Several of these men have been previously evacuated as unfit for military duties in this part of the country but have simply been sent back to their Regiment again.

At the end of the month, Colonel Pilkington took over command of the brigade, whilst Brigadier-General Ormsby went on leave. As Major Worthington was also going on leave, temporary command of the 6th Manchesters passed to the next most senior officer, Captain Blatherwick.

Until this point, the battalion's stay in Egypt had been most fortunate and there had been no deaths during 1916. However, news soon reached the men that one of their comrades had died in hospital in Alexandria on 1 October. George Gill was one of the drafts of replacements who had arrived in Egypt from Britain, earlier in the year. Aged thirty-eight and originating from the Wigan area, he died of malaria and nephritis.

Another man died a few days later but it was probably many months before his comrades learned of it. Bernard James Nobbs was a pre-war member of the battalion. Born in Wallasey in 1894, he and his parents later lived at 22 Canute Street, Stretford. Nobbs was taken prisoner at Gallipoli on 7 August 1915 and sent to a prisoner of war camp in Turkey. As with many others, he would have been put to work building a railway in Anatolia. The prisoners were kept in extremely harsh conditions and he died on 6 October[4]. The cause of death is unknown but epidemics of malaria and typhoid swept through the camp at around that time.

The weather started to become cold and damp at night and the men on outpost duty were pleased when greatcoats arrived by train early in the month. The Lewis gunners were also pleased when their establishment was increased by the issue of four additional guns during the month. In the middle of October, the battalion moved back to Romani. The battalion's war diary notes that halts were made on the hour and half hour and this allowed the men to rest and the journey was completed without any of the medical difficulties of their original advance. The month also saw the confirmation of the award of the Military Cross to Captain Arthur Norris, RAMC, the battalion's medical officer, for his work at Gallipoli. The citation, published in the *London Gazette* reads,

> *'For conspicuous gallantry and devotion to duty. He tended and dressed the wounded under very heavy fire, displaying great courage and determination. He has done very fine work throughout the campaign.*

From 18 October, a practice firing range was established a couple of miles away from camp. Many of the recently arrived new troops had only just been issued with their permanent rifles and had not yet been able to fire them. The practice 'gave them the opportunity of finding the good and bad points of the rifles with which they would have to fight' (Battalion war diary). It was also possible for the Lewis gunners to get some practice in with their new weapons.

Small drafts of new troops continued to arrive during the month and, on the 24th, the battalion moved to a rest camp on the coast at Mahamdiya for a few days. There was a short parade including rifle inspection each morning, followed by a bathing parade and the men were then free for the rest of the day. Many of the men were granted a day's leave to visit Port Said, some miles to the north west. The holiday was much appreciated by all ranks but, as with all holidays, it was over far too soon and the men were back in camp on the 28th. Orders arrived the same day that the battalion was to prepare for a move back into the desert to Bir-el-Abd, about twenty miles to the east of Romani. This area had been secured by ANZAC forces shortly after the Battle of Romani.

Port Said.

The march took three days and it was not until the morning of 2 November that the battalion took over the defensive positions. These were a series of small garrison posts manned by between fifty and a hundred men. The trenches were very rudimentary with little cover from either the sun or from enemy aircraft. Work to improve them started next day, with the men working for four hours each day. On the

5th, an enemy aircraft flew over the division's positions and dropped several bombs. The second to fall landed in the bivouac area of the 10th Manchesters, killing five soldiers. A fairly large draft of new troops arrived the next day. Amongst the seventy-nine men, were twenty members of the regimental brass band. Bandsmen would normally act as stretcher bearers when in the front line. The war diary has little to report over the following days. Work continued on improving the trench system at the garrison posts and the men started to erect barbed wire defences in front. Fifty-three new soldiers arrived on 19 November. *'These men were all in a very soft condition and quite unfit for desert marching.'*

After the defeat at Romani in August, the Turkish forces had fallen back to El Arish, on the Mediterranean coast of the Sinai peninsula. The British had not followed them to maintain contact but had only gradually moved forward, extending the railway from Romani to use as a supply route into the peninsula and, later, into Palestine. Another move was now ordered to El Mazar, about another twenty-five miles to the east.

Stanley Cooke, who had joined the battalion at Gallipoli in August 1915, had only

Turkish troops on exercise at El Arish.

made brief notes in his diary for several months but described the arrival at El Mazar during the afternoon of 24 November:

> *Arrive about 3pm, then D Company take up outpost about two miles further on. No rations up and none issued, but have a little bread and Machonochie. No fires or light allowed after dark. This is the furthest east the infantry have been so far. Bitterly cold night and only one blanket as greatcoats and second blanket not come up yet.*

D Company had deployed on the right of the outpost line. B Company took up the centre positions with A to their left. C Company and battalion headquarters remained at El Mazar. The march had gone well and even the men who had newly arrived from Britain and had had next to no desert experience were praised for their determination. They were soon all put to work digging trenches.

After a couple of days, the battalion moved forward again to take up defensive positions, ready to protect the military personnel and civilian workers pushing the vital railway eastwards. A signal station was established by 127 Brigade on Hill 133, protected by a small party of men from the battalion, under the command of Corporal Phillips. It was a valuable observation point and the mosque, at the Turkish held El Arish, could just be made out in the distance and Turkish patrols could be observed much nearer. Enemy aircraft continued their reconnaissance missions and the Turks would have been well aware of the progress of the railway construction and would have felt secure in the knowledge that, although an attack by British and Dominion forces was inevitable, it would not be imminent.

By the 17 December, preliminary arrangements were made for the final moves forward. Some of the difficulties in planning are highlighted by the conflicting information that was received from spies about Turkish strength at El Arish. It meant that two plans had to be drawn up.

> *One agent staked his reputation that Masaid and El*

Arish were only held by a force of less than 2,000 men and that El Arish was being evacuated. In this case, 127 Brigade …was to be ready to advance on ten minutes notice at any time and follow up the retreating enemy force. The second agent also staked his reputation that there were already 15,000 troops in El Arish, with many big guns and that reinforcements were arriving daily. In this case, a steady advance by 42nd and 52nd Divisions seemed probable. (Battalion war diary)

On 19 December, the men were ordered to bring their non-essential kit to a dump near the railway, so that they would have little to carry in the forthcoming advance. Second Lieutenant L E Back noted in his pocket book[5] that he had taken his haversack, greatcoat and spare blanket. Apart from his rifle and ammunition, he would take with him an oil sheet, mess tin, cutlery, iron rations and one day's ordinary rations. He reminded himself to carry a field dressing and an ampoule of morphine in his tunic pocket.

The Battalion war diary, 20 December 1916 records *'Great enthusiasm prevailed amongst all ranks in anticipation of an advance the following morning against enemy positions'*. In the event, the enthusiasm came to nothing. News came on the morning of the 21st, that the Turks had abandoned their positions and retreated without a shot being fired. Mounted troops attached to 52nd Division occupied El Arish whilst 42nd Division returned to El Mazar. They were back in time for Christmas.

All assemble at dinner and have a great feed. Play rugby in afternoon for battalion team against 5th Manchesters and got a slating. Have turkey and plum pudding at night and listen to concert. (Lance Corporal Stanley Cooke)

The concert that Cooke attended was not as elaborate as that staged by the original Pierrot Troupe two years before. Few, if any, of those performers were still with the battalion but a tradition had been maintained of a group entertaining their comrades and there had been a number of informal sing-songs and recitals in the desert, during the previous months. Two men had been the leading lights in organising the Christmas event. Sergeant 'Tickie' Evans, D Company, was described as being 'Choirmaster, Stage-Manager and Welshman'. Private William Tranter[6], A Company, had written the words for many of the songs – sung to the tunes of well

PASSED BY CENSOR.

SONGS OF THE SIXTH

BY

Pte. WILLIAM TRANTER, 1767.

"A" COY., 1/6th BATT., MANCHESTER REGT.

EGYPT.

ALEXANDRIA:
WHITEHEAD, MORRIS & COY. (EGYPT) LTD.
1917.

known songs but parodying well known members of the battalion and events in army life. He had arranged for them to be printed into a booklet for the audience and had dedicated it to Colonel Pilkington 'whose geniality and general popularity has been the mainspring of many desert sing-songs'. It was entitled *Songs of the Sixth* and there was none more topical than this example:

KEEP THE YULE LOG BURNING
(Tune: Keep the Home Fires Burning)

We had marched o'er miles of sand-dunes, for the last six months or so
With a patience monumental for we marched to meet the foe.
Oh, the killing kilometres, from Kantara to Arish
And to then be told to come straight back, the Turks were all "mafish"

We'd no campfire burning, to "drum up" we were yearning
Just a single blanket; frozen to the bone.
But we've all forgotten, times we thought so rotten
We've had a Christmas dinner just like they've had at home.

Oh, the Forty-second gathered, for the last and final crash
And with horse and foot and gunners there, we waited for the dash
We had drawn our extra "bully", and were ready for the fray
And we lay and slept and shivered, waiting for the dawn of day.

Hearts with bravery burning, every rumour learning
Talking of "Right Parry" in an undertone
When the dawn had broken, soon the news was broken
"Cobbers pinched El Arish, while we had dreamed of home."

We were very glad to hear it, for we longed to see the place
We had marched so many miles and much peril had to face
But the order was to "Imshi" back about ten miles or so
While the Jocks came up with pipes and drums to finish up the show

Keep the Yule log burning, soon we'll be returning
And we'll see El Arish 'ere we cross the foam
That is what the "gag" is, they can eat their haggis
When the New Year dawns that sees all the boys come home.

Private Jack Martin had spent Christmas at sea. He had landed at Gallipoli in May 1915 but had been wounded and, after treatment in Egypt, returned to Britain to recover. Fully fit once more, he left camp at Oswestry on 20 December and subsequently boarded the troopship *Ivernia* which was taking a large draft of replacement troops

Troopship *Ivernia.*

back to Alexandria. It had been a good voyage, stopping at Marseilles on the 28th, before continuing across the Mediterranean. Just after 10am on 1 January 1917, the ship was torpedoed by German submarine U47, whilst she was sailing off the coast of Greece. Martin later wrote to his wife telling what had happened[7]:

> *There were some awful scenes. We got the first boat away alright and then hauled the ropes up again to hook on to the other boat. This we managed to do and when the boat was full of men, we began to lower away and, just as the boat got halfway down, one of the ropes snapped and threw all the men into the water; the other rope then broke and the boat fell in the water upside down and buried the poor men under it and the poor men were drowned because they could not get up. The cries were awful and, to make matters worse, some of them got badly cut with the propellers.*

The ship sank within an hour with the loss of thirty-four crew members and eighty-four troops. Jack Martin jumped overboard and managed to reach one of the life rafts and, after about thirty minutes, was rescued by another ship. He spent nine days recovering on Crete before travelling to Alexandria to rejoin the battalion. Concluding the letter to his wife, he wrote

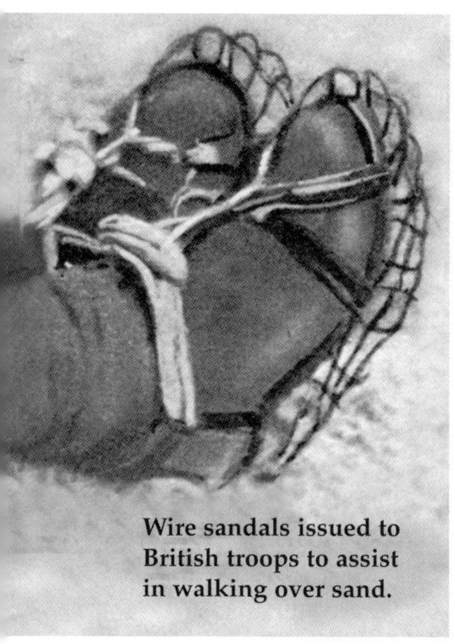
Wire sandals issued to British troops to assist in walking over sand.

> *I wonder what is going to happen next? Wounded twice at the Dardanelles; then later five operations for septic poisoning; nearly killed at Port Said and now torpedoed…Whatever else you do, don't go sailing while I am away."*

The first two weeks of the new year saw unseasonably cold and wet weather but the Manchesters continued with some training exercises which were not too taxing on the men. There was a problem of men reporting for medical attention suffering with septic sores. As many as ninety each day were seeing the medical officer for clean dressings. Other than this, the men's health was good. On 16 January 1917, the brigade marched towards new positions at El Bittia. Many of the men had been issued with wire sandals designed for walking across the sand.

> *These sandals proved very useful on really soft sand but whenever the sand is moist or inclined to be hard, they are of no use at all. As the wire road which extends from Mazar to Kilo 128 was reached about ½ hour after starting, the brigade was halted in order to allow men to take off their wire sandals which were, of course, useless on the wire road.* (Battalion war diary)

After camping overnight, the Manchesters reached El Bittia at about 2pm on the afternoon of the 17th. It was to be a pleasant move. As their positions were only two miles from the sea, it was possible for there to be regular bathing parades. The medical officer hoped this might help to alleviate the problem with septic sores. The number of men reporting daily for attention had now risen to over one hundred and there seemed to be no obvious cause. Within a few days, the problem started to disappear as quickly as it had started. On the 22nd, the men moved forward again, reaching El Arish later in the day. The area was now completely secure from Turkish attack and the battalion formed a general reserve of troops. Their stay would not be for long as news arrived that 42nd Division must now prepare to leave Egypt to enter a new theatre of war.

> *Battalion drill for an hour and speech by Blatherwick in which he tells us it is 10 to 1 we are bound for France.* (Lance Corporal Stanley Cooke)

Cooke also noted that his comrade, Walter Fiddes, was lucky to be alive. On 30 January, two enemy planes flew over El Arish, dropping eight bombs. One landed directly on Fiddes' bivouac – he had just left it to go on guard and escaped injury.

The closing days of January had been a busy time for Billy Warburton. A colour sergeant in 1914, he was one of a handful who had never left the Battalion to recover from illness or injury. Warburton had recently been promoted to the rank of Lieutenant and to the role of battalion quartermaster. Stores, equipment and surplus baggage had to be packed away and brought to a dump at the railhead and much of the responsibility for organising this fell to him. The troops started their move during the morning of 1 February when their train left for Kantara, which they reached by the evening. Further moves took them to El Ferdan and Moascar.

Although rumours were rife, the men still did not know exactly where they were heading but Stanley Cooke noted that on 8 February, they handed in their khaki drill uniforms and were issued with serge uniforms. It was, he believed, the confirmation that they were leaving Egypt for a colder climate and that Captain Blatherwick must have been right about France. While at Moascar, the men underwent some 'smartening up' drill and there were also specialist exercises for snipers, machine gunners and signallers. A separate specialist grenade platoon was formed and attached to D Company. There was some time for relaxation and, on the 14th, the battalion football team played a match against the 3rd Ghurkha Rifles. The Manchesters were soundly beaten by four goals to one.

The whole Division paraded on the 17th for an inspection by General Dobell, commanding the Eastern Forces in Egypt. Another parade, this time in front of the Commander in Chief of the Egyptian Expeditionary Force, took place on the 20th. Formalities over, there was little to do for the next week. At 9pm on 28 February, the battalion paraded for a final time in Egypt and then marched to the station. The train delivered them to the docks at Alexandria by early the next morning. Once again, they were at almost full strength – twenty-nine officers and 889 other ranks.

---

1 Frank Stretch is believed to have been born in the South Manchester area in 1892 and to have married Louise Curbishley at St Mary's Church, Cheadle, in 1920.

2 Born in Knutsford, Cheshire in 1887. Educated at Rugby School and later worked for cotton manufacturer, Robert Pullar & Sons. Joined the battalion in 1909. He was Mentioned in Despatches for his good work whilst in Egypt.

3 General Officer Commanding

4 After the war, the bodies of prisoners who had died in Anatolia were disinterred and reburied by the War Graves Commission at a cemetery in Baghdad. Nobbs is commemorated on the Stretford War Memorial.

5 The pocket book is held by the Regimental Archives

6 Tranter was a pre-war Territorial, living at 41 Temple Square, Cheetham, Manchester. He later served with the Army Service Corps and was invalided home in March 1918, suffering from fever. He returned to civilian life on 27 February 1919.

7 A transcript of Martin's letter is held by the Regimental Archives. Attempts have been made to contact the copyright holder without success.

Chapter 6

FRANCE and BELGIUM

WHEN THE BATTALION had been mobilised for overseas service in August 1914, many of the men hoped they would be going to France, where they felt the 'real war' was taking place. Instead the steamship *Corsican* had taken them from Southampton to Alexandria. Now *Corsican* was waiting for them again and, this time, they were bound for France at last. Embarkation was completed by 12.30pm on 1 March 1917 and the ship left the quay a few hours later. The night was spent at a mooring in the harbour but, by 8.30am, *Corsican* was under way, with an escort of two destroyers.

It was an uneventful voyage and the ship docked at Marseilles during the morning of the 9th. However, it was not until the evening that the men disembarked and joined the train waiting nearby. It was a slow journey, with many long halts, until they reached their destination. Pont-Remy was a small village some miles behind the front line of the Somme sector, with an imposing railway station. It started to rain heavily and the men soon found the area around the station deep in mud. It was something they

Pont Remy railway station front.

Pont-Remy railway station.

were going to have to get used to. They were served a welcome cup of tea and then moved off to billets at nearby Citerne. The men were accommodated in barns and other farm outbuildings. The officers had more luxurious billets provided by Monsieur Tagoux, the Mayor.

After being cooped up on the boat and train, the men were in need of some exercise and short marches were planned for the following days and, from 16 March, a training area was set up north of the village. This provided opportunities for bayonet practice and grenade throwing. There was also some new equipment:

> *The short Lee-Enfield rifle displaced the longer rifle with which the division had been armed; and the issue of two strange items, the 'tin hat' and the box respirator, provoked some hilarity.* (Divisional history)

Also on the 16th, approval was given for home leave for twenty-four men – none of whom had any leave since going overseas in September 1914. Their orders arrived at 9am and, within thirty minutes, the selected men were packed and on their way to the station at Pont Remy.

The battalion got its first opportunity since arriving in France for hot baths, the men marching to Oisemont on the 19th and 20th. In the middle of the month, half the battalion strength went to Pont Remy for several days instruction at the Musketry School. The course was said to be appreciated by all ranks, as they had been issued with the new rifles, but it was hard work, spending five hours a day on the firing ranges for six days. Their training and practice in Egypt had been for shooting over

Left and below: The Long Lee-Enfield equipped the Territorials until superceded by the Short Lee-Enfield MkIII.

long distances but there was the opportunity to practice short-range firing which would be the norm once they were in the trenches. The training was over at the end of the month and the battalion moved to Chuignes, some twenty kilometres east of the city of Amiens.

For many months, the Germans had been constructing a new heavily fortified line of defences well to the rear of the front occupied at the end of 1916. It was known to the British as the Hindenberg Line. The Germans started to gradually withdraw behind it from February 1917. As they did so, they laid waste to what had still been occupied French villages and flourishing farmland. Roads were destroyed as were their original defences. While the Manchesters were based at Chuignes, the men undertook daily working parties building and repairing the damaged roads or collecting and processing any military salvage they could find. It took them some time to acclimatise to the new conditions. After the heat of Egypt, they now had to cope with rain or snow on a daily basis.

A draft of new troops arrived on 8 April and the battalion war diary notes that, almost inevitably with recent drafts, some of the men were those who had previously been evacuated away as medically unfit. There was also the opportunity for specialist training during this part of the month and groups of men went to grenade and musketry schools. Second Lieutenant Frank Benton[1] and Lance Corporal Harold Williams received praise after their attendance at the Telescopic Sight School. Presumably the telescopic sight will have enhanced their sniping skills.

On the 10th, Second Lieutenant Whitamore took thirty-one men on what would prove to be something of a tiring and irritating wild goose chase. They were detailed to provide a working party for the Railway Transport Officer (RTO) at Warfusee but, after marching twelve miles to get there, they were told that not only were they not

Unknown 6th Battalion man who wears what appears to be the ribbon of the Military Medal.
Neil Drum

expected but that an RTO had never been based there. Whitamore was told that it was probably a Railhead Supply Officer (RSO) who had requested the working party. After some further delay, he established that an RSO had been at Warfusee until ten days before, but was now at La Flaque. He marched them off there and, eventually, they were put to work. A note was made in the battalion war diary that unnecessary fatigue had been caused to the men and this will have been seen by higher command.

Orders arrived, on 21 April: the battalion was to move to Herbecourt for a week's general training in trench warfare, prior to it going into the front line. However, this was cancelled within a few hours and the men returned to road building duties for a few days. New orders to move forward finally arrived and the men would get their training 'on the job', as their new positions were in the support trenches near the village of Saulcourt. They arrived there during the night of 27/28 April and spent the next day making final preparations to go into the line.

During the next night, C Company, under Captain J Gatenby, took up an outpost line in roughly made trenches west of Canal Wood. To their rear, B Company, commanded by Captain J R Bennett, was in the main line of resistance should there be a German attack. They had immediate support from A Company, with D being held in reserve. The battalion's strength was thirty-one officers and 720 other ranks. They spent a quiet day and night until 6am, on the 30th, when they spotted their first Germans some distance away in Ossus Wood.

The opening day of May 1917 saw the Manchesters come under an enemy bombardment for the first time. Lieutenant Richard Mawson and his men in No. 9 Platoon were holding a small trench near Red Ruin Farm. The shelling became so heavy that they left the usual safety of the trench and took up positions in shell holes in front of the position, just into No Man's Land. One man was badly wounded. This was probably Private Harry Blears who is recorded as having died on 4 May, of wounds received in action. He was twenty-two.

The battalion's first brief tour of duty on the Western Front came to an end during that evening when they were relieved by the 8th Battalion and went back to billets described in the war diary as 'any rough cover which could be found amongst ruined cellars and houses'. At about the same time the brigadier, General Ormsby came near to the front line on a reconnaissance mission and was hit by a piece of shrapnel from an exploding shell. He was taken to the nearby dressing station but died soon after. Vincent Ormsby was buried the next day in the civilian cemetery at Villers-Faucon. He was fifty-one. Four of the battalion's officers and ten other ranks attended the funeral.

On the night of 5/6 May, the men moved forward to relieve the 8th Battalion. As they were settling into the trenches, news came that Regimental Sergeant Major James Farthing, who had been attached to the battalion from the Shropshire Light Infantry had been awarded the Distinguished Conduct Medal for 'conspicuous devotion to duty'. The tour of duty in the trenches was uneventful. There was some enemy shelling and periodic bursts of machine-gun fire but there were no casualties. The night of 7/8 May was miserable. It rained heavily, flooding the trenches which became deep in mud. The next night, they were relieved back to billets in Saulcourt where, over the coming days, they undertook various working parties.

> *Stayed at Saulcourt all morning and Lieutenant Cadman had us on fatigues but, as he is quite 'potty', we had a good laugh.* (Lance Corporal Stanley Cooke)

When not on fatigues, there was little to do except check their equipment, repair clothing and undertake some fairly minimal training in platoons. The weather was fine and the men enjoyed the late spring sun. They were doubly fortunate in that they experienced no enemy shelling during this period. A small draft of new troops arrived on 14 May. It included Sergeant Robert Darbyshire who had left training camp at Ripon on 25 April[2]. He kept a diary in 1917 which is now held by the Regimental Archives. On arrival, he was posted to A Company: '...reported to CSM Kent who was a corporal when he left Southport and, of course, we had a few high words and cursed each other. Was then posted to No. 7 Platoon'.

On 19 May, the battalion moved to a new sector, taking over positions at Havrincourt Wood, about fourteen kilometres south west of the town of Cambrai. The war diary notes,

> *The trenches required a great deal of work on them, being badly cut, not drained and lacking in cover. The wiring in front of the trenches was also very weak and it was obvious that a lot of work would be required.*

Once it was dark, a patrol went out into No Man's Land to reconnoitre the immediate area but found nothing of interest. The first night in the trenches was quiet except for occasional bursts of machine-gun fire hitting the parapet. Private Percy Jackson[3]:

> *We took over our new area at night; passing over a log track through Havrincourt Wood. It was thick, extensive, full of tangled growth and beautiful 'rides'. The trenches lay forward of it just over a rise, whence a gentle declivity descended to the German lines. Our own trenches were newly formed; much of the front line remained to be dug for the division we relieved had followed up a German retreat that left ground to be entrenched. Everything was new; even the distance to the German lines unknown. Bullet wounds*

Unknown 6th Battalion man.
Neil Drum

were plentiful, but shelling was light. That night a number of us lay 200 yards in front of our line while the rest of the battalion dug the trenches under cover of our screen. Everything was quiet; there were no casualties and, after the colonel's inspection of the lines just prior to dawn, the screen was withdrawn and ordinary trench routine installed.

The men rested and tried to sleep during the day and worked on improving the trenches at night. Several patrols went out under the protection of the darkness and, late on the 21st, one had made its way about 300 yards from the British front line when it was surprised by a German patrol of about seven men. There was only five yards between them but the Manchesters quickly opened fire and made their escape.

Sergeant Robert Darbyshire was just starting out on a patrol when he came across the same group making their way back to the British line:

Teeming with rain, I was accompanied with three steady privates and we crossed over our front line trench, 400 yards to the right of my Company. I met a sergeant and his men returning from off patrol and he informed me that he had accountered [sic] *Johnnies and they were about 15 strong. So I decided not to go too far and to keep in touch with our line. Well, we returned at 3.30am, wet through to the skin and our clothes badly torn with the wire. It was a pitch dark night. Whilst we were out, we spotted the Bosh* [sic] *patrol.*

As they encountered more of the enemy, even if from a distance, the patrols started to be able to identify the approximate positions of the German lines. From sounds they heard, one patrol was able to confirm that a light railway was bringing supplies to the German positions and that horse-drawn transport was bringing up and depositing heavy material of some sort, possibly ammunition supplies.

Towards the end of the month, a strong fighting patrol was sent out, under the command of Lieutenant Stanley Bridgford, with orders to get very close to the German positions to investigate the railway. They were to be prepared to engage the enemy if challenged. With Bridgford's men from C Company were three of the battalion scouts. Percy Jackson was one of the scouts and it is probably this incident he described in his later account:

We began to crawl slowly along the German wire, parallel with it. There was a moon due up, but the clouds had so far obscured it. Just as we came to a small hillock, it burst from behind the clouds and flooded the country with light. We lay still and waited; a

German's bayonet gleamed from the trench, where his rifle lay pointed over the parapet – a sentry post. But the most thrilling thing of all was the sight we had of a road through a gap between two low hills behind the enemy lines. We could see guns and transports passing across the moonlit stretch; we could see men moving up and down, groups of them stopping and talking just as we did when moving behind our own lines. It was a glimpse of a forbidden land.

Suddenly, my pal touched my arm; we wriggled close together; he stretched his hand on the ground and slowly turned it to the right. Following it with a slow movement of the head, I saw shadowy figures between us and the moon – ten, fifteen, twenty, forty, fifty – we counted. They moved slowly towards our trenches. We followed them, hoping we could send some kind of warning to our own line. We followed them to within 100 yards of our trenches and were almost on the bank of the sunken road flanking us to the left when a Verey light threw us into silhouette. We had been seen, not by the patrol, but by a covering party to the patrol, who opened fire wildly on the spot we occupied. They must have formed the opinion that we were a large force attempting to cut them off. A signal sounded and the patrol retreated away to the right.

Then, for some minutes we lay, our hearts panting wildly while bullets thudded into the bank of the sunken road. They sang over us in a continuous volley, and we gauged the numbers of rifles as being about twenty.

The Manchesters had to lie still, hidden in the long grass that covered the area, until the British machine gunners opened a barrage on the German positions, allowing the patrol to crawl back to the safety of the trench. Lance Corporal Stanley Cooke:

At 10pm, Chatwood and I take gun over to C Company in the firing line to take place of a platoon which is out doing patrol work. Come back about 12.30am and find Mitchell[4] *lying in road badly wounded by a minenwerfer of which a lot had come over. He died about half an hour later."*

As Bridgford's patrol had not been successful, a further group was sent out during the late evening of 31 May. This time No. 10 Platoon, commanded by Second Lieutenant Richard Mawson would try to gain the necessary intelligence about the light railway. They left the British lines at 10.50 and made their way about 200 yards across No Man's Land. The British artillery and machine gunners were laying down a protective barrage just in front of them. This lifted to another point on the German defences and it allowed Mawson and his men to make a quick advance. While they were waiting for another lifting of the barrage, an enemy spotlight caught them and the German machine gunners opened fire, killing one man outright[5] and wounding two more. The British artillery lifted its barrage onto the machine gunners' positions and this allowed Mawson to lead his men forward. They were able to identify the exact position and nature of the railway and reported back. It is not recorded to what military use this information was put and it has to be hoped it was worth the deaths and injuries.

The beginning of June was spent in reserve positions and the men undertook working parties. Stanley Cooke wrote in his diary that there was heavy shelling in the morning of 1 June, which killed Private Bernard Buckley and mortally wounded Claude Carhart. He had paraded at 8.30am with about forty others and they were detailed to carry wire up to the front line. About 100 yards behind the support trench, they came under fire from enemy artillery, machine guns and rifles. They fell flat as they could, and had to wait for thirty minutes until Lieutenant Maule managed to secure orders authorising a withdrawal. The wire was left where they had dropped it.

The next day, Cooke[6] recorded that the shells dropped round their positions all morning. 'Poor Percy Courtman[7] – blown to bits by one about breakfast.' Robert Darbyshire found it pretty much a normal sort of day:

> *Got into the wood at 3am, where tea and rum was awaiting us. There we slept until 9am. Breakfast 10am. Lunch 1.30pm. Then slept again until 5pm. Tea 6pm. Went digging in advanced trench in front of 8th Manchesters. Jerry spotted us and opened machine guns on us, then we dug like hell to get under cover. Two of the 8th Manchesters killed. Returned to wood at 4am.*

For several nights from 7 June, the men of the 6th and 8th Battalions went out into the very wide No Man's Land and dug a new front line trench, some three hundred yards forward of the existing one. The war diary indicates that they were generally untroubled by the Germans during this time. On the night of 8/9 June, Private Arthur Mather became the only serious casualty in this period when he was killed by random machine-gun fire whilst digging. The work was finished by dawn on the 13th and the battalion withdrew to billets at Ruyaulcourt, where they spent the next seven days in reserve.

Lieutenant Richard Hooton Hankinson, aged 21, from Eccles. Buried in Ruyaulcourt Military Cemetery.
Photo of grave: Author.

During the evening of the 20th, the battalion went back into the front line, relieving the 8th Battalion. A number of men were wounded by shellfire during the relief and Corporal Edmund Butterworth[8], B Company, was killed. About 9am the next day, an enemy shell fell directly on the front line trench, killing Lieutenant Richard Hankinson. Sergeant Darbyshire described him being 'blown to pieces'.

Hankinson's personal belongings were sent home to his mother, Edith. They included a crucifix, cigarette case, wristwatch and a notebook of poems. His will left £5 to the 161st Manchester Troop of the Boy Scouts and the remainder of his estate to his mother. He had joined the battalion in Egypt in

Privates George Collins, William Grimshaw and Alfred Simm. Killed together when a shell landed on them. Buried in Ruyaulcourt Military Cemetery. Author

March 1916 and the war diary recorded that by his death the battalion had lost one of the most promising and keen young officers it had ever had.

Stanley Cooke witnessed the deaths of three comrades when a single shell dropped directly into the front line trench on 23 June. George Collins, William Grimshaw and Alfred Simm were killed instantly. They are now buried in adjacent graves at Ruyaulcourt Military Cemetery. Captain Hugh Brierley suffered the same fate the following day and is buried next to them.

The battalion was relieved back to Havrincourt Wood during the evening of the 28th. Almost immediately on arrival, a small party of twenty men was despatched as a working party for the Royal Engineers. Sergeant Robert Darbyshire:

> *Our job with the Engineers was to unload a train of trench stores but before we had been started many minutes, Jerry opened out with heavy shells and blew the train and stores to blazes. I gave the job up as a bad lot; got my men together and returned to the wood without having a casualty.*

The opening days of July saw the battalion being shelled each night, Darbyshire noting that, on the 2nd, 'Jerry shelled our cookers at the other side of the wood, so we got no dinner'. Orders were received that, on the 8th, the whole of 42nd Division would move to a new sector and the battalion remained in the line until the afternoon of that day. Before they moved off, news came that Major Blatherwick,

Private Francis Mahony, aged 27, from Seedley. Killed in action on 4 July. Buried in Ruyaulcourt Military Cemetery. Photo of grave: Author

Captain Molesworth, Second Lieutenant Lewis and Regimental Sergeant Major Farthing had all been honoured by being 'mentioned in despatches' for their work in Egypt. The battalion would be back in this sector the following year.

It was a fairly short march away from the front line and they arrived at a tented camp at Bertincourt at 9pm. Sergeant Robert Darbyshire:

> *Had tea, then a beer and rum issue. Everyone in the place was drunk. Lights should have gone out at 10pm but everyone seemed to be having too good a time. Here I found a spring mattress so I had a fairly decent night's sleep. Johnny Foster and Tommy Clapham[9] most laughable.*

Lieutenant Hugh Vipond, from Moss Side, Manchester. Died 28 July, aged 21. Buried in Achiet-le-Grand Cemetery.
Author

After two nights there, the battalion moved to a more permanent camp area at Achiet-le-Petit. The war diary describes the area assigned to the 6th Manchesters as:

> *The foulest that it had ever taken over. So much so that the Commanding Officer refused to put his troops into the bivouacs allotted. Permission was obtained to re-erect a camp on fresh ground and this was rapidly done and completed in the early afternoon.*

The Manchesters stayed at this camp until 20 August. A programme of training was put in place which, for the first week, was confined to general platoon and company exercises. After that, more specialist training in musketry, bayonet fighting and bomb throwing became the order of the day.

When fighting moved away from an area, the battlefields were searched for equipment that could be salvaged and put to re-use. This cost cutting would have disastrous results on 28 July when two salvaged grenades exploded prematurely during a training session. In the first explosion, the Bombing Officer, Second Lieutenant Hugh Vipond[10] was killed. Twenty minutes later, another explosion mortally wounded Corporal Fred Wilcox[11] and injured four other men less seriously. The war diary notes that Vipond was buried with full military honours the next day. It has nothing to say about Wilcox's burial in the same Cemetery, the following day, but Sergeant Darbyshire noted fifty of his comrades attended the burial.

Many members of the battalion were granted ten days leave to return to Britain, but Robert Darbyshire only got a day off. He went into Amiens where he had a haircut and shampoo, which cost him nearly three francs. A military policeman recommended a café where he could get a good meal for the same price. Darbyshire enjoyed a large lamb chop, two fried eggs, chips, two tomatoes, bread, butter and a beer. He left a contented man.

Sports were organised; a shooting competition was arranged. One of the prizes was carried off by a chum and myself, though there was little credit in this seeing that we had been using our rifles for sniping and scouting work for months, whereas the average Tommy rarely fired his unless an attack matured.

The prize was sixty francs and we repaired to a favourite estaminet and treated our pals after the time-honoured manner. That was the night my pal saw most distinctly two sentries on the gateway of the ruined chateau that lodged us. We had great difficulty in drawing him past before he was thrown into the guard-room. The single sentry became almost annoyed. (Private Percy Jackson)

Their period at rest over, the battalion packed up on 20 August and started a move that would take them to Ypres (now Ieper) in Belgium. A major British offensive had been launched here on 31 July. Intended to break through the German lines, British artillery had pounded the enemy defences for days. As at the Battle of the Somme the previous year, much of the first day's attack was in the hands of the Pals battalions, including those of the Manchester Regiment. Within hours, heavy rain had turned the battlefield to mud and the attack stalled. Attempts were made to renew the offensive over the coming days but the weather conditions prevented any significant progress. A further assault started on 16 August which, after four days of heavy fighting, brought some progress but at a heavy cost in casualties. The battalion and the other units of 42nd Division would provide much needed re-inforcements.

It was a long march which took Robert Darbyshire and his comrades from their rest camp to the railhead that would take them north. It was a hot day and the march over very rough tracks and roads.

Marched out of camp at Achiet-le-Petit in full marching order at 8.30am. Very stiff march. I fell out just over half way. We were marching towards Albert and, altogether, about 500 of the brigade fell out. Two died on the way and one shot himself.

Once at the railway, they were packed forty men to a truck 'in a most cramped uncomfortable position'. After a journey of over thirteen hours, the men arrived at Poperinghe and spent the remainder of the month in camps in the area. A feature of the Ypres battlefield was the German fortification of existing farm buildings into small garrisons and they had also constructed concrete strongpoints. These emplacements sheltered machine gun posts and, in any attack, had to be overcome so that advancing men were not fired on from the rear. The battalion concentrated its training in these days on the tactics of how to overcome such defences.

On 1 September, three companies moved off from camp towards the front line, where they would provide carrying parties for battalions of the Lancashire Fusiliers who were then in the trenches. During the evening of the next day, A Company also went forward, meeting a guide from the Fusiliers at the Menin Gate at 9.30pm. As they were marching along the road to Potijze, a shell dropped amongst them injuring thirteen men in the company headquarters section and in No. 1 Platoon. Privates Thomas Neill and Edward

Transports leaving the battered town of Ypres.

Sykes died from their injuries, later in the evening. It's probable that one of the wounded men was the officer commanding No. 1 Platoon, as Robert Darbyshire noted in his diary that he took over full command of the platoon the next day as there was no officer.

In his article published in *Everyman at War*, Percy Jackson also remembered going into the front line on the Passchendaele Ridge:

> *We went in little groups of five with intervals of more than 100 yards between each two. The Menin Road was a river of mud in which our boots sucked and slipped. Down one side of it came horses, limbers, wagons, ambulance cars, guns – all at full speed. The horses seemed to know they were coming from danger; their hoofs thrashed the mud about us as they flew down to the rear, their drivers sitting solidly, using the whip now and then, and smoking as they drove. Up the other side of the road, a slow procession of vehicles crawled, one behind the other; new guns going up to the positions, ammunition wagons full of shells, ambulances bound for the clearing stations, ration carts for the troops in the front line. Piccadilly could not have been more crowded.*
>
> *As we drew nearer to the Ridge, the howling in the sky grew more fierce. We had to pause while a shell dropped before us; rush on as one hurled down almost on top of us; dive for cover in the slimy ditch."*

Once in the support lines, the Manchesters were able to start work carrying ammunition, rations and other supplies up to the front line. Because this was newly

Private William Carter, from Chorlton-cum-Hardy. Killed in action, aged 20.

captured ground, the trench system had not yet been fully developed and protection from enemy shelling was minimal. What protection there was, came in the form of shell holes; sometimes merged with another hole; sometimes not. All were deep in water and thick with mud. Private Tom Holme, a 19 year old chauffeur from Kendal, did not escape the machine gun bullet which killed him instantly.

Robert Darbyshire lost several friends and comrades on 5 September:

> *Nothing much doing until about noon, when Jerry started to put a barrage on our trench – most awful. Dick Griffiths with his section, nine altogether, got a 5.9 shell to themselves and out of the nine, only two were living when we were able to get to them and one of them had both legs blown off. The other was wounded in forty places. Every bone in Carl Ashley's body was broken. Nick Carter had a hole in his stomach as big as a dinner plate. Dick had the left half of his face and left shoulder and arm blown clean off and was unrecognisable except for the two stripes on his right arm. A more ghastly sight I never saw and don't want to see again. This happened about 1pm and Jerry was still dropping shells into our trench, however the shelling slackened off until about 9pm when he opened out again for fifteen minutes. So, up to our report going in at midnight, we had one officer, two NCOs and about thirty men killed or wounded.*[12]

Dick Griffith's grave at Aeroplane Cemetery, Belgium. Author

At 7.30 the next morning, the battalions of Lancashire Fusiliers in the front line attacked three fortified German positions, known as Borry, Beck House and Iberian Farms. Beck House Farm was captured but a strong German counter-attack later in the morning forced a withdrawal. The attack on the other two positions failed under heavy enemy machine-gun fire. Throughout the day, the Germans continued

6 September 1917. The ground over which the Manchesters carried supplies to the Fusiliers. The buildings to the right and left are in the approximate positions of Borry and Beck House. Iberian Farm was further to the left. Author to re-inforce and counter attack and, by evening, the Fusiliers were almost back where they had started. The carrying parties of Manchesters had continued to bring up supplies and, as the previous day, there were significant casualties from shellfire.

Robert Darbyshire and his platoon had not been assigned carrying duties and were able to stay in the relative safety of the support trenches.

LOCAL WAR NEWS.

Casualties : Kendal.

KILLED IN ACTION.

HOLME, Pte. Tom, Manchester Regt., son of Mr. and Mrs. G. Holme, of 2, Granary Cottages, Kendal, was killed in action on September 2nd. He was struck by a machine gun bullet and died immediately. He was 19 last month and was chauffeur with Mr. R. Rimmer, in Kendal. His officer writes to his parents that he always showed a soldierly spirit and was cheerful under the most trying circumstances.

DIED OF WOUNDS

REED, Pte. Gilbert, King's (Liverpool) Regt., died of wounds on the 5th inst at a casualty clearing station in France. He had been out

At 7.10am, the most terrific barrage opened out, lasting until 2.30pm, being eight hours continual shelling. What a day! Talk about saying your prayers. One burst of shell hit me in five places but none of them hard enough to break the skin. Another shell fell on the top of the trench just over my head, but thank the Lord, which I did, it was a dud and only partly buried me with mud.

Darbyshire and his men had suffered no significant injuries during the day but the shelling started up again about 9pm and, over the next three hours, eight of the platoon were wounded. Perhaps unsurprisingly, he comments in his diary that he'd suffered from almost continual diarrhoea throughout the day.

Lieutenant Colonel Claude Worthington, received a letter on the 8th, from his counterpart commanding the 6th Battalion, Lancashire Fusiliers. Colonel Hammond-Smith expressed his regret at the high level of casualties sustained by the Manchesters whilst attached to his battalion.

Today, I asked for help to bury some of our dead, involving a carry of three-quarters of a mile through the barrage area. Seventy-two of your men volunteered and that speaks for itself. We could not bear to think of burying men in this area where they were bound to be blown up again, otherwise we should not have asked.

The next night, the battalion moved up to relieve the 8th Manchesters at Square Farm, so that the Ardwick battalion could practice for another attempt to capture Beck House and the other nearby strongholds still in German hands. They were, in turn, due to be relieved on the night of 11/12 but, late in the day, orders were received that they were to stay another twenty four hours, as the attack by the 8th Battalion had been cancelled. They spent the time in No Man's Land digging a new assembly trench to be used when the attack finally took place. A party from B Company found a private from the Inniskilling Fusiliers in a shell hole. He was wounded but still alive. The man had been there since an attack a month before[13]. He was safely brought back to the trench and evacuated to hospital. There is no information as to whether he survived. The remainder of the tour of duty was uneventful except that there was heavy enemy shelling from time to time.

After withdrawal from the front line, the battalion spent 14 September urgently digging a small trench between the Menin Road and Cambridge Road, in which telephone cables would be buried. The battalion war diary records that platoons were given a section to dig and it should be regarded as 'piece work' – once they had completed their section, the platoon could fully withdraw to rest billets at Toronto Camp.

James Cain, C Company, lived in Ancoats, Manchester and had been a member of the local Lads' Club. Killed in action on 6 September, aged 21.

This marked the end of the battalion's contribution to the fighting in the Ypres Salient and, on 22 September, it moved by lorry to the much quieter sector on the Belgian coast at Coxyde. In comparison with many other units, the involvement had been brief and the casualties light. Just prior to the move, Colonel Worthington received orders that he would be transferred from the battalion to take command of the 8th Battalion, Duke of Wellington's Regiment[14]. Colonel Wedgwood, commanding that unit, would take over command of the Manchesters. 'This news was received with great regret on the part of all ranks.' (Battalion war diary)

The battalion's billets were at Australia Camp, just to the west of Coxyde. On the opposite side of the road, Canada Camp accommodated the 5th Battalion, whilst the 7th and 8th Battalions were billeted in the town. They found themselves in the same sector as the Regiment's second line battalions. The history of the 2/6th Battalion is dealt with in the next chapter but it can be mentioned here that it had originally formed the reserve training battalion for the 6th Battalion and had been overseas on active service in its own right since the spring of 1917. The four second line battalions of the Manchester Regiment formed 199 Brigade of 66th Division and it is these troops that the first line troops relieved on the night of 24/25 September at Nieuport les Bains, north of Coxyde. In the changeover, there was an opportunity for old friends to meet; for hurried family gatherings and the opportunity to exchange anecdotes about their experiences since they had left Britain. The exchanges were quickly over and the second line territorials were soon on their way to Ypres.

About 100 men did not go north but were detached to work as labourers for the 2nd Australian Tunnelling Company. Although labouring did not carry the dangers of being in the front line, it was not safe work as the men were still well within range of the enemy artillery and, on 25 September, Private Walter Howe, from Farnworth near Bolton, was killed.

Flooded area of Belgium near the coast.

The men were not in the front line during this period and spent much of the time training and undertaking working parties. However, each day, officers took groups of soldiers to the front, so they could see the positions they would soon have to occupy. There was also some time for relaxation. 'Went out on pass to La Panne for the afternoon. Had a very good time. We could see Blighty off the promenade.' (Sergeant Robert Darbyshire)

Private David Morris. Killed in action 3 November. Buried in Coxyde Military Cemetery. Author

The move forward came on 2 October and the battalion took over trenches near the bank of the Yser canal which ran through Nieuport into the English Channel. The enemy positions were on the other side and, during the hours of darkness, Robert Darbyshire led a patrol across to reconnoitre:

We swam the canal, about thirty to forty yards, and crept up to his front line but found that he had evacuated. We then went a little further to the support line and also found that empty. We then decided to return and got across the canal alright and were getting dressed on the canal bank when he started to open out with gas shells and high explosive. We donned our gas masks and, whilst I was waiting, I was struck in the face. Of course, I dropped and when I awoke I found myself being bandaged up by a stretcher bearer out of the artillery. I was carried to our Aid Post and was attended to by a doctor and had my face redressed and had a good tot of rum off the doctor and was

put into a Red Cross ambulance and taken to 2nd Field Ambulance Hospital at Dunkerque.

The 'hospital' at Dunkerque was the main dressing station for 42nd Division and, after his wounds were examined there, he was taken to the well-equipped medical facility of one of the nearby field hospitals (casualty clearing stations). Here, his injuries were X-rayed and the shrapnel removed from his face. Robert Darbyshire was then evacuated back to hospital in Britain. He was discharged from the army on 3 March 1919, but it is not known if he was ever fit enough to return to duty before then.

Two days later, the battalion was relieved back to La Panne where the men spent several days training on the beach and amongst the sand dunes. During the period, five men received notification that they were to be awarded the Military Medal for their action near Ypres. They were Corporal Harry Maskell, Lance Corporal Edward Atherton and Privates Walter Farrand, Harold Jarvis and John Jones. This was the second time that Maskell had been considered for a gallantry award. He was an original member of the battalion, one of the Disley lacrosse players, and, in the closing months of the Gallipoli campaign, had dashed from the safety of the trench, although there was heavy shelling, to rescue Harold Richardson after he had been hit by shrapnel. There is no record that he was awarded a medal for his earlier bravery.

When not training, the men formed working parties for the Royal Engineers at Nieuport and, on the 19th, those who had been attached to the Australian tunnelling company rejoined the battalion. The following day, the men not on attachment to the Engineers marched to Nieuport where they took over the reserve positions behind the front line. Even here, fatigue parties continued with a hundred men working from just after midnight on the 21st to 5am, carrying cement and other materials for the

Drawing water from a well and filling petrol cans.

Engineers who were building a dam across the Yser River.

Over the coming days, enemy artillery shelling intensified and, on the 23rd, was successful in knocking out three bridges crossing the river. It was an arduous night for 150 of the men during the early hours of the 25th. They spent it carrying petrol cans, full of water, from the main supply dump to a position known as Tank House, where an emergency reserve was to be kept in case the shelling destroyed the piped supplies. The following evening, the battalion took over a sector of the front and support lines, relieving the 8th Battalion.

> *No trench line exists in either of these lines, the only protection being a badly battered breastwork with small concrete dugouts for use by day. The country surrounding these lines is badly broken up by shell holes and is also to a large extent under water and the approaches from the river are badly broken up and very exposed to the enemy's lines by day." (Battalion war diary)*

Almost immediately, Second Lieutenant Stuart Watson went out with a patrol of four men to reconnoitre the nearby area. They came up against deep entanglements of enemy barbed wire and, before they could creep away, came under grenade attack from a German sentry post. They made their escape without significant injuries – only Watson sustaining a minor wound.

The next night, another patrol into No Man's Land was able to search the body of a German who had been shot on the 24th. From evidence found, they were able to establish that it was the 14th Bavarian Regiment opposite them. Much of the remaining two days of the tour of duty was spent seeking what little protection could be found from the heavy enemy shellfire. However, the Manchesters were not the main target of the German infantry and they were fortunate to return to the reserve positions having suffered only one fatality – twenty-two year old James Hayward.

Private Arthur Haywood, from Levenshulme. Died of wounds, aged 23, on 8 November, whilst being treated at a field hospital at Zuydcoote. He is buried in the nearby military cemetery. He had worked for the family firm of Welcher & Heywood at Manchester's Smithfield Market.

They returned to the front line on 2 November and, the next day, two men from B Company were killed[15] when the Germans shelled the trench. The following day, another patrol from that company went out to reconnoitre the area. They came under machine-gun fire and so withdrew about one hundred yards, expecting a German patrol to come out to see if there were any casualties who could be captured for interrogation. The Manchesters hid themselves in the hope that they would be able to capture one of the Germans for similar reasons. A German patrol did venture out from their lines but did not come close enough for the men from B Company to take advantage. The war diary notes that *'one man was killed crossing Crowder Bridge in the afternoon. His body was not discovered until low tide in the evening'*. This was Private John Dearden, twenty-five, from the Blackley district of Manchester. The bridges were narrow affairs, made of duckboards mounted on floats, with no handrails. They would rise and fall several feet with the tide and it is, perhaps, no surprise that a man might slip and not even be missed.

The tour of duty ended during the evening of 6 November and, as they were withdrawing from the front line, Private Henry Johnson, from Cadishead, was also killed[16]. Captain R H Bedford was wounded in the foot by a shell nose cap which fell on his big toe when crossing one of the bridges.

Back in camp at Coxyde, the routine became much as before with training exercises undertaken when the men were not on working parties. On 9 November a small group of ten men joined the battalion. The war diary notes that, whilst these men had originally enlisted into one of the Service Battalions of the Regiment, they had been attached to the Royal Engineers for several months. 'They should prove useful men.'

There had been specific training for the Lewis gunners and, in the middle of the month, the divisional commander and the brigadier visited to watch a demonstration of the machine guns' use during an attack on an enemy strong point. Second Lieutenant Henry Chew commanded the gunners and he had arranged for each member of the team to wear large numbers on their backs so it was easy for the senior officers to follow the various roles.

On 16 November, 42nd Division was relieved from this sector by the French 133rd Division and, over the next three days, a move was made to the village of Lambres, to the northwest of the town of Bethune. Towards the end of the month, another move was made and the battalion went into camp in the grounds of the eighteenth century chateau at Gorre, to the east of the town. Training exercises were undertaken in the mornings, but the afternoons were free for football competitions.

The battalion returned to duty in the trenches on 3 December 1917, marching towards the front line in platoons, with a 300 yard gap between each one so as to avoid the possibility of high casualties if they were shelled. They were in position by 4.30pm and this was the first occasion that they had carried out a relief in daylight. It was found to be much easier than undertaking it in the dark. They found the defences were breastworks, rather than trenches, but they were in good condition and, it was hoped, would afford reasonably good protection. Three companies occupied the front line, whilst D Company took up a position in the support trenches and would undertake carrying all the rations and supplies forward to their comrades. Contact was quickly made with the battalion of Portuguese troops on the left.

A close examination of the defences concluded that there was some considerable work to be done as the breastworks were not bulletproof. Strengthening of the dug-outs was also needed because, as noted in the war diary, somewhat wryly, they were barely 'splinterproof'. The work was urgent as the battalion was coming under some shelling from trench mortars. This did not prevent inspection visits of the front line by the brigade and divisional commanding generals.

Private William Mackenzie, aged 24. Killed in action on 11 December 1917. Buried in Post Office Rifles Cemetery, Festubert, France.

On 9 December, the battalion moved to take up a key defensive role near Givenchy. Their positions were in the support area and, in case of a German attack in this sector, they would be the main counter-attacking force. A and B Companies had billets at Windy Corner and could move forward quickly once the details of an attack were known. D Company provided the garrison for the Givenchy Redoubts and their orders were to hold these posts 'at all costs', so as to form a pocket in any German attack, allowing the enemy to be attacked from its rear.

During the early hours of 11 December, the enemy fired gas shells at the Manchesters' positions. There were many casualties which the war diary attributes to 'insufficient gas discipline' – the men were too slow in putting on their gas masks. Amongst them was twenty-four year old William Mackenzie, originally from Stornoway on the Isle of Lewis, was one of the battalion Lewis gunners. He had trained as a pharmacist in Scotland before moving to Manchester, where he worked for a Mr Lockwood who owned several shops in the area. His officer later wrote to Mr and Mrs Lockwood saying he had been killed at about 2pm. *'He, along with a colleague, was serving his gun when the gun-pit was wrecked. His death was instantaneous. In losing him, we have lost one of our best.'*[17]

The Lewis gunners would continue to have a difficult time throughout the month:

At about 5.40am, an enemy party of about ten or fifteen men surprised our No. 5 Post. One Lewis gun drum was fired into the party when one man was wounded. As the gun could no longer fire from its position it was being moved to a point where it could come into action again when the No. 2, who was carrying it, slipped on the frozen duckboards, fell losing hold of his gun. Before he could recover himself, the enemy had picked up the gun and disappeared. (Battalion war diary, 19 December 1917)

On the 23rd, the battalion was relieved to billets at Beuvry, where they were able to spend their fourth Christmas overseas in some comfort as there were company mess huts. There was an inspection parade for Major General Solly-Flood on the 30th when he presented Military Medal ribbons to a number of men. The year ended with the adjutant undertaking one of his regular censuses of the battalion strength. There were thirty-eight officers and 794 other ranks. Of these, 131 were all that remained of the men who had left Britain in September 1914 and just three of them had had a charmed life, never being evacuated away from the battalion through illness or wounds. One is believed to have been Lieutenant and Quartermaster Billy Warburton, the pre-war colour sergeant.

Their rest over, the men started what would be the final year of the war going into trenches at the village of Cuinchy. The area had seen much fighting in the autumn of 1915 but was now relatively quiet. As usual, as soon as darkness fell, each company sent out small patrols to examine the protective barbed wire in front of the trench system. The positions came under very heavy shelling by trench mortars for several hours on 6 January 1918. There was a considerable amount of damage to the trench system, including the total destruction of about twenty yards of the front line. Several men were buried and Privates J Aldridge, Dennis McCarthy[18] and William Pounder

Royal Engineers repairing a lock on the La Basseee Canal at Cuinchy.

went to their rescue, digging them out. The three were later awarded the Military Medal. The battalion was fortunate to suffer only one fatality. Corporal William Fox, twenty-three, was a pre-war member of the battalion who had landed with his comrades at Gallipoli in 1915 and had been the first man from the unit to be awarded the Military Medal.

In the evening, Lieutenant Sidney Collier left the battalion to join the Royal Flying Corps. He had also seen action at Gallipoli, where he had led teams of bombers and had been awarded the Military Cross for his bravery. Collier was killed in action less than three months later, on 28 March 1918, when he was the observer flying in an RE8

Coming out of the trenches caked in mud these weary-looking soldiers pass a column taking supplies up to the front.

of the 5th Squadron, piloted by Second Lieutenant P Woodhouse. The men were on a reconnaissance mission for the artillery.

During the next tour of duty, the weather changed for the better but the result of the rapid thaw meant that the ground underfoot turned to mud and parts of the trench system again collapsed, necessitating much repair work. The remainder of the month of January continued along very similar lines, with the battalion undertaking tours of duty, interspersed with periods in reserve when they undertook working parties. In the front line, all opportunities were taken to patrol in No Man's Land to check the British wire had not been tampered with. More aggressive patrols went to find German listening posts, usually without success. One patrol, on 21 January, did find a small enemy post and heard movement. They threw over thirty grenades at and around the post but, before they could then investigate, the Germans fired Verey lights and opened fire. The patrol dropped to the ground and had to lay motionless for over half an hour before they could make a safe escape.

At the end of the month, the battalion withdrew to Bethune, where the men had very welcome hot baths. However, there was no clean clothing available so they had to put their very dirty uniforms back on. The whole of February was spent in reserve at first near Oblinghem and, later in the month, near Burbure – both villages to the west of Bethune. The war diary has little to report in this period and it seems to have been a reasonably relaxing time for the men, with the occasional route march and company training exercises. A rugby match was played on the 11th between the battalion's team and a team from the Royal Flying Corps. The RFC won 16 -5. A number of drafts of replacement troops arrived. Some of these new men were newly trained soldiers but a large draft of 200 men came from the 1/9th Battalion, which had been amalgamated with its second line unit. This was part of an army-wide re-organisation brought about by the severe drain on available manpower. All brigades were reorganised and reduced from four to three battalions. The 8th Battalion was the one designated to move from 127 Brigade and the Ardwick men now found themselves in 126 Brigade with the Oldham Territorials of the 10th Battalion and the 5th East Lancashires.

On the 21 February, Regimental Sergeant Major James Farthing left the battalion to return to Britain. He had been its senior warrant officer from the beginning of the war and his leaving was recorded in the war diary:

> *It was a matter for great regret that owing to the strain caused by active service conditions, it was necessary to replace him with a younger man. His service to the unit during the whole of his time with it and the conscientious way in which he performed all duties, whether in the line or not, are beyond praise.*

Company Sergeant Major William Kent was promoted in his place. The story of the 6th Battalion will continue in Chapter 8 but, like RSM Farthing, the reader must now return to Britain.

1 Frank Cyril Benton had joined the battalion the previous month. He survived the war rising to the rank of captain. In the early 1920s, he was living at 91 Dudley Road, Whalley Range, Manchester and is believed to have returned to work at the family firm of C Benton Ltd, 58 Peter Street, Manchester.
2 Darbyshire enlisted into the army on 21 January 1915 and is believed to have undertaken his training with the 2/8th Battalion.
3 First published in the book "Everyman at War", 1930. Jackson served with the battalion from 16 June 1915 until 8 October 1918, when he received a commission with the Lancashire Fusiliers. He survived the final weeks of fighting and returned to civilian life. In 1920, he was living at Rosedene, Windlehurst Road, High Lane, near Stockport.
4 Private F Mitchell, aged 24, from Higher Openshaw, Manchester.
5 Private Harry Barnes, aged 23, from Swinton
6 Stanley Cooke's diary ends around this time. He remained with the battalion until 1918, when he left to train to become an officer. He received his commission as a 2nd Lieutenant, after the armistice, on 2 February 1919 and served with the 28th Battalion, London Regiment (The Artists Rifles) until he returned to civilian life.
7 Percy Courtman was born in 1888 and was a noted international swimmer, winning a bronze medal at the 1912 Olympics for the 400M breaststroke.
8 Butterworth, aged 33, lived in Eccles and worked for Simon, Son & Co, 32 Oxford Street, Manchester
9 Foster – believed to be John Mathie Foster, an employee of C C Dunkerley Ltd, a Manchester firm of iron and steel merchants. Thomas Clapham – an employee of Stadelbauer & Co, 50 Bloom Street, Manchester. Enlisted into the battalion in April 1914 and was wounded later in 1917. Remained under medical treatment until discharged from the army in March 1919. His younger brother, Herbert, also served with the Regiment from the spring of 1917.
10 Vipond had been educated at Bangor College, North Wales and worked as an accountant for Peter Gregson & Co. He had lived with his parents at 44 Barton Street, Moss Side, Manchester. He was 21.
11 The Commonwealth War Graves Commission records Wilcox's death as being 31 July but the battalion war diary confirms the correct date.
12 Corporal Richard Griffiths had worked for Manchester Education Committee, although not as a teacher. Charles Carl Ashley, 23, was the son of a wealthy dress manufacturer, living in Heaton Mersey, near Stockport. The man recorded as "Nick" Carter is Private William Carter, 20, whose parents, William and Isabella, lived at 28 Cavendish Road, Chorlton cum Hardy, Manchester. Born on 10 December 1896, he had been educated at Manchester Grammar School and had enlisted on his 19th birthday.
13 The war diary records that the man had been in No Man's Land since 11 August, although it is more likely that the actual date was 16 August, when two battalions of Inniskilling Fusiliers took part in an attack on Beck House.
14 On 3 October 1918, Claude Worthington was mortally wounded whilst commanding the 5th Battalion, Dorsetshire Regiment. He died at a military hospital on 14 October and is buried at Mont Huon Cemetery, Le Treport.
15 Private William Holt, 19, from Rochdale and believed to have been an employee of Mather & Platt Ltd and Private David Morris, from Moss Side.
16 Johnson is commemorated on the Irlam & Cadishead war memorial
17 As reported in the Highland News, 12 January 1918
18 McCarthy had enlisted into the army in October 1915, going overseas in June 1917. He left the army in January 1919, returning to his home at 44 Bannerman Street, Cheetham, Manchester.

Chapter 7

THE 2/6th BATTALION

WHEN THE 6TH BATTALION left Britain in September 1914, about ten percent of its strength remained behind – men who, for whatever reason, had not volunteered for overseas service. These men now formed the nucleus of a new battalion which would be called the Second Sixth (2/6th Battalion Manchester Regiment). The intent, at least for now, was that the battalion would undertake a dual role. Firstly, it would take over the normal duties of the Territorial Force for home defence and, secondly, it would train new recruits who would join the first line battalion on active service overseas. Formal recruitment for the new unit was announced on 29 September 1914.

At first enlistment was slow. Many men who had not been able to join the first line battalion before it left for Egypt had now joined one of the Regiment's 'Pals' battalions which had started to be formed at the beginning of the month. These were also allowing the 'clerks and warehousemen of the City' to join together and serve together. By 13 October, when they assembled at Southport, the 2/6th Battalion and the equivalent units of the 5th, 7th and 8th Battalions could only muster a total of 700 men:

> *The men will be billeted in the town and are expected to arrive at 5.30. They will march from West Derby to Southport, a distance of about 18 miles. The men have a strenuous day before them. They will rise at 4am and will breakfast at West Derby at 8.30. They continue their march at 9.30 and are due at Scarisbrick at 12.30, where a halt of two hours will be made for dinner. The men will be accompanied by the bands of the 5th, 6th and 7th Battalions.* (Manchester Guardian)

The number of men enlisting did increase and, by 5 November, the *Manchester Evening News* was able to report that only twelve more men were needed to bring the 2/6th up to full strength of around 1,000 soldiers. During the autumn, the battalion and the other East Lancashire second line battalions were formed into the Army's 66th Division and they started to function as a unit, although it was a difficult period with few experienced officers and NCOs.

Lance Corporal Frank Thompson had joined the 6th Battalion before the War and was one of those still in Britain, using his experience to help train the new recruits at Southport. As mentioned in Chapter 3, he maintained a diary in 1915 and it shows him to have been a keen rugby player and a member of the battalion's team. On 27 February 1915, they played a match against a team from HMS *Conway*, a Royal Navy training ship. At halftime, Conway was winning 6 – 0, but the Manchesters made a

Officers of the 2/6th Battalion in the UK. Manchester Regiment Archives

strong comeback to win the game 23 – 6, with Thompson scoring a try. Training continued in the usual army pattern of drill, musketry practice and route marches to build up fitness. On 15 March, the men were scored on their shooting over different distances, including firing five shots within 25 seconds over a distance of 200 yards. Thompson finished top of his Company with 94 points from 100. He had applied to become an officer with one of the Salford 'Pals' battalions of the Lancashire Fusiliers and was invited to attend for an interview on 23 March but his request for a pass was refused. It would have been a wasted journey as, the next day, he received another letter from the Fusiliers, rejecting his application as he was considered too young.

Also this month, another new battalion was formed, the 3/6th, and this would become the main reserve battalion training troops for overseas service. The battalion never served overseas and was merged with other third line units during 1916. Few records of its activities now remain.

There was an inter-battalion rugby match on 27 March between the 2/6th and the 2/10th Battalions. The 2/10th won a resounding victory, 41 – 5, but Thompson points out the 10th Battalion's team contained eight members of the Oldham rugby team, then a leading member of the game's Northern Union.

In mid-April, Thompson was able to return to Salford for a couple of days leave. On the evening of the 15th, he caught the train back to Southport and was back in time for the company 'smoker' at the Scarisbrick Hotel, on the town's Lord Street. Smokers were usually informal social events where the men would provide their own entertainment but, this evening, there were a number of professional acts from the Pavilion on the pier and the Palladium Theatre, also on Lord Street. The next night, the battalion practised a night attack until 3am. There was another similar exercise on 22 April.

Overnight on 15/16 May, the battalion moved to camp at Crowborough in Sussex. 'Camp arrangements nearly perfect. Hot and cold baths and showers. Not allowed out of camp. Wrote to mother.' (Lance Corporal Frank Thompson).

The men had had a fairly easy time at Southport but this was soon put behind them. On 19 May, they went on a 14 mile march. 'Very tired. Hills terrible.' Over the following two days, they constantly practised attacks. On the 22nd, Thompson records 'Huts cleared out for Brigade Major inspection. Scrubbed floors, bed planks, etc. He didn't turn up'. The final days of the month were spent on route marches, attack practices or, again, preparing for inspections.

On 1 June, the first draft of men left to go overseas to join the first line battalion at Gallipoli and Thompson was notified that he would be in the second draft. He was allowed a few days home leave, before returning to Crowborough for final training. He celebrated his 21st birthday on 28 June, receiving a number of presents from family. Two days later, Thompson and sixty-one other men drew sun helmets and other stores and paraded to march to the local railway station. The train took them to Devonport where, on 4 July, they set sail for Gallipoli. As recorded in Chapter 3, Thompson and his comrades disembarked at Cape Helles 23rd July. On 7 August, he was killed in action.

There are only scant records of the battalion's activities for the remainder of 1915 and most of 1916. Men would arrive after initial training with the 3/6th Battalion, to be made ready for active service and then be sent overseas to the first line unit at Gallipoli and, from early 1916, Egypt. Also in early 1916, the battalion and the remainder of 66th Division assumed responsibility for guarding the south east coast and were based around Colchester. As the year progressed, it was decided that the division would, in due course, go on active service in its own right. However, the constant demands for replacement troops by the frontline units meant that their own ability to become battle-ready continued to be hampered. It was only towards the end of the year that a period of relative peace in Egypt reduced the need for drafts to be sent and the second line units could concentrate on their own needs. By January 1917, the division was declared ready for active service and, on 3 March, an advance party of three officers and seventy-eight other ranks left camp for Boulogne. The remainder of the battalion followed two days later and, from this point, a war diary of activities was maintained[1].

There was to be no gentle introduction to the war for Captain John Haworth Whitworth, commanding B Company. He had written to his wife, Ida, just after arriving and, on the 10th, wrote again, as quoted in his biography[2]:

> *Things have moved somewhat since I last wrote to you. Yesterday morning, forty men per company and a number of officers, including myself, were put on motor lorries and rushed to the firing line. Last night, we spent in the support line – nothing of incident has happened so far.*

Born on 26 September 1879 at Alderley Edge, Whitworth had lived in Bowden,

Captain John Haworth Whitworth.

Cheshire, for a number of years and practised as a barrister in Manchester. He may have been a Quaker as his marriage to Ida King, in 1913, had been conducted at the Friends Meeting House in Ulverston. He joined the Manchester University Officer Training Corps on 10 September 1914 and, by the end of the following month, had received his commission and immediate promotion to the rank of Captain.

Private Walter Greenhalgh[3], serving in 13 Platoon, D Company, had also been to the front line with his comrades. They spent two days attached to the 16th Battalion, Royal Warwickshire Regiment being instructed in trench warfare. The instruction for the whole battalion was completed in a few days and, by 16 March, they were in billets near the French town of Bethune where Greenhalgh spent the evening gambling at Crown & Anchor and other games. He was not successful and seems to have lost all his money as, recounting the march away from the battalion's first tour of duty in the front line, he writes 'Utterly exhausted. No money. Fred Lee bought me a basin of coffee at an estaminet'.

The next tour of duty started during the evening of 31 March. The men were in a front line trench known as 'Old Boots', near the village of Cambrin. It rained heavily and the water was quite deep in the bottom of the trench. Walter Greenhalgh records an unusual and unsettling encounter with his company commander:

> *On Stand To at night, as I stood back to let Captain Blayney[4] pass, he snatched my rifle and passed it to his runner, Dixon, who was already carrying four or five rifles. After "stand down", Corporal Hartley and six of us whose rifles had been pinched were summoned to Company HQ dugout and lectured by a maudlin Blayney. All Company officers appeared to be "tight", except Oughtred[5], who watched these proceedings very miserably it seemed to me.*

On 4 April, the battalion was relieved from the front line. Two companies moved back to the support line acting as a reserve unit for the 2/7th Battalion. The other two companies withdrew into the reserve at Cambrin. The next day, they suffered their first fatality. A party was out in No Man's Land during the night, improving the barbed wire defences and Private Benjamin Kay was killed, most probably by random enemy fire.

The Battalion's first fatality. Private Benjamin Kay, a 31 year old married man from Blackpool, was killed on 5 April and is buried in Vermelles British Cemetery. Author

The area in which the Manchesters found themselves had been hard fought over in the autumn of 1915 but, by 1917, it had become a quiet sector, neglected by both sides, its landscape dominated by slag heaps from the nearby coal mines. To the north, Ypres continued to be a major battle area and, to the south, there had been many casualties during the Battle of the Somme. When they were not holding the front line, the men undertook working parties to improve the trench systems, which had been damaged by shellfire over the many months of fighting.

In an account written many years after the war, Private P R Hall[6] recounted that the working parties were much troubled by a German sniper hidden in No Man's Land. Hall had volunteered for the army in 1915 but was not called-up until after his 18th birthday in 1916. He was a good shot, although not yet one of the battalion's recognised snipers. Hall says that Captain Blayney asked him to try and deal with the German. Using binoculars, he identified a slight rise in No Man's Land where the German might be hidden. His plan was to crawl out and conceal himself near to the sniper's position. He would wait for the German to fire and would then aim just behind the rifle flash. The plan seemingly works as the German is later seen to be limping back towards his own trench, assisted by two comrades. After this success, he became a regular sniper working along the whole of the Brigade sector.

Another tour of duty ended on 21 April. There had been little to report over the previous days except that, on the evening of the 17th, two Prussians had deserted across No Man's Land and had been escorted away to the rear as prisoners of war. The men now took up reserve positions in a quarry near Cambrin. During the day, an enemy shell landed amongst them, killing 19 year old Private Edwin Lowe and mortally wounding Oliver Williams, who died the next day.

The grave of 19 year old Edwin Lowe, from Chorlton-on-Medlock. Author

Assisted Edgerley[7] and Riley to carry Lowe to Vermelles where we sewed him up and left him for burial. (Private Walter Greenhalgh)

The men were getting the trench system into much better shape by the end of the month but the improvements were not enough to protect Richard Ravenscroft from being mortally wounded by a shell on 27 April. Walter Greenhalgh was lucky to escape injury 'Whizzbang hit parados, buried him and covered me with earth'. Ravenscroft, 19, came from the West Derby district of Liverpool. Greenhalgh wrote that they got 'Ravey' out but his leg was severed below the knee. They bandaged him up as best they could and the stretcher bearers took him. He died on the 30th at a nearby field hospital.

Although most members of the battalion were still volunteers who originated from the Manchester area, the army's growing number of casualties had required conscription to be introduced in 1916 and this inherently meant that an increasing number of recruits were assigned to battalions that were unrelated to their home area. Another Liverpudlian, Joseph Hooley, was fatally wounded on 4 May. He was a thirty-seven year old married man who had earned his living as house painter. Hooley was one of four to be killed or wounded that day, probably by shellfire. He died of his injuries on the 6th, also at a nearby field hospital.

The tour of duty which started on 6 May proved to be a busy time. Each day, there was major shelling of the enemy positions with the intent of cutting the German defensive wire and disrupting their normal routines, in preparation for a raid on the enemy trench. Much of the firing was undertaken by the divisional trench mortar batteries but the heavier artillery stood by in case the Germans undertook significant retaliation. Each night the battalion commander sent patrols out into No Man's Land, the war diary recording that 'a great deal of enterprise was shown, but the main object – a prisoner – was not attained. No Man's Land became very definitely ours'.

With the battalion having the advantage of dominating No Man's Land, the plan was developed to raid the enemy trenches. Such raids were commonplace in the quieter sectors of the Western Front. Groups would creep across to the enemy positions, try to capture prisoners to gain intelligence and, otherwise, cause as much death and destruction as they could before it became imperative to return to their own lines. It was a good tactic that was enthusiastically adopted by both sides. On the one hand, it ensured that the fighting spirit of the attackers was maintained whilst the defenders could never relax safe from the possibility of a raid. The raid planned for 27 May would involve two parties from B Company, under the command of Lieutenant Frank Stockdale[8] and Second Lieutenant L Wilson.

The key to a successful raid was the ability to get across No Man's Land without being detected. As far as that went, the raid that night was not a success. They were spotted and the Germans opened fire on them with rifles and grenades but they pressed on and still managed to get into the enemy trench. The raiders on the right found the Germans had pulled back behind a defensive 'block' in the trench system and, from there, started to throw more grenades at the Manchesters. Fire was returned in kind. On the left, there was no sign of the Germans but there was sufficient kit lying about for their unit to be identified as the 65th Regiment. This was sufficient intelligence to take back and a successful withdrawal to the British line was made by both groups. Only three men had been wounded – all minor injuries.

Later the same day, Walter Greenhalgh received a ticking off from Corporal Hartley. He doesn't record what he had done wrong but the matter had blown over within a couple of days. 'Hunting rats by putting cordite down holes. Resumed normal relations with Hartley, offering him some of my preserved strawberries which I had just had a tin from home.'

The month of June opened with perfect summer weather. It was dry and warm and, of more interest to the men, the enemy artillery was relatively quiet. Although the battalion had a nominal strength of forty-five officers and 723 other ranks, its strength in the trenches was only thirty-two officers and 528 men. The others were away recovering from wounds or illness; on leave or seconded to other brigade or divisional units. 'Not much doing. Usual trench mortar and artillery activity' (Battalion war diary).

On 7 June, the Germans shelled with gas but, fortunately, only three men were badly affected. Joseph Carron, John Dean and Cyril Walton were all admitted to a military hospital. Walton recovered sufficiently to be able to transfer to home duties with the Royal Defence Corps. Carron, a twenty-two year old plasterer from the Hulme area of Manchester, was never able to return to duty and was discharged from the army in November 1918, still suffering from regularly vomiting after he had eaten. Nothing is known about Dean's future.

The next day, the 2/5th Battalion moved troops up to the front line to conduct a raid on the enemy trench. The 2/6th men moved back to the support line except for the battalion's Lewis gunners who stayed to give additional covering fire for the raiders. The raid was a great success, with many casualties being caused to the German garrison.

During the early hours of 11 June, the Germans opened a heavy artillery barrage on the Manchesters' positions, causing several injuries. Walter Greenhalgh received a minor wound and went to the Regimental Aid Post to be treated by the battalion's medical officer. Whilst he was there, a much more seriously wounded man was brought in. Harold Dunkley[9] 'had abdominal wounds from splinters and part of his foot had been blown off. The stretchers bearers took him to 1st Field Ambulance at Cambrin Church, where he died soon after.'

There was little to report over the coming days. It was generally quiet on both sides, although the British periodically shelled the Germans with trench mortars. They retaliated firing 'aerial darts' which caused some injuries.

On 21 June, the battalion was relieved from the trenches and moved away to rest billets at Allouagne, a village west of the town of Bethune, where a draft of 122 new troops was waiting to join. Amongst them was Oswald George Billingham. He had enlisted at Northampton, near his home at Kislingbury, on 15 January 1917 and was assigned to the Norfolk Regiment. After training, he went overseas on 29 May and remained at Boulogne until he was reassigned to the Manchesters. He maintained a diary[10] during his service and his entry on 21 June records that he was assigned to D Company. 'Very cushy day. Nothing to do at all.'

On the 26th, the battalion moved by train to the Channel coast and took over billets in a corn warehouse at St Pol-sur-Mer, now a suburb of Dunkerque. They spent several days in training, no doubt for the benefit of the new troops who had arrived in three separate drafts. The 2/6th Manchesters were now at almost full fighting strength – thirty-four officers and 927 other ranks. Training continued for the first two weeks of July. It was a pleasant time and drills took place on the beach and amongst the sand dunes and then, on the 15th, they moved to take over coastal defences at Dunkerque Bains, to the east.

Second Lieutenant Herbert Bate[11] was serving with A Company and later wrote that, whilst at the coast,

The whole battalion undressed on the beach to swim in the sea. Having no bathing costumes, we took to the water naked. Five or six hundred young men naked together on a beach is a wonderful sight, as impressive and comic as a beach packed with penguins. Two French or Belgium young women who happened to pass by obviously thought the same, by their giggles and shrieks of mirth.

Once at Dunkerque, 200 men from D Company were attached to the 2nd Australian Tunnelling Company. Private P Hall was one of the men sent to work with the Australians. He later wrote that many of them were silver miners and everybody worked shifts of two hours on and four hours off, round the clock. They were well within range of the German artillery:

The noise these shells made coming through the air was like an express train rushing through a small country station and the explosion when the shell burst was deafening and the shock was like a small earthquake. At the height of the bombardment, I saw one of our men coming towards us across a large hollow in the sand dunes. A shell burst quite close to him and I saw him fall and thought he was wounded so I went down and pushed him up and carried him up to the shelter of the tunnel. There was no wound on him but he was dead. Then someone shouted 'Gas' and we all started to put on our gas masks. By this time, I was retching violently and could not put my mask on. Two of the others saw my predicament and realised I had breathed very deeply in struggling to climb out of the hollow with the dead man on my back. They grabbed me and rushed me along the tunnel to where it was close to the beach and left me on the sand close to the water. There was a slight breeze off the sea so the air was clear of gas. I was violently sick and felt terrible but the tide was coming in so I crawled a few yards at a time towards the dunes. Each time I stopped, I was sick again. The advancing tide forced me to keep moving and the effort and the vomiting must have emptied my stomach and lungs….I managed to reach the dunes before becoming unconscious and the search party found me and carried me back to my billet where I fell into a deep sleep. In the morning, I thought I had recovered, although I still felt rather groggy.

On the evening of 24 July 1917, the battalion paraded and marched a few miles north towards the front line at Nieuport. The town stood at the northern end of the whole western front which snaked southwards through Belgium and France to the Swiss border. Passing through Nieuport, to empty into the English Channel, is the strategically important River Yser, formed into a canal as it flowed to the sea. In December 1914, the Allies had crossed the canal to establish their frontline on the northern bank around the village of Lombartzyde. It was to this area that the Manchesters headed to relieve another battalion from the front line.

As the battalion reached Nieuport, enemy gas shells started to fall in the town. It was decided to wait for an hour before trying to cross the canal on its flimsy floating wooden bridges. The shelling stopped and C Company led the way forward but as the men were crossing Putney Bridge and Vauxhall Bridge, the Germans opened fire again

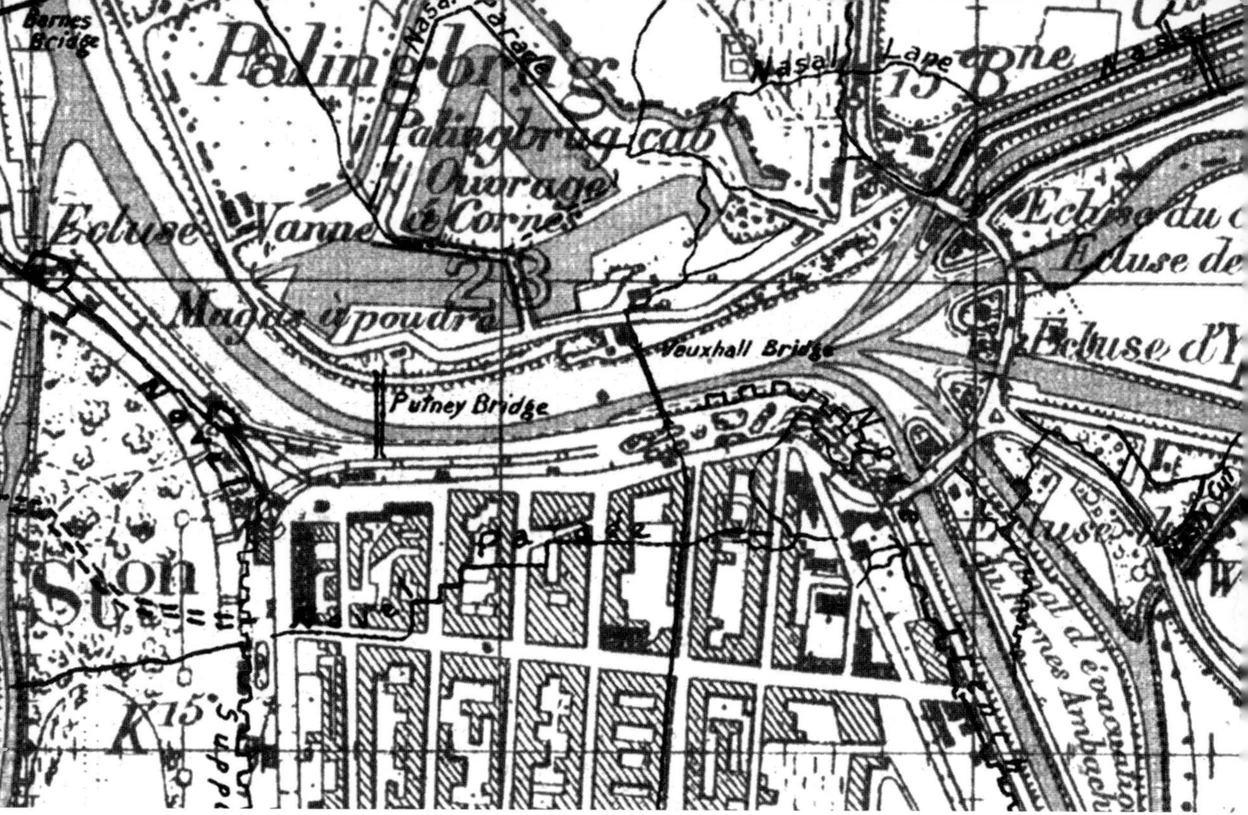

Trench map of the Nieuport sector, showing the bridges across across the Yser.

with gas and high explosive shells. Herbert Bate recorded what happened to him:

> *To get across the Yser Canal was a difficult operation…all bridges had long been destroyed* [and] *the Engineers had put across floating duckboards. Shells were falling and exploding on the banks and in the water. Mingled with high explosives were gas shells which could be detected by the pungent smell in the smoke filled air and the 'popping' sound as they hit the ground. We put on our gas masks, dashed across the duckboards, splayed out on the far side and rushed forward. It was not easy to see in a respirator and impossible to shout. I was obliged to remove mine several times to shout orders, though this did not account for what happened. Our respirators were designed for protection from chlorine and phosgene gas. The Germans were using, for the first time, mustard gas.*
>
> *Soon, my eyes began to water and feel sore and become painful, then my sight began to fail and, finally, my eyes became fast closed and I was totally blind. I began to stagger and stumble, aimlessly and helplessly, falling over the broken and churned up ground and into shell holes. In this plight, someone clutched my arm, whether friend or foe I didn't know, but was relieved to hear him say 'I am Major Melvill*[12]*. Hold on to my belt and follow me'. Others in the same condition were collected and joined up in single file. In this manner, we were led back to the canal bank. To re-cross, it was slow, hard-going and perilous. The canal was tidal and the tide was now lower than when we attacked, so there were now banks to climb up and down. The duckboards had been damaged and*

Putney Bridge. Courtesy of Kristof Jacobs, author *Nieuwpoort Sector 1917.*

broken by the shelling so there was a risk of falling into the water. At each step forward, one had to feel for a firm spot. Slow and tedious though it was, we reached the other side and, as far as I know, no-one was lost. From that moment, my mind became blank and I was oblivious of everything until I awoke in a bed in the 1st Eastern Military Hospital at Cambridge.[13]

Although affected by the gas himself, Major Melvill continued to direct the battalion and those still able to do so undertook the relief of the other battalion. They were in position by 4am on the 25th. Many men had been affected by the gas and a casualty report filed with the war diary shows twelve officers and 135 men unfit for duty. They included Melvill, Captain John Whitworth and Captain William E. Fitzgerald, the battalion's medical officer. All three men were awarded the Military Cross for their 'gallantry and devotion to duty'. Lieutenant Frank Stockdale was amongst the men who were wounded by exploding shells or rifle fire whilst getting into position. He was evacuated away to be treated at a field hospital behind the lines. After surgery there, he was sent to 2nd General Hospital in Manchester. The wound was serious, but not life-threatening. A medical report in April 1918 concluded 'The left shoulder is healed but is absolutely frail and useless. It is never likely to be fit for any useful military purpose. The whole left upper limb is at present useless'.[14]

Second Lieutenant John Francis Horsfield, from Buxton. Killed in action on 26 July and buried in Cozyde Military Cemetery.

Private Stanley Rawlinson, from Higher Broughton, was another badly affected. He was never able to return to frontline duty but, in due course, transferred to the Army Service Corps as a clerk working in Britain.

The battalion held the front line here until the night of 30/31 July. Casualties continued to mount and, during the tour of duty, eight men were killed. They included Charles Bradley, a twenty year old from Grantham, Lincolnshire, who had enlisted at the end of 1915 and had joined the battalion on 30 June as one of the new replacement drafts. The men now withdrew to billets at Nieuport Bains for three days. Walter Greenhalgh recalled that, while they were there, two Australian soldiers in nearby billets "managed to get hold of" two jars of army ration rum. Everyone got a tot but the Australians and Corporal Bert Hartley continued to drink until all three passed out. The Australians were put on a charge and Hartley was "out" for two days and felt very much the worse for wear afterwards.

The next move was to take up the coastal defence positions at Coxyde Bains. This was easy work, with the trenches in and amongst the sand dunes, facing out to the English Channel in case of a German invasion attempt. The relaxed atmosphere resulted in another drinking incident, remembered by Walter Greenhalgh. Sergeant Tommy Dicks and Private John T McNulty went out one evening and returned to billets very drunk. The next morning, the senior sergeant tried to wake them, but they refused to get up and were abusive to him. Both were arrested. Dicks apologised to the company commander and was lucky to receive only a stern admonishment. McNulty insisted on arguing with the officer and was sent to the colonel. He was sentenced to Field Punishment No. 1. This would have involved McNulty having to undertake "hard labour" each day for a period of time and, also, being tied to a wagon wheel for two hours each day.

The final resting place of Horace Buddery at Ramscappelle Road Military Cemetery, Nieuwpoort, Belgium.
Author

On 13 August, the Manchesters moved back to Nieuport Bains and, during their time in the trenches, enemy artillery shelling increased, killing a number of men. One was 29 year old Horace Buddery from Great Yarmouth[15]. He had trained with the Norfolk Regiment and had joined the battalion only a few weeks before, as part of one of the replacement drafts. He was a Lewis gunner and had been on duty in the front line when he was killed at about 4am on the 18th. His Lieutenant had the unfortunate, but increasingly regular, duty of writing to his family. "*It is my sad and painful duty to inform you of the death of your brother, No. 270060, Pte. H Buddery.......The shell hit the ground about two yards from him, killing him instantly. I can honestly assure you that he suffered no pain at all. I cannot tell you how sorry we all are to have lost such a cheerful companion – cheerful both in safety and in danger, and a companion always. He was one of the best men in the company and I recognised him as a "good man", and that is a great compliment to anyone in the Army.*"

The tour of duty finished on the night of 20/21 August and the battalion spent the rest of the month in billets at Coxyde, where training exercises were undertaken. On the 29th, D Company returned from its long duty with the Australian Tunnelling Company. They had spent the previous weeks assisting with the construction of large dug-outs built into and under the sand dunes, to be used by the coastal defence infantry as sleeping quarters. The opening days of September were spent back on the coastal defences but, from the 4th, the battalion moved back to billets near Coxyde and, later in the month, to Middlesex Camp near Oost Dunkerque Bains.

Second Lieutenant Joseph Arnold Rowbottom. Killed when a shell hit B Company's officers' mess. Amanda Hancox

On the night of 23/24 September, the camp came under intermittent heavy shelling from long range German guns. One landed directly on the hut used as the B Company officers' mess. It killed four officers and six orderlies. Captain John Whitworth wrote home the next day to assure his wife that he was uninjured:

We had a terrible tragedy last night. A shell burst in the middle of our company mess in the middle of the night. Four officers were killed and three wounded and six orderlies killed and two wounded. I am hoping you will get this before you hear any rumours from outside. The story is going round that all the B Company officers have been killed from which it is a very easy thing to say that I have been killed. B… and M… have gone.. I think they were the only two you knew. We buried them this morning before we left. It was quite a nice funeral service.

It is not known if the army censor deleted the names of the two officers from Whitworth's letter, or if he did this himself. The two men were Captain Thomas S Beaumont, on temporary attachment from the 2/8th Battalion, and Second Lieutenant Edgar Maitland. The other two officers killed were Second Lieutenants Clement Cunliffe and Joseph Arnold Rowbottom. Rowbottom was a pre-war member of the battalion and, in civilian life, worked as a clerk with the Great Central Railway Ltd and lived in the Gorton area of Manchester. He had served at Gallipoli as a private and been wounded three times, also contracting enteric fever and spent over three months in hospital in London. Returning to duty, he was attached to the 2/5th Battalion, becoming an officer and transferring to the 2/6th Battalion only on 29 May 1917. Arnold Rowbottom was 22.

Little is known of the six privates who were also killed – Sydney Barber[16], Warren Baxter, Albert Bradshaw, Fred Stacey, Joseph Stone and James Worthington. All ten men were buried at what is now Ramscappelle Road Military Cemetery, maintained

Ramscappelle Road Military Cemetery. Author.

by the Commonwealth War Graves Commission. After the funerals, the battalion moved to a new camp at nearby Ghyvelde, a little way to the west into France, where training exercises were carried out. The battalion war diary notes that there was a 'considerable amount of practice in advancing behind a barrage'.

It is said that every British Army division fought around the Belgian town of Ypres at some point in the war and the 66th Division now moved towards that sector to play a brief role. Heavy fighting had been underway since 31 July in a series of "bite and hold" assaults on the German positions. Rather than the massive attacks on a wide front which had characterised the Battle of the Somme the previous year, the new tactics required smaller concentrations of troops undertaking assaults with more limited objectives, but the men had still become exhausted and successive divisions were brought forward from the reserves.

On 4 October, British and Australian troops undertook another successful attack up the Passchendaele Ridge. The next day, the 2/6th Manchesters were ordered forward to relieve the 41st Australian Battalion from the front line. They marched from their overnight camp at Brandhoek, through Ypres to the Menin Road, where they were then guided to the front line. It was a dangerous time.

> *It was utterly stupid and daft. The idea was to split the battalion into parties of twelve men. Each group had to leave a gap of fifty yards behind and in front, so there was room for shells to burst. Meant that if one party stopped, all the parties had to stop which gave the enemy gunners plenty of time to adjust their sights and concentrate on one party at a time.*

View from the position taken up by the Battalion on 5 October. Author

> *Thus A, B and C Companies had heavy casualties…but D Company's commander (an Ulsterman) had adopted Australian ideas enthusiastically. He ordered everyone to proceed individually choosing their own route and dodging across from one trench to another, like as common sense dictates.* (Private P R Hall)

Five men were killed during the move to the front line, including Corporal William Currie and Private Arthur Dean, both close comrades of Oswald Billingham. Born in Nantwich in 1888, Alfred Bowdler had moved to Manchester by the time of the war and was working as a barman at the Bull's Head in Hulme. He enlisted into the army in October 1916 and served with the 23rd Battalion. After several weeks, he was invalided home suffering with 'trench foot'. Once recovered, he was transferred to the 2/6th Battalion and had only been with his new comrades since 9 September.

The position the battalion took up was adjacent to Tyne Cot, a series of now captured German pill boxes and, today, the site of the largest cemetery maintained by the Commonwealth War Graves Commission. It consisted of four trenches hurriedly dug by the Australians after their advance. Three companies occupied the front line, with A Company in close support.

> *The weather was wet and the ground heavy. The line was held without difficulty – no counter attack being made – shelling was persistent and a certain number of casualties were sustained. (Battalion war diary)*

They held this position until darkness fell on the evening of the next day when they were relieved to a support position. *'Absolutely rotten day. Slept in shell hole half full of water.'* (Private Oswald Billingham). Whilst in support at Hill 40, to the south of the village of Zonnebeke, Captain Archibald Brooks[17] was killed by shrapnel. Oswald Billingham was one of the men who buried him. *'Carried body back from Regimental Aid Post. Afterwards got lost so slept on Zonnebeke Road until dawn.'*

Private Percy Macefield.

Private Percy Macefield was also unlucky to be killed whilst in support at Hill 40. Thinking that they were relatively safe, he and a few comrades were sitting on the edge of a shellhole when he was shot through the heart, by a sniper. The others buried him there but, over the course of the war, the location of his grave was lost and his name is now inscribed at the Memorial to the Missing at Tyne Cot Cemetery. Aged thirty-five, he lived in Skipton with his wife Jessie and their child and had worked as a tram conductor for Bradford City Tramways. In his spare time he was a keen playing member of Skipton Cricket Club. His platoon officer, Lieutenant J R Thompson wrote to Mrs Macefield expressing condolences. *'His quiet unassuming manner won him the respect of all his comrades. He took his part bravely and never hesitated about giving a comrade a helping hand when needed.'*

On the night of 8/9 October, the battalion was further withdrawn to a field near the Menin Road. From the time they had arrived at the front line position until this withdrawal, eighteen men had been killed and another fifty-six wounded. They would play no part in the attack launched by their divisional comrades just before 5.30 on the morning of the 9th. It would later be officially designated as the Battle of Poelcapelle and the attack was carried out by eleven divisions, totalling around 300, 000 men. The 66th Division attack would be carried out by the battalions of East Lancashires and Lancashire Fusiliers, together with the 2/9th and 2/10th Battalions, Manchester Regiment.

Private Charles William Fletcher. Before the war, he had been living in Rhode Island, USA, but had returned to join up. Killed on 10 October.

For the men of the 2/9th, preparations for their first time in a major action had started the day before. The men had started their march from the reserve positions, through heavy rain. As day turned to night, men slipped off the roadways, fell into shell holes and had to be pulled free by their mates. The going was slow and it was not until 4.45am that they were fully in position. They had been 'on the go' for eleven hours and were cold, wet and hungry. All four companies lined up in the front trenches ready to go over the top in the first wave. At 5.20am, the artillery started shelling the German lines and, four minutes later, the infantry advanced through the quagmire up the Passchendaele Ridge.

Private Percy Bailey, a married man, was living in Chorlton-on-Medlock when he enlisted. Died of wounds 12 October.

They immediately came under severe enemy artillery and machine gun fire and, as they neared the German lines, they were fired on by German snipers scattered in shellholes in advance of their own trenches. The Manchesters continued on, in spite of mounting casualties, capturing their first objective. They cleared enemy dugouts and captured some prisoners. At around midday, they were due to continue the advance to a further objective, but the men were so exhausted and their numbers depleted that it was impossible. Other units managed to make some progress but they were later ordered to return to the first objective where all the troops now dug-in and consolidated their gains. In the early evening, the Germans counter-attacked but this was driven off by rifle and artillery fire. A total of 113 members of the 2/9th Battalion had been killed.

Although they had been fortunate to escape the carnage of the attack, over the coming days there was a gruesome aftermath for working parties from the 2/6th Battalion. The advance now meant the bodies of men who had been killed in this and previous attacks could be recovered from what had been No Man's Land.

> *It was the practice to dig a trench where the dead were thickest. Then we towed them into it, after putting their discs and what we found in their pockets into little white ration bags. A regular 'Burial Sergeant' was in charge. When at first we were reluctant to handle men who had been dead more than two months, he would say 'Go on, get a move on, those lads won't hurt you'. When they were in, the sergeant would read three or four sentences from the C of E burial service, while we all stood round bare-headed. Then he would say 'Cover their faces and fill in'. When all recognisable bodies had been dealt with, we often had to collect widely spread fragments of other bodies and put them in the trench.* (Private Walter Greenhalgh)

The burial parties remained near Ypres until 16 October when they rejoined their comrades who had moved by train, on the 13th, to billets at Arques, some miles south east of Calais. A re-inforcing draft of ninety-four men and four officers joined the battalion here and all members of the unit undertook training over the following days. Particular attention was given to specialist training for signallers, stretcher bearers and Lewis gunners. As the casualties had continued to mount from the fighting around Ypres, replacement drafts had been rushed from Britain so the offensive could be maintained. The time given to training recruits appears to have been shortened with the effect that the new arrivals were not always as well prepared as the troops who had gone overseas earlier in the year. In what would be a successful attempt to improve the situation, many brigades and divisions established their own training schools. The brigade of which the 2/6th Battalion was part, 199 Brigade, was one which formed such a school and, on 22 October, Captain John Whitworth was seconded as its first commandant.

At the end of the month, an announcement was made that five members of the battalion were to be awarded the Military Medal for gallantry and devotion to duty during the operations at Ypres earlier in the month. The recipients were Company Sergeant Major Charles Collins, Corporal Jonathon Beckham and Privates Robert Black, Charles Brierley and A B Smith.

Training continued into November until the 10th, when the battalion returned to the Ypres area. For most of the month, it provided working parties near the Ypres Canal for the Canadian 9th Railway Battalion. They undertook ballasting and general maintenance of a light railway which ran nearby. The Canadian battalion's war diary notes that there was heavy shelling throughout the time. Two of the Manchesters were killed. They were Privates Edward Eason and George Lee. Albert Lamming, from Grimsby, was seriously injured and died on the 18th at a field hospital.

The pattern continued for the remainder of the year with the battalion remaining around the general area of Ypres, undertaking either training exercises or providing working parties to improve trench defences.

Of the week or two till Christmas, I have no special recollection except the extremely cold conditions, the rain and cold and flooded shell holes. I do remember that we were told to celebrate Christmas on 23 December because that was the last day of our rest period and we would be in the line on Christmas Day. I recall I decided to start the celebrations with a shave, but even that was a very cold one, sitting on a frozen pond and breaking the ice to dip my lather brush in the water. I think we had extra rations but I forget what they were. (Private P R Hall)

The burial place of Corporal Nathan Parr, from Davyhulme. He is remembered on the war memorial in the garden of St Mary's Church, Davyhulme. Author

In the event, the battalion spent Christmas Day still in the reserve area. However, Oswald Billingham recalled that his platoon was called out to patrol the streets of Reninghelst in the evening. Nearby, labourers of the Chinese Labour Corps had conspired to kill their Sergeant Major, as they believed him to be an extortioner who also worked them too hard. A riot ensued which was declared to be a mutiny. A company of Royal Welch Fusiliers had rounded up many of the mutineers and others had been shot out of hand. However, many were still in the area, armed with improvised weapons, and the Manchesters were called out to keep the peace.

31 December – my friend, Nathan Parr, who had been promoted corporal that day, was killed by a shell at Yorkshire Dump. (Private Walter Greenhalgh)

The period of quiet continued throughout January 1918 and

Malcolm Melvill, now promoted to Lieutenant Colonel and commanding the battalion, was able to write his summary for the month very quickly:

> *During the month, the battalion put in some useful company training and also one complete tour in the line. The time in the line was successful in spite of bad weather and adverse conditions. A useful patrol was carried out by Second Lieutenant Gregsten*[18] *and twenty other ranks who succeeded in locating a machine gun which had been giving trouble – this was fired on the next day and has not been reported as active since. Health and morale of the battalion has been very good.*

After their brief tour of duty in the line, during which Oswald Billingham had been pleased to have 'clicked for a good dugout', the battalion had withdrawn to Halifax Camp near Poperinge. There they spent what the war diary describes as a 'pleasant few days, resting and cleaning up, only supplying working parties on the last two days of the month'.

The fighting around Ypres during 1917 had left the British Army with an acute manpower shortage. Newly trained troops were not arriving at a rate able to replace casualties. Battalions such as the 2/6th Manchesters were now at less than half normal strength. At the beginning of February, the battalion had an effective strength of just 453, including twenty-two officers. It had become clear that a major reorganisation of army structure was needed and this started to be put into place during February. Brigades were reduced from four to three battalions and many battalions were disbanded with their troops being reassigned to other units. These were often, but not always, battalions from the same regiment. The 2/6th was to continue in existence and would receive re-inforcing drafts mainly from the 2/8th Battalion which had been completely disbanded by the end of the month

On 17 February, the battalion, now nearly at full strength, left Belgium and moved to a new camp near the French village of Harbonnieres, between Amiens and St Quentin.

Circumstances had combined to give the German Army a temporary supremacy over the Allies. The British and French forces were starved of reinforcements. American troops were arriving in Belgium and France at a much slower rate than hoped – it would be months before they could take to the field in numbers and, on the German side, peace with Russia after its revolution had released many thousands of troops to be moved west. Both sides knew a major German offensive was only a matter of time. The only question was where it would be launched.

> *The general situation on the Russian and Italian fronts, combined with the paucity of reinforcements which we are likely to receive will in all probability necessitate our adopting a defensive attitude for the next three months. We must be prepared to meet a strong and sustained hostile offensive.* (Field Marshal Sir Douglas Haig, 3 December 1917)

With the need for defence assuming great importance, new tactics had been developed by the British. There would no longer be a single heavily defended front line trench, with comparatively little by way of defensive structures in the support lines to the rear. Instead, there would now be 'defence in depth'. German attackers would first encounter a 'forward zone'. This would be defended in sufficient strength to oblige the Germans to mount preliminary artillery attacks against it and, when the assault began, to commit large numbers of infantry to overcome it. Within this zone, the British would deploy half their strength in small outposts. The remaining half would be in much better defended redoubts. Their job was to inflict the maximum number of casualties on the enemy before withdrawing. They would then fall back to a 'battle zone' some 2000 – 3000 yards to the rear and their efforts would have given sufficient warning to the larger concentrations of troops already there that an attack was under way. Approaching the 'battle zone' the German attackers would have to cross ground cleared to allow heavy artillery, machine gun and rifle fire to be poured on them from prepared positions.

Richard Cartwright's death was reported by the *Warrington Guardian*, 9 March 1918.

After settling into the new camp at Harbonnieres, the battalion carried out large scale training exercises with the 2/5th and 2/7th Battalions in the new tactics. There was also a practice counter-attack in which the 2/6th supported the 2/5th. On 26 February, they took over support positions in the Battle Zone near the village of Villeret, about twenty kilometres north of St Quentin. As they were going into the line, Private Richard Cartwright, a twenty year old grinder from Warrington, was killed by shrapnel. Second Lieutenant Furness wrote to his father:

> *Your lad was unfortunately hit yesterday afternoon and passed away a few hours later in hospital. He was buried this afternoon near to where he fell, a service being held. He will be much missed by us and his comrades here. The other company officers join me in sending our deepest sympathy in this your sad bereavement.*

On the final day of the month, there was an attack alert, with all ranks being warned to prepare to go to their battle positions at short notice. It was a practice to see how quickly the battalion would react.

On 2 March 1918, the battalion relieved the 2/5th Battalion in the front line and stayed there until the 6th. Each night, patrols were sent out into No Man's Land and they were able to keep the enemy positions under close observation. As elsewhere, German preparations for their forthcoming offensive were being undertaken in such secrecy that the patrols detected nothing untoward. They were relieved back to huts at the village of Montigny where, on the night of 8/9th, there was another practice 'attack alert'.

20 March 1918 is described in all available accounts as a pleasant quiet day. On the previous day, Colonel Melvill had returned to Britain on leave and Major John

Whitworth was now in command of the battalion. One of the apparently few officers who did not expect an attack soon was the commander of 66th Division, Major General Neill Malcolm. The nine battalions should have been deployed with three in the Forward Zone and the other six firmly entrenched in the Battle Zone. However, he had insisted that this was not necessary and that half of the Battle Zone battalions could remain at rest in the reserve area. One of them was the 2/6th Manchesters.

It was payday and the men received their francs at camp to the rear of the Battle Zone. Walter Greenhalgh went off to spend them:

> *In the afternoon, Charlie Randall, Jack Beetham and I went to the canteen in Roisel. At night, before going to bed, the three of us had a long conversation, being joined by Brierley and Bill Bamford, who was acting orderly sergeant that day. We were ordered to sleep in our clothes and not take our boots or puttees off.*
>
> *The five of us had a long light-hearted and hilarious discussion about everything on earth, except battles and spring offensives. The Germans might have been ten thousand miles away, instead of three.*
>
> *Within the next week, Bamford was killed, Brierley was desperately wounded (he would lay in a German hospital until 1919), Randle was wounded and Beetham and I were prisoners.*

Their peace and quiet would be shattered at 4.45 on the morning of 21 March. *Kaiserschlacht* – the Kaiser's Battle – had begun. The Germans had secretly moved vast numbers of artillery pieces into position during the previous days and these now opened a ferocious barrage of high explosive and gas shells which fell on the British front line and support areas. It did not take long for orders to 'Man Battle Positions' to reach the 2/6th Battalion, in the reserve area behind the Battle Zone.

> *We marched up the hill from Montigny towards Hervilly with some distances between platoons, No. 13 – mine – leading. Randle and I were at the rear of the platoon, the last two men. I recall our conversation, which illustrates our complete lack of anxiety about the morning's events so far. We agreed it was going to be a hungry morning. Randle said "As soon as we get back to Montigny, the first job for you is to make a mess-tin of burgoo" – I regarded myself as an expert at making oatmeal porridge. The general idea in the ranks seemed to be that the Germans were just trying to make themselves 'a bloody nuisance'.*
>
> *Faces, generally wearing gas-masks, peered at us from the high bank at the right of the road. I suppose*

HUN GUNS START

From St. Quentin to the Scarpe.

PRELUDE TO ATTACK.

Heavy Bombardment of Our Front This Morning.

From SIR DOUGLAS HAIG.

A heavy bombardment was opened by the enemy shortly before dawn this morning against our whole front, from the neighbourhood of Vendeuil (south of St. Quentin) to the River Scarpe.

[Vendeuil is ten miles to the south of St. Quentin. The Scarpe runs around Arras. The total distance of the bombarded area—in a direct line as distinct from the military line—is about 50 miles.]

A successful raid was carried out by us last night in the neighbourhood of St. Quentin. Thirteen prisoners and three machine-guns were brought back by our troops.

Prisoners were also taken by us in patrol encounters south-east of Messines and in another successful raid carried out by us south of Houthulst Forest.

A raid attempted by the enemy in the neighbourhood of Armentieres was repulsed.

The German attack reported by the *Manchester Evening Chronicle*.

there were battery positions there. We donned our masks two or three times. In about twenty minutes we turned right into a field near Hervilly village. The village was under very heavy shellfire, much of it 5.9 overhead shrapnel. In isolation, we should have heard such shells coming well before they burst, but that morning they merged into a continuous roar. As the bursts were becoming uncomfortably near, our platoon was moved across the shallow valley to the side of Hervilly Wood. There we lay down to await further orders.

(Private Walter Greenhalgh, quoted in *The Kaiser's Battle* by Martin Middlebrook)

In the Forward Zone, the battalions were finding it impossible to see. The smoke caused by the heavy shelling was made worse by a thick mist and the 2/8th Lancashire Fusiliers had their headquarters surrounded and the men taken prisoner before they realised the German infantry attack was underway.

By 11am, the battalion had taken up its position in the Battle Zone and casualties had, so far, been light with Second Lieutenant Gilbert Carmichael being the only

Germans advancing their artillery during the opening stages of the attack.

The 21 March battlefield. Cote Wood in the far distance. Fervaque Farm was near to the clump of tree on the right. Author

The 21 March battlefield. Carpeza Copse in the distance on the left. Author

officer reported killed. Within fifteen minutes, the situation had dramatically changed. Taking advantage of the mist, the Germans had picked their way through the British wire and forced their way through between A and C Companies, moving round to surround both of them. Fierce hand-to-hand fighting was taking place with many killed and wounded on both sides. It was a desperate but unequal struggle.

> *As soon as the barrage eased off a bit, we stood on the fire-step and opened up. I had two or three men filling magazines and I kept pegging away at the Germans… until my Lewis gun refused to continue. [I] stripped the gun down. I discovered that the barrel was choked with carbon deposits. I got a rod with a bit of four-by-two and, after a quick clean, it agreed to resume work.*
>
> *But, by this time, the Germans had got very close and I saw, a little distance away, a*

Modern map of 21 March battlefield.

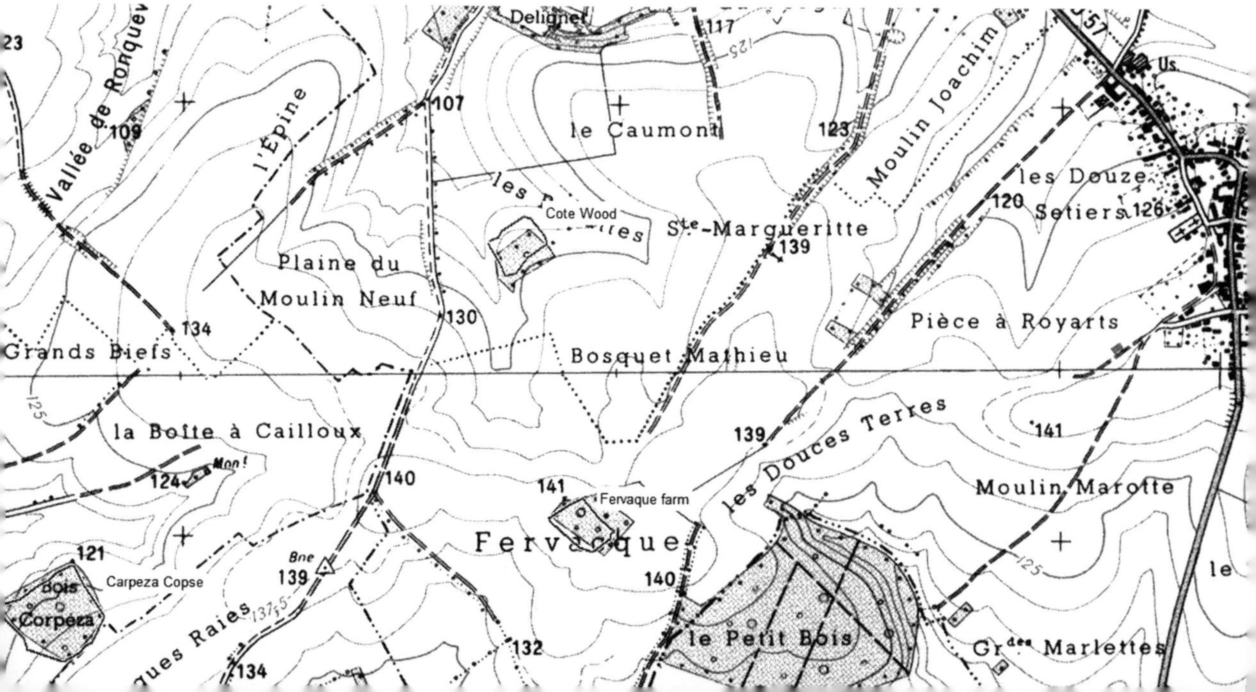

Private Frank Wroe, from the Moston area of Manchester. Killed in action serving with D Company, 22 March, aged ninteen. He had worked in the offices of the Great Northern Railway.

> *sergeant and some men climb out of the trench with their hands up. I tried to escape along the trench but the way through was blocked by dead bodies. Among these was a corporal who had put me on a charge two weeks earlier. He had been hit in the middle of the forehead and both his eyeballs were hanging down his cheeks. When I turned in the opposite direction, I saw two German soldiers approaching, spraying the trench ahead with liquid fire. One held the nozzle and the other had the cylinder on his back.*
>
> *There was often talk among the lads that, to be captured with a Lewis gun, you didn't stand a chance. You'd be finished off at once. So I dumped it into a water-filled shell hole and put my hands up. I was sorry to lose that gun; it was nearly new and I had become very fond of it.* (Private Charles H Martin, quoted in The Kaiser's Battle, by Martin Middlebrook)

Battalion headquarters formed a defensive line around the northern edge of Cote Wood and this allowed the remnants of the battalion to make a temporary escape and take up a new line between Fervaque Farm, near a wood of the same name and Carpeza Copse. The Germans concentrated their attack on the troops at Fervaque Farm and Fervaque Wood but were beaten off several times before the flamethrowers forced a surrender by the defenders. A few got away to join their comrades around Carpeza Copse. Oswald Billingham was one who had become separated and he was not able to make his way back to the others until darkness fell. He was tired, shocked and very hungry having had nothing to eat in the previous twenty four hours. During the night, two squadrons of dismounted cavalry joined John Whitworth's now much depleted force as very welcome re-inforcements. At least for a few hours, the German advance had been halted. But it had been at a very heavy cost. The 2/6th Battalion, Manchester Regiment now numbered just 162 men, including twelve officers.

Later records show that sixty members of the battalion had been killed. Many more were wounded or, like Walter Greenhalgh, now prisoners of war.

The position was held overnight but, by 8am on 22 March, the Germans were on three sides of the British at Carpeza Copse and orders were received to withdraw. As they passed through the nearby village of Hesbecourt, there were further heavy casualties, no doubt from enemy artillery fire. The withdrawal continued and the battalion spent the night of the 23rd outside the town of Peronne.

Captain Samuel Collier. Killed on 22 March. His brother, Samuel, was killed six days later while serving as an observer with the Royal Flying Corps.

On the 24th, a further withdrawal brought the battalion to the banks of the River Somme, where they took up defensive positions on the far side with the 2/5th Manchesters on their right and the 5th Battalion, Border Regiment on the left. The advancing Germans reached their positions in the middle of the afternoon and there was more desperate fighting. Oswald Billingham wrote that there were many casualties in the trench from artillery and machine-gun fire.

> *Fritz coming over about 4 o'clock and we fought and held on until almost surrounded when we surrendered with Lieutenant Harland, Simmonds and Holland – about twenty of us left. Grundy killed last minute[19]. Dobson shell-shock. M Wood killed. Sergeant Hartley wounded. Marched through Peronne and carried wounded. Marched to Roisel and put in hut."*[20] (Private Oswald Billingham)

Private William Grimshaw was another man taken prisoner. Joining the army only in March 1917, he had been assigned to the battalion in the autumn. He was sent to Antwerp where the Germans put him to work carrying shells. He was released in December 1918 and was demobilised in March 1919, returning to his home at 9 Rennie Street, West Gorton.

Another withdrawal was made in the evening to near the village of Herbecourt. Major John Whitworth's battalion now consisted of himself, one other officer and thirty four men. Other retreating units had been similarly reduced in strength. At about 9am on 26 March, a large body of Germans were spotted advancing about 500 yards away. The British immediately fell back. They had gone no more than 100 yards when Whitworth was shot in the back. His orderly was also wounded in the side. Whitworth was carried to a truck on a light railway line where he was evacuated from the combat area and taken to 8th General Hospital at Rouen. He died there on 31 March.

Captain Charles Anderton and the twenty remaining men withdrew with the small

Edward Marlor, killed in action on 26 March. Most of his service was with the 9th Battalion and the photograph was taken during that time and is reproduced courtesy of Jean Marlor and Peter Whitehead.

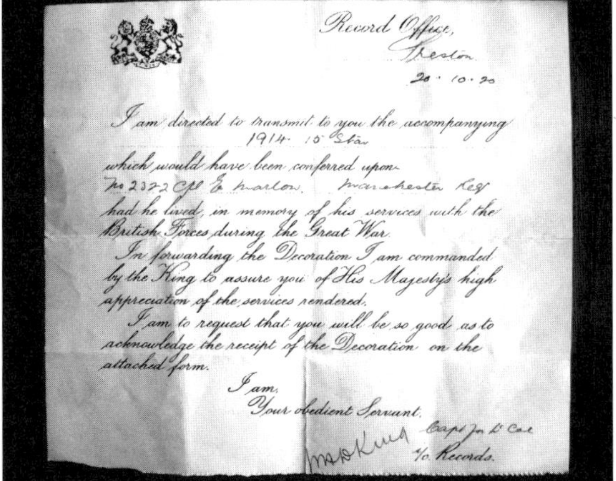

Record Office,
Preston
20 · 10 · 20

I am directed to transmit to you the accompanying
1914 · 15 Star
which would have been conferred upon
No 2372 Cpl E Marlor, Manchester Regt
had he lived, in memory of his services with the British Forces during the Great War.

In forwarding the Decoration I am commanded by the King to assure you of His Majesty's high appreciation of the services rendered.

I am to request that you will be so good as to acknowledge the receipt of the Decoration on the attached form.

I am,
Your obedient Servant,
[illegible] Capt for Lt Col
i/c Records.

Letter which accompanied Edward Marlor's service medal. Reproduced courtesy of Jean Marlor and Peter Whitehead.

NCOs from the 6th and other battalions of the Regiment at a Prisoner of war Camp in Chemnitz, Saxony. Cliff Hobson

number of comrades left in 66th Division but they managed to launch a counter-attack on the 27th which was successful in holding up the enemy advance for a while. It bought time for a further retreat to be made.

By the end of the month, the German attack was fizzling out. Their advance had been so rapid that the supply lines had become over-stretched. More significantly, they had also suffered heavy casualties and their ability to draw on reinforcements in the immediate area was at an end. The Manchesters were now on a defensive line between Hangard and Villers-Bretonneux. Stragglers who had become detached from the battalion had rejoined, as had a number of men whose wounds had been slight and their numbers were now five officers and 200 men. It enabled them to take part in a divisional counter-attack. It was not successful and the battalion was again forced to fall back. Another nineteen men were recorded as having died on 31 March.

The 2/6th Battalion, Manchester Regiment was now withdrawn from the fighting to the reserve. Although soldiers who had served with it, continued to fight and die they did so attached to other units. The battalion never saw action again.

1 National Archives reference: WO95/3144

2 "The Life of Major John Haworth Whitworth, DSO, MC". W L Mackennal, 1918. Publisher; Sherratt & Hughes, Manchester.

3 Walter Greenhalgh's diary is held by the Liddle Collection, University of Leeds and extracts are quoted with permission.

4 Joseph J Blayney, born in the Oldham area in 1885.

5 Lieutenant Eric Oughtred, born in the South Manchester area in 1889 and an employee of Tootal, Broadhurst, Lee & Co.

6 The papers of Private P R Hall are held by the Department of Documents, Imperial War Museum and extracts are used with the permission of the copyright holder.

7 Probably Private Horace Edgerley and Private A Riley. Riley is believed to have been invalided home in July 1917 after being gassed. He later transferred to the RAF and returned home to 6 Trafalgar Street, Eccles, in February 1919. Edgerley is also understood to have survived.

8 Born in 1891, Stockdale had lived in Cheadle Hulme, Cheshire before the war. Educated at Manchester Grammar School, he had practised as an accountant. He had joined the 1/6th Battalion, as a private, on 3 September 1914; saw action at Gallipoli and, as recorded in Chapter 4, returned to Britain on 12 August 1915 to train as an officer.

9 Dunkley, 20, was one of the Stockport lacrosse players who had joined up in the early weeks of the war. He had worked for the Royal Insurance Company at its branch at Exchange Street, Manchester

10 Oswald Billingham's papers are held by the Liddle Collection, University of Leeds, which gives permission for extracts to be quoted.

11 2nd Lieutenant Herbert Bate's papers are held by the Department of Documents, Imperial War Museum and extracts are quoted with the permission of the copyright holder. He had originally joined the Artist's Rifles and, whilst still in training in December 1915, had been selected to become an officer. He joined the 2/6th Battalion whilst it was at Crowborough.

12 Major Malcolm Melvill, temporarily commanding 2/6th Battalion whilst Colonel Wilson was seconded to brigade command.

13 Herbert Bate recovered from the effects of the gas and, promoted to Lieutenant, was transferred to the 9th Battalion, Royal Sussex Regiment. He was awarded the Military Cross in April 1919. After leaving the army, he became ordained as an Anglican minister and was rector of Welwyn Parish Church from 1931 to 1963.

14 Stockdale never fully recovered from his wound and was discharged from the army. He died in 1969. His widow, Irene, was later living at Burlington Place, Eastbourne.

15 Before enlisting, Buddery had been employed by Great Yarmouth Council as Inspector of Weights and Measures, a position his father had previously held for forty years.

16 Barber had enlisted in May 1916 and lived at 14 Gladstone Street, Eccles.

17 Born in 1890, Brooks had lived with his parents and older brother, Rowland, at the Manor House, Hale Barns, Cheshire. He practised as an architect in Manchester before enlisting in September 1914, into the 2/6th Battalion. Rowland Brooks had been killed in 1915 serving with the 1/6th Battalion at Gallipoli. Both men are commemorated on the Hale and Hale Barns war memorials. Archibald is further commemorated on the memorials at Manchester University and UMIST.

18 Ernest Bernard Gregsten, born in Middlesex in 1895

19 According to a letter written later in the year by Private Arthur Dobson, Grundy was accidentally killed by a bullet from a British Lewis gun - shot "through the heart from behind."

20 The records of the Commonwealth War Graves Commission do not record any soldier of the regiment called Wood being killed around this time. Sergeant Herbert Hartley avoided capture and was invalided home. He later returned to duty serving as a grenade instructor at a training camp at Filey until he returned to civilian life in February 1919.

Chapter 8

1918 – ATTACKS

THE READER LEFT THE 6TH BATTALION at the end of Chapter 6, towards the end of February 1918, relaxing near the village of Burbure, to the west of Bethune. March 1918 opened with a shooting competition, with one platoon from each company taking part, under the rules laid down by the Army Rifle Association. It was judged by Captain Stacpoole, brigade major of 127 Brigade. The next day, he inspected the platoons for general efficiency and, totalling the scores together from both days, declared the platoon from D Company to be the winner. On the 4th, a move was made to a new camp at L'Ecleme, about eight kilometres away.

Although still in the reserve, the battalion had orders that it might be needed to go into action if the Portuguese troops holding the front line in this sector came under serious attack and, almost immediately on arrival at L'Ecleme, company officers and senior NCOs went to reconnoitre the area. Mention was made in the previous chapter of the expectation of a German offensive and training now started to be directed towards that. Anticipating that the battalion would be rushed to the front line to assist whilst an attack was under way, a practice route march was undertaken by two companies wearing gas masks. The men reported that it had not appreciably slowed them down or tired them out.

On the 7th, Captain Farwell was hospitalised suffering with diphtheria. Successful vaccines against this contagious and potentially fatal disease were not yet common at this time and it meant that the other Headquarters officers and troops had to be isolated for several days. He survived and it would seem no other members of the battalion contracted the disease.

During the night of 11/12 March, orders were received that the battalion must make ready to move two hours later to go into action. The men turned out in fighting kit and the battalion was ready to go in just over an hour. It was another practice and one that had been entirely successful. The alert that came during the late evening of 22 March was not a practice.

> *Before dawn on March 21 1918, a terrific bombardment along more than fifty miles of the British front, from east of Arras to south of St Quentin, heralded the opening of the mightiest attack in the history of warfare. More than one hundred divisions, including many transferred from the Russian front - highly trained for the special purpose for which they were to be used, were suddenly launched against less than fifty. The German storm-troops were concentrated in depth on narrow fronts opposite what were judged to*

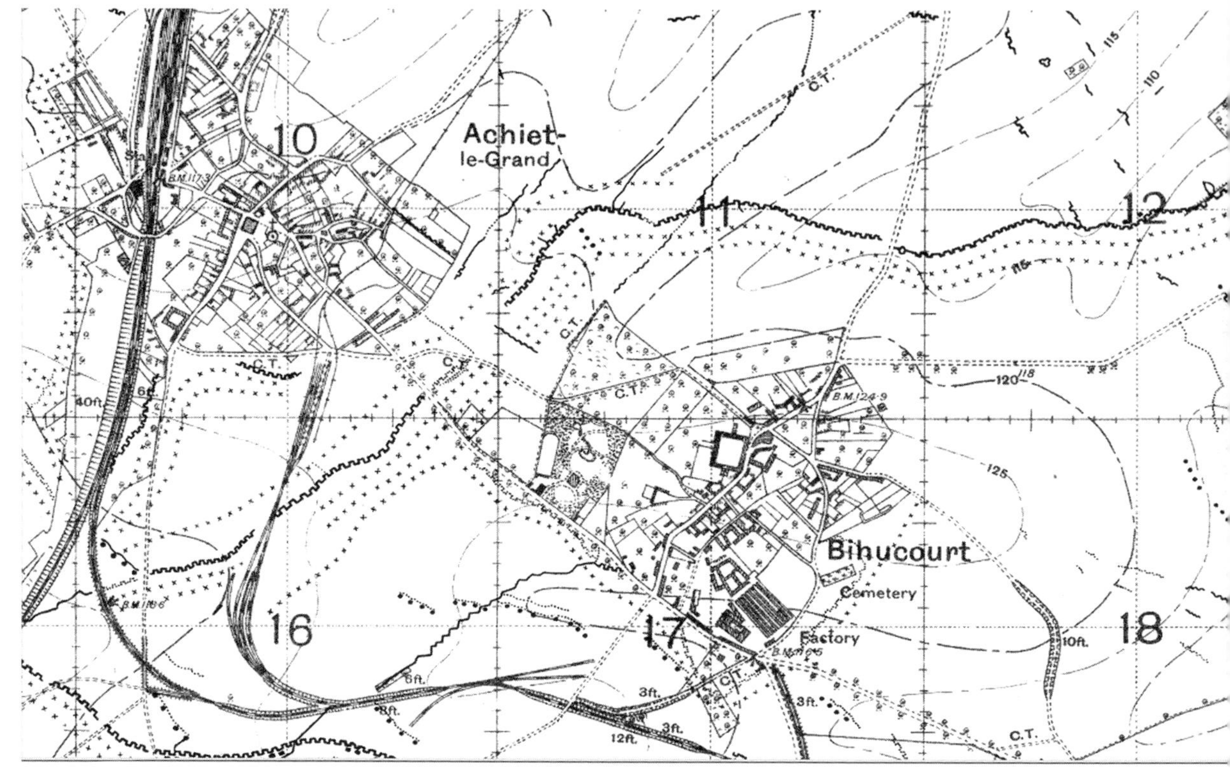

Trench map showing the area around Achiet-le-Grand and Bihucourt. Bihucourt Wood is not shown, being further away from the village.

> *be the most vulnerable points in the British line; fresh troops passing through those of the exhausted or shattered divisions that had been used to break open the gaps. Before they could be brought to a standstill, still further troops, with hordes of machine-guns, moved forward through the wreckage of the others, forcing their way to the flanks and even to the rear of the British positions.* (42nd Division history)

The troops in the front line were soon fighting a desperate retreat as land that had been captured over many months of 1916 and early 1917 was lost within hours.

The Manchesters marched off at 9am on 23 March, joining the other battalions of 42nd Division to be rushed forward on buses and lorries. The transport column headed south to Doullens, before turning to its designated objective – the village of Ayette, some eight miles south of Arras and the same distance northwest of Bapaume. They reached there at about midday and the battalion's four companies deployed along the ridge running between Ayette and Moyenville. As the divisional history records, the men who had joined since August 1915 were about to find 'the few remaining days of March more crammed with incident and fighting than the whole of their previous careers'.

Overnight, 127 Brigade received orders to move to Mory to relieve troops there but, after moving off at 5am and reaching Gomiecourt, found the orders cancelled. Fierce

Bihucourt Wood. Author

fighting had been going on around Mory for nearly two days, with the Germans capturing the village twice, only to be driven out again by British counter-attacks. However, another determined German assault had again taken it and there were reports that the British were now withdrawing. The 5th, 6th and 7th Manchesters were diverted to positions between the villages of Achiet-le-Grand and Bihucourt and dug in for the night.

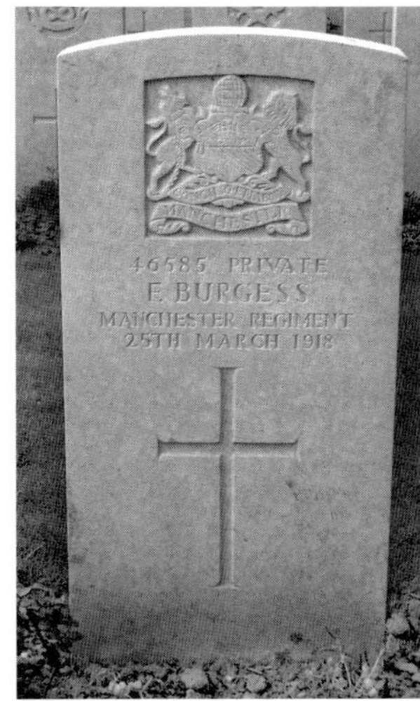

Private Frank Burgess, killed in action 25 March.

At 10.30 next morning, Second Lieutenant Rupert Kirsch led a patrol of twenty men towards both villages to try to ascertain the situation. Second Lieutenant George Nickson took ten men to similarly reconnoitre towards Biefvillers. Returning about noon, Kirsch had found no signs of the enemy but Nickson's patrol had seen small groups of Germans near the road running between Biefvillers and Bapaume. At about 2pm, the battalion was ordered to move and engage the Germans who were now to be seen advancing on the Achiet – Bihucourt road. Moving immediately and extending into line as they crested a small ridge, A and B Companies took up positions in and around Bihucourt Wood, in front of the village. C and D Companies deployed at Achiet.

The Germans came on an hour later and very heavy fighting took place. Under severe pressure, Captain Stanley Bridgford, commanding one of the companies at Bihucourt Wood, was forced to order a small withdrawal. He immediately led his men in a counter-

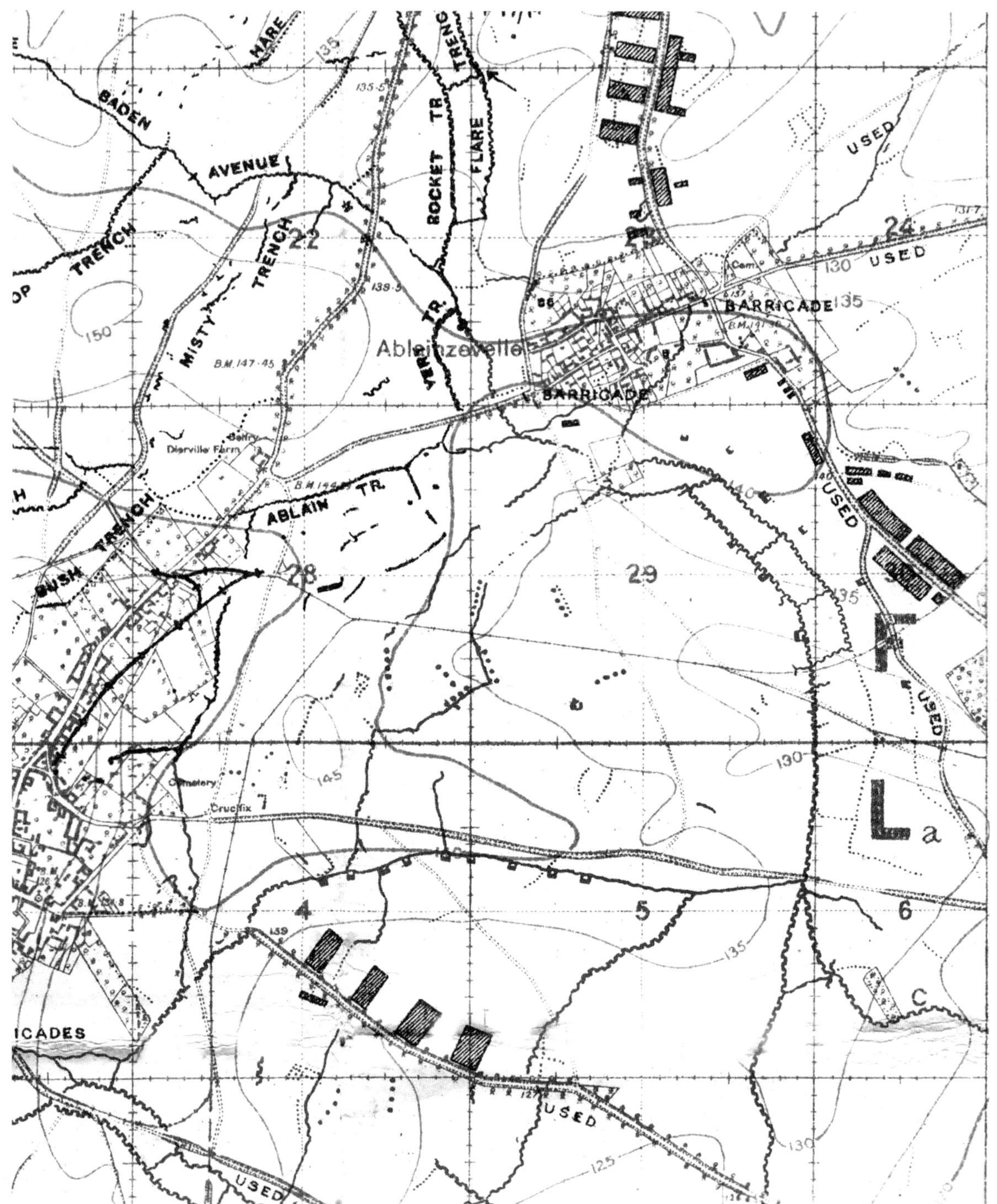

The Ablainzevelle battlefield. The 6th Battalion took up positions in and around Ablain Trench.

Ablainzevelle. View as would have been seen by the Manchesters. Author.

attack, driving the Germans back with a determined bayonet charge and more hand-to-hand fighting. However, the enemy's overwhelming numbers meant that they would once again force the Manchesters to withdraw, but precious time had been bought which allowed reserves to get to the fighting area and prevent the enemy making any significant progress from Bihucourt. During the fighting, Bridgford was badly wounded and taken prisoner, as were the two stretcher bearers who were attending to him. He died of his wounds on 8 April at a German military hospital at Ghent, Belgium. Fighting continued throughout the afternoon and well into the evening, in spite of British tanks being ordered into action and causing many German casualties in their support of the Manchesters.

Ablainzevelle in the distance. Battalion took up positions around the road.

The German advance had been temporarily checked but thirteen members of the battalion were known to be dead. Another fifty two were wounded. There was no news of another twenty-nine men who, at that time, were simply posted as missing – later records show that seventeen of them had also been killed. One of these seventeen, whose body was later found, was Private Henry Hindley. He had run a scrap metal business before enlisting at the end of 1915. He was originally posted to the Regiment's 2nd Battalion but returned to Britain for hospital treatment suffering with trench foot. After recovering, he had joined the 6th Battalion in the previous July.

By 11pm, the situation had become relatively quiet. Colonel Gilbert Wedgwood reported to the Brigadier and received orders that the battalion must now evacuate to a new position before the Germans could regroup. They slipped quietly away at 2am on 26 March making their way to the railway station at Achiet-le-Grand, where they moved by train to nearby Ablainzevelle. At about the same time, an old friend of the battalion was killed. Philip Holberton was the battalion's adjutant in September 1914, when it had first gone overseas. Promoted to Lieutenant Colonel, he was now in command of the 1/5th Battalion, Lancashire Fusiliers. His battalion was dug-in nearby at Gomiecourt when it came under another sustained attack. He was shot through the head and died instantly[1].

Private Henry Raymond. Killed in action on 27 March 1918. Buried in Douchy-les-Ayette British Cemetery. Author

After arriving at Ablainzevelle, the men took up a defensive line in trenches south east of the village. This was about 3am and they remained there for a few hours before moving to a stronger position west of the village, in the middle of the morning, after the enemy had been sighted moving in that direction towards Bucquoy. The 7th Battalion was to the right, with the 5th Battalion a little to the rear in close support. The positions were shelled heavily all day and they received a considerable amount of machine gun and rifle fire from nearby high ground. At about 7pm, the advancing German infantry was at last spotted coming into range over the crest of a low hill to the south. The advanced outposts and forward companies of the 6th and 7th Battalions opened a heavy fire on them, breaking up the attack formation and the Germans retreated to find cover.

With this attack broken, there were no further advances made by the Germans, although artillery shelling and machine gun fire was maintained on the Manchesters' positions. Casualties had been light during the day but another six men had been added to the toll of those killed.

Early on the morning of 27 March, the Germans were seen massing for an attack near Nissen huts close to Logeast Wood. The Manchesters urgently called for artillery support and, within minutes, British howitzers and 18-pounder guns were delivering extremely accurate fire onto the Germans. The preparations for attack were completely broken up and many casualties were

James Peover.

observed. However, throughout the morning, small detachments of Germans worked their way towards their front line. Lewis gun and rifle fire was directed at them with some success. At about 2pm, the enemy had brought together sufficient troops to launch a local attack on the positions held by A Company but this was beaten off with sustained rifle fire. Private William Barker, one of the battalion's original members, kept a diary for 1918. *'Bombardment of position with 9.4 trench mortars. Attack driven off. Bob Stott and Hookey Walker killed.'*[2]

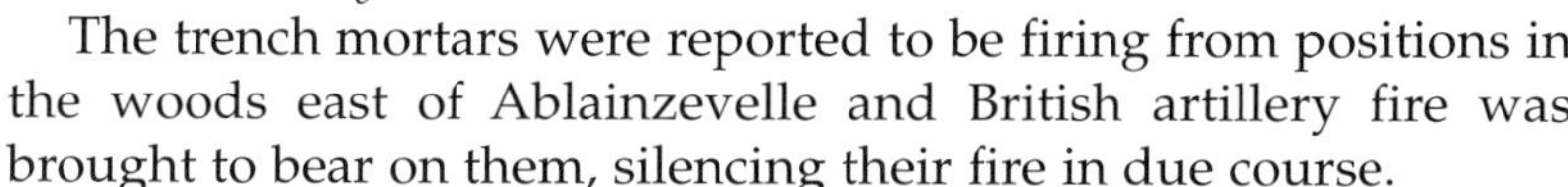

The trench mortars were reported to be firing from positions in the woods east of Ablainzevelle and British artillery fire was brought to bear on them, silencing their fire in due course.

Later in the afternoon, troops from A and D Companies, led by Captain Fox, of the 5th Battalion, and Lieutenant William Wynne, of the 6th, entered Ablainzevelle. Moving along the main street, they came across two parties of German machine-gunners and immediately opened fire. There were a number of enemy casualties with the remainder dropping their guns and running away. The machine guns were captured and taken back to the British lines. Fox was the only British casualty, being severely wounded just before reaching the safety of the trench. He is thought to have survived.

Before the war, James Peover, twenty-one, had lived with his parents in Crumpsall and had been training to become a pharmacist. He had joined the battalion at Gallipoli in September 1915. Now one of the headquarters runners, he had spent the day taking messages to and from the front line under heavy fire. He was badly wounded and, after receiving treatment just behind the front line, was evacuated to 55th General Hospital at Boulogne, where he died on 3 April.

Private Frederick Hodgson, 19, from Blackburn. Wounded in the recent fighting, he died at a military hospital on the Channel coast on 3 April.

During the early morning of 28 March, large numbers of Germans were again seen assembling on the battalion's front, near to the Nissen huts. Artillery fire was brought down on them with such force that the enemy had no practical option but to withdraw. But, about 11am, German infantry were spotted working their way down a disused trench towards the positions held by Lieutenant Robert Maule. He let them move much closer and then, in a singular act of bravery, he leapt out of his trench and, standing on the parapet, called to his men to follow him. They quickly did so and the Germans were caught by surprise. Taking on two Germans himself, Maule wounded the officer and another soldier, taking both prisoner. His men engaged the others, killing fifteen and only four Germans managed to escape. Meanwhile, to the left, D Company was successfully fighting off another small attack. They had spotted that one of the men escaping Maule's party had been wounded in the leg and was still in No Man's Land. As soon as it was safe to do so, some of the Manchesters went out and took him prisoner, bringing him back to the trench for treatment. Maule received the Military Cross for his bravery in the action and was promoted to captain.

Later in the day, a formal note was received from the divisional commander, Major General Solly-Flood, congratulating 'most heartily the 1/6th Manchester Regiment on soldier-like spirit shown by their patrol which entered Ablainzevelle killing Bosches and capturing two M.G.s'. (Battalion war diary)

> *While one of the hottest attacks of the day was in progress, Corporal A Brooks[3], 6th Manchesters, noticed that his men were short of rifle-oil and that the bolts of the rifles, from incessant use, were not working freely. In the face of the enemy machine guns and rifles, the corporal calmly moved along the line of his platoon with an oil-can, personally oiled the bolts – and survived.* (Divisional history)

About 6pm, the battalion came under intense shelling for fifty minutes, but it ceased as abruptly as it had started and the anticipated German infantry attack did not materialise. The evening was quiet and, at 10pm, the battalion was relieved from the front line by the 5th Battalion together with men from the divisional company of Royal Engineers who had been fighting as infantry since the action began. Along the whole of the British front, the German attack had, at last, been generally held.

There would be many medals awarded for gallantry and devotion to duty over these days. Company Sergeant Major Jack Martin, whose rescue after being torpedoed was described in Chapter 5, was to receive the Distinguished Conduct Medal.

> *For conspicuous gallantry and devotion to duty. During three days especially, this warrant officer was of greatest assistance to his company officer. When the shelling was heaviest, he went about placing his men to the best advantage. He was seriously wounded but continued his work until again wounded. He showed the highest courage and determination." Martin had been wounded on 25 March and evacuated to a field hospital at Gezaincourt, where he died three days later.*

Second Lieutenant Henry Martin, MC.

Also receiving the DCM, was Lance Sergeant Rupert Dennerley who had taken charge of two platoons when the officers had become casualties. He had led them in at least one of the numerous small counter-attacks, killing four Germans with his own bayonet. Similarly, Acting Company Sergeant Major Sydney Wilson found that all the company officers had been killed or wounded and he also took charge of the men, displaying conspicuous gallantry and devotion to duty during this critical period.

Second Lieutenant Henry Martin[4] was awarded the Military Cross. He had charge of one of the forward trenches and, as officer casualties mounted, took command of the company. *'His contempt of danger and care for his men kept them going through a difficult time. He showed fine courage.'*

Frank Crossley had started the war as a private with the battalion, going into action in May 1915 at Gallipoli. Now a Lieutenant and serving as the battalion's transport officer, he was also awarded the Military Cross. *'For a week, this officer regularly brought up rations and ammunition under heavy fire of all descriptions regardless of personal danger. His courage, coolness and steady work were a splendid example to his section.'*

The battalion spent its first day back in the reserve cleaning up and resting but their positions were still within range of the German artillery and there was considerable shelling, most of which fell on neighbouring units and casualties amongst the Manchesters were minimal. On the 30th, they were further relieved and took up positions at Fonquevillers. They found the trenches in very poor condition and flooded in parts. There were no dug-outs and the only protection from the weather were trench covers which had been left by the outgoing battalion. But, at least, there was hardly any shelling, apart from an occasional salvo of high explosive and shrapnel, which wounded five men during the day. The final day of March was again quiet and it allowed casualty returns to be properly submitted to brigade headquarters. The war diary records that, since the battalion had gone into action on the 23rd, thirty-eight men were known to have died, another 183 were wounded and a further forty-six were still missing and it would be some time before their fates became known. Records held by the Commonwealth War Graves Commission show seventy-eight men had died in the period, including those who had died of their wounds at field hospitals.

The first few days of April were spent in several different locations around Fonquevillers and Gommecourt, both areas which saw fierce fighting during the Battle of the Somme in 1916. It was much quieter now and, though very weary from lack of sleep, the men were put to work clearing and improving the trenches.

> *Rained hard. Sent from post to sunken road to get a sleep at night. If Germans had attacked during last few days, I don't think our boys would have been in a fit state to stop them getting through.* (Private William Barker, diary entry, 6 April 1918)

The enemy shelling was so light as to be almost non-intrusive, compared with recent days. On 8 April, a draft of 10 officers and 88 men arrived from the 18th Battalion, Manchester Regiment which, like many others, was being disbanded. A further draft of 140 men arrived on 11 April. These men had come directly from Britain, having just finished their training with the 51st Graduated Battalion. They were all young men, recently conscripted and none aged over nineteen. The need for replacements had been so urgent that a number had not yet reached their 18th birthday which, under normal circumstances, would be the minimum age for overseas service. These young soldiers were weeded out and sent to the reserve areas for safety until their birthday.

On the 15th, preparations were made for a move back to the front the next day and officers and senior NCOs from each company went to reconnoitre the new area. The battalion moved off at 4.30pm on the 16th and had reached Sailly-au-Bois five hours later. They had to halt here for some time as their route was being shelled by the Germans, but they were in position by midnight and had suffered no casualties. The next day, intelligence received suggested that the Germans were planning an attack for the following day. To resist this, the 6th and 7th Battalions moved to the village of Hebuterne, with B Company of the 6th deploying in the village and the other companies in trenches, some hastily dug, around it. In the event, the rumours proved false and there was no enemy attack.

Over the coming days, a number of men received notifications that they were to be awarded gallantry medals for their bravery and devotion to duty around Ablainzevelle the previous month. On the 18th, eighteen heard they had been awarded the Military Medal: Sergeants A Johnson and H Berry, Lance Sergeant D Gorman, Corporal J Foster, Lance Corporal F Dugdale and Privates T Beresford, A Brooks, S Butterworth, G Dutton, W Fletcher, H Hancock, S Irwin, T Ralphs, W Smith, S Tomlinson, B Stubbs, H Warburton and H Wilson.

Back in the front line on the night of 20 April, Second Lieutenant Babbage led a patrol of twelve men out into No Man's Land. Their mission was to try and find an enemy post and, if possible, raid it. However, the raiders were spotted and came under fire and had to return to the trench, when they were effectively 'chased off' by the German patrol. Three nights later, another raid was attempted on enemy machine gun posts. It was carried out by a platoon from B Company, under Second Lieutenant Leonard Burrows and another from D Company, commanded by Second Lieutenant Leonard Bodell. To allow them to get safely across No Man's Land, a protective artillery barrage was opened on the Germans in several bursts between 1.20am and 2.30am. At 2.40, the shelling changed to a box barrage, firing immediately behind the German front line, cutting off the enemy posts from the possibility of being reinforced or, indeed, from the Germans being able to make an escape. Both platoons of Manchesters stormed into the German positions but found they had already been evacuated. The body of one German was found and he was carrying sufficient identification to establish he was serving with the 126th Infantry Regiment. There were no casualties on the British side.

In the evening of 24 April, New Zealand troops moved up to relieve the Manchesters who withdrew to rest billets at Coigneux, where they remained until the 29th.

Much of May 1918 was spent at a reserve camp near the village of Henu, approximately midway between Amiens and Arras. Although the German assault which started on 21 March had ground to a halt by the end of that month, the enemy attacked again, on 9 April, in Northern France and the area south of the Belgian town of Ypres, in what was later officially designated as the Battle of the Lys. As before, it was initially overwhelmingly successful, prompting Field Marshal Sir Douglas Haig to issue a critical Special Order of the Day on 11 April:

Many among us are now tired. To those I would say that victory will belong to the side which holds out the longest. The French Army is moving rapidly and in great force to our support. Every position must be held to the last man. With our backs to the wall and believing in the justice of our cause, every one of us must fight on to the end. The safety of our homes and the freedom of mankind alike depend upon the conduct of each one of us at this critical moment.

Private Arthur Bradshaw, from Besses o'th' Barn. Died of wounds on 29 May at an army hospital on the Channel coast. Believed to have previously served with the 9th Battalion.

With that in mind and in the context that the enemy might attack again on the Somme front, Henu would be no rest camp for the Manchesters. They spent the time training and the main focus was in defensive fighting and counter-attack. Officers and NCOs from each platoon went to fully reconnoitre the area which they would be required to defend against any German assault in this sector.

Other than this, the war diary has little to record for the month, although there were some casualties on the night of 15/16 May, when a German plane dropped six bombs on the camp area. Several men were wounded, including some serious injuries, and later records show that three men[5] died of wounds in the following days whilst in military hospitals.

The battalion's experience was put to good use for three weeks from 17 May, when two companies of the 2nd Battalion of the American 307th Regiment were attached for battle training. The Regiment consisted of men from New York and they had arrived in France on 20 April 1918.

Company officers and specialist instructors were detailed to assist them in musketry, physical training and bayonet fighting. This was commenced during the morning. They have apparently had little musketry instruction and particular attention is to be paid to this part of their training. Elementary rifle practices were carried out in the afternoon. The men appear particularly keen to acquire knowledge. (Battalion war diary)

Jack Ratcliffe, 18, from Lower Broughton. Probably wounded in the night attack on 19 July, he died three days later in hospital.

There was a parade on the 26th in front of Major General Solly-Flood when he presented medal ribbons to all the men who had received gallantry awards for the actions in the March fighting. The same day, Colonel Wedgwood, who had been in command of the battalion for the previous eight months, was promoted Brigadier General and left to take command of 126 Brigade. Tom Blatherwick, was promoted to Lieutenant Colonel to take his place. It was a popular promotion.

The Manchesters returned to trench duty during the late evening of 6 June 1918, deploying near the village of Hebuterne. It was to be a quiet month, marked only by occasional heavy enemy shelling which caused a few casualties. On most nights when they were in the front line, patrols were sent out into No Man's Land to try to pinpoint the location of enemy machinegun posts and other strongpoints. There was an alert on the 25th, when reports were received from brigade headquarters that German storm troops had been spotted in the Hebuterne sector. Soldiers on guard duty were warned to exercise extra vigilance in case there were signs of an attack or raid being prepared but there were none. However, just in case there was a hidden build-up of German infantry, the British artillery heavily shelled the enemy lines and support areas on four separate occasions during the night.

There was a period away from the front line at the beginning of July and, on their first day in the reserve area, the men had the opportunity for hot baths at Courcelles. Over the following days, they continued to supply working parties; improving trenches, dug-outs, etc.

A number of men started to fall ill with influenza and needed to be hospitalised. Although the consequences could not have been known at that time, they were among the first victims of what would become a worldwide pandemic of Spanish flu, which caused millions of deaths from the autumn onward.

The Manchesters returned to the front on 18 July, taking over trenches near Colincamps. The next night, the battalion supported a small attack by the 7th Battalion to capture a number of advanced enemy posts and incorporate them into the British line. C Company secured its objectives without opposition but D Company had a few minutes of stiff fighting before they overcame the defenders in the trench known as Nairn Street. One man was killed[6] and others wounded. Although not taking part in the attack, Captain Hay was severely wounded. Frederick Hay's early service was detailed in Chapter 3. During the fighting, Company Sergeant Major Herbert Whitford, a pre-war member of the battalion, had shown great courage for which he was awarded the Distinguished Conduct Medal. The citation records:

> *He led a party under heavy machine-gun fire to bring in a man lying in No Man's Land and led another party with ammunition and rations through to the garrison holding the new posts. Throughout the operations, he set a fine example of courage and resource to the men of his company.*

The next two days were spent consolidating the gains, including a few very small advances, intended to do no more than straighten out the line. A number of patrols were sent out to explore the immediate area, including one from B Company on the evening of 23 July. It was commanded by an officer and included Sergeant Thomas Pygott, a holder of the Military Medal, and four other men. They accidentally stumbled across a German outpost and were challenged. The Germans immediately opened fire, throwing a large number of grenades which killed or mortally wounded Pygott. The British officer emptied his revolver at the enemy over their barricade but then ordered the patrol to withdraw for their own safety, leaving Pygott behind[7]. The officer and another man had also been wounded in the incident, although not too seriously. Later on, a patrol from A Company went out along the same route to see if they could find Pygott and rescue him but there was no trace and he was never heard of again. The next evening, the battalion was replaced in the front line by the 5th

Battalion and moved back to the support line, where it remained for the remainder of the month.

The Battle of Amiens, which started on 8 August, was the commencement of an Allied offensive which would bring the war to an end, just three months later. The British III Corps, Australian Corps, Canadian Corps and French 1st Army all attacked, supported by heavy artillery, tanks and aircraft and, in an echo of the German offensives in the spring, overwhelmed the enemy, forcing them back several miles within the first few hours. It would be some days before the Manchesters had a part to play in this battle and they spent the day training in the reserve areas. This was training for the new style of war that was expected to be needed with the anticipated breakthrough. The days of trench warfare would soon be over and the open warfare of moves across unknown terrain, not seen since 1914, would return. The soldiers who had seen service with the battalion in Egypt would recognise many of the tactics needed to advance whilst being unsure exactly where the enemy would be found and the Manchesters would be better placed than some other units which had only seen action on the Western Front. The Brigadier visited the training area during the afternoon of the 8th and two platoons from C Company put on a demonstration of the tactics for him.

The battalion returned to the front line on 12 August. Just before they arrived, the outgoing unit had advanced the line, establishing four new posts. As B Company was in the process of taking over these positions, the Germans counter-attacked on three separate occasions, using many grenades, but they were repulsed, mainly by accurate fire from the Lewis gunners. Corporal Matthew Shea had served for most of the war with the 9th Battalion but had been transferred earlier in 1918 and was now in charge of one of the Lewis guns. Although wounded in the first German attack, he remained at his post, directing the fire. In extreme pain, he refused to go to the Aid Post for treatment until the attacks were finally beaten off. He was awarded the Military Medal for his devotion to duty.

Although there had been no significant action in the Manchesters' sector, reports started to be received on the morning of 14 August that the Germans were withdrawing from their front line. Strong patrols were sent out in the afternoon to check the situation and they reported that the enemy had, indeed, retreated. One of these was led by Alfred Wignall, the Scout Sergeant. He and his men went forward some 2,500 yards, bringing back most useful information about the terrain in front of the battalion[8]. As a result, the whole Brigade started an advance to try to regain fighting contact with the Germans. It was not until the next morning that they established exactly where the enemy was. The Germans had again taken up previously prepared defensive positions and opened a heavy artillery and machine-gun barrage on the advancing British, killing four members of the battalion.

By the early morning of 16 August, the situation had again become uncertain, with confusing and contradictory reports being received about the location of the Germans and the relative positions of neighbouring Allied troops. It was decided to halt the battalion's advance near the village of Serre and send out Sergeant Wignall and his scouts again to try to establish where the other battalions of the brigade were. He returned an hour later having found the troops on the right, who had lost their correct direction during the enemy shelling. The British remained in place overnight and throughout the next day, until they were relieved in the evening by the 7th Battalion.

Around this time, Sergeant William Roberts undertook acts of bravery for which he was awarded his first Distinguished Conduct Medal:

William Roberts, DCM and Bar. Manchester Regiment Archives.

For conspicuous gallantry and good leadership whilst in charge of fighting patrols to keep in touch with the enemy and advance the line. He led his men to the second objective under very heavy fire and, despite the fact that both his flanks were unprotected, owing to other patrols not being able to advance, he held on under very difficult circumstances. Later, his platoon officer being wounded, he assumed command and handled the platoon with great skill. He set a very fine example to his men.

A general advance of the whole British line on a ten mile front was ordered for the morning of 21 August. It would later be known as the Battle of Bapaume and was the second phase of the offensive started on the 8th of the month. On 127 Brigade's front, the 6th Manchesters would attack on the right, with their comrades from the 7th Battalion on their left. Once the leading two companies from each battalion had captured the German front line, the remaining two would overlap them to continue the advance to a second objective, with further units then taking up the attack. The battalion moved into assembly positions during the morning of the 20th.

The Royal Artillery opened fire at 4.55am and, fifty minutes later, the battalion went over the top. There was a thick mist and this helped to screen the attackers, who were moving across No Man's Land, keeping close behind the protection of the artillery barrage which rolled forward relentlessly towards the German defences.

A very difficult ravine had had to be crossed with steep gradients down to and up from the Beaucourt-Puisieux road. This broken ground was defended by nests of machine-guns but the friendly mist rendered their fire far less deadly than usual and the Manchesters were able to get to close quarters. Many of the enemy were killed with the bayonet and a large number captured. (Divisional history)

As A and C Companies moved forward, three enemy machine guns were firing heavily into them from the left flank. Sergeant Herbert Holden and Private T J Davis charged the enemy post, killing six of the gunners and taking the remainder of them prisoner. Their act of singular courage played a large part in the success of the attack and they were both awarded the Distinguished Conduct Medal. Private James Ingham, from Stockport, is another believed to have won his DCM for action on this day. As one of the battalion's Lewis gunners, he had covered the flank until other troops arrived, although under heavy shellfire throughout. His fire kept about seventy Germans pinned in their dug-outs and they were able to be taken prisoner.

By 7.45, A and C Companies reported that they had secured the first objective but, an hour later, there was still no sign of B Company. The latter had lost its way in the mist and, as the men moved forward, they had come across a well fortified German defensive position and had suffered many casualties. A gap between B Company and the other two companies of some 800 yards had opened up and the company commander spread his men very thinly to secure the line as best he could. Although the units on either side of the two Manchester battalions had been able to make significant progress, heavy machine gun fire was preventing any further move by the 6th Battalion. Positions were held overnight, in front of Miraumont, so that British artillery could be brought up to assist in clearing the way. Casualties had been relatively light but ten men had been killed during the day, mostly from B Company. Private Stanley Moores had found himself facing a small party of the enemy and had, single-handed, attacked it, killing its officer and two other men and taking prisoner the remaining four. After handing them over, he spent the rest of the day acting as a company runner, taking messages under heavy fire. He was another worthy winner of the Distinguished Conduct Medal.

In fact, it was the German artillery which first came into action significantly on the morning of 22 August, opening a heavy bombardment on the British line, forcing the battalion on the right of the Manchesters to withdraw a short distance. The bombardment was maintained for most of the day but there was little action, except for a weak attempt at a counter attack on the positions held by B Company. In the early hours of 23 August, reports from fighting patrols indicated that the Germans were falling back from their positions. This was later confirmed and, the following morning, the battalion again advanced.

Sergeant William Roberts had led one of the patrols and, whilst out, they had come across an enemy machine gun post. They attacked it, killing the crew and bringing back the gun. He was awarded his second Distinguished Conduct Medal for the action. Born in 1886, Roberts had originally enlisted into the Lancashire Fusiliers but was transferred to the 18th Battalion, Manchester Regiment on going overseas in 1916. In January 1917, he was court-martialled for drunkenness and going absent without leave and was reduced to the rank of private. It took him twelve months to regain the rank of sergeant and he had transferred to the 6th Battalion, when the 18th had been disbanded earlier in 1918. He was wounded in early September and Colonel Tom Blatherwick, the battalion commander, wrote to him at home congratulating him on

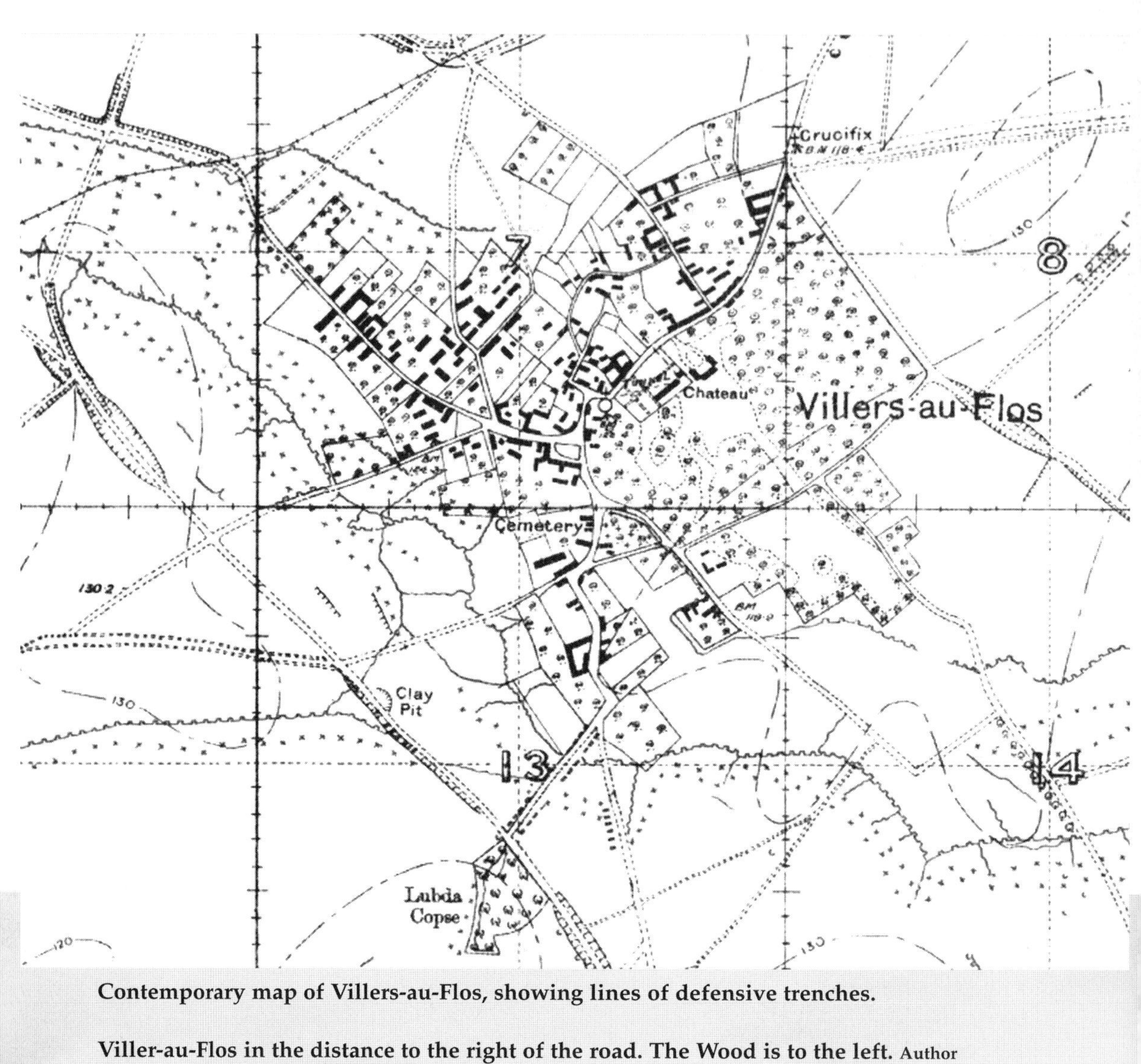

Contemporary map of Villers-au-Flos, showing lines of defensive trenches.

Viller-au-Flos in the distance to the right of the road. The Wood is to the left. Author

The Villers-au-Flos battlefield. The view is as would have been seen by the German defenders. The camera position is in the Wood and what is now a German military cemetery. Author.

both awards of the DCM:

> *I offer you my most hearty congratulations on a very well earned honour. Your work with the battalion has always been most excellent and I sincerely hope we may see you back again. I hope your wounds are improving.*[9]

The advance carefully continued through the next day. The village of Miraumont was encircled and captured by early afternoon, with significant numbers of prisoners being taken. In the late afternoon, on reaching the outskirts of Warlencourt, the battalion came under heavy machine gun fire from the left as well as from the front. An attack could not be considered until the troops were reinforced and it was not possible to remain in such a precarious position overnight. Orders were given to withdraw the Manchesters a little way to high ground. The next morning, patrols from neighbouring units established that the Germans had vacated Warlencourt, but were still shelling the area from artillery positions well to their rear. The advance continued but the Manchesters were relieved from the front line for a couple of days rest.

Private Thomas Bailey, from Salford. Killed in action on 2 September. Buried in Bancourt British Cemetery. Author.

With the battalion back in the support line on the morning of the 29th, Second Lieutenant Stanley Heyhoe led a patrol towards the town of Bapaume. He was able to confirm that the Germans had vacated the area and the advance continued. It was an action which would win him the Military Cross. *"His energy and disregard for danger were an example to all"*. Heyhoe had been commissioned into the 18th Battalion in November 1917, transferring when it was

The grave of Leopold Sitford at Manchester Cemetery, Riencourt-les-Bapaume. Author

disbanded.

The next objectives were the villages of Riencourt and Villers-au-Flos and a move towards them was made on the morning of the 30th, but Riencourt was found to be heavily defended and a halt was called to the Manchesters' advance, whilst other units dealt with the Germans. Colonel Tom Blatherwick had personally led his men forward towards the village and was awarded the Distinguished Service Order for this and an earlier action:

He displayed the greatest courage and skill when personally supervising the crossing of a river in the face of a position strongly held by the enemy. Later, his battalion was ordered to relieve another battalion at short notice in an attack on positions which had not been previously reconnoitred. He went forward and made a personal reconnaissance, amidst heavy shell bursts and machine-gun fire and returning led the battalion successfully forward under extremely difficult circumstances.

The 6th Manchesters next found themselves in the vanguard of the attack on the morning of 2 September. Supported by three tanks, A and B Companies advanced towards Villers-au-Flos at about 6am, the war diary recording that they had secured their objective, on the eastern edge of the wood on the outskirts of the village, by 6.10 "with great dash". Neighbouring units had not had the same success and their failure to advance as quickly had left the battalion exposed to enfilade machine gun fire from both northern and southern flanks. In particular, "A" Company came under heavy fire from a group of Germans in positions in and around a group of huts.

Viller-au-Flos German Cemetery. Author

Second Lieutenant William Greenough would serve with the Battalion for less than a month before being killed on 21 October. Author

The situation on the southern flank eased later in the morning when 21st Division cleared the Germans from Lubig Wood but it was early afternoon before a raiding party from the neighbouring New Zealand battalion attacked and captured the huts. Throughout this time, there had been a problem with the British artillery firing short and a not inconsiderable number of casualties amongst the Manchesters was caused by this, as well as from the expected German bombardment of the newly captured positions. Twenty eight men had been killed, including Second Lieutenant Leopold Sitford[10]. He enlisted into the 8th Battalion in 1915, aged 26 and his service papers show him to have been a short man, just over five foot three inches tall, with a sallow complexion, blue eyes and dark hair. He worked as a Maker Up, possibly a position in Manchester's garment trade. He was transferred to the King's Liverpool Regiment when he went overseas in 1916 and was commissioned into the 6th Manchesters the following year. Only a few weeks before his death, he had been at home on leave and had married his fiancée, Edith Read.

The battalion was relieved from the front line overnight and withdrew to rest positions near Warlencourt, where it remained until 21 September, mainly undertaking the usual training courses in musketry, signalling, etc. During this time, the battalion received several reinforcing drafts totalling nearly 200 men, including five new second lieutenants. One of the newly commissioned officers was William Gladstone Greenough[11]. He had served as a Sergeant with the 21st Battalion,

The Havrincourt battlefield, where the Battalion attacked from left to right on 27 September.

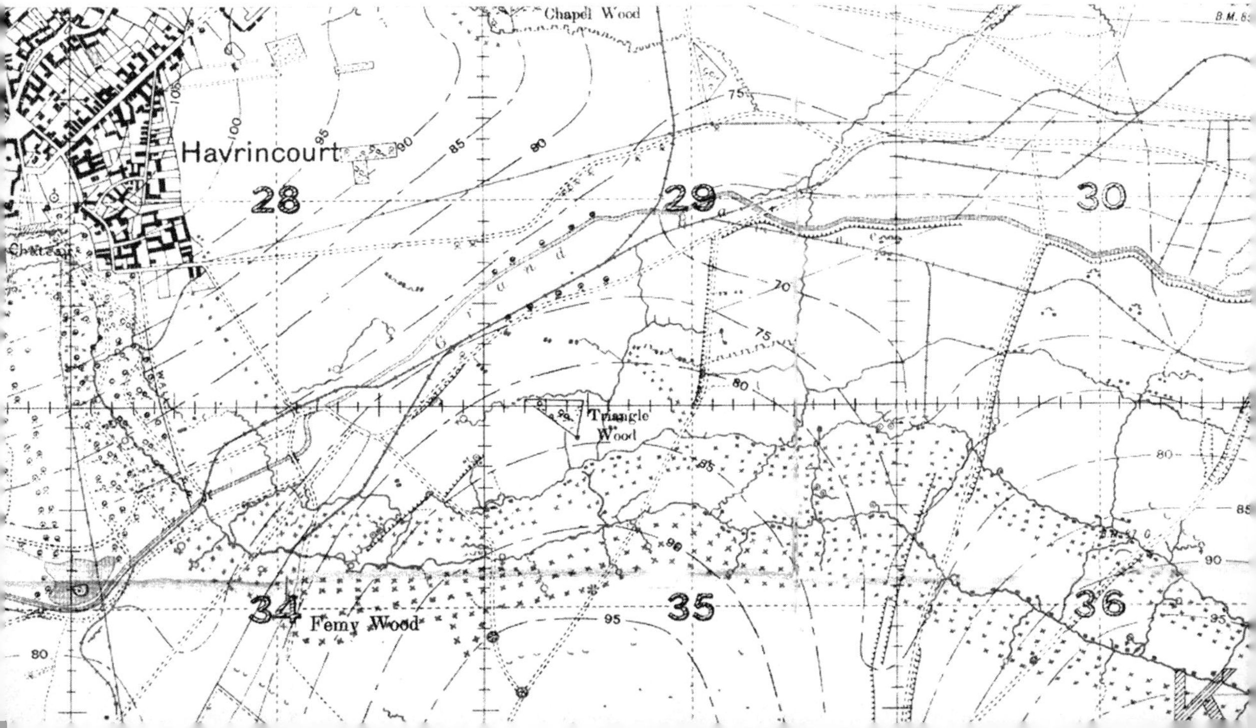

Early photograph of what is now Ribecourt Road Cemetery.

the sixth of the Pals Battalions, and had been awarded the Distinguished Conduct Medal in early 1917. Second Lieutenant Greenough was killed in action on 21 October.

Captain George Kershaw was one of several men who were notified that their recent bravery was to be recognised by the award of a medal, in his case with the Military Cross. The citation, published in the London Gazette, in October, reads:

> *During recent operations, the company commanded by him was repeatedly engaged. He organised his attacking parties with great skill and, at one period when, owing to casualties inflicted by heavy machine gun and rifle fire, the advance was checked, he personally took charge of the attacking party and, by his determined example and fine leadership, successfully drove out the enemy and established a strong point 800 yards in front of the old line. He did splendid work.*

Ribecourt Road Cemetery, On 27 September, the Manchesters attacked from left to right here.

Born in Harrogate, Herbert Stone was living in Liverpool when he enlisted. He was killed in action at Havrincourt on 27 September, aged nineteen.

The battalion left camp on the morning of 21 September, making its way towards the front line, which had been advanced several miles since the Manchesters had last been in action. The Germans had slowly fallen back towards their defensive positions, known to the British as the Hindenberg Line. It had been a costly few weeks for both sides, with some of the severest fighting of the whole war. After a few days in reserve, the Manchesters moved into assembly positions near Havrincourt ready to take part in a major attack the next morning – 27 September. The men knew the area well, having been here in May 1917, when it had then also formed the front line.

On 42nd Division's front, the attack would be led by the 6th and 7th Battalions, together with two battalions of Lancashire Fusiliers from 125 Brigade. Zero hour for the British attack was set for 5.20am but 42nd Division would not go into action until some three hours later. The reason for this was the ground over which they were to attack was in plain view of the Germans entrenched on the vantage point of the Flesquieres

Ridge. These positions would first need to be captured. Private William Barker: 'Went over the top at 8.20am. Battalion advanced two miles and got plenty of prisoners and machine guns, etc.' The official records confirm the battalion's success as recorded by Barker. D Company, still under the strong command of George Kershaw, had quickly reached its objective where they found many Germans wanting to do nothing more than surrender.

By 10.30, C Company, commanded by Captain F Whitamore, had also had similar success in taking its objective. A and B Companies passed through these positions to continue to press home the attack. Large numbers of German prisoners were now being escorted to the rear and, by mid-morning, the numbers exceeded 200, including four officers. The entire attack had been a success for the battalion and, by 3pm, all objectives had been fully secured. It had, however, cost the lives of thirty four men and many more wounded. B Company had suffered heavily and the company strength holding its objective on the Yellow Line was just two officers and thirty other ranks.

> *It had been a soldier's battle of ding-dong fighting against an enemy possessing the advantage of the strongest possible positions combined with superiority in numbers of men and machine guns. To win success against such odds required skill with weapons – bullet, bayonet and bomb – and also the finest qualities of initiative, resource, determination and endurance on the part of subordinate leaders and men, and this skill and these qualities had been shown to a high degree. When company, platoon and section commanders fell, junior NCOs and even privates proved they could lead.* (42nd Division history)

The next morning, it was clear that the Germans had made a significant withdrawal from the area and there was almost no enemy shellfire. Other units took up the advance, but the Manchesters made their way back to rest positions, where they remained for a few days. The Hindenberg Line had been breached and the men had proved the divisional motto to Go One Better.

The battalion left its rest area during the morning of 8 October, to begin a three day march to the front. After an overnight stop at Vaucalles, they continued toward Le Grand Pont, a hamlet about twenty kilometres south east of the town of Cambrai. As they neared it, signs of very recent hand-to-hand fighting were evident. The New Zealand Canterbury Regiment had been amongst those in action in the area with men under the command of Second Lieutenant James Mitchell clearing the village of the enemy whilst it was still being shelled by the Allied artillery. Groups of German dead were still lying on the road and in the adjacent fields as the Manchesters marched through to their positions on the far side of the hamlet. The next two days were spent resting, although parties were sent out to collect any discarded munitions and other equipment that could be salvaged.

The next major obstacle to the British advance was the River Selle, in the vicinity of Le Cateau – the location of a major battle in August 1914. It had to be crossed and the Germans held heavily defended positions to its east. The German High Command publicly asserted that an honourable peace could only be achieved by strong resistance to the Allied advance, offering a tough defence to any attack. Major General Solly-Flood passed the German statement on to the troops of 42nd Division adding 'The Division, as it has always done, will overcome the toughest defence the already shaken Hun can offer and teach him once more what the Divisional Motto means'.

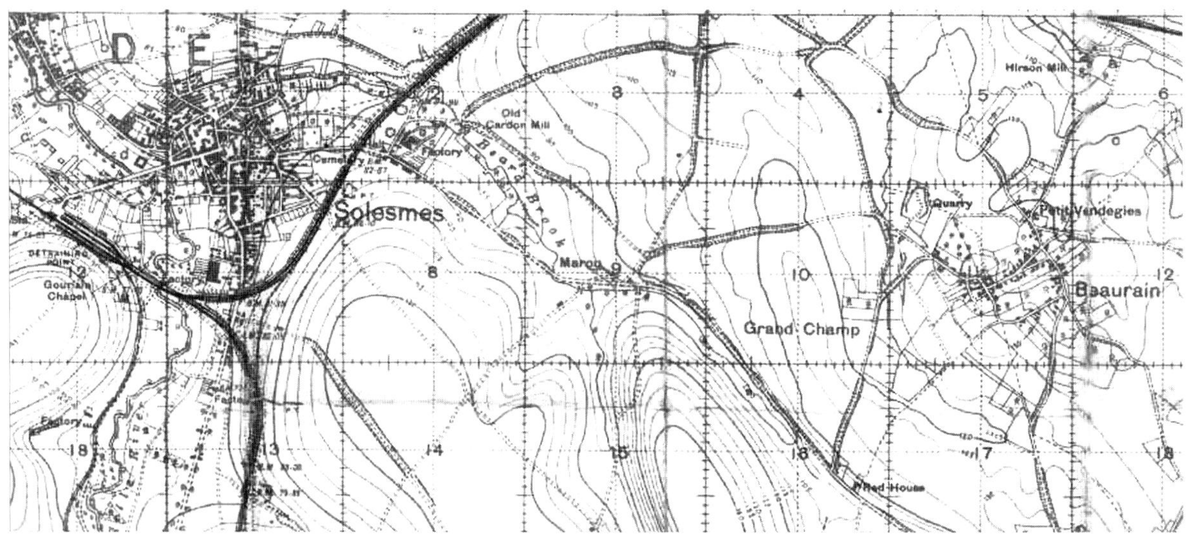

Map dated September 1918, showing the area of action on 20 October.

Marou and the Old Cardon Mill. Photo taken from the Battalion's positions in the late afternoon. Author

By 12 October, small detachments of British and Dominion troops had crossed the river and, during the following night, companies of Lancashire Fusiliers, from 42nd Division, moved up to relieve them. Throughout the 13th, the Germans made desperate counter-attacks to try to force them back, but without success. With the eastern bank increasingly secure, posts were established from Briastre to south of Solesmes and these were able to protect parties of Royal Engineers who put in strenuous efforts building pontoon bridges across the river. Everything was finished in time for the scheduled major advance starting in the early hours of 20 October.

On 42nd Division's front, the attack would be carried out in three phases. The initial phase would be undertaken by 126 Brigade capturing the first two objectives, known by the markings on the planning map as the Blue Line – a railway cutting running south from Solesmes – and the Green Line – high ground running parallel to the railway and a total of 1,500 yards from the starting point. The three battalions of Manchesters forming 127 Brigade would then take up the advance to the Red Line at Marou and then to the Brown Line – a crossroads on the top of a hill between Marou and Romieres. The final phase, beyond the Brown Line, would be undertaken by 125 Brigade and was left to be determined as circumstances suggested at the time.

The 6th Battalion moved off from billets to the assembly positions in the late evening of 19 October. It was raining hard and news soon arrived that the River Selle was rising and there was a danger of the bridges being washed away. A halt was called on the western bank around midnight and it was possible to serve the men with a hot meal and tea. The bridges had held and the men crossed the river at about 4am on the 20th and, although there was heavy enemy shelling in the area, no casualties were incurred. The initial phase of the attack had started at 2am and had been successful

The Sunken Lane. A strong German defensive position which had to be overcome. Author

with all objectives being secured, so it was now possible for the 6th Manchesters to follow the route taken by 126th Brigade. This was uphill and, soaked to the skin from the rain and crossing the river, the men found it heavy going, particularly climbing down and up the railway cutting on the Blue Line. They were in position at 6.50, just in time as their covering barrage was due to open up at 7am.

As soon as they went over the top, the 5th and 6th Battalions came under a fierce machine-gun barrage from the German positions which were obviously strongly held. The 5th Battalion, on the right, was particularly hard hit, as the division on its right had had to temporarily withdraw, leaving the flank of the Wigan battalion in the air. The 6th Battalion was also soon suffering casualties as the Germans put up a skilled defence. The battalion's rifle grenade specialists were now

The Grand Champs. *'The remainder of the garrison – 400 strong – was seen running away for all they were worth.'* Author

Private John Magee, a 34 year old married man from Chorlton-on-Medlock. He had previously served with one of the Pals battalions. Killed in action on 21 October – one of the last two to be killed.

brought into action under the command of Lieutenant Frank Benton. Sergeant William Tinsley led his section to attack one of the machine gun posts, through heavy fire. They captured it with Tinsley bayoneting five Germans. He was later awarded the Distinguished Conduct Medal for his bravery. In a short while, they had cleared the German garrison in front allowing the advance to continue with the capture of thirty prisoners.

As casualties continued to mount, Private Albert Brewer took charge of his section, leading it throughout the remainder of the day, including in an attack on another machine gun post where he and his men took twelve prisoners and captured the gun. Private Stanley Marlor, from Oldham, had also led an attack to capture a German strongpoint. Both men were also awarded the DCM

Photograph of Richard Coppock, left in the visitors book at Belle Vue British Cemetery, Briastre.

"A" and "B" Companies soon secured the Red Line at the hamlet of Marou and the nearby Old Cardon Mill. "C" and "D" Companies now moved up to join them but the heavy fire and determined German resistance was preventing any further move forward. At 2pm, reports were received that the Germans appeared to be assembling for an attack around the fields known as Grand Champs. Heavy and accurate artillery fire was quickly brought down on them, breaking up any prospect of an early counterattack.

Throughout the day, Sergeant Selwyn Sturgess, a pre-war member of the battalion, had been in charge of the signallers. He was another soldier to be awarded the Distinguished Conduct Medal for his actions:

> *By his gallantry, great devotion to duty and cheerfulness, he was largely responsible for ensuring that signal communication was maintained between battalion headquarters and companies under very trying conditions. In spite of very heavy fire he organised his cable parties so successfully that he ensured telephone communication with companies the moment they reached their objectives.*

The situation had stabilised somewhat by mid-evening and Colonel Blatherwick decided that he could continue the attack to the final objective. The main German defences were now in a sunken road and an artillery bombardment was ordered to be fired on them at 9.10pm.

This advance was carried out skilfully and successfully by C Company on the right and D Company on the left.....A very successful assault was made on this position and one machine gun and twenty five prisoners were captured. The remainder of the garrison – 400 strong – was seen running away for all they were worth on the far heights of Grand Champs Ridge. (Battalion war diary)

The Manchesters held their gains throughout the night and the next day until they were relieved in the evening of the 21st. Although there were no German counter attacks, enemy snipers and artillery remained active and, during this time, John Magee and Hubert Roper were killed. Although their comrades must have felt that victory was not far away, they could not know when the war would end, nor could they know that Magee and Roper would be that last men from the battalion to be killed in action.

Nearly thirty other soldiers had been killed on the 20th and a hundred wounded[12]. It was a long and tiring march to the billets at Beavois.

The battalion again marched away towards the front line on the morning of 3 November, along with the other units of 42nd Division. It had continued to rain and the roads were thick with mud. Two days later, they had reached the Forest of Mormal. It was a thickly wooded area, near to the border between Belgium and France, and the retreating Germans had blown large craters at every crossroads of the few routes through.

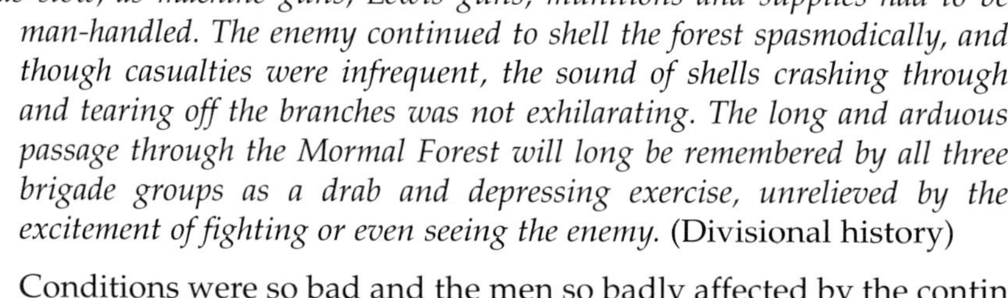

Progress was slow, as machine guns, Lewis guns, munitions and supplies had to be man-handled. The enemy continued to shell the forest spasmodically, and though casualties were infrequent, the sound of shells crashing through and tearing off the branches was not exhilarating. The long and arduous passage through the Mormal Forest will long be remembered by all three brigade groups as a drab and depressing exercise, unrelieved by the excitement of fighting or even seeing the enemy. (Divisional history)

Wilhelm Grotjahn, a German casualty of the fighting on 20 October. Buried at Quievy. Author

Conditions were so bad and the men so badly affected by the continual cold rain, that the battalion was sent to billets at Le Carnoy, to recuperate for two days. Meanwhile, the other brigades of the division, which had continued to advance, had seen some fighting. By the morning of the 8th, these units had captured the village of Hautmont and the surrounding area. The 6th Battalion now left Le Carnoy and moved to billets at Hargnies which was also now secure as the Germans had retreated a considerable way.

It spent the next two days there, cleaning up and continuing to rest. During the morning of 11 November, all troops received this order:

Hostilities will cease at 11am today. Troops will stand fast on the line

reached at that hour. Defensive precautions will be maintained. There will be no intercourse of any description with the enemy.

The bands of the three Manchester battalions assembled outside church at Hargnies to the obvious interest of many local people who gathered to watch. A few minutes before 11am, two parties of about thirty German prisoners passed through the village.

> *Armistice commenced at 11am. Band plays 'Cease Fire' and 'No Parade Today' outside village church."* (Private William Barker)

The fighting was over.

Hargnies Church.
Author.

---

1 The Fusiliers had no time to bury their commander before retreating but, months later, when the British again advanced, a German burial marker was found on the spot where he was known to have been killed. The marker, in German, read "Here rests the body of an unknown British field officer". Philip Holberton was reburied at Achiet-le-Grand on 18 September 1918. The funeral was attended by many of his brother officers, including his friend, Tom Blatherwick, now commanding the 6th Battalion.

2 Barker's diary is held by the Regimental Archives, which gives permission to quote extracts. Robert Stott and Francis James Walker were two of the thirteen members of the battalion who

The Band at Hautmont, November 1918. **Manchester Regiment Archives.**

died on 27 March.

3 Asa Brooks, an original member of the battalion. Awarded the Military Medal on 18 April 1918.

4 Henry Rowland Martin lived in the Pendleton area of Salford and was a chemist by profession. He had joined the battalion in 1913 but did not go overseas in September 1914. He transferred to the Royal Warwickshire Regiment and, in October 1917, was commissioned into the 9th Battalion, Manchester Regiment. He returned to the 6th Battalion in February 1918. In September 1918, he was invalided to Britain suffering from debility and returned to civilian life in April 1919.

5 John Benson, Arthur German and Percy Link

6 Believed to be Alfred French, a 25 year old married man from Hounslow, Middlesex, although his date of death is officially recorded as 20 July. He had enlisted in late autumn of 1915 and had served with the regiment's 18th Battalion until it was disbanded in February 1918. He had previously been wounded in the back in April 1917.

7 Pygott, from the Hulme district of Manchester, had originally joined the Regiment's 18th Battalion, the third "Pals" battalion, transferring when that battalion was disbanded at the beginning of 1918. His medal had been awarded for actions during the Battle of Arras in April 1917.

8 For this and several subsequent scouting patrols, Wignall received the Distinguished Conduct Medal

9 Roberts returned to civilian life in March 1919 and is believed to have lived in Irlam o' th' Heights for many years, before moving to Keighley in 1959. He died there, aged 78, on 17 August 1963. His medals are held by the regimental museum.

10 As with many of those killed on 2 September, Sitford is buried at Manchester Cemetery, Riencourt-les-Bapuame, which overlooks the area where he was killed. His headstone carries an inscription "Only goodnight, Leo, not farewell. Your true wife, Edith. Rev. 21 -4"

11 Believed to have worked for steelwork manufacturers, Edward Wood & Co, Ocean Ironworks, Manchester.

12 In 2009, the author visited Belle Vue Cemetery to photograph graves, including that of Private Richard Coppock. Filed with the cemetery visitors' book was a copy of Coppock's photograph and a copy of a note written by someone who had visited the cemetery in the 1920s. It read "He was hit about 1/4 mile S E of Solesmes, but most of the bodies were carried to the Belle Vue Cemetery near Briastre. He was hit by a sniper when carrying a message and was felled outright. There is a decent cross over his grave and when I saw it not long ago some French civvies had left two very nice floral bouquets on the grave. A small slip of paper said in French "To a brave English hero who helped deliver us on 20th October 1918. All thanks to him and to God." There was no indication of the identity of the modern visitor who had left the copies.

Chapter 9

RETURNING HOME

HOSTILITIES HAD ENDED ON 11 NOVEMBER 1918 with an armistice being signed. Technically only a temporary cessation in the fighting, it allowed peace negotiations to start and these would not be concluded until 1920. It was not until 31 August 1921 that Parliament formally ratified the peace treaty. Until then, the war was not over and troops would need to remain on the Western Front for a considerable time.

The 6th Battalion spent the next day moving to new billets in a school at nearby Hautmont. It may have had a military feel to it as the German Army had only vacated it a few days before as it retreated.'The billets were extremely dirty but when cleaned out provided very good accommodation.' (Battalion war diary) There was little to do for the remainder of the month except for some basic training exercises and three route marches each week. On the 16th, troops from B and C Companies took part in a ceremonial parade at Hautmont where the guns captured by the division in the final days were presented to the mayor. Perhaps unsurprisingly, the atmosphere amongst the men was becoming increasingly relaxed. It was a situation which the officers would not allow to continue.

Hautmont, November 1918. Photo: Manchester Regiment Archives.

Battalion officers, Hautmont, November 1918. Manchester Regiment Archives.

'Battalion in state of discontent owing to tightening of discipline.' (Private William Barker. Diary entry 30 November 1918)

The King and the Prince of Wales visited the divisional area on 1 December and the three Manchester Regiment battalions of 127th Brigade lined the part of his route nearest to where they were met by divisional and brigade generals. The King walked past the battalion's positions.

Private Joseph Turley, aged 20. Died on 26 November – a victim of the Spanish Flu pandemic.

The next day, in Manchester, there was a ceremony when the Lord Mayor handed back the Regimental Colours to representatives of the battalion. They had been deposited with him for safe keeping before the battalion had left for Egypt in September 1914 and they were now to be escorted to France. In charge of the escort was Captain J H Helm, whose short service at Gallipoli was described in Chapter 3. The presentation was made outside the Town Hall and the colour party then left for France from Victoria Station.

One hundred new troops joined the battalion on 4 December. These were mainly men who had previously been exempted from overseas service due to their health. The colour party arrived from Manchester on the 6th and the day also saw a memorial tablet erected inside the church at Hargnies commemorating the battalion's presence in the village on 11 November. The oak plaque had been carved by Private H L Jones. Private Cyril Farmer painted the inscription, which is surmounted with the coat of arms of the City of Manchester,

Devant cette eglise le Sixieme Bataillon du Regiment de Manchester a commemore la cessation des hostilities de la Grande Guerre.

Le XI Novembre a onze heures du matin, MCMXVIII

The commemorative plaque at Hargnies church.
Author.

The next day, William Barker's platoon played a platoon from the 7th Battalion in the final of the brigade football competition. After extra time, the score was 1 – 1, so a replay was arranged for the next day. Neither side scored this time and, in the days before penalty shoot-outs, a further replay was needed. This took place on the 10th, with the 6th Battalion's team triumphing 3 - 0. Although there is no mention of discontent amongst the men being recorded in the battalion's war diary, Barker notes on the 10 December:

Battalion have a sort of strike and go on parade in drill order, instead of full marching order. The General takes our complaints. Leather jerkins and trench gloves taken from us.

On the 14th, the Manchesters started a long route march to the Belgian village of Fleurus, to the north east of the city of Charleroi. It took them until the afternoon of the 19th to reach it. An advance party had already arranged for all troops to be billeted with civilians. A large building nearby was used as mess rooms and, over the next few days, it was decorated for the coming festive season. Seventeen men would be glad not to celebrate Christmas with their comrades – leaving on the 22nd, they were the first members of the battalion to return to Britain to be demobilised. A full traditional meal was served on Christmas Day, followed by a battalion concert. New Years Eve was celebrated with a dance with many of the local young woman being invited to attend as guests.

On the first day of 1919, the men went on a route march in the morning. Educational classes started in the afternoon and men would be excused parades if they were attending one. These were practical courses in subjects such as boot repairing, sign writing, tailoring and horse shoeing – possibly reflecting the changing social class of the battalion's members from the accountants, stockbrokers and bank clerks who had made up many of the original pre-war numbers. Towards the end of January, groups of men left for demobilisation in Britain every few days. The parties varied in size from four men to several dozen. In the middle of February, another draft of 100 new troops arrived. This allowed the speeding-up of the return home of long service men and, by the 20th, it was decided to close the education classes as there were too few men now

The cadre prepares to return to Manchester. Manchester Regiment Archives

interested. At the end of the month, almost all of the men eligible for demobilisation had left the battalion.

A move to Charleroi was made on 7 March with the men being again billeted with civilians. Morning parades were held but the men had no other significant duties. On the 27th, the battalion's cadre, comprising six officers and forty-nine other ranks, left to return to Manchester with the regimental colours.

> *No instructions have been received in regard to the remainder of the battalion, comprising 11 officers and 243 other ranks, who are retainable for the Army of Occupation. They were concentrated into brigade groups pending instructions.* (Battalion war diary. Final entry 28 March 1919)

Although many people watched the arrival of the battalion cadre on 8 April, there was no official welcome. Amongst the group were several who had served throughout the war, including Billy Warburton, the pre-war colour sergeant from Cheadle and now a Lieutenant and the battalion's quartermaster.

> *Despite the lack of official recognition by the civic authorities, Manchester was today prepared to receive the second contingent of the famous 42nd Division and the people demonstrated what they can do spontaneously. There were expressions of surprise yesterday at the supposed lack of courtesy on the part of the Corporation.* (Manchester Evening Chronicle, 8 April)

With that final act, the story of the 6th Battalion, Manchester Regiment, in the Great War, comes to an end. Men became civilians again and tried to rebuild their lives – returning to employment, getting married and raising families. At the end of 1919, Billy Warburton received the award of a Military Cross in recognition of his service throughout the war. He had returned to the Cheadle area where he died in 1935, aged fifty-three.

Captain Henry Hammick, one of the battalion's officers at Gallipoli, had transferred to the Royal Engineers. Once more a civilian, he married Mabel Pilditch in the spring of 1919 in the Chertsey area of Surrey. He died in 1968 and is buried at the Municipal Cemetery in Weybridge.

Ridley Sheldon, whose account of his service in Egypt and Gallipoli is held by the regimental archives, returned to civilian life on 26 March 1919. After recovering from his wounds, he spent the latter part of the war with the Royal Engineers. He came back to live in Broughton, Salford where, in 1923, he is believed to have married Constance Cottam at St Clement's Church.

Oswald Billingham, who had been taken prisoner whilst serving with the 2/6th Battalion, returned to Kislingbury, near Northanpton in December 1918 and was formally demobilised the following month. In 1924, he married Elizabeth Rose.

For many men, a return to normality was impossible. Their wounds meant they could not return to normal employment or, indeed, enjoy a happy life. For many others, the effects of wounds or illnesses contracted whilst on military service meant that their lives would be shortened. The Commonwealth War Graves Commission cares for the cemeteries in Belgium, France, Turkey and many other countries where men served and died and where they are now buried. It regards all deaths of serving troops, from whatever cause, between 4 August 1914 and 31 August 1921, as 'war deaths'. It also treats as 'war graves' many burials in Britain. These are the graves of men who died in this country, prior to the ratification of the peace treaty on 31 August 1921, whilst still serving in the forces or those who died from a cause directly attributable to their service, after they had been discharged.

Corporal Hector Fraser is believed to be the latest death, commemorated by the Commission, of a man known to have served with the 6th Battalion. Born in Cork, he was a pre-war member of the battalion and had worked as a shipping clerk for a cotton

Memorial inscription to Hector Fraser at Manchester's Southern Cemetery. Author

goods firm[1]. He saw action in the early months at Gallipoli but, with failing health, returned to Britain in the latter part of 1915. The remainder of his army service was spent at home working as a clerk but he was discharged in 1917 suffering from tuberculosis. He died of the disease on 20 October 1920 at Ladywell Sanatorium, Salford and is buried at Southern Cemetery, Manchester.

The war had left such an impact on British society that communities, large and small, quickly put in hand arrangements to remember the dead. At the first national Peace Day celebration in London, a wood and plaster cenotaph was temporarily erected in Whitehall to mark the end of the victory parade. By the following year, a permanent structure had replaced it and it continues to be the focus for national remembrance.

On 21 January 1920, a bronze memorial to the memory of men of the 6th Battalion was unveiled at St George's Church at Mustapha Barracks in Alexandria:

> *To the memory of the officers, warrant officers, non-commissioned officers and men of the I/VIth Battn Manchester Regiment TF who fell for King and Country in the Gallipoli campaign of MCMXV this monument was placed here by their comrades. The battn was quartered in these barracks from September 27th MCMXIV to January 19th MCMXV and embarked for Gallipoli from the port of Alexandria May 3rd MCMXV.*

A detachment of the Regiment's 22nd Battalion attended the formal unveiling, together with a small number of officers who had served with the 6th Battalion. They included Captain William Cadman who had been wounded on 3 June 1915 and Lieutenant (then Corporal) Eric Hartshorn who had won a Distinguished Conduct Medal at Gallipoli. The memorial was removed to Britain in 1946 and was re-erected at the battalion barracks in Hulme and is now at University Barracks.

It is alongside a memorial to those who fell which was unveiled at the battalion's barracks on 12 June 1921. It consists of seven oak panels recording the names of 1,057 soldiers who died serving with the battalion during the war. It was unveiled by Major General Herbert Shoubridge, then commanding 42nd Division, but the main address was given by the Chaplain, Reverend Edwin Kerby who had served at Gallipoli as the chaplain to the 7th Battalion:

> *In its personnel, the battalion was unique. I can speak as an attached officer. It contained in its ranks the flower of the young citizenship of Manchester. In it were enshrined the hopes of most of the leading families of this city. It was a battalion inspired by the spirit of our great public schools – to do one's best and play the game. It was a battalion in which almost every man had the true soldier spirit and was rather to lead than to be led. It was a battalion singularly conspicuous in its members' devotion to religious duties and for patriotism of the highest and noblest order. It was something more than a battalion – it was a brotherhood, a fellowship in which gratification of self was subordinated to the welfare and efficiency of the whole.*

Many men who came home did return to a normal life and never really spoke again of their wartime experiences. It was, presumably, a way of coping with the most frightening and appalling of times. For others, the bond of comradeship was strong and they would meet in annual reunions. Walter Greenhalgh, who had served with "D" Company of the 2/6th Battalion and whose diary is held by the Liddle Collection, revisited the battlefields in 1926 and found the villages were still in ruins and only a small number of civilians had moved back to start their lives again. He went again in 1959 and found what he described as a "lovely and thriving countryside". "D" Company's "Old Comrades" were one of the groups that met annually until the late 1950s.

"Boys" of "D" Company meet again . . . Members of "D" Company 2/6th Battalion the Manchester Regiment, Old Comrades Association seen at their thirty-seventh reunion at the Town Hall Hotel, in Tib Lane.

Old Comrades get-together in 1959. D Company of the 2/6th Battalion. *Manchester Evening News.*

An unknown poet amongst the former soldiers wrote the following which was published in the Regimental Gazette:

They went from Hulme to Hebuterne, from Sale to Sinai
They wrote their name at Krithia – the name will never die

Helles Memorial, Turkey. **Commonwealth War Graves Commission**

We lived, and laughed, and fought the Hun, away from and kind –
Let's drink a toast to "Absent Chums" – the lads we left behind.

Beside the waters of the straits in loneliness they lie
A field of Christian crosses underneath a crescent skye
And some are where a "sleepy Somme", its peaceful course may wind
Untroubled by a brutal foe, the lads we left behind

And Holberton and Holt still live and Davies shows the way
And Jackson, Kessler, Bazley, Mills – are with us every day
For Turk or Hun can not destroy what lives within the mind
The band of gallant gentlemen – the lads we left behind.

In the years immediately following the war, many communities remembered their local dead by the erection of war memorials. *Ad hoc* committees were formed to raise money, commission the memorial and collect names of the local men who were to be included. Today, they often form a focus for Remembrance Sunday commemorations and are a fascinating resource for local historians. It was whilst researching the names on the memorial in Cheadle, Cheshire, that the author first developed an interest in the 6th Manchesters. He realised that, whilst Sergeant Tom Worthington, extensively mentioned in the early chapters, was commemorated on the memorial, he was not included on the country's Debt of Honour Register, maintained by the War Graves Commission. Worthington was not buried in one of the Commission's cemeteries, nor was his name inscribed on the Memorial to the Missing at Gallipoli. It took many months of further research to collate the documentation which would prove that Worthington had indeed been killed in action. It was submitted to the Commission and the Ministry of Defence in 2005 and, with the assistance of Cheadle's Member of Parliament, the official bodies agreed to include him in the Register. Tom Worthington's name was added to the Helles Memorial to the Missing at the beginning of 2008. He is now 'in from the cold' and his death properly recognised by his country.

In the immediate aftermath of the war, the National Publishing Company started to publish a series of books containing brief biographies of many of the men who served, whether they died or not. It is probable that the biographies were collected by door-to-door salesmen and charges were made for entries, as well as for buying the finished book. Several volumes were published including one for Manchester. The family of Private George Bailey, of 33 John Street, Hulme, Manchester, was one family who arranged for an entry in the book. Bailey had enlisted in August 1916 and had gone overseas with the 2/6th Battalion the following year. He was wounded and captured on 21 March 1918 and died four days later. His entry ends with an epitaph which the author borrows to end the book.

Whilst we remember, the sacrifice is not in vain.

---

1 Probably Heynssen, Martienssen Ltd, Manchester. The Company's entry, in the Manchester City Battalions Book of Honour, lists a Private H Fraser amongst its employees who served with the battalion.

ROLL OF HONOUR

of men known or believed to have
been serving with the battalions
at date of death

This Roll of Honour has been compiled from the records of the Commonwealth War Graves Commission and the CD-ROM "Soldiers Died in the Great War". It does not purport to be a complete listing nor can the accuracy be absolutely guaranteed. A number of men recorded by the Commission as serving with the battalions have been excluded as their date of death and/or place of burial suggests that they were attached to other units at the time. Similarly a number of men are included even though the Commission records them serving with a different unit.

NAME	RANK & NO.	UNIT	DATE	CAUSE[1]	BURIAL/MEMORIAL
AINSWORTH, William	Pte 2491	1st/6th	05/06/1915	KIA	Helles Memorial
ALDERMAN, Horace	Pte 1478	1st/6th	05/06/1915	KIA	Helles Memorial
ALEXANDER, John	Pte 63492	1st/6th	03/09/1918	DOW	Bagneux Brit. Cem.
ALLEN, Arthur	Cpl 250905	2nd/6th	22/03/1918	KIA	Pozieres Memorial
ALLEN, Frank E	Pte 1903	1st/6th	27/05/1915	KIA	Helles Memorial
ANDERSON, Arthur E	Sgt 2343	1st/6th	12/08/1915	Died	East Mudros Mil. Cem
ANDERSON, Robert C	Pte 2350	1st/6th	16/11/1915	Died	Pieta Mil. Cem.
ANTROBUS, Stephen J	Pte 252254	2nd/6th	18/08/1917	KIA	Ramscappelle RoadMil. Cem.
APPLEBY, Robert	L/Cpl 270164	2nd/6th	23/03/1918	Died	Pozieres Memorial
ARBON, George F	Pte 270075	2nd/6th	21/03/1918	KIA	Pozieres Memorial
ARNOLD, Charles W	Pte 252375	2nd/6th	04/05/1917	KIA	Cambrin Mil. Cem.
ARNOLD, Eric D	Pte 250620	2nd/6th	07/10/1917	KIA	Tyne Cot Memorial
ARNOLD, Ernest W	Pte 2235	1st/6th	07/08/1915	KIA	Helles Memorial
ASHLEY, Charles C S	Pte 250328	1st/6th	06/09/1917	KIA	Tyne Cot Memorial
ASHTON, William	Pte 2296	1st/6th	05/06/1915	KIA	Helles Memorial
ASPINWALL, Rupert A	Pte 1802	1st/6th	07/08/1915	KIA	Helles Memorial
ATHERTON, James	Pte 2452	1st/6th	05/06/1915	KIA	Helles Memorial
ATKINS, Robert W	Pte 252472	2nd/6th	22/03/1918	KIA	Pozieres Memorial
ATKINSON, Charles	Pte 54645	2nd/6th	04/06/1918	Died	Le Cateau Mil. Cem.
ATKINSON, Ralph	Pte 250873	1st/6th	28/03/1918	KIA	Arras Memorial
ATKINSON, Sidney	L/Cpl 1556	1st/6th	07/08/1915	KIA	Helles Memorial

AUSTIN, Herbert G	Pte 2369	1st/6th	05/06/1915	KIA	Twelve Tree Copse Cem.
BAILEY, George W	Pte 252349	2nd/6th	25/03/1918	DOW	Hancourt Brit. Cem.
BAILEY, Howarth	Pte 251270	1st/6th	06/09/1917	DOW	Aeroplane Cem
BAILEY, Percy V	Pte 252483	2nd/6th	12/10/1917	DOW	Lijssenthoek Mil. Cem.
BAILEY, Thomas	Pte 63495	1st/6th	02/09/1918	KIA	Bancourt Brit. Cem.
BAKER, James E	Pte 1931	1st/6th	05/06/1915	KIA	Helles Memorial
BALLANTINE, George	Pte 1491	1st/6th	07/08/1915	KIA	Helles Memorial
BALLINGALL, Arthur S	L/Cpl 2130	1st/6th	12/09/1915	DOW	Alexandria (Chatby) Mil. Cem
BAMFORD, Job	Pte 303550	2nd/6th	05/02/1918	DOW	Menin Road South Mil. Cem.
BAMFORD, Norman	Pte 2283	1st/6th	05/06/1915	KIA	Helles Memorial
BAMFORD, William	Cpl 251763	2nd/6th	22/03/1918	KIA	Pozieres Memorial
BANKS, Stanley E	Pte 251027	1st/6th	27/03/1918	KIA	Arras Memorial
BARBER, George H	Pte 47184	1st/6th	27/09/1918	KIA	Ribecourt Road Cem.
BARBER,Leonard H	2/Lieut	1st/6th	05/06/1915	KIA	Helles Memorial
BARBER, Norman	Pte 47843	2nd/6th	10/10/1917	DOW	Tyne Cot Memorial
BARBER, Sydney	Pte 252152	2nd/6th	24/09/1917	KIA	Ramscappelle Road Mil. Cem.
BARDSLEY, Norman	Pte 1831	1st/6th	05/06/1915	KIA	Helles Memorial
BARKER, Lees	Pte 303582	2nd/6th	18/10/1918	Died	Tournai Comm. Cem.
BARKER, William R	Pte 1731	1st/6th	12/06/1915	DOW	Helles Memorial
BARLOW, Charles	Pte 1927	1st/6th	07/08/1915	KIA	Helles Memorial
BARLOW, George	Cpl 1513	1st/6th	04/06/1915	KIA	Helles Memorial
BARLOW, Henry	Pte 251625	1st/6th	23/10/1918	n/k	Peel Green Cem.
BARNES, George	L/Cpl 250906	2nd/6th	22/03/1918	DOW	Peronne Comm. Cem. Ext.
BARNES, Harry	Pte 251529	1st/6th	01/06/1917	KIA	Thiepval Memorial
BARRATT, Arthur	Pte 252410	1st/6th	20/10/1918	KIA	Belle Vue Brit. Cem.
BARRATT, William	Sgt 300058	2nd/6th	25/03/1918	KIA	Pozieres Memorial
BARTER, Harry J	Pte 270128	2nd/6th	21/03/1918	KIA	Pozieres Memorial
BATES, Charles B	L/Cpl 2093	1st/6th	07/08/1915	KIA	Helles Memorial
BATESON, Ernest	Pte 2370	1st/6th	04/06/1915	KIA	Helles Memorial
BATTYE, Wilfred T	Pte 251368	1st/6th	05/09/1917	KIA	Aeroplane Cem
BAUGH, James T	2/Lieut	6th (n/k)	03/11/1918	DOW	St Souplet Brit. Cem.
BAXTER, Warren	Pte 252114	2nd/6th	24/09/1917	KIA	Ramscappelle Road Mil. Cem.
BAZLEY, Walter N	Capt	1st/6th	23/05/1915	DOW	Lancashire Landing Cemetery
BEBBINGTON, Thomas	Pte 2253	1st/6th	20/05/1915	KIA	Helles Memorial
BEDFORD, Robert H	Capt	2nd/6th	25/03/1918	KIA	Pozieres Memorial
BEESTON, Frank	Pte 251900	1st/6th	29/03/1918	Died	Ontario Cem.
BELL, Arthur	Sgt 250599	1st/6th	25/03/1918	KIA	Arras Memorial
BELL, Edwin F	Pte 1968	1st/6th	05/11/1915	Died	Alexandria (Chatby) Mil. Cem
BELL, Frederic A	Pte 251536	1st/6th	02/09/1918	KIA	Bancourt Brit. Cem.
BELL, Thomas C	Pte 252373	2nd/6th	21/03/1918	KIA	Pozieres Memorial

BELSHAW, Albert	Pte 251501	1st/6th	06/09/1917	DOW	Aeroplane Cem
BENNETT, John	Sgt 2033	1st/6th	07/08/1915	KIA	Helles Memorial
BENSON, John W	Pte 251430	1st/6th	17/05/1918	DOW	Doullens Comm. Cem 2
BENT, James A	Pte 252710	2nd/6th	29/12/1917	KIA	Menin Road South Mil. Cem.
BERRY, Arthur J	Sgt 250959	1st/6th	22/04/1918	KIA	Couin New Brit. Cem.
BERRY, Stanley C	Pte 2764	1st/6th	09/10/1915	Died	Alexandria (Chatby) Mil. Cem
BESWICK, Charles E	Pte 252460	2nd/6th	31/03/1918	KIA	Pozieres Memorial
BICKERTON, James A	Pte 251718	2nd/6th	22/05/1917	KIA	Cambrin Mil. Cem.
BICKERTON, Norman	Pte 2198	1st/6th	04/06/1915	DOW	Lancashire Landing Cemetery
BINNS, Charles F	Pte 1439	1st/6th	05/06/1915	KIA	Helles Memorial
BIRCH, George R	Pte 1404	1st/6th	05/06/1915	KIA	Helles Memorial
BISPHAM, John	Cpl 250666	2nd/6th	31/03/2018	KIA	Not known
BLACKLOCK, James	Pte 1742	1st/6th	07/08/1915	KIA	Helles Memorial
BLACKWELL, George	2/Lieut	2nd/6th	30/03/1918	KIA	Pozieres Memorial
BLADES, Harry	Pte 245089	1st/6th	20/07/1918	KIA	Bertrancourt Mil. Cem.
BLAIKIE, Murray	Pte 2248	1st/6th	09/05/1915	KIA	Helles Memorial
BLAKE, Harry	Sgt 250793	2nd/6th	31/03/1918	KIA	Pozieres Memorial
BLEACKLEY,Edward O	Pte 1977	1st/6th	25/07/1915	KIA	Alexandria (Chatby) Mil. Cem
BLEACKLEY, Worsley	L/Cpl 1369	1st/6th	05/06/1915	KIA	Redoubt Cem
BLEARS, Harry	Pte 251076	1st/6th	04/05/1917	DOW	Villers-Faucon Comm. Cem.
BLEASE, Frank S	Pte 251066	1st/6th	29/09/1918	DOW	Grevillers Brit. Cem.
BOODSON, Laurence	L/Cpl 1345	1st/6th	04/06/1915	KIA	Helles Memorial
BOOTH, William H	Pte 1866	1st/6th	13/06/1915	DOW	Pieta Mil. Cem.
BOOTHMAN, Richard H	Pte 302398	2nd/6th	01/04/1918	DOW	Le Cateau Mil. Cem.
BOSWELL, Percy W I	Sgt 1764	1st/6th	07/08/1915	KIA	Helles Memorial
BOURNE, William	Pte 2154	1st/6th	30/09/1915	DOW	Helles Memorial
BOWDLER, Alfred	Pte 39891	2nd/6th	05/10/1917	KIA	Tyne Cot Memorial
BOWERS-TAYLOR, Archibald	Capt	1st/6th	07/06/1917	KIA	Ypres (Menin Gate) Memorial
BOWLING, John	Sgt 250776	2nd/6th	31/03/1918	KIA	Villeret Old Chuchyard
BOWYER, Sam	L/Cpl 303377	2nd/6th	21/03/1918	KIA	Pozieres Memorial
BOYD, Leonard D	Sgt 2083	1st/6th	04/06/1915	KIA	Redoubt Cem
BOYES-VARLEY, Cecil	Sgt 1717	1st/6th	13/07/1915	KIA	Lancashire Landing Cemetery
BRABBS, Albert H	Pte 270156	2nd/6th	21/03/1918	KIA	Pozieres Memorial
BRADBURY, George S	Sgt 1009	1st/6th	05/06/1915	KIA	Twelve Tree Copse Cem.
BRADLEY, Charles W	Pte 42601	2nd/6th	30/07/1917	KIA	Nieuport Memorial
BRADLEY, Wilfred	Sgt 60517	2nd/6th	24/03/1918	KIA	Pozieres Memorial
BRADSHAW, Albert	Pte 32467	2nd/6th	24/09/1917	KIA	Ramscappelle Road Mil. Cem.
BRADSHAW, Arthur	Pte 352216	1st/6th	29/05/1918	DOW	Etaples Mil. Cem.

BRANDRETH, Alfred	Pte 252100	2nd/6th	01/04/1918	DOW	Hancourt Brit. Cem.
BRIDGFORD, Stanley L	Capt	1st/6th	08/04/1918	DOW	Gent City Cem.
BRIERLEY, Frank	Pte 75202	1st/6th	27/09/1918	KIA	Ribecourt Road Cem.
BRIERLEY, Hugh C	Capt	1st/6th	23/06/1917	KIA	Ruyaulcourt Mil. Cem.
BRIMBLECOMBE, Thomas L	Pte 251337	1st/6th	26/03/1918	KIA	Arras Memorial
BRITTAIN, Leonard A	Pte 1620	1st/6th	05/06/1915	KIA	Helles Memorial
BROADBENT, Fred	Pte 75103	1st/6th	27/09/1918	KIA	Ribecourt Road Cem.
BROCKLEBANK, Thomas I	Pte 251896	2nd/6th	25/09/1917	DOW	Ramscappelle Road Mil. Cem.
BROMHEAD, Thomas P	L/Cpl 1639	1st/6th	12/08/1915	KIA	Redoubt Cem
BROOKE-TAYLOR, Arthur C	Lieut	1st/6th	04/06/1915	KIA	Helles Memorial
BROOKS, Archibald B	Capt	2nd/6th	07/10/1917	KIA	Ypres Reservoir Cem.
BROOKS, Rowland C	2/Lieut	1st/6th	04/06/1915	KIA	Helles Memorial
BROOKS, Walter H	Pte 2374	1st/6th	05/06/1915	KIA	Helles Memorial
BROOME, George E	Pte 1665	1st/6th	10/09/1915	KIA	Helles Memorial
BROWN, David	L/Cpl 270059	2nd/6th	13/10/1917	DOW	Mont Huon Mil. Cem.
BROWN, Samuel	Sgt 250680	2nd/6th	22/07/1917	KIA	Coxyde Mil. Cem.
BROWN, Samuel O	Pte 251290	1st/6th	22/08/1918	KIA	Queens Cem, Bucquoy
BROWN, William E	Pte 2209	1st/6th	04/06/1915	KIA	Awtg. commem.
BRYAN, Charles T	Pte 250482	1st/6th	02/09/1918	KIA	Bancourt Brit. Cem.
BUCKLEY, Alfred	Pte 2221	1st/6th	05/06/1915	KIA	Helles Memorial
BUCKLEY, Bernard C	Pte 250269	1st/6th	01/06/1917	KIA	Neuville-Bourjonval Brit. Cem
BUCKLEY, Joseph	Pte 50282	1st/6th	25/03/1918	KIA	Achiet-le-Grand Com. Cem
BUCKLEY, Reginald W	Sgt 1196	1st/6th	05/06/1915	KIA	Helles Memorial
BUDDERY, Horace M	Pte 270060	2nd/6th	18/08/1917	KIA	Ramscappelle Road Mil. Cem.
BUERDSELL, Arthur	Pte 251605	1st/6th	02/04/1918	KIA	Arras Memorial
BULLOCK, Alfred	Pte 251586	1st/6th	25/03/1918	KIA	Arras Memorial
BURGESS, Frank	Pte 46585	1st/6th	25/03/1918	KIA	Gommecourt Wood Cem.
BURGESS, John A	Pte 1558	1st/6th	22/09/1915	KIA	Twelve Tree Copse Cem.
BURNE, Victor	L/Cpl 250491	1st/6th	12/09/1917	KIA	Tyne Cot Cem.
BURNS, James	Pte 250754	2nd/6th	21/03/2018	KIA	Pozieres Memorial
BUSSEY, Harry	Pte 270082	2nd/6th	18/10/1918	Died	Tournai Comm. Cem.
BUTCHER, George S	L/Cpl 270061	2nd/6th	21/03/1918	KIA	Pozieres Memorial
BUTTERFIELD, Sam	Pte 54339	1st/6th	27/09/1918	KIA	Ribecourt Road Cem.
BUTTERWORTH, Edmund C	Cpl 250558	1st/6th	20/06/1917	KIA	Ruyaulcourt Mil. Cem.
BYROM, George	Pte 251342	1st/6th	25/03/1918	KIA	Arras Memorial
CADMAN, Clifford	Pte 303977	1st/6th	20/10/1918	KIA	Belle Vue Brit. Cem.
CAIN, James	Pte 251393	1st/6th	06/09/1917	KIA	Tyne Cot Memorial
CANTRILL, Charles E	Sgt 252171	2nd/6th	02/04/1918	DOW	Le Cateau Mil. Cem.
CARD, Samuel	Pte 203651	2nd/6th	21/03/1918	KIA	Pozieres Memorial
CARHART, Claude S	Pte 250293	1st/6th	01/06/1917	DOW	Neuville-Bourjonval Brit. Cem

CARMICHAEL, Gilbert	2/Lieut	2nd/6th	21/03/1918	KIA	Pozieres Memorial
CARR, Bertram E	Cpl 252492	2nd/6th	21/03/1918	KIA	Pozieres Memorial
CARTER, Thomas	Pte 350451	1st/6th	23/03/1918	KIA	Arras Memorial
CARTER, William	Pte 251697	1st/6th	06/09/1917	KIA	Aeroplane Cem
CARTWRIGHT, Richard	Pte 201976	2nd/6th	26/02/1918	DOW	Hargicourt Brit. cem.
CAUSER, Edgar B	Cpl 251253	1st/6th	27/09/1918	KIA	Flesquieres Hill Brit Cem
CAWLEY, Harold T	Capt	1st/6th	23/09/1915	KIA	Lancashire Landing Cemetery
CAWTHORNE, Richard	Pte 3911	6th (n/k)	13/12/1916	n/k	Agecroft Cem, Salford
CHAMBERLAIN Roland	Pte 302111	2nd/6th	25/03/1918	KIA	Pozieres Memorial
CHILTON, Thomas F	Pte 1450	1st/6th	01/06/1915	KIA	Helles Memorial
CHURCH, Eric	L/Cpl 251217	1st/6th	20/12/1919	n/k	St Mary's, Bowden
CLARK, Fred M	Pte 2205	1st/6th	02/07/1915	KIA	Twelve Tree Copse Cem.
CLARK Sidney	Pte 2276	1st/6th	05/06/1915	KIA	Helles Memorial
CLARK William J	Pte 251146	1st/6th	29/04/1918	KIA	Couin New Brit. Cem.
CLARKE, Alfred	Sgt 59397	2nd/6th	21/03/1918	KIA	Pozieres Memorial
CLARKE, John	Sgt 250537	1st/6th	23/04/1918	KIA	Pozieres Memorial
CLARKE, John H D	L/Sgt 143	1st/6th	07/08/1915	KIA	Helles Memorial
CLARKE, Victor	Pte 2285	1st/6th	07/08/1915	KIA	Helles Memorial
CLARKSON, Arthur H	L/Cpl 252364	2nd/6th	11/06/1917	KIA	Cambrin Mil. Cem.
CLAYTON, Colin B	Pte 1578	1st/6th	04/06/1915	KIA	Helles Memorial
CLAYTON, Stanley C	Pte 1480	1st/6th	04/06/1915	KIA	Helles Memorial
CLEGG Herbert,	Pte 252771	2nd/6th	12/06/1917	DOW	Chocques Mil. Cem.
CLEGG John,	Sgt 93	1st/6th	04/06/1915	KIA	Helles Memorial
CLEVELAND, Richard	L/Cpl 50940	2nd/6th	31/03/1918	DOW	Abbeville Com Cem. Ext
CLINCH, Henry P	Cpl 682	1st/6th	29/05/1915	KIA	Helles Memorial
CLOY, Harry	CSM 252	1st/6th	07/08/1915	KIA	Helles Memorial
CLUFF, Albert	Pte 1753	1st/6th	04/06/1915	KIA	Helles Memorial
COHEN, Jacob	Pte 252663	2nd/6th	21/03/1918	KIA	Assevillers New Brit. Cem.
COLLARD, Ernest	Pte 2030	1st/6th	05/06/1915	KIA	Helles Memorial
COLLIER, Samuel F	Capt	2nd/6th	22/03/1918	KIA	Pozieres Memorial
COLLINGE, Arthur	Pte 2340	1st/6th	30/05/1915	KIA	Helles Memorial
COLLINS, George F	Pte 251401	1st/6th	23/06/1917	KIA	Ruyaulcourt Mil. Cem.
COMPTON-SMITH, Roger N	2/Lieut	1st/6th	27/05/1915	DOW	Redoubt Cem
CONNOR, John	Pte 203666	2nd/6th	15/02/1918	DOW	Lijssenthoek Mil. Cem.
CONNOR, Patrick J	Pte 1247	6th (n/k)	16/05/1915	n/k	Lancaster Cemetery
CONST, William	Pte 251589	1st/6th	25/03/1918	KIA	Arras Memorial
COOK, Arthur	L/Cpl 302719	2nd/6th	31/03/1918	KIA	Pozieres Memorial
COOKE, William H	Sgt 250701	2nd/6th	09/10/1917	DOW	Lijssenthoek Mil. Cem.
COONEY, John D	Pte 2486	1st/6th	29/05/1915	KIA	Redoubt Cem
COOPER, Charles H	Pte 1810	1st/6th	12/05/1915	KIA	Helles Memorial
COOPER, Richard H N	Pte 2060	1st/6th	02/08/1915	KIA	Redoubt Cem
COOPER, Will	Pte 2748	1st/6th	07/08/1915	KIA	Helles Memorial
COOPS, Harry	Pte 2378	1st/6th	26/05/1915	KIA	Helles Memorial
COPE, Charles	Pte 252377	2nd/6th	31/03/1918	KIA	Pozieres Memorial

COPPOCK, Richard	Pte	351720	1st/6th	20/10/1918	KIA	Belle Vue Brit. Cem.
CORBISHLEY, Robert P	Pte	2397	1st/6th	08/12/1915	KIA	Lancashire Landing Cemetery
CORBITT, Hugh	Cpl	251426	1st/6th	25/03/1918	Died	Achiet-le-Grand Com Cem
CORDT, Thomas H	Pte	24433	1st/6th	27/09/1918	DOW	Ruyaulcourt Mil. Cem.
CORNES, Harold W	Pte	61210	1st/6th	27/09/1918	KIA	Ribecourt Road Cem.
CORNWELL, James	Pte	2961	1st/6th	07/08/1915	KIA	Helles Memorial
CORY, Bernard C	L/Sgt	1184	1st/6th	06/06/1915	KIA	Helles Memorial
COSGROVE, Thomas W	Pte	252758	2nd/6th	22/03/1918	KIA	Pozieres Memorial
COTTRILL, Geoffrey H	Pte	2039	1st/6th	07/08/1915	KIA	Helles Memorial
COURTMAN, Percy	Pte	250755	1st/6th	02/06/1917	KIA	Neuville-Bourjonval Brit. Cem
COUTTS, John	L/Cpl	33680	2nd/6th	29/03/1918	DOW	St Roch Comm Cem
COWELL, Harold	Pte	251399	1st/6th	02/09/1918	KIA	Bancourt Brit. Cem.
COXHIL, Oliver R	Pte	57438	1st/6th	21/08/1918	KIA	Queens Cem, Bucquoy
COYLE, Arthur	Pte	44944	2nd/6th	30/07/1917	KIA	Nieuport Memorial
CRADDOCK, Francis L	Pte	251911	1st/6th	20/10/1918	KIA	Belle Vue Brit. Cem.
CRAMPTON, Thomas	Cpl	250025	6th (n/k)	28/03/1917	n/k	Southern Cem, Manchester
CRAVEN, Thomas R	Pte	303068	1st/6th	22/08/1918	KIA	Queens Cem, Bucquoy
CRAYTHORNE, James	Pte	63517	1st/6th	20/10/1918	KIA	Belle Vue Brit. Cem.
CRESSY, Reginald P	Pte	2266	1st/6th	05/06/1915	KIA	Helles Memorial
CREWE, Phillip	Pte	1613	1st/6th	05/06/1915	KIA	Helles Memorial
CRIGHTON, Richard	Pte	252258	2nd/6th	05/03/1917	Died	Yew Tree Cem, Liverpool
CROMPTON, Robert S	Pte	251520	1st/6th	04/09/1918	DOW	Bagneux Brit. Cem.
CROMPTON, Wilfred	Sgt	250521	1st/6th	06/09/1917	KIA	Tyne Cot Memorial
CROMPTON, William	Pte	55836	1st/6th	27/03/1918	KIA	Arras Memorial
CROOK, John	Pte	251565	1st/6th	31/03/1918	DOW	Gezaincourt Comm. Cem. Ext.
CROSBY, Walter J	Pte	54469	2nd/6th	31/03/1918	KIA	Pozieres Memorial
CROSS, Charles A	Pte	2087	1st/6th	04/06/1915	KIA	Helles Memorial
CROWDER, Charles E	L/Cpl	251458	1st/6th	26/03/1918	KIA	Arras Memorial
CUMMOCK, Archie F	Pte	1525	1st/6th	30/05/1915	DOW	Lancashire Landing Cemetery
CUMPSTY, Stephen H	Pte	1509	1st/6th	28/05/1915	KIA	Helles Memorial
CUNDALL, Walter L	L/Cpl	2126	1st/6th	05/06/1915	KIA	Helles Memorial
CUNLIFFE, Clement W	2/Lieut		2nd/6th	24/09/1917	KIA	Ramscappelle Road Mil. Cem.
CURLISS, James	Pte	1905	1st/6th	07/08/1915	KIA	Helles Memorial
CURRIE, David	Pte	51267	2nd/6th	21/03/1918	KIA	Pozieres Memorial
CURRIE, William G	Cpl	250770	2nd/6th	05/10/1917	KIA	Tyne Cot Memorial
DABER, Alfred	Pte	2287	1st/6th	05/06/1915	KIA	Helles Memorial
DALE, Frank	L/Cpl	250811	2nd/6th	30/07/1917	KIA	Coxyde Mil. Cem.
DALTON, Norman E	Pte	251764	2nd/6th	03/08/1917	KIA	Ramscappelle Road Mil. Cem.

DARCY, James	Pte 351140	1st/6th	27/03/1918	KIA	Arras Memorial
DARLINGTON, Harry C	L/Cpl 2098	1st/6th	06/08/1915	KIA	Helles Memorial
DAVENPORT, Ernest B	L/Cpl 252311	2nd/6th	10/10/1918	Died	Le Quesnoy Comm. Cem.
DAVIES, Arthur	Pte 53753	2nd/6th	03/04/1918	DOW	Premont Brit. Cem.
DAVIES, Arthur L	Pte 2013	1st/6th	07/08/1915	KIA	Redoubt Cem
DAVIES, Robert	Pte 1630	1st/6th	07/08/1915	KIA	Helles Memorial
DAVY, Arthur	L/Cpl 1757	1st/6th	07/08/1915	KIA	Helles Memorial
DAWES, Walter	Pte 2446	1st/6th	20/05/1915	KIA	Redoubt Cem
DAWSON, John	Pte 2451	1st/6th	05/06/1915	KIA	Helles Memorial
DAYSH, Joseph P	Pte 252511	2nd/6th	25/03/1918	KIA	Pozieres Memorial
DEAN, Arthur	L/Cpl 252103	2nd/6th	05/10/1917	KIA	Tyne Cot Memorial
DEARDEN, Frank	Pte 2852	1st/6th	29/09/1915	Died	Portianos Mil. Cem.
DEARDEN, John	Pte 251450	1st/6th	04/11/1917	KIA	Coxyde Mil. Cem.
DENHAM, John D	Pte 1998	1st/6th	17/05/1915	DOW	Helles Memorial
DENNETT, William	Pte 251042	1st/6th	25/03/1918	KIA	Achiet-le-Grand Com Cem
DERRY, William	Pte 2578	1st/6th	07/08/1915	KIA	Helles Memorial
DICK, Harry	Pte 2025	1st/6th	22/09/1915	Died	Twelve Tree Copse Cem.
DOBSON, Luke	Pte 252000	1st/6th	28/03/1918	KIA	Gommecourt Wood New Cem
DODD, William W	Pte 868	1st/6th	07/08/1915	KIA	Helles Memorial
DOHERTY, Francis	Pte 302131	2nd/6th	21/03/1918	KIA	Pozieres Memorial
DOHERTY, Patrick B	Pte 252091	2nd/6th	11/05/1918	Died	Etaples Mil. Cem.
DOIG, Alexander M	Pte 1738	1st/6th	11/08/1915	DOW	Helles Memorial
DONALD, Alan J I	2/Lieut	1st/6th	04/06/1915	KIA	Helles Memorial
DUGGIN, Michael	Pte 2319	1st/6th	31/05/1915	KIA	Helles Memorial
DUNBAR, Harold	Pte 251120	1st/6th	15/09/1917	DOW	Etaples Mil. Cem.
DUNKERLEY, John	Pte 2359	1st/6th	04/06/1915	KIA	Helles Memorial
DUNKLEY, Harold	Pte 250607	2nd/6th	11/06/1917	KIA	Cambrin Mil. Cem.
DUNN, John W	Pte 251302	1st/6th	27/09/1918	KIA	Ribecourt Road Cem.
DURRANT-ROSE, William E	Pte 870104	2nd/6th	21/03/1918	KIA	Pozieres Memorial
DYER, Frank	Pte 75156	1st/6th	27/09/1918	KIA	Ribecourt Road Cem.
DYSON, Charles	Pte 1893	1st/6th	04/06/1915	KIA	Twelve Tree Copse Cem.
EARL, Jeffery	Pte 54407	1st/6th	25/03/1918	KIA	Arras Memorial
EASON, Edward	Pte 203509	2nd/6th	17/11/1917	KIA	Hooge Crater Cem.
ECKERSLEY, Thomas	Pte 2431	1st/6th	05/06/1915	KIA	Helles Memorial
EDGAR, Robert G	Capt	1st/6th	04/06/1915	KIA	Redoubt Cem
EDWARDS, Frank	L/Cpl 251959	1st/6th	13/08/1918	KIA	Bertrancourt Mil. Cem.
EDWARDS, John G	Pte 2489	1st/6th	04/06/1915	KIA	Helles Memorial
EGERTON, John W	Pte 75293	1st/6th	20/10/1918	KIA	Belle Vue Brit. Cem.
EGERTON, William	Pte 302794	2nd/6th	31/03/1918	KIA	Pozieres Memorial
ELLIOTT, Fred	Pte 201449	2nd/6th	21/03/1918	KIA	Pozieres Memorial
ELLIS, William	Sgt 400430	1st/6th	25/03/1918	KIA	Arras Memorial
ELTON, John F	Pte 1619	1st/6th	01/06/1915	KIA	Helles Memorial
ENTWISLE, Arthur C	Pte 35705	2nd/6th	27/03/1918	DOW	Abbeville Com Cem. Ext

ENTWISTLE, James H	Pte 252437	2nd/6th	21/03/1918	KIA	Villeret Old Chuchyard
EVANS, George	L/Cpl 2118	1st/6th	16/06/1915	DOW	East Mudros Mil. Cem
EVANS, James	Pte 38408	1st/6th	28/03/1918	KIA	Arras Memorial
EVANS, Leonard	Pte 1602	1st/6th	07/08/1915	KIA	Helles Memorial
EVANS, William	Pte 1953	1st/6th	12/07/1915	DOW	Hatherlow URC Cemetery
EVANSON, Walter	Pte 40531	1st/6th	28/03/1918	DOW	Arras Memorial
FAGEN, Thomas	L/Sgt 250570	1st/6th	25/03/1918	DOW	Arras Memorial
FAIRY, William	Pte 57141	1st/6th	02/04/1918	KIA	Arras Memorial
FANCOURT, Lawrence	Pte 2898	1st/6th	29/10/1918	Died	Peel Green Cem.
FARRANCE, Thomas	Pte 76090	1st/6th	11/10/1919	n/k	St Pierre Cem, Amiens
FARRINGTON, William	2/Lieut	1st/6th	25/03/1918	KIA	Arras Memorial
FELTON, Norman	Pte 57145	1st/6th	20/10/1918	KIA	Belle Vue Brit. Cem.
FERGUSON, Albert	Pte 1444	1st/6th	01/03/1915	Died	Cairo War Mem. Cem
FERGUSON, Donald	Pte 2915	1st/6th	01/10/1915	Died	East Mudros Mil. Cem
FERN, John H	L/Cpl 350814	1st/6th	27/09/1918	DOW	Ribecourt Road Cem.
FEW, Horace A	Cpl 270087	1st/6th	20/10/1918	KIA	Romeries Comm. Cem. ext.
FIDDES, Herbert	Pte 250801	1st/6th	27/09/1918	KIA	Ribecourt Road Cem.
FIELDS, James S	Pte 53346	1st/6th	20/10/1918	KIA	Belle Vue Brit. Cem.
FILDES, James	L/Cpl 252326	2nd/6th	05/10/1917	KIA	Tyne Cot Memorial
FINLAYSON, Henry A	L/Cpl 252185	2nd/6th	10/05/1917	KIA	Cambrin Mil. Cem.
FINNINGLEY, Arthur	Pte 1565	1st/6th	07/08/1915	KIA	Helles Memorial
FITTON, Leonard	Pte 251448	1st/6th	15/08/1918	KIA	Vis-en-Artois Memorial
FLEMING, Arthur J	Sgt 316	1st/6th	18/06/1915	DOW	Alexandria (Chatby) Mil. Cem
FLETCHER, Charles W	Pte 250690	2nd/6th	10/10/1917	DOW	Tyne Cot Memorial
FLETCHER, Reginald	Pte 275752	1st/6th	27/09/1918	KIA	Ribecourt Road Cem.
FOLEY, Charles	Pte 303651	2nd/6th	21/03/1918	KIA	Pozieres Memorial
FOLEY, John C	Pte 2081	1st/6th	06/06/1915	KIA	Helles Memorial
FORBES, Stuart H	Pte 2247	1st/6th	05/06/1915	KIA	Helles Memorial
FOX, William	Pte 351953	1st/6th	26/03/1918	KIA	Arras Memorial
FOX, William H	L/Cpl 250129	1st/6th	07/01/1918	KIA	Gorre Brit. & Indian Cem.
FRASER, Hector R	Cpl 250111	6th (n/k)	20/10/1920	n/k	Southern Cem, Manchester
FREEMAN, Harry	Pte 46691	1st/6th	20/10/1918	KIA	Belle Vue Brit. Cem.
FRENCH, Alfred R	Pte 43670	1st/6th	20/07/1918	KIA	Bertrancourt Mil. Cem.
FROGGATT, George	L/Cpl 252743	2nd/6th	21/03/1918	KIA	Bellicourt Brit. Cem.
FRY, Alfred H	Pte 1374	1st/6th	02/06/1915	KIA	Helles Memorial
GAFFNEY, Richard L	Pte 250844	2nd/6th	02/05/1918	DOW	Le Cateau Mil. Cem.
GALLEY, George	Pte 59537	1st/6th	27/09/1918	KIA	Flesquieres Hill Brit Cem
GAME, George H	Pte 270090	2nd/6th	10/10/1917	KIA	Tyne Cot Memorial
GANDER, Frederick A	Pte 54199	2nd/6th	27/03/1918	DOW	Le Cateau Mil. Cem.
GANT, Albert	Pte 1434	1st/6th	04/06/1915	KIA	Helles Memorial
GARNER, Joseph L	Pte 42616	2nd/6th	28/03/1918	KIA	Assevillers New Brit. Cem.

GARNER, Thomas H	Pte	2325	1st/6th	05/06/1915	KIA	Twelve Tree Copse Cem.
GARSIDE, Charles	Pte	59608	1st/6th	07/11/1918	Died	Terlincthun Brit. Cem.
GASKELL, Frederick	Pte	251895	1st/6th	21/08/1918	KIA	Queens Cem, Bucquoy
GASKELL, Thomas	Pte	250977	1st/6th	02/04/1917	KIA	Achiet-le-Grand Com Cem
GERMAN, Arthur K	Pte	8149	1st/6th	16/05/1918	DOW	Doullens Comm. Cem 2
GERRARD, Norman W	Pte	2458	1st/6th	07/08/1915	KIA	Helles Memorial
GIBSON, Arthur	Pte	50340	1st/6th	04/09/1917	KIA	Aeroplane Cem
GILBERT, Joseph	Pte	2174	1st/6th	28/05/1915	DOW	Lancashire Landing Cemetery
GILL, George	Pte	4958	1st/6th	01/10/1916	Died	Alexandria Hadra War Cem
GILLAND, John T	Pte	400526	1st/6th	02/09/1918	KIA	Manchester Cem.
GLOVER, James F	Pte	57146	1st/6th	20/10/1918	DOW	Belle Vue Brit. Cem.
GOODALL, Edmund L	Pte	2151	1st/6th	07/08/1915	KIA	Helles Memorial
GOODALL, Ernest	Pte	375434	1st/6th	26/03/1918	DOW	Bac-du-Sud Brit. Cem.
GOODIER, John	Pte	203323	1st/6th	04/09/1918	DOW	Varennes Mil. Cem.
GOODRICH, Walter M	2/Lieut		2nd/6th	25/03/1918	KIA	Assevillers New Brit. Cem.
GOODWIN, John T	Pte	1310	6th (n/k)	11/10/1915	n/k	Darwen Cemetery
GOUDE, Frank	Pte	2762	1st/6th	07/08/1915	KIA	Helles Memorial
GRADISKY, Frederic C	Pte	2801	1st/6th	07/08/1915	KIA	Helles Memorial
GRAHAM, Frederick	Pte	1959	1st/6th	04/06/1915	KIA	Helles Memorial
GRAHAM, William	Pte	245108	2nd/6th	20/08/1918	Died	St Roch Comm. Cem
GRAY, Douglas	Pte	2829	1st/6th	07/08/1915	KIA	Redoubt Cem
GREAVES, Norman	Pte	61236	1st/6th	02/09/1918	DOW	Manchester Cem.
GREAVES, William	Pte	351354	1st/6th	20/10/1918	KIA	Vis-en-Artois Memorial
GREEN, John H G	Pte	351481	1st/6th	25/08/1918	KIA	Warlencourt Brit. Cem
GREENHALGH, Fred	Pte	252432	2nd/6th	30/10/1918	Died	Hautmont Comm. Cem.
GREENOUGH, William	2/Lieut		1st/6th	21/10/1918	KIA	Belle Vue Brit. Cem.
GREGORY, Archibald G	Sgt	250700	2nd/6th	28/03/1918	DOW	Le Cateau Mil. Cem.
GREGORY, James	Pte	2745	2nd/6th	06/10/1917	DOW	Brandhoek New Mil. Cem. 4
GRIFFITH, George	Pte	2434	1st/6th	04/06/1915	KIA	Helles Memorial
GRIFFITH, Richard F	Cpl	250935	1st/6th	06/09/1917	n/k	Aeroplane Cem
GRIFFITHS, Harold	Pte	1805	1st/6th	04/06/1915	KIA	Helles Memorial
GRIMES, Charles R	Pte	1466	1st/6th	04/06/1915	KIA	Helles Memorial
GRIMSHAW, Edward M	Pte	2210	1st/6th	05/06/1915	KIA	Helles Memorial
GRIMSHAW, William	Pte	270024	1st/6th	23/06/1917	KIA	Ruyaulcourt Mil. Cem.
GROGAN, Thomas	Pte	57152	1st/6th	27/03/1918	KIA	Arras Memorial
GROOME, T M	Capt		6th (n/k)	01/06/1916	N/K	Rake Lane Cem, Wallasey
GROOMES, Samuel J	Pte	63537	1st/6th	15/08/1918	KIA	Vis-en-Artois Memorial
GROVE, David V	L/Cpl	57147	1st/6th	25/03/1918	KIA	Arras Memorial
GRUNDY, Henry C	Pte	250967	1st/6th	02/11/1918	Died	St Stephen's, Kearsley Moor

GRUNDY, Herbert W	Pte	33997	2nd/6th	21/03/1918	KIA	Pozieres Memorial
GRUNDY, Walter	Pte	250854	2nd/6th	25/03/1918	KIA	Pozieres Memorial
GUNN, Robert	Pte	1792	1st/6th	25/10/1915	Died	Pieta Mil. Cem.
HACKETT, Joseph	Pte	1980	1st/6th	07/08/1915	KIA	Helles Memorial
HACKWELL, William J	Pte	302916	2nd/6th	31/03/1918	KIA	Villers-Bretonneux Mil. Cem.
HADFIELD, Edgar	Pte	251088	1st/6th	04/09/1917	KIA	Aeroplane Cem
HADFIELD, Frank	Sgt	307	1st/6th	05/06/1915	KIA	Helles Memorial
HAHN, Walter F	L/Cpl	2716	1st/6th	13/08/1915	DOW	Lancashire Landing Cemetery
HAIGH, Ernest	Pte	57165	1st/6th	27/03/1918	KIA	Gommecourt Wood Cem.
HALL, Alfred E	L/Cpl	250533	2nd/6th	26/05/1917	DOW	Bethune Town Cem.
HALL, George B	Pte	29406	2nd/6th	31/03/1918	KIA	Villeret Old Chuchyard
HALL, James	Pte	1545	1st/6th	05/06/1915	KIA	Helles Memorial
HALLIDAY, Frank H	L/Cpl	2219	1st/6th	05/06/1915	KIA	Helles Memorial
HAMBLETON, William	Pte	2335	1st/6th	05/06/1915	KIA	Helles Memorial
HAMER, John	Pte	376772	2nd/6th	19/04/1918	DOW	Chambieres French Nat. Cem.
HAMMOND, George L	Pte	78118	1st/6th	06/03/1919	n/k	Chadderton Cem.
HAMMONDS, William	L/Cpl	42659	2nd/6th	26/03/1918	DOW	St Sever Cem. Ext.
HANKINSON, Richard	Lieut		1st/6th	21/06/1917	KIA	Ruyaulcourt Mil. Cem.
HANLEY, Cyril A	Pte	251003	1st/6th	25/03/1918	KIA	Arras Memorial
HARDAKER, Rufus	Pte	44864	2nd/6th	31/10/1917	DOW	Wimereux Comm. Cem.
HARDMAN, Thomas	Pte	252022	2nd/6th	13/07/1918	Died	Cologne Southern Cem.
HARMAN, Arthur G	2/Lieut		1st/6th	20/10/1918	KIA	Belle Vue Brit. Cem.
HAROLD, Owen	Pte	44225	1st/6th	04/09/1917	KIA	Ypres Town Cem. Ext.
HARRISON, Benjamin	Pte	250815	1st/6th	28/03/1918	KIA	Gommecourt Wood Cem.
HARRISON, Thomas	L/Cpl	250441	1st/6th	29/03/1918	DOW	Gezaincourt Comm. Cem. Ext.
HARROP, Joseph	Pte	251876	1st/6th	28/03/1918	KIA	Gommecourt Wood Cem.
HARWOOD, John W	Pte	53320	1st/6th	27/09/1918	KIA	Ribecourt Road Cem.
HAUGHTON, Alfred	Pte	1688	1st/6th	01/06/1915	KIA	Helles Memorial
HAUGHTON, Tom M	Pte	251172	1st/6th	29/03/1918	DOW	Doullens Comm. Cem 1
HAWORTH, Frank	Pte	57157	1st/6th	25/03/1918	KIA	Arras Memorial
HAWORTH, Harry	Pte	43056	1st/6th	05/09/1917	DOW	Lijssenthoek Mil. Cem.
HAWTHORN, PERCY	Pte	352071	1st/6th	25/03/1918	KIA	Arras Memorial
HAYDEN, Charles	Pte	252436	2nd/6th	02/04/1918	DOW	Netley Mil. Cem.
HAYES, Arthur	Sgt	88	1st/6th	08/07/1915	DOW	Cairo War Mem. Cem
HAYES, Wilfred	Pte	1676	1st/6th	04/06/1915	KIA	Helles Memorial
HAYNES, Harold	Pte	1618	1st/6th	05/06/1915	KIA	Helles Memorial
HAYWARD, Frederick	Pte	887	1st/6th	07/08/1915	KIA	Helles Memorial
HAYWARD, James H	Pte	251242	1st/6th	29/10/1917	KIA	Coxyde Mil. Cem.
HAYWARD, Thomas B	Pte	885	1st/6th	25/05/1915	KIA	Helles Memorial

HEALD, Eli J	Pte	252327	2nd/6th	21/03/1918	KIA	Pozieres Memorial
HEAP, Ernest A	Pte	1678	1st/6th	09/06/1915	DOW	Alexandria (Chatby) Mil. Cem
HEAP, Nathan P	Pte	57159	1st/6th	27/03/1918	KIA	Arras Memorial
HEARD, Robert L	Cpl	250155	1st/6th	27/03/1918	KIA	Arras Memorial
HEATH, Herbert	Pte	2714	1st/6th	07/08/1915	KIA	Helles Memorial
HEELEY, Arthur E	Pte	2637	1st/6th	23/09/1915	KIA	Twelve Tree Copse Cem.
HENDERSON, John	Pte	203657	2nd/6th	21/03/1918	KIA	Pozieres Memorial
HERFORD, George	Cpl	250860	2nd/6th	10/07/1917	Died	Dunkirk Town Cem.
HEWITSON, Ben	Pte	252028	2nd/6th	04/05/1917	KIA	Cambrin Mil. Cem.
HEWITT, John	Pte	250906	1st/6th	02/09/1918	KIA	Vis-en-Artois Memorial
HEYDON, Sidney	L/Cpl	2142	1st/6th	06/06/1915	KIA	Helles Memorial
HEYES, William	Pte	252124	1st/6th	25/03/1918	KIA	Douchy-les-Ayette Brit. Cem.
HEYWOOD, Arthur	Pte	251739	1st/6th	08/11/1917	DOW	Zuydcoote Mil Cem.
HEYWOOD, Arthur G	Major		1st/6th	12/09/1918	DOW	St Sever Cem
HEYWOOD, Walter	Pte	2092	1st/6th	07/08/1915	KIA	Helles Memorial
HICKMAN, Fred P	Pte	2050	1st/6th	05/06/1915	KIA	Helles Memorial
HICKSON, John F	Pte	1818	1st/6th	04/06/1915	KIA	Helles Memorial
HIGGINBOTTOM James	Pte	270125	2nd/6th	21/03/1918	KIA	Pozieres Memorial
HIGGINS, Harold W	Pte	2460	1st/6th	06/06/1915	DOW	Helles Memorial
HIGGINSON, Arthur	Pte	351946	1st/6th	26/03/1918	KIA	Arras Memorial
HIGHET, William W	L/Sgt	252051	2nd/6th	25/03/1918	KIA	Pozieres Memorial
HILL, George A	Pte	1817	1st/6th	07/06/1915	DOW	Helles Memorial
HILL, Victor	Pte	53757	2nd/6th	13/07/1918	Died	Tincourt New Brit. Cem.
HILTON, Herbert	Pte	201166	1st/6th	08/11/1917	DOW	Zuydcoote Mil Cem.
HINCHLIFFE, Charles V	Pte	352544	1st/6th	02/09/1918	DOW	Euston Road Cem.
HIND, Robert B	Pte	1544	1st/6th	11/12/1915	KIA	Twelve Tree Copse Cem.
HINDLEY, Henry J B	Pte	41455	1st/6th	25/05/1918	KIA	Achiet-le-Grand Com Cem
HIRST, Jack	Pte	250380	1st/6th	25/07/1917	n/k	Bournemouth East Cem.
HOBDEY, Alfred M	Pte	1413	1st/6th	06/06/1915	DOW	Helles Memorial
HOCKNELL, Thomas	Pte	2241	1st/6th	04/06/1915	KIA	Helles Memorial
HODGSON, Frederick	Pte	57158	1st/6th	03/04/1918	DOW	Wimereux Comm. Cem.
HODGSON, Philip M	Pte	252048	2nd/6th	22/03/1918	KIA	Pozieres Memorial
HODGSON, Thomas	Pte	250920	1st/6th	29/01/1918	n/k	St Anne's Churchyard, Clifton
HOLDEN, George A	Pte	2176	1st/6th	04/06/1915	KIA	Helles Memorial
HOLDSWORTH, Arthur	Pte	252723	2nd/6th.	21/03/1918	KIA	Pozieres Memorial
HOLDSWORTH, Harold	Pte	231182	1st/6th	06/09/1917	KIA	Bedford House Cem.
HOLLAND, Thomas	Pte	251942	1st/6th	02/11/1917	DOW	St Anne's Churchyard, Sutton
HOLLAND, Thomas D	Pte	1851	1st/6th	05/06/1915	KIA	Helles Memorial
HOLLIDAY, Ernest	Pte	42708	2nd/6th	31/03/1918	KIA	Pozieres Memorial
HOLME, Thomas	Pte	63542	1st/6th	02/09/1918	KIA	Bancourt Brit. Cem.
HOLME, Zaccheus	Pte	2166	1st/6th	04/06/1915	KIA	Redoubt Cem

HOLT, Joseph	Capt	1st/6th	04/06/1915	KIA	Helles Memorial
HOLYOAKE, Frank	L/Cpl 2149	1st/6th	07/08/1915	KIA	Helles Memorial
HONNIBALL, Walter	Pte 2351	1st/6th	07/08/1915	KIA	Helles Memorial
HOOLEY, Joseph	Pte 252240	2nd/6th	06/05/1917	DOW	Noeux-les-Mines Comm. Cem
HOPWOOD, Samuel	Pte 251510	1st/6th	21/06/1919	n/k	Philips Park Cem, Manchester
HORNBROOK, Harold	Pte 2399	1st/6th	05/06/1915	KIA	Helles Memorial
HORNE, James L	Pte 2000	1st/6th	04/06/1915	KIA	Helles Memorial
HORROCKS, William T	Pte 2410	1st/6th	04/06/1915	KIA	Helles Memorial
HORSFIELD, John F	2/Lieut	2nd/6th	26/07/1917	KIA	Coxyde Mil. Cem.
HOUGH, Ernest	Pte 3617	2nd/6th	21/04/1918	Died	Wimereux Comm. Cem.
HOUGH, John	Pte 2031	1st/6th	06/06/1915	DOW	East Mudros Mil. Cem
HOUSEMAN, William	Pte 270193	2nd/6th	21/03/1918	KIA	Pozieres Memorial
HOWARTH, Arthur	Pte 63541	1st/6th	02/09/1918	KIA	Bancourt Brit. Cem.
HOWARTH, Arthur	Pte 36793	2nd/6th	10/10/1917	KIA	Tyne Cot Memorial
HOWARTH, Norman D	Pte 1876	1st/6th	12/07/1915	KIA	Redoubt Cem
HOWE, Walter	Pte 28433	1st/6th	25/09/1917	KIA	Coxyde Mil. Cem.
HOWE, Walter W	L/Cpl 252094	2nd/6th	21/03/1918	KIA	Pozieres Memorial
HOWELL, Arthur H	Pte 1909	1st/6th	05/06/1915	KIA	Helles Memorial
HOYES, Fred	Pte 252001	2nd/6th	30/12/1917	DOW	Lijssenthoek Mil. Cem.
HUDDLESTON, Lorimer	Pte 2255	1st/6th	05/06/1915	KIA	Helles Memorial
HUFF, Leonard	Pte 1441	1st/6th	01/06/1915	KIA	Helles Memorial
HULSE, Charles	L/Cpl 351959	1st/6th	27/09/1918	KIA	Hermies Hill Brit. Cem.
HUMPHREYS, John L	Pte 250244	1st/6th	05/06/1915	KIA	Helles Memorial
HUNTER, Arthur D	Capt	1st/6th	07/08/1915	KIA	Redoubt Cem
HURST, Herbert G	L/Cpl 358	1st/6th	04/06/1915	KIA	Helles Memorial
HYMAN, Harold	Pte 251597	1st/6th	20/10/1918	DOW	Belle Vue Brit. Cem.
IRLAM Lewis,	Pte 45014	1st/6th	09/09/1917	KIA	Ypres Reservoir Cem.
ISHERWOOD, Joseph C	Pte 250939	6th (n/k)	15/03/1917	n/k	Ripon Cem
ISMAY, Thomas	Pte 44259	1st/6th	02/09/1918	KIA	Bancourt Brit. Cem.
JACKSON, Alfred	Pte 251881	1st/6th	06/09/1917	KIA	Tyne Cot Memorial
JACKSON, Malcom R	2/Lieut	1st/6th	25/03/1918	KIA	Arras Memorial
JACKSON, Stanley F	Capt	1st/6th	04/06/1915	KIA	Twelve Tree Copse Cem.
JACKSON, William	Pte 1638	1st/6th	07/08/1915	KIA	Helles Memorial
JAGGER, James H	Pte 63555	1st/6th	02/09/1918	KIA	Vis-en-Artois Memorial
JARRATT, Harold	Pte 29809	1st/6th	28/03/1918	KIA	Arras Memorial
JEFFERIS, Thomas F	Pte 2238	1st/6th	07/08/1915	KIA	Helles Memorial
JEFFERS, Joseph P	Pte 54941	2nd/6th	19/05/1918	KIA	Etaples Mil. Cem.
JOHNSON, Henry	Pte 251046	1st/6th	06/11/1917	n/k	Coxyde Mil. Cem.
JOHNSON, Lawrence A	Pte 2380	1st/6th	07/08/1915	KIA	Helles Memorial
JOHNSON, Sidney R	Pte 57173	1st/6th	25/03/1918	DOW	Douchy-les-Ayette Brit. Cem.
JOHNSTON, James	Pte 345038	1st/6th	22/09/1918	DOW	Grevillers Brit. Cem.
JONES, Ernest	Pte 1768	1st/6th	05/06/1915	KIA	Helles Memorial
JONES, George H	Pte 64285	1st/6th	27/09/1918	KIA	Ribecourt Road Cem.

JONES, Harold	Pte 1845	1st/6th	07/08/1915	KIA	Skew Bridge Cem.
JONES, James	Pte 1838	1st/6th	02/06/1915	KIA	Helles Memorial
JONES, Percy G	Pte 345037	2nd/6th	28/04/1918	Died	Cologne Southern Cem.
JONES, Peter	Pte 251173	1st/6th	28/03/1918	KIA	Achiet-le-Grand Com Cem
JONES, Robert E	Pte 250302	1st/6th	04/09/1918	DOW	Bagneux Brit. Cem.
KAY, Benjamin	Pte 252725	2nd/6th	05/04/1917	KIA	Vermelles Brit. Cem.
KAY, Harold	Pte 2386	1st/6th	06/06/1915	KIA	Lancashire Landing Cemetery
KELSEY, John	Pte 2252	1st/6th	11/08/1915	DOW	Helles Memorial
KENT, Gilbert	Sgt 250645	1st/6th	20/10/1918	KIA	Belle Vue Brit. Cem.
KENYON, James	2/Lieut	2nd/6th	21/03/1918	KIA	Pozieres Memorial
KERSHAW, Frederick	Sgt 1469	1st/6th	07/08/1915	KIA	Helles Memorial
KERSHAW, Roland	Pte 43809	1st/6th	27/09/1918	KIA	Ribecourt Road Cem.
KERSHAW, Stanley	Pte 1729	1st/6th	27/05/1915	KIA	Helles Memorial
KERWIN, John	Pte 1755	1st/6th	06/06/1915	DOW	Lancashire Landing Cemetery
KESSLER, Edgar	Capt	1st/6th	04/06/1915	KIA	Redoubt Cem
KILLICK, Richard	2/Lieut	1st/6th	15/05/1915	KIA	Helles Memorial
KING, Ernest	Pte 270034	1st/6th	01/07/1918	KIA	Bertrancourt Mil. Cem.
KITCHEN, Cyril J	L/Cpl 40099	1st/6th	21/10/1918	DOW	St Aubert Brit. Cem.
KITSON, Frederick	Pte 2459	1st/6th	07/08/1915	KIA	Helles Memorial
KNIGHT, Arthur	Pte 1741	1st/6th	11/05/1915	DOW	Helles Memorial
KNIGHT, Harold H	Lieut	1st/6th	27/03/1918	KIA	Douchy-les-Ayette Brit. Cem.
KNIGHT, Thomas	Pte 251213	1st/6th	05/09/1917	KIA	Aeroplane Cem
KNOTT, Ernest	Capt	2nd/6th	22/03/1918	KIA	Pozieres Memorial
LAIMBEER, Herbert N	Pte 1996	1st/6th	04/06/1915	KIA	Helles Memorial
LAMB, Joseph	Pte 351472	1st/6th	26/03/1918	KIA	Arras Memorial
LAMMING, Albert V	Pte 42626	2nd/6th	18/11/1917	DOW	Lijssenthoek Mil. Cem.
LANCASTER, Donald G	Pte 2389	1st/6th	21/05/1915	KIA	Helles Memorial
LANGFORD, Gerald H G	Pte 57179	1st/6th	20/10/1918	KIA	Belle Vue Brit. Cem.
LANGSTON, John	Pte 252792	2nd/6th	21/03/1918	KIA	Pozieres Memorial
LAWES, Victor J	Pte 270096	2nd/6th	03/05/1918	DOW	Le Cateau Mil. Cem.
LAWRENCE, Harry H	Pte 42686	2nd/6th	21/03/1918	KIA	Pozieres Memorial
LAWSON, William F	L/Cpl 1395	1st/6th	05/06/1915	KIA	Helles Memorial
LAYCOCK, Fred	Pte 44867	2nd/6th	21/03/1918	KIA	Pozieres Memorial
LEACH, Harry A	Pte 1473	1st/6th	06/08/1915	DOW	Lancashire Landing Cemetery
LEAVER, Hartley	Pte 302370	2nd/6th	22/07/1918	Died	Niederzwehren cem.
LEE, George F	Pte 42627	2nd/6th	16/11/1917	KIA	Tyne Cot Memorial
LEE, James W S	Pte 1878	1st/6th	04/06/1915	KIA	Helles Memorial
LEE, John	Pte 57176	1st/6th	02/09/1918	KIA	Manchester Cem.
LEE, Samuel	Pte 59240	1st/6th	02/09/1918	KIA	Bancourt Brit. Cem.
LEEK, Walter	Cpl 76095	1st/6th	18/11/1919	n/k	Burngreave Cem, Sheffield

LEEKS, George	Pte 270097	2nd/6th	12/01/1918	Died	Longuenesse Souvenir Cem
LEESE, John S	Pte 2193	1st/6th	07/08/1915	KIA	Helles Memorial
LEESON, William	Pte 251777	2nd/6th	11/06/1917	KIA	Cambrin Mil. Cem.
LEIGH, Thomas B	Pte 250855	1st/6th	06/09/1917	KIA	Tyne Cot Memorial
LEIGH, William	L/Cpl 1490	1st/6th	04/06/1915	KIA	Helles Memorial
LEIGHTON, William	Pte 1911	1st/6th	05/06/1915	KIA	Twelve Tree Copse Cem.
LEWIS, Graham	Pte 203615	2nd/6th	31/03/1918	KIA	Villeret Old Chuchyard
LILLEY, Leo,	Pte 1967	1st/6th	05/06/1915	KIA	Helles Memorial
LINGARD, John R	Lieut	1st/6th	21/08/1915	KIA	Helles Memorial
LINK, PERCY	Pte 54357	1st/6th	15/05/1918	KIA	Couin New Brit. Cem.
LISTER, John B	Pte 2289	1st/6th	05/06/1915	KIA	Helles Memorial
LITCHFIELD, Edward J	Pte 252669	2nd/6th	10/10/1917	KIA	Tyne Cot Memorial
LITTLER, Thomas B	Pte 42497	2nd/6th	29/03/1918	DOW	St Roch Comm. Cem,
LIVINGSTONE, Jacob	Pte 251846	1st/6th	09/12/1917	DOW	Bethune Town Cem.
LIVSEY, Arthur	Pte 251473	1st/6th	25/03/1918	KIA	Arras Memorial
LLEWELLYN, Frank	Pte 3018	1st/6th	07/08/1915	KIA	Helles Memorial
LLOYD, Harold	Cpl 26406	2nd/6th	22/03/1918	KIA	Pozieres Memorial
LLOYD, Norman V	Pte 2164	1st/6th	27/05/1915	KIA	Helles Memorial
LOMAS, George G	Lieut	2nd/6th	22/03/1918	KIA	Pozieres Memorial
LOMAX, Albert	Pte 48822	2nd/6th	21/03/1918	KIA	Pozieres Memorial
LOUGHLAND, Harry V	Pte 2797	1st/6th	07/08/1915	KIA	Helles Memorial
LOUIS, Reginald	Pte 252540	2nd/6th	29/12/1917	KIA	Menin Road South Mil. Cem.
LOVE, James E	2/Lieut	1st/6th	02/09/1918	KIA	Manchester Cem.
LOWE, Edward J	Pte 250095	2nd/6th	16/11/1918	DOW	Southern Cem, Manchester
LOWE, Edwin	Pte 252336	2nd/6th	21/04/1917	KIA	Vermelles Brit. Cem.
LOWE, William A	L/Sgt 982	1st/6th	05/06/1915	KIA	Helles Memorial
LOWN, Sydney	Pte 251579	1st/6th	28/03/1918	KIA	Douchy-les-Ayette Brit. Cem.
LUCK, George	Cpl 252674	2nd/6th	18/08/1917	KIA	Ramscappelle Road Mil. Cem.
MACEFIELD, Percy E	Pte 270145	2nd/6th	07/10/1917	Died	Tyne Cot Memorial
MACKENZIE, William	Pte 251809	1st/6th	11/12/1917	KIA	Post Office Rifles Cem.
MAGEE, John H	Pte 36543	1st/6th	21/10/1918	KIA	Quievy Comm. Cem. Ext.
MAHONY, Francis	Pte 251582	1st/6th	04/07/1917	KIA	Ruyaulcourt Mil. Cem.
MAITLAND, Edgar F	Lieut	2nd/6th	24/09/1917	KIA	Ramscappelle Road Mil. Cem.
MALONEY, Henry	CSM 7385	1st/6th	05/06/1915	KIA	Helles Memorial
MANTLE, Joseph	Pte 400663	1st/6th	23/07/1918	DOW	St Sever Cem. Ext.
MARLOR, Edward	Pte 350735	2nd/6th	26/03/1918	DOW	Pozieres Memorial
MARSDEN, Cyril	Pte 2363	1st/6th	04/06/1915	DOW	Pink Farm Cem.
MARSDEN, Thomas F	Pte 2277	1st/6th	04/06/1915	KIA	Twelve Tree Copse Cem.
MARSH, Albert	L/Cpl 275382	1st/6th	20/10/1918	KIA	Belle Vue Brit. Cem.

MARSLAND, William	Pte 39721	2nd/6th	31/03/1918	KIA	Pozieres Memorial
MARTIN, John R	CSM 250371	1st/6th	28/03/1918	DOW	Gezaincourt Comm. Cem. Ext.
MARTIN, Joseph	Pte 1482	1st/6th	05/06/1915	KIA	Helles Memorial
MARTIN, Robert	L/Cpl 773	1st/6th	04/06/1915	KIA	Helles Memorial
MASON, Frank	Pte 50344	1st/6th	14/07/1918	KIA	Bertrancourt Mil. Cem.
MASSEY, Thomas	Pte 251491	1st/6th	02/09/1918	KIA	Euston Road Cem.
MASTERS, Harry L	Sgt 300940	2nd/6th	06/10/1917	KIA	Tyne Cot Memorial
MATHER, Arthur S	Pte 251611	1st/6th	09/06/1917	KIA	Ruyaulcourt Mil. Cem.
MATTHEWS, James	Pte 2059	1st/6th	17/10/1915	DOW	Helles Memorial
MATTHEWSON, Jack A	Pte 2108	1st/6th	05/06/1915	KIA	Twelve Tree Copse Cem.
McDOUGALL, Sidney	Lieut	1st/6th	07/08/1915	KIA	Helles Memorial
McGARRY, James	L/Sgt 300809	2nd/6th	21/03/1918	KIA	Pozieres Memorial
McGUIRE, John B	Pte 1535	1st/6th	05/06/1915	KIA	Helles Memorial
McHALE, Thomas	Pte 302618	2nd/6th	31/03/1918	KIA	Pozieres Memorial
McINTYRE, Peter S	Sgt 966	1st/6th	05/06/1915	KIA	Helles Memorial
McMILLAN, Sidney	L/Cpl 1281	1st/6th	05/06/1915	KIA	Helles Memorial
McNAB, John	Pte 350684	1st/6th	25/03/1918	KIA	Arras Memorial
McNAUGHTON, W. M,	Sgt 109	1st/6th	07/08/1915	KIA	Helles Memorial
McNULTY, Edward	Pte 270037	1st/6th	28/03/1918	DOW	Bac-du-Sud Brit. Cem.
McNULTY, John T	Pte 252777	2nd/6th	19/04/1918	DOW	Premont Brit. Cem.
McSPIRIT, George P	Pte 251291	1st/6th	30/03/1918	DOW	Etaples Mil. Cem.
MEEK, Alfred C	Pte 270099	2nd/6th	01/05/1918	Died	Cologne Southern Cem.
MELLOR, Cyril L	Pte 2312	1st/6th	04/06/1915	KIA	Helles Memorial
MELLOR, John	L/Cpl 252705	2nd/6th	31/07/1917	DOW	Coxyde Mil. Cem.
MERCER, William D	Pte 1654	1st/6th	31/05/1915	KIA	Helles Memorial
MERRILL, Thomas A	L/Cpl 252097	2nd/6th	02/08/1917	DOW	Coxyde Mil. Cem.
MERRON, Edward	Pte 17976	1st/6th	27/09/1918	DOW	Ribecourt Road Cem.
METCALFE, George E	Pte 44936	1st/6th	21/03/1918	KIA	Arras Memorial
METCALFE, Haydn G	Pte 2270	1st/6th	07/08/1915	KIA	Redoubt Cem
METCALFE, John	Pte 63572	1st/6th	21/08/1918	KIA	Queens Cem, Bucquoy
METCALFE, William	Pte 245230	1st/6th	20/10/1918	KIA	Belle Vue Brit. Cem.
MILLAR, Arthur F	Pte 252125	2nd/6th	30/11/1917	Died	Mendighem Mil. Cem.
MILLER, Cyril W	L/Cpl 1271	1st/6th	31/07/1915	KIA	Helles Memorial
MILLS, Bernard W	Pte 53593	2nd/6th	21/03/1918	KIA	Pozieres Memorial
MILLS, Frederick T	L/Cpl 2097	1st/6th	05/06/1915	KIA	Helles Memorial
MILLS, Robert	Pte 248041	1st/6th	04/09/1918	DOW	Mont Huon Mil. Cem.
MILLS, Tom R	Lieut	1st/6th	04/06/1915	KIA	Helles Memorial
MILLS, William	Pte 252335	2nd/6th	21/03/1918	KIA	Pozieres Memorial
MILNE, Alexander N	Capt	1st/6th	07/08/1915	KIA	Helles Memorial
MITCHELL, Andrew	Pte 252477	2nd/6th	21/11/1917	DOW	Lijssenthoek Mil. Cem.
MITCHELL, Frank	Pte 250562	1st/6th	31/05/1917	DOW	Neuville-Bourjonval Brit. Cem
MOIR-BROWN, William	Pte 2209	1st/6th	04/06/1915	KIA	Helles Memorial
MOLYNEUX, William	Pte 48484	1st/6th	15/08/1918	KIA	Vis-en-Artois Memorial
MOORE, Norman	Pte 252407	2nd/6th	20/07/1918	n/k	Philips Park Cem, Manchester

MOORES, Stanley	Pte 251740	1st/6th	28/09/1918	DOW	Grevillers Brit. Cem.
MOORHOUSE, William	Pte 2674	1st/6th	07/08/1915	KIA	Helles Memorial
MORETON, Bertrand W	L/Cpl 2254	1st/6th	07/08/1915	KIA	Helles Memorial
MORRELL, Fred	Pte 302442	2nd/6th	21/03/1918	KIA	Pozieres Memorial
MORRIS, David	Pte 250553	1st/6th	03/11/1917	KIA	Coxyde Mil. Cem.
MORRIS, William	Pte 252716	2nd/6th	24/07/1917	KIA	Coxyde Mil. Cem.
MORRIS, William T	Pte 251578	1st/6th	02/09/1918	KIA	Vis-en-Artois Memorial
MORTIMER, Harry	Pte 1311	1st/6th	30/06/1915	KIA	Helles Memorial
MOSS, Frederick	Pte 352325	1st/6th	27/09/1918	KIA	Ribecourt Road Cem.
MOSS, Frederick B	Pte 2358	1st/6th	07/08/1915	KIA	Helles Memorial
MOSS, Herbert	Pte 251557	1st/6th	25/03/1918	KIA	Achiet-le-Grand Com Cem
MOTTERSHEAD, James	Pte 252348	2nd/6th	07/10/1917	KIA	Tyne Cot Memorial
MOULD, Herbert	L/Cpl 1316	1st/6th	06/06/1915	KIA	Helles Memorial
MULLINS, Patrick	Cpl 250370	1st/6th	21/08/1918	KIA	Vis-en-Artois Memorial
MURPHY, Frederick	Pte 1164	1st/6th	07/08/1915	KIA	Helles Memorial
MUSGRAVE, Walter	Pte 1548	1st/6th	07/08/1915	KIA	Helles Memorial
MUSGRAVE, William	L/Cpl 251706	2nd/6th	21/03/1918	KIA	Pozieres Memorial
NEAVES, Charles A	Pte 2089	1st/6th	29/05/1915	KIA	Helles Memorial
NEEDHAM, Frank	Pte 1812	1st/6th	05/06/1915	KIA	Helles Memorial
NEILL, Thomas	Pte 251203	1st/6th	02/09/1917	DOW	Ypres Reservoir Cem.
NEWLOVE, George	Cpl 421	1st/6th	05/06/1915	KIA	Helles Memorial
NICHOLS, William J	Pte 42747	2nd/6th	21/03/1918	KIA	Pozieres Memorial
NICHOLSON, Samuel	Pte 459	1st/6th	04/06/1915	KIA	Helles Memorial
NIGHTINGALE, Frank	Pte 3391	1st/6th	19/11/1915	Died	Helles Memorial
NIGHTINGALE, Robert	Pte 2484	1st/6th	04/06/1915	KIA	Helles Memorial
NOBBS, Bernard J	Pte 1997	1st/6th	06/10/1916	Died	Baghdad (North Gate) Cem
NORBURY, Joseph E	Pte 251366	1st/6th	27/09/1918	DOW	Flesquieres Hill Brit Cem
NORTON, Ernest	Sgt 778	1st/6th	04/06/1915	KIA	Helles Memorial
OATES, Ernest	Pte 350475	1st/6th	25/10/1918	DOW	Ashton-under-Lyne Cem.
O'CONNOR, John	Pte 303391	2nd/6th	21/03/1918	KIA	Pozieres Memorial
OGDEN, Arnold	Pte 352330	1st/6th	27/09/1918	KIA	Ribecourt Road Cem.
OLLERENSHAW Robert	Pte 3296	1st/6th	07/08/1915	KIA	Helles Memorial
O'LOUGHLIN, William	Pte 44735	1st/6th	22/08/1918	KIA	Vis-en-Artois Memorial
ORME, Joseph	Sgt 218	1st/6th	06/06/1915	KIA	Helles Memorial
ORMEROD, William	Pte 57268	2nd/6th	21/03/1918	KIA	Pozieres Memorial
OWENS, Thomas	Pte 1887	1st/6th	07/08/1915	KIA	Helles Memorial
PALMER, Thomas	Pte 2455	1st/6th	07/08/1915	KIA	Helles Memorial
PARKER, Alfred J	Pte 252127	2nd/6th	31/07/1917	DOW	Coxyde Mil. Cem.
PARKER, Gerald	Pte 1869	1st/6th	04/06/1915	KIA	Helles Memorial
PARKER, Gerald C	L/Cpl 250552	1st/6th	01/11/1918	Died	Awoingt Brit. Cem.
PARKER, Jonathon N	Pte 51423	1st/6th	26/03/1918	KIA	Arras Memorial
PARKES, Alfred	Pte 252050	2nd/6th	27/05/1918	Died	Cologne Southern Cem.
PARR, Nathan F	Cpl 251710	2nd/6th	31/12/1917	KIA	Menin Road South Mil. Cem.

PARTT, Ernest	Pte 1538	1st/6th	05/06/1915	KIA	Helles Memorial
PAYNE, Alfred R	Pte 3048	1st/6th	07/08/1915	KIA	Helles Memorial
PAYNE, William P	Pte 42663	2nd/6th	31/03/1918	DOW	St Sever Cem. Ext.
PEAKE, Robert	Pte 252043	2nd/6th	21/03/1918	KIA	Pozieres Memorial
PEAT, Charles J	L/Cpl 251621	1st/6th	28/03/1918	KIA	Arras Memorial
PEEL, Stephen	Pte 251859	1st/6th	06/09/1917	KIA	Tyne Cot Memorial
PEERS, William	Pte 63581	1st/6th	02/09/1918	KIA	Bancourt Brit. Cem.
PENN, Herbert	Pte 2161	1st/6th	31/05/1915	KIA	Redoubt Cem
PENNY, Thomas H	Pte 2336	1st/6th	12/05/1915	KIA	Helles Memorial
PEOVER, James W	Pte 250963	1st/6th	03/04/1918	DOW	Wimereux Comm. Cem.
PERCIVAL, Arthur	Pte 251974	1st/6th	28/03/1918	KIA	Arras Memorial
PHILLIP, Herbert F	L/Cpl 302390	2nd/6th	22/03/1918	KIA	Pozieres Memorial
PHILLIPS, David	Sgt 251211	1st/6th	26/03/1918	KIA	Arras Memorial
PICKUP, John B	L/Cpl 840	1st/6th	04/06/1915	KIA	Helles Memorial
PIERPOINT, Harold W	Pte 251047	1st/6th	05/09/1917	KIA	Tyne Cot Memorial
PILKINGTON, Hugh B	Capt	1st/6th	04/06/1915	KIA	Helles Memorial
PILLING, Harry	Pte 250559	1st/6th	31/12/1917	Died	Longuenesse Souvenir Cem
PILLING, Joseph	Pte 63435	1st/6th	21/06/1918	DOW	Gezaincourt Comm. Cem. Ext.
PILLING, Stuart B	Pte 1806	1st/6th	04/06/1915	KIA	Helles Memorial
PINDER, Charles N	Cpl 302695	1st/6th	28/09/1918	DOW	Grevillers Brit. Cem.
PLACE, Walter A	Pte 57199	1st/6th	20/04/1918	KIA	Couin New Brit. Cem.
PLANT, Henry M	L/Cpl 976	1st/6th	11/05/1915	DOW	Helles Memorial
PLEVIN, Henry	Pte 2145	1st/6th	24/05/1915	DOW	Helles Memorial
POGSON, George	Pte 270179	2nd/6th	21/03/1918	KIA	Pozieres Memorial
POLLARD, George	Pte 302373	2nd/6th	21/03/1918	KIA	Pozieres Memorial
POLLARD, Joseph	Pte 64364	1st/6th	27/09/1918	KIA	Ribecourt Road Cem.
POLLITT, Francis C	Pte 300644	2nd/6th	01/04/1918	DOW	Etaples Mil. Cem.
POLLOCK, Francis	Pte 2109	1st/6th	05/06/1915	KIA	Helles Memorial
POOLE, Arthur	Pte 1112	1st/6th	05/07/1915	KIA	Twelve Tree Copse Cem.
POOLE, James	Pte 250745	2nd/6th	09/10/1917	DOW	Nine Elms Brit. Cem
PORTER, Thomas C	Pte 2212	1st/6th	04/06/1915	KIA	Helles Memorial
POULSON, John T	Pte 57269	2nd/6th	21/03/1918	KIA	Pozieres Memorial
POUNDER, William H	Pte 251408	1st/6th	28/03/1918	KIA	Gommecourt Wood Cem
PRATT, Frederick	Pte 252276	2nd/6th	02/08/1917	DOW	Coxyde Mil. Cem.
PRESCOTT, Norman	Pte 250315	1st/6th	21/08/1918	KIA	Queens Cem, Bucquoy
PRESTON, Henry	L/Cpl 252173	2nd/6th	20/04/1917	KIA	Cambrin Mil. Cem.
PRICE, Enoch H	Cpl 251680	1st/6th	20/10/1918	DOW	Belle Vue Brit. Cem.
PRIME, Charles	Pte 38501	1st/6th	27/03/1918	KIA	Arras Memorial
PRINCE, James	Pte 37594	2nd/6th	21/03/1918	KIA	Serre Road Cem. 2
PUGH, David	Pte 63582	1st/6th	21/08/1918	KIA	Queens Cem, Bucquoy
PYGOTT, Thomas	Sgt 10951	1st/6th	23/07/1918	KIA	Pozieres Memorial
RABBITT, Charles C	Pte 57282	2nd/6th	21/03/1918	KIA	Pozieres Memorial
RAE, Colin W	Pte 250281	1st/6th	15/09/1917	DOW	Ypres Reservoir Cem.
RAINBOW, John	2/Lieut	1st/6th	07/08/1915	KIA	Helles Memorial

RALPHS, Herbert	Pte 2934	1st/6th	07/08/1915	KIA	Helles Memorial
RALPHS, Thomas	Pte 50395	1st/6th	07/04/1918	KIA	Pozieres Memorial
RANKIN, William M	Pte 1897	1st/6th	05/06/1915	KIA	Twelve Tree Copse Cem.
RATCLIFFE, Jack	Pte 63589	1st/6th	22/07/1918	DOW	Gezaincourt Comm. Cem. Ext.
RATCLIFFE, Sydney	Pte 251769	2nd/6th	21/03/1918	KIA	Le Cateau Mil. Cem.
RAVENSCROFT Richard	Pte 252621	2nd/6th	30/04/1917	DOW	Bethune Town Cem.
RAYMOND, Henry A	Pte 270046	1st/6th	27/03/1918	KIA	Douchy-les-Ayette Brit. Cem.
READE, Herbert E	Pte 57209	1st/6th	27/09/1918	KIA	Flesquieres Hill Brit Cem
REBBITT, Henry R	Pte 1889	1st/6th	07/08/1915	KIA	Helles Memorial
REDFERN, Robert L	Pte 2461	1st/6th	04/06/1915	KIA	Helles Memorial
REDHEAD, John	Pte 2295	1st/6th	05/06/1915	KIA	Helles Memorial
REID, William C	Pte 2327	1st/6th	07/08/1915	KIA	Helles Memorial
REISS, Willoughby E	Capt	1st/6th	08/08/1915	DOW	Lancashire Landing Cemetery
RENWICK, Thomas	Pte 2401	1st/6th	04/06/1915	KIA	Helles Memorial
RHODES, Richard C	Pte 3021	1st/6th	08/08/1915	DOW	Helles Memorial
RICHARDS, Alfred G	L/Cpl 2303	1st/6th	11/07/1915	KIA	Helles Memorial
RICHARDS, George A	Sgt 2453	1st/6th	05/06/1915	KIA	Helles Memorial
RICHARDSON, Arthur V	Pte 1735	1st/6th	07/08/1915	KIA	Helles Memorial
RICHARDSON, Sydney	Pte 251477	1st/6th	27/03/1918	KIA	Arras Memorial
RIGBY, Stephen G	Pte 50366	1st/6th	28/03/1918	KIA	Arras Memorial
RILEY, Joseph A	Pte 57205	1st/6th	01/05/1918	DOW	St Sever Cem. Ext.
ROBERTS, Bertie	Pte 401105	1st/6th	27/09/1918	KIA	Ribecourt Road Cem.
ROBERTS, Charles	Pte 251849	1st/6th	07/09/1918	DOW	Bagneux Brit. Cem.
ROBERTS, Griffith A	Pte 1667	1st/6th	20/06/1915	DOW	East Mudros Mil. Cem
ROBERTS, Henry	Pte 252739	2nd/6th	10/10/1917	DOW	Godewaersvelde Brit. Cem.
ROBERTS, William	L/Cpl 1147	1st/6th	05/06/1915	KIA	Twelve Tree Copse Cem.
ROBINSON, Edgar I	Pte 57204	1st/6th	25/08/1918	KIA	Warlencourt Brit. Cem
ROBINSON, James	Pte 375053	1st/6th	20/10/1918	KIA	Belle Vue Brit. Cem.
ROBINSON, Rudolph	Pte 57276	2nd/6th	21/03/1918	KIA	Pozieres Memorial
ROBINSON, Walter R	Pte 250869	1st/6th	14/12/1917	KIA	Gorre Brit. & Indian Cem.
ROBINSON, Walter T	Pte 1391	1st/6th	04/06/1915	KIA	Helles Memorial
RODWELL, James W	Pte 270114	2nd/6th	13/05/1918	DOW	St Mary's Church, Denver
ROGERS, Samuel	Pte 2685	1st/6th	07/08/1915	KIA	Helles Memorial
ROGERSON, Eric	Pte 250627	1st/6th	25/03/1918	KIA	Arras Memorial
ROPER, Hubert	Pte 21446	1st/6th	21/10/1918	KIA	Romeries Comm. Cem. Ext.
ROSCOE, Frederick N	Pte 250509	1st/6th	21/08/1918	KIA	Queens Cem, Bucquoy
ROSE, William	Pte 270104	2nd/6th	21/03/1918	KIA	Assevillers New Brit. Cem.
ROTHWELL, James H	Pte 121	6th (n/k)	01/01/1915	n/k	Warrington Cem.
ROTHWELL, John	Pte 64321	1st/6th	20/10/1918	KIA	Belle Vue Brit. Cem.
ROTHWELL, William E	Sgt 20210	6th (n/k)	17/11/1915	n/k	Weaste Cem, Salford

ROWBOTTOM, Joseph	2/Lieut	2nd/6th	24/09/1917	KIA	Ramscappelle Road Mil. Cem.
ROWLAND, Frederick	Pte 351264	1st/6th	27/09/1918	DOW	Ribecourt Road Cem.
ROWLINSON, John G	Pte 2279	1st/6th	07/08/1915	KIA	Helles Memorial
ROYLE, George	Pte 252107	2nd/6th	12/07/1918	Died	St Roch Comm. Cem
RUSSELL, William	L/Sgt 301400	2nd/6th	26/03/1918	KIA	Pozieres Memorial
RUTHERFORD, William	Pte 552	1st/6th	05/06/1915	KIA	Helles Memorial
RUTTER, Claude A G	Cpl 1479	1st/6th	25/05/1915	KIA	Helles Memorial
RYDER, Archibald D	Pte 1761	1st/6th	05/06/1915	KIA	Helles Memorial
RYDER, James A	L/Cpl 303395	2nd/6th	21/03/1918	KIA	Pozieres Memorial
RYDER, Walter	Pte 250503	1st/6th	05/09/1917	DOW	Ypres Reservoir Cem.
RYDING, Frederick	Pte 250774	2nd/6th	26/07/1917	KIA	Nieuport Memorial
RYLANDS, Archibald	Sgt 250017	1st/6th	20/10/1918	DOW	St Aubert Brit. Cem.
SAGAR, William	Pte 57283	2nd/6th	21/03/1918	KIA	Pozieres Memorial
SALE, Alfred	Pte 50024	2nd/6th	21/03/1918	KIA	Pozieres Memorial
SAMES, Herbert C	Pte 2309	1st/6th	23/06/1915	DOW	Alexandria (Chatby) Mil. Cem
SAVILLE, Arthur	Pte 270133	2nd/6th	02/11/1918	Died	Berlin South-western Cem.
SCOLDING, Henry W	Pte 54480	1st/6th	21/03/1918	KIA	Arras Memorial
SCOTCHFORD, George	Pte 251049	1st/6th	06/09/1917	KIA	Tyne Cot Memorial
SCOTT, John	Pte 9925	1st/6th	02/09/1918	KIA	Bancourt Brit. Cem.
SENIOR, James K	Pte 758	1st/6th	04/06/1915	KIA	Helles Memorial
SHARPLES, Albert	Pte 251153	1st/6th	28/03/1918	KIA	Arras Memorial
SHAW, Henry	Cpl 303273	2nd/6th	21/03/1918	KIA	Pozieres Memorial
SHAWCROSS, Joseph	Sgt 250818	1st/6th	14/06/1918	KIA	Bertrancourt Mil. Cem.
SHENTON, Robert	Pte 2851	1st/6th	07/08/1915	KIA	Helles Memorial
SHEPPARD, Laurence	Pte 10456	1st/6th	23/04/1918	KIA	Serre Road Cem 1
SHIRLEY, John A	Pte 345046	2nd/6th	21/03/1918	KIA	Pozieres Memorial
SIDDALL, John S	Pte 252350	2nd/6th	22/03/1918	KIA	Pozieres Memorial
SIDEBOTTOM, Edward	Pte 24844	1st/6th	20/10/1918	KIA	Belle Vue Brit. Cem.
SIDES, Willoughy	Pte 2002	1st/6th	07/08/1915	KIA	Helles Memorial
SIMM, Alfred	Pte 251482	1st/6th	23/06/1917	KIA	Ruyaulcourt Mil. Cem.
SINCLAIR, David C	Pte 2177	1st/6th	07/08/1915	KIA	Helles Memorial
SITFORD, Leopold J	2/Lieut	1st/6th	02/09/1918	KIA	Manchester Cem.
SLATER, Eric C H	Pte 2366	1st/6th	28/05/1915	KIA	Twelve Tree Copse Cem.
SLATER, George H	Pte 350761	1st/6th	04/09/1918	DOW	Varennes Mil. Cem.
SLATER, William	Pte 60795	1st/6th	03/10/1918	DOW	Thilloy Road Cem.
SMITH, Alfred	Pte 49920	2nd/6th	26/03/1918	KIA	Jeancourt Comm. Cem. Ext.
SMITH, Andrew B	Cpl 1801	1st/6th	07/08/1915	KIA	Helles Memorial
SMITH, Arthur G	Pte 251207	1st/6th	27/09/1918	KIA	Flesquieres Hill Brit Cem
SMITH, Douglas	Cpl 250382	1st/6th	24/06/1918	KIA	Bertrancourt Mil. Cem.
SMITH, George	Pte 63454	1st/6th	02/09/1918	KIA	Bancourt Brit. Cem.
SMITH, George S	Pte 2413	1st/6th	02/07/1915	KIA	Twelve Tree Copse Cem.
SMITH, Harold M	Cpl 1159	1st/6th	05/06/1915	KIA	Helles Memorial

SMITH, Harry	Pte 63467	1st/6th	27/09/1918	KIA	Ribecourt Road Cem.
SMITH, Herbert	Pte 303577	2nd/6th	21/03/1918	KIA	Pozieres Memorial
SMITH, John	Pte 52634	2nd/6th	29/12/1917	KIA	Menin Road South Mil. Cem.
SMITH, Leonard T	L/Cpl 250059	2nd/6th	05/10/1917	KIA	Tyne Cot Memorial
SMITH, Mark	Cpl 2085	1st/6th	05/06/1915	KIA	Helles Memorial
SMITH, Walter	Pte 64251	1st/6th	27/09/1918	DOW	Vis-en-Artois Memorial
SMITH, William	Pte 251901	1st/6th	22/08/1918	KIA	Queens Cem, Bucquoy
SMITH, William F	Pte 50278	1st/6th	27/03/1918	KIA	Douchy-les-Ayette Brit. Cem.
SNAPE, William	Pte 1925	1st/6th	05/06/1915	KIA	Helles Memorial
SOLOMON, Baron	Pte 251908	1st/6th	28/03/1918	KIA	Arras Memorial
SORTON, Ernest	Sgt 176	1st/6th	05/06/1915	KIA	Helles Memorial
SOUTHAM, Percy	Pte 55851	1st/6th	23/08/1918	KIA	Queens Cem, Bucquoy
SPENCE, Alexander	Pte 252431	2nd/6th	13/09/1917	KIA	Ramscappelle Road Mil. Cem.
SPRING, William H	Pte 251403	1st/6th	08/10/1917	DOW	Zuydcoote Mil Cem.
STABLES, Stanley G	Pte 1870	1st/6th	05/06/1915	KIA	Helles Memorial
STACEY, Fred	Pte 250838	2nd/6th	24/09/1917	KIA	Ramscappelle Road Mil. Cem.
STACEY, James	Pte 250292	1st/6th	23/08/1918	KIA	Queens Cem, Bucquoy
STAFFORD, John W	Pte 64146	1st/6th	18/10/1918	DOW	Audenshaw Cem.
STANSFIELD, James E	Pte 57284	2nd/6th	25/03/1918	DOW	Rosieres Brit. Cem.
STEAD, Joseph R	Pte 1523	1st/6th	05/06/1915	KIA	Helles Memorial
STEAR, Robert	Pte 2804	1st/6th	03/08/1915	KIA	Twelve Tree Copse Cem.
STEWARD, Percy	Pte 251566	1st/6th	05/09/1917	DOW	Ypres Reservoir Cem.
STONE, Herbert	Pte 59875	1st/6th	27/09/1918	DOW	Ribecourt Road Cem.
STONE, Joseph	Pte 252119	2nd/6th	21/03/1918	KIA	Pozieres Memorial
STONE, Joseph E	Pte 251023	2nd/6th	24/09/1917	KIA	Ramscappelle Road Mil. Cem.
STOPFORD, Albert	Pte 252357	2nd/6th	14/10/1918	Died	Belgrade Cem.
STOREY, George W	Pte 49602	2nd/6th	15/09/1917	DOW	Vlamertinghe New Mil. Cem.
STOTT, Robert	Sgt 250254	1st/6th	27/03/1918	KIA	Arras Memorial
STRINGER, Bernard	Pte 50345	2nd/6th	28/03/1918	DOW	St Souplet Brit. Cem.
SUMMERS, George	Pte 251780	1st/6th	21/10/1918	DOW	Awoingt Brit. Cem.
SUTTON, Fred	Pte 49104	1st/6th	24/06/1918	KIA	Bertrancourt Mil. Cem.
SUTTON, James	Pte 302481	2nd/6th	21/03/1918	KIA	Pozieres Memorial
SWANWICK, Horace	Pte 252105	2nd/6th	18/08/1917	KIA	Ramscappelle Road Mil. Cem.
SWIFT, William	Pte 252782	2nd/6th	05/10/1917	KIA	Tyne Cot Memorial
SYKES, Edward	Pte 250303	1st/6th	02/09/1917	DOW	Ypres Reservoir Cem.
TABB, PERCY	Pte 2471	1st/6th	27/05/1915	KIA	Helles Memorial
TALBOT, Thomas	Pte 251685	1st/6th	25/03/1918	KIA	Arras Memorial
TATLOW, Harry	Pte 2477	1st/6th	05/06/1915	KIA	Helles Memorial
TATTERSALL, George	Pte 1871	1st/6th	29/06/1915	DOW	Lancashire Landing Cemetery

TAYLFORTH, William	Sgt 142	1st/6th	31/05/1915	KIA	Helles Memorial
TAYLOR, Arthur	Pte 251562	1st/6th	25/03/1918	KIA	Arras Memorial
TAYLOR, Charles H	Pte 2256	1st/6th	26/05/1915	KIA	Helles Memorial
TAYLOR, Frank	Pte 1517	1st/6th	05/06/1915	KIA	Helles Memorial
TAYLOR, Frank	Pte 251168	1st/6th	28/06/1917	KIA	Thiepval Memorial
TAYLOR, George E	Pte 2344	1st/6th	07/08/1915	KIA	Helles Memorial
TAYLOR, John	Pte 44941	2nd/6th	21/03/1918	KIA	Pozieres Memorial
TAYLOR, John H	Pte 4204	2nd/6th	31/07/1916	Died	Southern Cem, Manchester
TAYLOR, Percy E	Pte 1704	1st/6th	07/08/1915	KIA	Helles Memorial
TAYLOR, Robert	L/Cpl 252392	2nd/6th	22/07/1917	KIA	Coxyde Mil. Cem.
TAYLOR, Thomas	Pte 2095	1st/6th	05/06/1915	KIA	Helles Memorial
TAYLOR, Thomas H	Pte 2152	1st/6th	04/06/1915	KIA	Helles Memorial
TAYLOR, Wilfrid	Pte 2897	1st/6th	19/08/1915	KIA	Alexandria (Chatby) Mil. Cem
TAYLOR, William	Pte 130	6th (n/k)	25/12/1914	n/k	Southern Cem, Manchester
TAYLOR, William H	Pte 251508	1st/6th	06/09/1917	KIA	Potijze Chateau Grounds Cem.
TEARE, Thomas A	Sgt 337	1st/6th	06/06/1915	KIA	Helles Memorial
TEBB, George W	L/Cpl 49810	2nd/6th	10/04/1918	DOW	Tourgeville Mil. Cem.
THIRLWALL, George H	Cpl 251736	1st/6th	20/10/1918	KIA	Belle Vue Brit. Cem.
THOMPSON, Arthur	Pte 2423	1st/6th	08/03/1915	Died	Cairo War Mem. Cem.
THOMPSON, Frank	L/Cpl 1643	1st/6th	07/08/1915	KIA	Redoubt Cem
THOMPSON, George S	Pte 2297	1st/6th	05/06/1915	KIA	Helles Memorial
THOMPSON, Herbert	Cpl 252138	6th (n/k)	22/02/1919	n/k	Urmston Cem.
THOMPSON, Walter	Capt	1st/6th	07/08/1915	KIA	Helles Memorial
THORBURN, Edward F	Lieut	1st/6th	10/06/1915	KIA	Helles Memorial
TINDALE, Matthew	Pte 252722	2nd/6th	23/04/1918	DOW	St Sever Cem. Ext.
TINKER, William	Pte 252455	2nd/6th	24/03/1918	KIA	Pozieres Memorial
TOLLITT, William	Pte 302962	1st/6th	27/09/1918	KIA	Flesquieres Hill Brit Cem
TOMLIN, Ernest	Pte 1631	1st/6th	07/08/1915	KIA	Helles Memorial
TORKINGTON, Richard	Pte 2175	1st/6th	03/06/1915	KIA	Helles Memorial
TOZER, Norman S F	Pte 2306	1st/6th	04/06/1915	KIA	Helles Memorial
TOZER, Stanley M	Pte 252789	2nd/6th	29/01/1918	KIA	Tyne Cot Memorial
TREACHER, Harry	Pte 19282	1st/6th	21/10/1918	DOW	Awoingt Brit. Cem.
TROWSE, Frank W	L/Sgt 44945	2nd/6th	21/03/1918	KIA	Pozieres Memorial
TRUEMAN, Stanley	Pte 1670	1st/6th	04/06/1915	KIA	Helles Memorial
TUE, Gladstone	Pte 252501	2nd/6th	21/03/1918	KIA	Pozieres Memorial
TULK, Leslie	Pte 1430	1st/6th	14/07/1915	DOW	Helles Memorial
TURLEY, Joseph G	Pte 302747	1st/6th	26/11/1918	n/k	St Sever Cem. Ext.
TURNBULL, George C	Pte 44940	2nd/6th	21/03/1918	KIA	Pozieres Memorial
TURNBULL, PERCY	Sgt 250944	2nd/6th	07/10/1917	DOW	Tyne Cot Memorial
TURNER, Richard W	Pte 2540	1st/6th	01/09/1915	KIA	Helles Memorial
TURNOCK, John	Pte 376436	1st/6th	27/09/1918	DOW	Ruyaulcourt Mil. Cem.
TURTLE, Harry	Pte 252135	2nd/6th	21/03/1918	KIA	Villeret Old Chuchyard

TURTON, Charles G	Pte 2143	1st/6th	04/06/1915	KIA	Helles Memorial
TYLDESLEY, John H	Pte 2407	1st/6th	11/08/1915	DOW	Helles Memorial
TYRRELL, Richard A	Pte 252121	2nd/6th	26/07/1917	KIA	Nieuport Memorial
UTTLEY, Christopher	Pte 1709	1st/6th	04/06/1915	KIA	Helles Memorial
VALENTINE, Charles K	Sgt 253	1st/6th	05/06/1915	KIA	Helles Memorial
VASS. William	Major	6th (n/k)	23/09/1917	Died	Southern Cem, Manchester
VAUGHAN, John C	L/Cpl 251778	2nd/6th	27/03/1918	DOW	Abbeville Com Cem. Ext
VEITCH, Alfred P F	Cpl 1512	1st/6th	10/08/1915	DOW	Helles Memorial
VICKERS, Benjamin	Pte 252380	2nd/6th	26/07/1917	KIA	Coxyde Mil. Cem.
VIPOND, Hugh	Lieut	1st/6th	28/07/1917	Died	Achiet-le-Grand Com Cem
WADE, George	Pte 251724	1st/6th	28/09/1918	DOW	Grevillers Brit. Cem.
WAINE, William H	Capt	1st/6th	07/08/1915	KIA	Helles Memorial
WAISTER, John J	Pte 270182	2nd/6th	26/03/1918	DOW	Honnechy Brit. Cem.
WALKER, Arthur J	Capt	1st/6th	07/08/1915	KIA	Redoubt Cem
WALKER, Francis J	Pte 250239	1st/6th	27/03/1918	KIA	Arras Memorial
WALKER, Frederick J	Pte 2121	1st/6th	25/08/1915	DOW	Helles Memorial
WALLACE, Fred	Pte 250879	1st/6th	01/03/1918	DOW	Etaples Mil. Cem.
WALLEY, Alfred	L/Cpl 1301	1st/6th	05/06/1915	KIA	Helles Memorial
WALLEY, Frank	Pte 203220	1st/6th	27/09/1918	DOW	Ribecourt Road Cem.
WALTERS, Arthur J	Pte 1901	1st/6th	05/06/1915	KIA	Helles Memorial
WALTERS, William	L/Sgt 250926	1st/6th	21/08/1918	KIA	Queens Cem, Bucquoy
WALTON, Cyril	Pte 1591	1st/6th	05/06/1915	KIA	Redoubt Cem
WALTON, George	Pte 1929	1st/6th	07/08/1915	KIA	Helles Memorial
WARBURTON, Herbert	Pte 251963	1st/6th	02/10/1918	DOW	Grevillers Brit. Cem.
WARD, William E	Pte 1949	1st/6th	04/06/1915	KIA	Helles Memorial
WARDLEY, Charles S	Pte 1971	1st/6th	12/06/1915	DOW	Alexandria (Chatby) Mil. Cem
WARNER, Charles	Pte 54235	2nd/6th	21/03/1918	KIA	Pozieres Memorial
WARRINGTON, Bert	Pte 8332	1st/6th	15/08/1918	KIA	Queens Cem, Bucquoy
WARWICK, Richard	Pte 270054	1st/6th	04/09/1917	DOW	Mendighem Mil. Cem.
WATERLAND, Sydney	Pte 251277	1st/6th	30/05/1918	Died	St Sever Cem. Ext.
WATERS, George E	Pte 250555	1st/6th	03/09/1918	DOW	Bagneux Brit. Cem.
WATKINSON, John S	Pte 252381	2nd/6th	09/10/1917	DOW	Lijssenthoek Mil. Cem.
WEBSTER, Arthur	Pte 1217	1st/6th	05/06/1915	KIA	Helles Memorial
WEBSTER, Thomas	Pte 63477	1st/6th	21/10/1918	DOW	Awoingt Brit. Cem.
WELCH, Edward	Pte 302151	2nd/6th	21/03/1918	KIA	Pozieres Memorial
WELCH, John G	Pte 55815	2nd/6th	02/12/1918	DOW	Terlincthun Brit. Cem.
WETHERALL, John	Pte 252666	2nd/6th	13/04/1917	DOW	Cambrin Mil. Cem.
WHITBREAD, Leslie G	Pte 3090	1st/6th	11/09/1915	Died	Helles Memorial
WHITEHEAD, Edgar L	Pte 251587	1st/6th	24/07/1918	KIA	Bertrancourt Mil. Cem.
WHITLA, Charles M	Pte 2036	1st/6th	05/06/1915	KIA	Helles Memorial
WHITTAKER, Arnold D	Pte 250927	1st/6th	25/03/1918	KIA	Arras Memorial
WHITTAKER, George	Pte 1680	1st/6th	05/06/1915	KIA	Helles Memorial
WHITTAKER, James	Pte 303910	2nd/6th	22/03/1918	KIA	Pozieres Memorial

WHITWORTH, John H	Major	2nd/6th	31/03/1918	DOW	St Sever Cem
WILCOX, Fred	Cpl 250787	1st/6th	31/07/1917	DOW	Achiet-le-Grand Com Cem
WILD, Charles P	Pte 2463	1st/6th	07/08/1915	KIA	Helles Memorial
WILD, Edmund	L/Cpl 251841	1st/6th	31/10/1918	Died	Etaples Mil. Cem.
WILD, John W	Pte 203297	1st/6th	02/09/1918	KIA	Bancourt Brit. Cem.
WILDE, John A V	L/Cpl 252066	2nd/6th	08/10/1917	KIA	Tyne Cot Memorial
WILKINS, Harold A T	Pte 303272	2nd/6th	21/03/1918	KIA	Pozieres Memorial
WILKINSON, Alfred	Pte 252376	2nd/6th	26/05/1917	KIA	Cambrin Mil. Cem.
WILKINSON, William	Pte 1932	1st/6th	01/06/1915	DOW	Lancashire Landing Cemetery
WILLIAMS, Edward	Pte 251951	1st/6th	06/09/1917	KIA	Aeroplane Cem
WILLIAMS, Edward	L/Cpl 251633	1st/6th	25/03/1918	KIA	Arras Memorial
WILLIAMS, Ernest	Pte 2062	1st/6th	31/05/1915	KIA	Helles Memorial
WILLIAMS, Frank N	Pte 1915	1st/6th	30/05/1915	DOW	Helles Memorial
WILLIAMS, Harry	L/Cpl 1857	1st/6th	17/10/1915	Died	Portianos Mil. Cem.
WILLIAMS, Herbert	Pte 251854	1st/6th	25/03/1918	KIA	Arras Memorial
WILLIAMS, Hugh	Pte 251246	1st/6th	26/03/1918	KIA	Arras Memorial
WILLIAMS, Oliver S	Pte 252286	2nd/6th	22/04/1917	DOW	Bethune Town Cem.
WILLIAMS, William H	Pte 57312	2nd/6th	01/11/1918	Died	Robermont Cemetery, Liege
WILLIS, Benjamin	Pte 252265	2nd/6th	21/03/1918	KIA	Pozieres Memorial
WILSON, Colin	L/Cpl 1035	1st/6th	05/06/1915	KIA	Helles Memorial
WILSON, Hugh	Pte 51419	1st/6th	28/03/1918	KIA	Arras Memorial
WILSON, James	L/Cpl 944	1st/6th	05/06/1915	KIA	Helles Memorial
WILSON, James	Pte 251200	1st/6th	20/10/1918	KIA	Vis-en-Artois Memorial
WILSON, John W	CQMS 57	1st/6th	01/06/1915	KIA	Helles Memorial
WILSON, William F	Pte 252650	2nd/6th	03/04/1918	DOW	Vadencourt-et-Boheries Cem.
WINDSOR, Thomas	L/Cpl 252061	2nd/6th	06/10/1917	KIA	Tyne Cot Memorial
WISE, George H	Pte 252378	2nd/6th	22/03/1918	KIA	Pozieres Memorial
WOOD, Ernest	Pte 39775	1st/6th	20/10/1918	KIA	Belle Vue Brit. Cem.
WOOD, Ernest	L/Cpl 2243	1st/6th	04/06/1915	KIA	Helles Memorial
WOOD, Frank	Pte 63479	1st/6th	27/09/1918	DOW	Grevillers Brit. Cem.
WOOD, John	Pte 252766	2nd/6th	13/04/1917	KIA	Cambrin Mil. Cem.
WOODCOCK, George	Pte 251264	1st/6th	07/09/1917	DOW	Brandhoek New Mil. Cem. 3
WOODHEAD, Cyril S	Cpl 1539	1st/6th	31/05/1915	KIA	Helles Memorial
WOODWARD, Harry F	Pte 54515	2nd/6th	21/03/1918	KIA	Pozieres Memorial
WOOLLERTONFrederick R	Sgt 250432	2nd/6th	22/03/1918	KIA	Roisel Comm. Cem. Ext.
WORLEY, George O	Pte 49637	2nd/6th	14/08/1917	KIA	Coxyde Mil. Cem.
WORRALL, Rupert	Pte 252424	2nd/6th	18/10/1917	DOW	Etaples Mil. Cem.
WORTHINGTON, James	Pte 252480	2nd/6th	24/09/1917	KIA	Ramscappelle Road Mil. Cem.
WORTHINGTON, Thomas R	Sgt 637	1st/6th	07/08/1915	KIA	Helles Memorial
WRIGHT, Albert E	L/Cpl 2509	1st/6th	06/09/1915	Died	Helles Memorial

WRIGHT, Richard	Pte	251835	1st/6th	19/05/1918	Died	Boulogne Eastern Cem.
WRIGHT, Thomas H	Pte	10472	1st/6th	02/09/1918	KIA	Bancourt Brit. Cem.
WROE, Frank	Pte	57309	2nd/6th	22/03/1918	KIA	Pozieres Memorial
WYLIE, Richard	Pte	57313	2nd/6th	21/03/1918	KIA	Pozieres Memorial
WYNNE, Robert	Pte	63486	1st/6th	23/08/1918	DOW	Bagneux Brit. Cem.
YARDLEY, Harold	Sgt	251353	1st/6th	21/08/1918	KIA	Queens Cem, Bucquoy
YATES, Alfred	CSM	250074	1st/6th	04/09/1918	DOW	Varennes Mil. Cem.
YATES, Arthur C	Pte	2286	1st/6th	08/07/1915	DOW	Pieta Mil. Cem.
YATES, Richard	Sgt	250763	1st/6th	22/08/1918	KIA	Vis-en-Artois Memorial
YATES, William C	Pte	2337	1st/6th	07/08/1915	KIA	Helles Memorial
YOUNG, Edmund T	Lieut		1st/6th	10/06/1915	KIA	Helles Memorial
YOUNG, John	Pte	1902	1st/6th	21/12/1915	KIA	Twelve Tree Copse Cem.
YOUNG, William	Pte	252306	2nd/6th	30/04/1917	KIA	Cambrin Mil. Cem.

1 KIA – Killed in action. DOW – Died of wounds. Died – usually indicating a death from natural causes unconnected with combat. Note that the original information is known to contain errors and the details here cannot be relied on with certainty.

INDEX

(Note: Ranks are generally those at first mention in the text)